# THE SPIRITUAL ARCHETYPES

# THE SPIRITUAL ARCHETYPES

*A Guide to Discovering and Illuminating the
Patterns, Psyche, and Inspirations of the
Twenty-Two Spiritual Paths
Through Myths, Stories, and History*

## CHRISTIAN KURZ

*Published in the United States by:* Vaquero Publishing www.VaqueroMinistries.com

*Cover design:* Barbara LeVan Fisher  |  *Edited:* Jenna Love-Schrader and Vanessa Ta
*Interior design:* Jordan Wannemacher  |  *Cover and interior artwork:* Christian Kurz
*All of the artwork of the Spiritual Archetypes was created by Christian Kurz,*
*as well as The Moon tarot image used for The Recoverist.*
*All other tarot images are from the Rider–Waite–Coleman Tarot deck*
*Image on page 77 is called the Flammarion Engraving aka The Vision of Ezekiel from Camille Flammarion's*
*1888 book L'atmosphère: météorologie populaire ("The Atmosphere: Popular Meteorology")*

The photograph of Dr. Helen Schucman on page 220 is used with permission by the Foundation for
Inner Peace, 448 Ignacio Blvd., #306, Novato, CA 94949, www.acim.org.

Deer Hunter and White Corn Maiden" translated by Alfonso Ortiz; from AMERICAN INDIAN
MYTHS AND LEGENDS by Richard Erdoes and Alfonso Ortiz, copyright © 1984 by Richard Erdoes
and Alfonso Ortiz. Used by permission of Pantheon Books, an imprint of the Knopf Doubleday Publishing Group, a division of Penguin Random House LLC. All rights reserved.

The charities and foundations listed on page 445 are shared with
the permission of the organizations.

Unless otherwise noted, scripture quotations are taken from
the King James Version of the Bible.
Scripture quotations marked AMP are taken from the Amplified® Bible (AMPC).
Copyright © 1954, 1958, 1962, 1964, 1965, 1987 by The Lockman Foundation.
Used by permission. www.Lockman.org.

The author of this book does not dispense medical advice or prescribe the use of any technique or spiritual
practice as a form of treatment for mental, emotional, physical or medical concerns, without the advice
of a medical physician, either directly or indirectly. The intent of the author is to share information of a
general nature to assist you on your spiritual journey. In the event you use any of the information in this
book for yourself, the author and the publisher assume no responsibility for your actions.

*Publisher note:* In this book, you will find that the terms and names such as satan, lucifer, enemy, and ego
are all lowercase. This is done intentionally to show the insignificance, and lack of power, that the enemy
has. We believe that it is worth being grammatically incorrect to emphasize this point.

Library of Congress Cataloging-in-Publication Data

Names: Kurz, Christian, author, artist
Title: The Spiritual Archetypes:
Description: 1st edition | Monument, Colorado: Vaquero Publishing 2023.
Identifiers: LCCN 2022916334 ISBN 979 8 9868549 0 8 (hardback)

Hardcover ISBN: 979-8-9868549-0-8
Paperback ISBN: 979-8-9868549-1-5
eBook ISBN: 979-8-9868549-2-2

Printed in the United States of America

# PRAISE FROM THE
# SPIRITUAL ARCHETYPES

This page is generally dedicated to sharing praise, testimonials, and reviews of the book. However, since praise always belongs to God, I would instead like to share quotes about God and spirituality by some of the best and most respected teachers and spiritually devoted people who embodied their Spiritual Archetype.

"Love is qualified as an attribute of that force, power or influence known as God. Thus as man makes application of love in his daily experience, he finds God a personal God."
—EDGAR CAYCE

"An enlightened man had but one duty - to seek the way to himself, to reach inner certainty, to grope his way forward, no matter where it led."
—*DEMIAN* BY HERMANN HESSE

"May today there be peace within. May you trust God that you are exactly where you are meant to be. May you not forget the infinite possibilities that are born of faith. May you use those gifts that you have received, and pass on the love that has been given to you. May you be content knowing you are a child of God. Let this presence settle into your bones, and allow your soul the freedom to sing, dance, praise and love. It is there for each and every one of us."
—ST TERESA OF AVILA

"God, When I was alone and had nothing, I asked for a friend to help me bear the pain, No one came, except God. When I needed a breath to rise, from my sleep, No one could help me... except God. When all I saw was sadness, and I needed answers, No one heard me, except God, So when I'm asked.. who I give my unconditional love to? I look for no other name, except God."
—TUPAC SHAKUR

"I would urge you to give priority to the search for God. Allow his spirit to permeate your being... If you do not have a deep and patient faith in God, you will be powerless to face the delays, disappointments, and vicissitudes that inevitably come."
—MARTIN LUTHER KING, JR.

"Sir, my concern is not whether God is on our side; my greatest concern is to be on God's side, for God is always right."
—ABRAHAM LINCOLN

"There is no higher religion than the truth."
—H. P. BLAVATSKY

"God is in everything I see because God is in my mind."
—A COURSE IN MIRACLES

"I believe God is managing affairs and that He doesn't need any advice from me. With God in charge, I believe everything will work out for the best in the end. So what is there to worry about."
-HENRY FORD

"It wasn't me, it was the Lord! I always told Him, 'I trust to you. I don't know where to go or what to do, but I expect You to lead me,' and He always did."
– HARRIET TUBMAN

# CONTENTS

# SPECIAL CONSIDERATIONS

## Word Choice

In writing a book that encompasses the range of personalities and backgrounds of spiritual paths such as this, there is naturally going to be a variety of preferences in terms of word choices. While I use the word *God* and reference God mostly as *Him*, others may prefer the term *universe*, or *spirit*, or might use a term like *father mother God*. Alternatively, I use words like *the enemy* while others might use the word *ego*, *devil*, or *satan*. Although it may be tempting to focus on these details and allow ourselves to get into a mindset of separation, I would like to note that truth is truth, and although we may use different words to express our beliefs, it does not take away from the truth. I believe that if we could look past ourselves and see the similarities in our thoughts, words, and beliefs, we would all see just how connected we truly are. It is incredible how the threads of our paths, regardless of their appearance, actually knit us together as a collective and how we all say the same things in our own individual voices.

So, in reading this book, I would like to extend an invitation to focus on the all-encompassing, all-inclusive stories, myths, expressions, words, and beliefs that are honored and represented in this book. Please feel free to insert the word you prefer and perhaps even examine the sameness, connectedness, and oneness of it all. When we focus on what unites us, and the connections between us, we ultimately learn more about ourselves and one another, which is also part of the beauty of the spiritual path.

## Resonating with the Spiritual Archetypes

In taking the quiz you may be surprised by your Spiritual Archetype and how it relates to your gender or race. Please keep in mind that the Spiritual Archetypes are not gender or nationality specific. The Spiritual Archetypes, and their names, are not solely referring to gender or nationality but are based on the teachings, as well as the common experiences of each path. The people represented as the Spiritual Archetypes are some of the most famous on those paths, but do not necessarily indicate the appearance of each person who embodies and resonates with that Spiritual Archetype.

# INTRODUCTION

In 2016 I awoke to the words *Spiritual Archetypes*. Although my husband and children were asleep, I heard these words spoken as clearly as though someone were in the same room. I began to see visions of each of the Spiritual Archetypes vividly. Having been in the spiritual field and involved with a variety of spiritual communities for over thirty years, each Spiritual Archetype was familiar to me. I could picture individuals I knew as each Spiritual Archetype and had a clear definition of each. I spent the morning outlining the Spiritual Archetypes as I knew them, their common strengths, behaviors, fears, and things they resonated with, and spent the next month detailing them. At that time, I had one toddler and one newborn, which made it a little challenging to find the time to write. I began waking up at four o'clock every morning and writing for two hours before my children woke up, and I would steal any additional moments when possible. Regardless of how much or how little I could write each day, there was one practice I committed to every time I wrote: Each time I sat down at my computer, I prayed, "God, please give me the words to write. If no one ever reads this, I will be okay just knowing they exist in the world because you told me to write them." I used those words as a compass and committed to that intention until the first guidebooks were completed.

To share the guidebooks, I created a quiz called "What is Your Spiritual Archetype?" By taking the quiz, a person could find out their main Spiritual Archetype and download the corresponding eight-page guidebook. Upon finishing the quiz and guidebooks, I shared them on a few social media sites. Within two weeks of launching the quiz, it went viral, gaining over ten thousand new subscribers to my newsletter. I received messages and emails from throughout the US, as well as from Romania, Nova Scotia, the UK, all over Africa and everywhere in between, testifying to the impact the information had on people's lives, spirituality, relationships, and businesses.

The response from the initial quiz and guidebooks taught me two things. First, when we put something in God's hands with an attitude of surrender and commitment to do God's Will, He will always exceed our expectations. The quiz has now been taken over one million times and has far exceeded my original vision. I never get tired of reading the testimonials of people who have discovered my quiz and hearing how it has helped them on their spiritual path.

Second, the world wants, and needs, more of this kind of material. After the quiz and initial guidebooks were released, I was constantly asked for more information, guidance, and elaboration on the Spiritual Archetypes. This is ultimately why I created this book! This book is for those first million people who loved the Spiritual Archetypes and wanted more, as well as anyone else seeking more information on their spiritual path.

Thank you to everyone who supported the beginning of my journey writing the Spiritual Archetypes and to everyone reading this who is letting me be a part of your journey. It is an honor and a privilege.

## PART ONE
# THE QUEST
# FOR GOD

# THE GIRL WHO SOUGHT
# GOD IN ALL THINGS

*To fall in love with God is the greatest romance; to seek him the greatest adventure; to find him, the greatest human achievement.*
—SAINT AUGUSTINE

Once, there was a girl who wanted to find God; she set out on a grand spiritual quest to look for Him. She began her journey in hopes of speaking with God. Thereafter, she met a group of people who told her, "We know how to talk to God. He is in our cards, our crystals, and the stars. Listen to these things, follow this path, and you will find Him." And so, she did. She learned the ways of the ancient arts and followed the modalities of different teachers and leaders. But the more she learned about these things, the further away she felt from God's voice. She told the group that she could not hear the voice of God and that perhaps He was not in the cards and stones but something else. She was shunned by the group for her beliefs and told not to return. She left that path in pursuit of another.

Since she could not hear God in the earthly objects, she thought to herself, "Perhaps I will seek his Word instead; maybe that is how I will find Him." So, she set out on a path to seek his Word. She went to churches and temples, met with religious leaders, and told them she wanted to know God's Word. "We have God's Word. He is in our doctrine. Abide by our doctrine, and you will find him." And so, she did.

She followed that path, studied various religions, and read all of the doctrines on Earth. But the more she studied, the further away from His Word she felt. She told the churches and temples that while she had gained knowledge, she did not feel God in her heart. She began asking questions, but the religious leaders did not like her questions because they challenged what they knew. She was shunned by the churches and temples and told not to return. She left that path in pursuit of another.

Lonely and outcast, she thought, "Perhaps I will pursue a path to seek His love." So, she set out to seek love. On this path, she surrounded herself with friends and people she believed she could trust and love. She loved freely and gave her love to others, but they did not deserve it. They used her love and disposed of it as freely as she gave it. The more she was rejected, the more she wanted to love and be loved. She lowered her standards and gave herself to anyone who would take her just so that she had a glimmer of love in her life. When the glimmer left, she felt broken and empty. She left that path in pursuit of another.

Hurt and angry, she thought, "If none of these paths leads to God, then I will be my own God and reign over my own life." So, she lived her life carelessly, in debauchery, believing only in herself, and giving in to her desires. It did not take long before that path became painful, empty, and meaningless. Desperate, she decided to try something she had never done before; she fell to her knees and surrendered.

In her despair, she prayed, "Please God, I just need you." At that moment, God appeared to her and said, "My child, why are you so distraught?" In her distress and disbelief, she asked, "Where have you been? I have walked every path looking for you!"

God smiled sweetly and compassionately and placed a hand on her shoulder. "My child, each path you pursued gave you exactly what they produce after their kind.

You pursued my creations like the stars and the stones, but that is not where I dwell. Those are my creations, but they are not me.

You studied doctrines and gained knowledge and wisdom, but those are only words. My Word cannot just be read. It must be felt.

You sought love and looked for it in others, but you defiled yourself for scrapes of affection from people who treated you in ways I never would. That is conditional love, not my love, which is unconditional.

And you attempted to make yourself your own authority, and to walk away from your path, only to feel powerless.

You did all of these things and walked many paths, but there is one path you did not pursue."

She thought back on the quest and could not think of any paths she could have missed. When He saw she did not know the answer, He looked her lovingly in the eyes and kindly replied,

"You were always focused on the paths, but those are man-made roads full of error, confusion, and strife. When you walk those paths, I will still be with you, guiding you, loving you, and leading you in the direction you should go, but they will always be full of hardship and pain because man makes paths to look for what already exists. To find me, you must seek me in your heart, then instead of following one path, a path will be made for you."

# THE SPIRITUAL PATH

*"Sir, shall I ever leave the spiritual path?" inquired a doubt-filled
disciple. Paramahansa Yogananda answered: "How could
you? Everyone in the world is on the spiritual path."*
—PARAMAHANSA YOGANANDA

Every person, in every moment, regardless of whether they are consciously aware of it or not, is on a spiritual path. Life and how we act or react on our spiritual path are part of our initiations. For those who understand their path, purpose, and initiations, and the aspects and fundamentals of what is happening or unfolding for them, life—and the spiritual journey—will be much more proactive, productive, and conducive to their highest and best good. Each event, hardship, blessing, situation, and experience are elements of our spiritual path. Although everyone has a spiritual path, each path will differ in appearance, experiences, background, interests, or lifestyle, yet they all have one common thread; they are all in an attempt to know and understand God.

The Spiritual Archetypes are the twenty-two most prominent spiritual paths people walk in their pursuit of God. The Spiritual Archetypes are personal identities with conscious and unconscious characteristics, behaviors, and beliefs, serving as doorways into our consciousness, which, when we walk through them, provide divine revelation. We gain the ability to understand ourselves better, our path, our patterns, our beliefs, and our reasoning. However, the Spiritual Archetypes are not just personal attributes; they also serve as aids in the quest for God and our spiritual path. Understanding our Spiritual Archetype gives us insight and clarity to bypass common hardships and recalibrate our quest when needed. Doing so can create the most rewarding path and spiritual experience.

The Spiritual Archetypes embody specific mindsets, beliefs, psychology, experiences, understandings, and characteristics. They also clarify the soul's purpose and enable God to speak to us in a language that is sensible, grows our faith, and calls us back to our path. Knowing our Spiritual Archetype gives us insights into ourselves, our path, and our relationship with God, which develops and strengthens not only our knowledge and understanding spiritually and personally, but, most importantly, helps us to cultivate and deepen our relationship with God. By approaching our spiritual path in this manner, we can have a relationship with God that is advantageous yet still speaks our language. God speaks to each of His children in ways that are relative, sensible, and necessary. Like a good parent, God speaks to His children based on their needs, skill, and understanding. That is not to say that God changes, for He does not change. He is the same God now and forever. We are all different; therefore, God sees and loves each of His children and will do everything in His power to address us in the ways we need. God gives and communicates with us according to each person's faith and unbelief. God is infinitely creative in how He communicates with us, gets our attention, or provides revelation. Just as in the Bible, God chooses his prophets, leaders, kings, teachers, priests, messengers, healers, and disciples from varying backgrounds, educations, and lineages. He communicates with His people through dreams, prophetic visions, nature, the elements, and numbers. He also addresses His prophets differently. Some have dreams; others are visited by angels. Some are spoken to directly by him; others are spoken to through the elements. God utilizes His creation to speak to us, provide signs, and address us in ways relevant to us and our path. Whichever path we are on, God will exercise His resources to call to us and speak to us in a language we understand in an attempt to bring us toward our destination and soul's purpose.

Unfortunately, God is not the only one who speaks to us in ways that resonate. The enemy (the devil, ego, evil) is fully versed in our thoughts, feelings, fears, and weaknesses and will use these vulnerabilities to lead us into temptation and away from our soul's purpose. It is similar to the November 1960, episode of *Twilight Zone* entitled, "The Howling Man." In the episode, a man named David Ellington stumbles upon an old monastery during a terrible storm in the night. Ellington goes to the building to seek sanctuary from the storm. He finds that it is run by the order of the Brothers; a group of men with long hair, long beards, and white robes. Ellington asks for shelter from the storm and is brought inside to meet with Brother Jerome, the highest-ranking Brother. While waiting to meet Brother Jerome, Ellington hears a loud wolf-like howl throughout the halls. Ellington cannot see where the noise is coming from but is greatly perturbed. His anxiety is interrupted when someone comes to take him to Brother Jerome. He is brought to Brother Jerome, who tells him that, unfortunately, they cannot help him and that Ellington must leave at once. Sick and tired from the storm, Ellington faints before leaving the room. The Brothers decide that Ellington can stay one night as he recovers and take him to a room.

Upon waking in the monastery, Ellington hears the howling again and decides to investigate. Ellington secretly roams the halls following the sound when he finds an older disheveled man locked away in a jail-like cell. The man claims to be a prisoner of the Brothers and says that Brother Jerome is essentially an insane cult leader who keeps him locked up and beats him with his staff. Ellington is caught speaking with the man and is again taken to Brother Jerome. Ellington tells Brother Jerome that he talked to the man they are holding prisoner, but Brother Jerome insists, "That is no man." Ellington threatens to tell the police everything unless he gets further explanation about who the man is and why he is locked away. Brother Jerome declares again, "That is no man!" and begrudgingly agrees to tell Ellington the truth. He explains to Ellington that the man in the cell is the devil himself. He explains that after World War I, the devil had come to the village and Brother Jerome saw him for what he truly was. He managed to capture him with his Staff of Truth and has kept him locked away since. Ellington now believes Brother Jerome is insane, just as the prisoner said, but pretends to believe Jerome. Brother Jerome catches on and sees that Ellington does not believe or understand the situation so he assigns him a guard to keep watch over him through the rest of the night, insisting Ellington leave in the morning. Ellington waits for his guard to fall asleep and sneaks back to the prisoner. Upon seeing Ellington, the man pleads for him to let him out. Ellington rushes to the cage and sees that the door is held shut by only a stick and no actual lock. He asks the man why he doesn't just free himself, but the man urges Ellington repeatedly to let him out before it is too late. Ellington quickly removes the staff and is immediately thrown to the floor as the man is released from the cell. As the prisoner walks away, he transforms into his authentic appearance, which is the devil. Ellington then spends the rest of his life trying to recapture the evil that tricked him into letting it out.

The enemy (devil, ego, satan) is our howling man. It will take any appearance or form that will garner sympathy or pardon. To the naked eye, we generally do not see anything but surface appearances, just as Ellington saw a disheveled man being held hostage when the reality was that the man was the devil and Brother Jerome saw his authentic appearance. Part of the spiritual path is being able to see behind surface appearances and see the bigger picture. Things are never as they seem in our minds and may not even be what most people assume or believe in this physical and material world. There is always something greater at work and play. If we see things as they appear, we get caught up in worldly appearances and not the truth.

Jesus Himself was faced with temptation during His forty days in the desert. When He was hungry, parched, and tired, the enemy came to tempt Him, using tricks that were customized to Jesus's vulnerabilities in hopes of thwarting His mission and purpose. The devil used the Word of God as a weapon against the Son of God to attempt to trick Him and lead Him off His spiritual path. Likewise, each Spiritual Archetype has common distractions that can lure us from our highest potential, tempt us, and keep us from our soul's purpose. Just as we all have ways God calls us to our fullest potential, we also have ways the enemy attempts to divert us from our highest selves. Awareness of the common struggles and blocks we will face and then being wise to how the enemy uses them against us places the enemy's battle plan in our hands. With this information, we can create a strategy, just as in any battle, and come out victorious. Thus, knowing and understanding our Spiritual Archetypes allows us to triumph both personally and spiritually.

Just as in the story of "The Howling Man," the one thing that keeps "the devil" held prisoner is the truth. Not a key, not a specialized weapon, but the truth. Our greatest weapon against our enemy (ego, devil, satan) is spiritual truth. When we know the truth, and understand our authority to exercise it, we gain unwavering power over our enemy and howling man. If we sit and listen to its stories, its thoughts, or its lies, we risk letting it out into our consciousness. If the enemy is released into our consciousness, it runs freely into our lives and on our spiritual path until we recapture it with the truth and lock it back into its place. However, keeping the enemy at bay is always easier than recapturing it after we have let it loose. The Spiritual Archetypes give us the ability to see some of the specific ways the enemy howls in our consciousness and the authoritative truth over it, thus allowing us to lock it away and walk our path more freely, powerfully, and aligned.

PART TWO

# THE POWER OF ARCHETYPES

# WHAT IS AN ARCHETYPE?

*"Archetypes are complexes of experience that come upon us like
fate, and their effects are felt in our most personal life."*
—CARL JUNG

W e tend to think of ourselves and our spiritual path singularly, with only personal consciousness and unconscious. This is true, of course, we each have our own life, path, gifts, and experiences. However, as well as having our own conscious and unconscious, we also have a collective unconscious. Together, everyone in the world makes up a collective whole, which acts out various forms of our unconsciousness in different ways. Similarly to how we create our experience in our own lives with our thoughts, words, beliefs, and actions, whether conscious or subconscious, we also create and manifest collectively. Archetypes are themes and manifestations of the collective consciousness. They consist of patterns, images, and personalized collective experiences and can be found in stories, tales, myths, folklore, and spirituality.

The definition of *archetype* in Merriam-Webster's dictionary states, "the original pattern or model from which all things of the same kind are copied or on which they are based; a model or first form; prototype." The word *archetype* first entered the English language in the 1540s, but psychologist Carl Jung created the classic psychological archetypes in 1919. Jung believed that there were twelve universal psychological archetypes that symbolize human motivations, visions, and goals. He defined archetypes as "a collectively inherited unconscious idea, pattern of thought, image, etc., universally present in individual psyches." Jung found that most, if not all, people exhibited multiple archetypes and characteristics of their archetypes in their personality. Through the study and exploration of archetypes, people have learned the importance and value of understanding ourselves on a conscious and subconscious level. Knowing and understanding human motivations, needs, and desires can be incredibly beneficial in our relationships with others but also in our own personal and spiritual development. Discovering our true nature and essence has been one of man's greatest motivations and conquests throughout existence. By illuminating and unearthing our patterns, reasonings, and motivations, then seeing why we resonate with the people, places, and practices we do, we become equipped to understand new depths of ourselves.

The Spiritual Archetypes symbolize our motivations, visions, and goals both personally and spiritually. Each person who identifies with a specific Spiritual Archetype may find that they identify with that archetype's intentions, blocks, and belief systems. One of the primary purposes of the Spiritual Archetypes is to identify those struggles and provide information, guidance, and healing resources that will resonate with that specific archetype to achieve the utmost success. The Spiritual Archetypes are conscious identities with conscious and subconscious behaviors, blocks, and beliefs. Due to their similarities, each archetype is partial to specific colors, beliefs, and aspects of psychology and spirituality that further their progression. By utilizing these, each Spiritual Archetype can bypass common mental, emotional, spiritual, and even physical struggles while leaning into their strengths.

Although not related to the original psychological archetypes of Jung, the Spiritual Archetypes do integrate original psychological factors. Every human problem, motivation, or perspective has a deeper root that can be healed, transmuted, or released with a spiritual resolution. Therefore, everything addressed in the Spiritual Archetypes shows the human aspect and provides spiritual perspectives, solutions, and truths.

By putting God at the forefront of our solutions, we create limitless possibilities for ourselves personally, emotionally, mentally, physically, and spiritually. Essentially Spiritual Archetypes act as a map, but integration, communion, and relationship with God are the greatest journeys we will ever embark upon.

## Do We Only Have One Spiritual Archetype?

The Spiritual Archetypes are similar to astrology in that they have a prominent sign (which is your sun sign), an ascendant sign, a moon sign, houses, etc. The Spiritual Archetypes have a main influence, followed by other secondary, Spiritual Archetypes. You will likely have one main Spiritual Archetype, yet as you explore the characteristics and traits, you may also find that you are on the cusp of another. Also, as with astrology, you may feel some features fit you exceptionally well while others are not predominant factors in your sign or Spiritual Archetype. These may differ depending on where you are on your spiritual path. You may find one of your traits is something you have already worked on, so it is not as active in the present moment, yet it is still a part of your overall past or life pattern. Perhaps a Spiritual Archetype has appeared in your life or has not appeared yet. Life, and the spiritual path, are not linear. They work in cycles and spirals, bringing us through themes and, later, circle back again. Themes can build on one another and happen in layers, depending on our experience. A specific theme of a Spiritual Archetype may be prevalent in your life, or it may spiral through later and build upon other themes on your path. Thus, you may find that you resonate completely with one Spiritual Archetype and identify with a different one years later. Each of the Spiritual Archetypes identifies a part of our spiritual path; therefore, as you travel on your path, your Spiritual Archetype might change to reflect that. While these signify different lessons, you do not have to experience each Spiritual Archetype. Some will never relate to your personality, but you will recognize them in other people. You may also find that your main life lessons reside in one Spiritual Archetype and hardly stray or step outside of that framework. Our Spiritual

Archetypes represent the current state of our consciousness and what style of learning we resonate with. As we change on our path, so can our Spiritual Archetypes.

## Is One Spiritual Archetype Better Than Another?

When I initially finished the Spiritual Archetype quiz, I gave it to a friend to test. He was my best friend. I had known him for years and worked with him professionally, so I knew undoubtedly that he was the Eastern Philosopher. After taking my quiz, he called to tell me he had gotten the Theologist. Upon hearing this, I asked which answers he picked. He confessed that he had taken the quiz multiple times and received the Eastern Philosopher the first couple of times. However, after reading the Spiritual Archetype descriptions, he was determined to receive the Theologist. He altered his answers until he received it because he believed that particular Spiritual Archetype was the most "enlightened." Since he strived to be more like the Theologist, he answered the questions as though he was already where he hoped to be, not where he currently was on his path. Another person I knew exceptionally well answered the questions based on how she aimed to be rather than where she was, because she wasn't happy with her life, so she answered them based on her goal, not her reality.

One Spiritual Archetype is not superior to another. Every Spiritual Archetype has positive and less-than-positive traits, blocks, and challenges. My friend longed to be further along on his path, so he wanted a Spiritual Archetype that embodied his goal but not the reality of his current consciousness. However, we must recognize where we are to decide best where to go.

In the book *Alice's Adventures in Wonderland* by Lewis Carroll, Alice asks the Cheshire Cat, "Would you tell me, please, which way I ought to go from here?" The Cheshire Cat responds, "That depends a good deal on where you want to get to." Alice tells him, "I don't much care where." The Cheshire Cat tells her, "Then it doesn't much matter which way you go." Alice responds, "So long as I get somewhere." And the Cheshire Cat says, "Oh, you're sure to do that, if only you walk long enough."

Knowing where we want to go and having goals is invaluable in life and spirituality, but we must also meet ourselves where we are to be able to get directions to where we want to go. The Spiritual Archetype we currently resonate with holds certain parts of the path our soul knows we need to experience to point us in the direction we know we want to go. Pretending to be something we are not is essentially the same as saying, "You'll get there if only you walk long enough." The word *path* has multiple definitions. It can mean "a continual motion of walking or movement," or "a course of action." We don't want to merely "walk long enough" on our spiritual path. We influence where we go by knowing where we want to go, but the first step is acknowledging where we are *now*. In a less "Cheshire Cat" way of speaking: You must honor yourself by recognizing where you are on your path, then allow yourself to be fully present in that place. From that point, you can approach your path with a goal and let God lead you to where you ought to go.

## The Spiritual Archetypes + Others

After the Spiritual Archetypes quiz was released, I received hundreds of letters, emails, and messages from people sharing their testimonies about the power of the resulting information and what it had healed, inspired, or propelled in their spiritual lives and relationships. One of the most profound testimonials I received was from a middle-aged man who had given the Spiritual Archetype quiz to his mother. He wrote to me and explained that he and his mother had endured a strained relationship throughout his life. When he was younger, he tried to mend their differences, but after years of unsuccessful attempts, he decided they were too different to reconcile their relationship. When he took the quiz and downloaded his personalized guidebook, he was in awe of how accurately his Spiritual Archetype described himself and his path. It shed light on his thoughts, feelings, and behaviors that he could never understand—until reading his guidebook. Feeling inspired, he decided to give the quiz to his mother. His mother, who was not a deeply spiritual person, was shocked by how much she identified with the material in her guidebook, which produced different results than her son's. Feeling like their Spiritual Archetypes perfectly suited them both, they decided to try something utterly foreign to their relationship. They let one another read their Spiritual Archetype guidebook. He told me that after reading about her Spiritual Archetype, and her reading about his, for the first time in their lives they felt like they understood and "saw" each other. For over thirty years, they avoided talking about their strained relationship. But they finally saw each other and looked forward to how their relationship would progress with their new insights and understanding.

We do not see things as they are; we see things as we are. And while we may have the best intentions to love or support the people in our lives, sometimes we cannot see past our own lens. This can feel disheartening if we do not understand why they are the way they are and how to best communicate with them in that place. Sometimes, a misunderstanding signifies a lack of realization, which can be refocused to provide clarity and harmony. We all have experiences in our lives where we wish someone could see us clearly and love us in that space. Holding space for someone's human afflictions while holding truth for them on a spiritual level is one of the most spiritual actions we can make. This is a powerful act in any relationship: between parent and child, romantic partners, friends, siblings, coworkers—the list goes on. By gaining a better understanding of each other's strengths, we are able to better work together. By understanding each other's struggles, we can remove some of our own opinions and biases. As with the case with the gentlemen and his mother, they had spent almost a lifetime fighting to be seen, yet choosing to hide from each other out of the false belief that the other person couldn't see them or love them as they were. The Spiritual Archetypes are not just about revealing our inner self and soul path; they allow us to witness, love, and support other people's inner self and soul path. By revealing the holiest parts of ourselves and testifying to the holiness in others, we create space to peel back our layers of fear, guilt, shame, or confusion that penetrate the belief in *separation* and create a bridge for *connection* and oneness.

While you may choose to only read about your Spiritual Archetype, I encourage everyone to read them all regardless of what your beliefs, opinions, or preconceived notions may be about another person or group. This can be enlightening and healing in and of itself. Oftentimes, we may believe we know the truth about another person, group, or community. But, if we surrender our ideas and make room for information, we also create space for understanding, empathy, and compassion.

PART THREE

# THE SPIRITUAL ARCHETYPES

# WHAT IS YOUR SPIRITUAL ARCHETYPE?

T o provide the most accurate results, I created the *What is Your Spiritual Archetype?* quiz on an online platform. In doing so, I could use the best resources to ensure the utmost success. I realize this may feel like an inconvenience or hassle, but I assure you that this will give you the best outcome. Therefore, please go to VaqueroMinistries.com and return here after discovering your Spiritual Archetype.

# THE NEOTERIC SHAMAN

The Neoteric Shaman embodies the spirit of the counselor and advisor of shamans and medicine men and women. Shamans are revered and sought after for their council. Throughout history, they have held a position that was honored and appreciated among their people. The Neoteric Shaman may find that they embody these traits in their life and work. The Neoteric Shaman finds they attract others who are seeking guidance and support without even offering it. People may be drawn to them without explanation. Because they channel this ancient energy, others are drawn to it, seeking their wisdom and counsel.

The Neoteric Shaman harnesses the energy of the tribal medicine men and women who heal their people through prayer, herbs, intuition, vision, and connection with God. Shamans deeply understand the spirit realm and are believed to walk in both worlds. Similarly, the Neoteric Shaman has a strong connection to the spirit world and feels driven to connect others to this realm also. They believe the Earth and the stories of people hold immense value. They are fascinated by old-world life-styles and love ancient relics and antiquities.

The Neoteric Shaman is generally an introvert who mainly opens up to those closest to them. They usually have a lot happening internally. They think a lot and may have trouble expressing the emotions they feel. This is partially why they may be more comfortable in their personal space rather than when given too much centralized attention, which is difficult because people are so intensely drawn to them. They enjoy connecting with nature and animals over being in the city or surrounded by people. Living in the woods, lakeside, or where they can regroup is sacred to them.

Being connected to the spirit and physical world requires staying well grounded. Shamans endured many personal initiations for the sake of their tribe, which included painful sacrifices. The Neoteric Shaman must stay grounded in the physical world to fully commit to their health and well-being. This stability will increase their connection without depleting their body or self. It is part of their destiny to learn that they no longer need to suffer for their wisdom or to benefit others.

**Most Common Ascendant Spiritual Archetypes:** the Witch, the Recoverist, the Christian Mystic

**Colors of the Neoteric Shaman:** red, burnt orange, gray, clay brown, bright yellow, dark brown/almost black, bright green, forest green, lava

**When Balanced, You May Feel or Experience:** grounded, stable, reliable, centered, focused on self-care, physically active, able to manifest, able to process emotions

**When Unbalanced, You May Feel or Experience:** anxiety, fear, fight-or-flight, insecurity, low self-esteem, anger

**Governs:** genitalia, feet, bladder, colon, and legs or knees

**Common Physical Ailments:** knee pain, sciatica, constipation, underactive sex drive, infertility and reproductive issues, poor immune system, laziness, and irritable bowel

## Correlating Essential Oils

**Tobacco:** ceremony, respect, peace, unity
**Sandalwood:** spiritual vitality
**Patchouli:** love, prosperity, grounding
**Cedarwood:** strength, faith, healing of infections
**Cinnamon:** stimulation of root chakra, dry heat for the body, love, and abundance
**Sage:** protection, cleansing, releasing

## Correlating Stones

**Moqui Marble (aka the Shaman stone):** found in abundance in the Navajo desert and offers a balancing energy
**Tigers Eye:** action, discernment, courage, and fearlessness
**Bloodstone (aka Christ's stone):** Legend says that when Jesus was crucified, His blood hit the stone beneath the cross.
This caused the fusion of stone and blood, thus birthing the bloodstone.
This gemstone symbolizes sacrifice and comfort during our sacrifices.
**Black Obsidian:** a shield against negativity
**Turquoise:** intuition, wisdom, inner peace, communication
**Red Jasper:** stamina, strength, endurance
**Lodalite:** communication with oneself

## Correlating Plants

- **Yucca:** transmutation, protection, purification
- **Wood:** protection, purification, love
- **Palo Santo:** release, healing, initiation
- **Agave:** nectar of life

## Correlating Animal: THE BEAR

The Bear has close ties to shamans in various countries, including in North America and Siberia. Bear represents strength, solitude, healing, connection and communication with Spirit, and hibernation. The Neoteric Shaman has tendencies of codependency and often lacks boundaries. The Bear is a reminder to connect with God first and be strong within yourself before giving to others. You cannot serve from an empty well. Bear encourages you to seek solitude and practice self-care.

**Power Words:** self-care, wisdom, support, transparent, honest, loyal, space holder, nature, grounded

### People, Places, and Periods That May Resonate with You

- **People:** Native American, Druid, Aboriginal, blacksmith, metal worker, inventor, cowboy, frontiersmen
- **Places:** Peru, Arizona, Colorado, Mexico, Brazil, Australia, Africa
- **Periods:** Ancient civilizations, 2600 BC; early American Frontier, the late 1800s through the early 1900s.

### Common Struggles

**Common Triggers:** being taken advantage of, not feeling needed, not having boundaries, feeling unlovable, being unappreciated, feeling neglected

**When Triggered, the Neoteric Shaman Can Become:** selfish, manipulative, withdrawn

**Common Personal Struggles:** Those who have The Neoteric Shaman Spiritual Archetype struggle with the internal battle of having to live in a world that is no longer supportive of the old ways of life. It is as though you were born at the wrong time and would prefer to be living centuries ago. You may feel confused by modern technology and the current proceedings of the world. Some Neoteric Shamans feel overwhelmed by what may seem like simple, everyday tasks, such as running errands or using the Internet because their mind is not geared toward modern life. You feel like an outsider, in part, because of the priorities of our present society, and may even feel hurt by the lack of empathy others have for the old ways of life. Your values, thought process or ideals are reminiscent of the past, and it may feel like you are working against the grain. There is a remarkable beauty in the old-world ways that you wish more people valued and respected, and it may even feel like a personal attack when they do not.

The Neoteric Shaman sees the fruits of their labor as evidence of their worth. Therefore, the more they do, create, or make, reaffirms this belief in their mind and the more worthy they feel. When it comes to healing, The Neoteric Shaman will go to great lengths to heal, grow, or expand, sometimes even putting themselves through unnecessary discomfort because they feel like they can take it. Some with the Neoteric Shaman Spiritual Archetype may even be proud of their pain and wear it as a badge of honor, as though suffering makes them more dedicated, stronger, or able.

The Neoteric Shaman often comes from an upbringing where they needed to be the emotional support for others in their life or witnessed others doing so, which taught them the behavior. This could be from emotionally absent parents, abusive parents, having to play the caregiver to family, friends, or siblings—or feeling like the people in their life relied on them in a big way. The Neoteric Shaman had to grow up quickly and may feel like they didn't really have a childhood because of this. They are always the adult to everyone around them, which leads to growing up and still feeling like they must mentally, physically, spiritually, and/or emotionally support others. This may also manifest as having a difficult time creating boundaries for themselves because they feel bad doing so.

Lastly, The Neoteric Shaman worries about basic survival needs, such as money or being able to provide, and operates in fight-or-flight mode when their basic needs are being threatened.

**Common Spiritual Struggles:** To reach the level of wisdom that was required of shamans and medicine people, they were expected to go through painful emotional, physical, mental, and spiritual initiations, sometimes beginning in early childhood. The mentality was that it was for the greater good of the tribe and only the strongest, bravest, or wisest could make such sacrifices. The Neoteric Shaman Spiritual Archetype struggles with this same "greater good" mentality. You find yourself making sacrifices for others and believe you must even sacrifice yourself and your desires for the greater good of others. Indigenous tribes had a strong survival mentality because they had to endure harsh conditions and also lived without excess. They believed in only having what they needed to survive and couldn't understand the need others had for material possessions. The Neoteric Shaman believes they require very little to survive, yet they also have fears about survival. Unfortunately, when we live in survival mode, we may selfishly take what we want because we fear the outside world will not provide for our basic needs.

## Mythology, Folklore, Symbolism, or Correlating Story

*The following story is from the book* American Indian Myths and Legends *and was translated by Richard Erdoes and Alfonso Ortiz from the Tewa, a group of Pueblo Native Americans.*

Long ago in the ancient home of the San Juan people, in a village whose ruins can be seen across the river from present-day San Juan, lived two magically gifted young people. The youth was called Deer Hunter because even as a boy, he was the only one who never returned empty-handed from the hunt. The girl, whose name was White Corn Maiden, made the finest pottery and embroidered clothing with the most beautiful designs of any woman in the village. These two were the handsomest couple in the village, and it was no surprise to their parents that they always sought one another's company. Seeing that they were favored by the gods, the villagers assumed that they were destined to marry.

And in time they did, and contrary to their elders' expectations, they began to spend even more time with one another. White Corn Maiden began to ignore her pottery making and embroidery, while Deer Hunter gave up hunting at a time when he could have saved many of his people from hunger. They even began to forget their religious obligations. At the request of the pair's worried parents, the tribal elders called a council. This young couple was ignoring all the traditions by which the tribe had lived and prospered, and the people feared that angry gods might bring famine, flood, sickness, or some other disaster upon the village.

But Deer Hunter and White Corn Maiden ignored the council's pleas and drew closer together, swearing that nothing would ever part them. A sense of doom pervaded the village, even though it was late spring and all nature had unfolded in new life.

Then suddenly White Corn Maiden became ill, and within three days she died. Deer Hunter's grief had no bounds. He refused to speak or eat, preferring to keep watch beside his wife's body until she was buried early the next day.

For four days after death, every soul wanders in and around its village and seeks forgiveness from those whom it may have wronged in life. It is a time of unease for the living, since the soul may appear in the form of a wind, a disembodied voice, a dream, or even in human shape.

To prevent such a visitation, the villagers go to the dead person before burial and utter a soft prayer of forgiveness. And on the fourth day after death, the relatives gather to perform a ceremony releasing the soul into the spirit world, from which it will never return.

But Deer Hunter was unable to accept his wife's death. Knowing that he might see her during the four-day interlude, he began to wander around the edge of the village. Soon, he drifted farther out into the fields, and it was here at sundown of the fourth day, even while his relatives were gathering for the ceremony of release, that he spotted a small fire near a clump of bushes.

Deer Hunter drew closer and found his wife, as beautiful as she was in life and dressed in all her finery, combing her long hair with a cactus brush in preparation for the last journey. He fell weeping at her feet, imploring her not to leave but to return with him to the village before the releasing rite was consummated. White Corn Maiden begged her husband to let her go because she no longer belonged to the world of the living. Her return would anger the spirits, she said, and anyhow, soon she would no longer be beautiful, and Deer Hunter would shun her.

He brushed her pleas aside by pledging his undying love and promising that he would let nothing part them. Eventually, she relented, saying that she would hold him to his promise. They entered the village just as their relatives were marching to the shrine with the food offering that would release the soul of White Corn Maiden. They were horrified when they saw her, and again they and the village elders begged Deer Hunter to let her go. He ignored them, and an air of grim expectancy settled over the village.

The couple returned to their home, but before many days had passed, Deer Hunter noticed that his wife was beginning to have an unpleasant odor. Then he saw that her beautiful face had grown ashen and her skin dry. At first, he only turned his back on her as they slept. Later, he began to sit up on the roof all night, but White Corn Maiden always joined him. In time, the villagers became used to the sight of Deer Hunter racing among the houses and through the fields with White Corn Maiden, now not much more than skin and bones, in hot pursuit. Things continued in this way until one misty morning a tall and imposing figure appeared in the small dance court at the center of the village. He was dressed in spotless white buckskin robes and carried the biggest bow anyone had ever seen. On his back was slung a great quiver with the two largest arrows anyone had ever seen. He remained standing at the center of the village and called, in a voice that carried into every home, for Deer Hunter and White Corn Maiden. Such was its authority that the couple stepped forward meekly and stood facing him.

The awe-inspiring figure told the couple that he had been sent from the spirit world because they, Deer Hunter and White Corn Maiden, had violated their people's traditions and angered the spirits; that because they had been so selfish, they had brought grief and near-disaster to the village. "Since you insist on being together," he said, "you shall have your wish. You will chase one another forever across the sky as visible reminders that your people must live according to tradition if they are to survive." With this, he set Deer Hunter on one arrow and shot him low into the western sky. Putting White Corn Maiden on the other arrow, he placed her just behind her husband.

That evening, the villagers saw two new stars in the west. The first, large and very bright, began to move east across the heavens. The second, a smaller, flickering star, followed close behind. So it is to this day, according to the Tewa; the brighter one is Deer Hunter, placed there in the prime of his life. The dimmer star is White Corn Maiden, set there after she had died; yet she will forever chase her husband across the heavens.

Like White Corn Maiden, The Neoteric Shaman does not prioritize themself and their needs. Although White Corn Maiden knew she must transition into the afterlife, she agreed to stay because of the grief of her husband. She allowed herself to waste away so that he could be sustained. The Neoteric Shaman can also allow themself to ignore their own needs and let their dreams, wishes, and selves decay for the needs, desires, and wants of others. Just as in the story, there is balance and harmony in the world, and by doing what is right for ourselves, we allow others the opportunity to change, grow, heal, and commune with God in ways they may not otherwise. Only by following the path that honors ourselves do we give others these opportunities in the most divinely planned way.

## Spiritual Guidance

The Neoteric Shaman must connect the physical world with the spiritual world. They often rely on their keen sense of survival instead of asking for guidance and support from God. By accepting more from God, The Neoteric Shaman may unload some of the weight on their shoulders. Instead of entering fight-or-flight mode, you could pause to breathe and ask for support, love, abundance, health, or whatever it is you need. Expect that you will receive it by giving gratitude along with your prayer.

Being in nature has a profound effect on you; enter nature as frequently as possible. Additionally, being around animals can be incredibly soothing and comforting to you. Animals have long been believed to have healing properties, and each animal holds its own medicine, which has been used for guidance, support, and wisdom for centuries. By practicing animal medicine, we can build a bridge between the spiritual and physical world. Ask for guidance on where you should focus your healing intention, then see which animals present themselves to you.

Do what you can to care for others while giving them room to take care of themselves. Often, people can miss their lessons, expansion, and growth if someone else does all the work. As the saying goes, you can give a man a fish and he will be fed for that meal, but if you teach him how to fish, he will be fed for life. Do your best to teach others to fish instead of always giving them your fish and leaving yourself hungry.

### Affirmations:

- *I am grounded. I am safe. I am protected in this world.*
- *I release my fear to God and know that God loves, protects, and supports me.*
- *I am not responsible for others. I will do my best, and my best is good enough. I lovingly release others to God and trust God to provide everything for them.*

### Prayer:

"Lord, guide and direct me in all things so that I may surrender my will and seek Yours above everything."

### Additional Resources:

*Animal Speak* by Ted Andrews
*Codependent No More* by Melody Bettie
*The Four Agreements* by Don Miguel Ruiz

*The Secret Science Behind Miracles* by Max Freedom Long
*Black Elk Speaks* by John G. Neihardt
*Kateri Tekakwitha The Iroquois Saint* by Pierre Cholonec
*Samson Occom and the Christian Indians of New England*
     by William DeLoss Love
*More Than I Asked For: The Life of Isabel Crawford*
     by Marilyn Fardig Whiteley
*Boundaries* by Henry Cloud and John Townsend

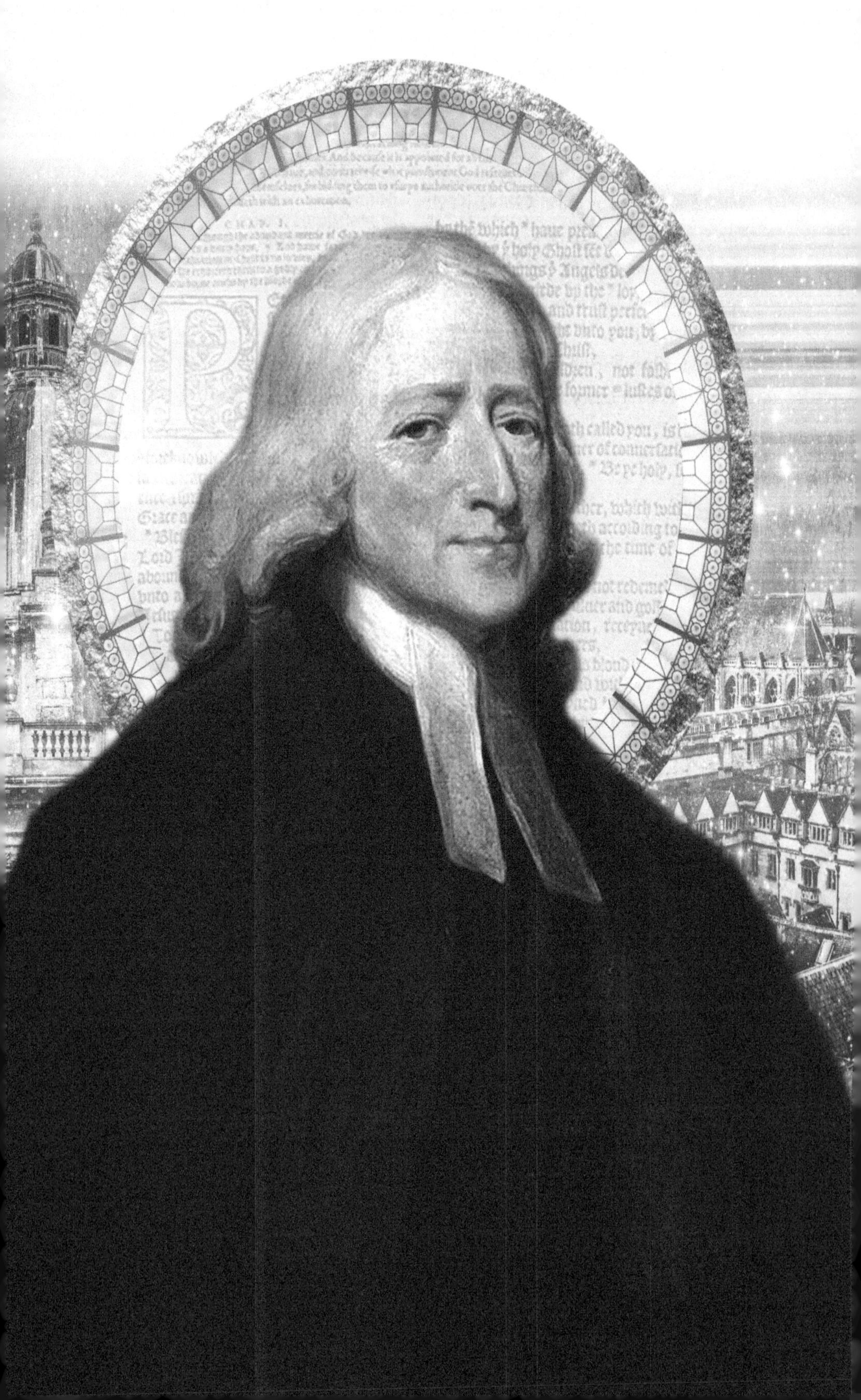

# THE RECOVERIST

The Recoverist is the Spiritual Archetype whose main introduction to spirituality is through recovery programs such as Alcoholics Anonymous (AA) and Narcotics Anonymous (NA). Although they may have had prior experience with religion or spirituality, it was through the trials of life and their surrender of addiction that led them to pursue faith for themself. The Recoverist is a sensitive soul who may or may not realize their sensitivities. Many people who struggle with addiction are unaware of their intuitive or empathic nature, or are incredibly emotional people who do not know how to harness their feelings. People who struggle with addiction may even feel as though they are possessed by an outside force when they use or desire to use because of the intensity behind the emotions, some of which are not their own because they may also be picking up on the emotions of their environments. This is especially prevalent with people in Al-Anon or who have childhood experiences with emotionally unstable caregivers.

The Recoverist has a deep desire to fit into the world and is haunted by the feeling that they do not. Most Recoverists do not understand that they do not feel like they fit into the world because they are not meant to. This world is a physical world, but we are physical beings with a spiritual nature. While our body is real and must abide by the laws of this physical world, we are souls encased by the body and are not our bodies themselves. This inner knowing of our divine origin and the breath of life breathed into our souls, yet living in the physical world, can lead people to feel like outsiders.

The Recoverist's inner world is constantly spinning. Unconsciously, they seek stability in the internal chaos and either try to slow it down or match the speed outside that is hurtling within. They are charismatic in nature, attracting and pulling people into their lives. If this energy and power can be used for good, the Recoverist can succeed in their lives, relationships, and work. However, if used in correlation with their addiction, the Recoverist may pull others into their addictions, behaviors, and patterns and negatively affect the people around them.

**Most Common Ascendant Spiritual Archetypes:** the Neoteric Shaman, the Crusader, the Neonate

**Colors of the Recoverist:** royal blue, regal blues, black, white, gray, red, purple

**When Balanced, You May Feel or Experience:** healthy, clear-headed, goal-oriented, successful, positive, motivated, helpful

**When Unbalanced, You May Feel or Experience:** scattered, unhealthy, useless, helpless, depressed, hopeless, selfish, chaotic

**Governs:** lower back, heart, knees, circulatory system, liver, kidneys

**Common Physical Ailments:** liver issues, low-back pain, kidney infections, blood issues, circulatory system problems, body aches, knee problems, weak heart

## Correlating Essential Oils

**Black pepper Oil:** personal identity, emotional strength, and perseverance

**Juniper Berry Oil:** Juniper is a sacred tree where an angel of the Lord visited Elijah. This reminds us to be present and listen to the word of God despite our situations.

**Frankincense:** oil of truth; speaking the truth and knowing the truth of God

## Correlating Stones

**Amethyst:** Amethyst is derived from Greek origin, meaning "not drunk," because they believed the stone kept people from intoxication. Therefore, it is the "stone of sobriety."

**Amazonite:** good for those who struggle with addiction and find water healing

**Carnelian:** encouragement, leadership, motivation

**Smoky Quartz:** "the grounding stone," grounds those in need of being present in one's life and with one's goals

**Peacock Ore:** joy, happiness, being comfortable in one's own skin

## Correlating Plants:

- **Bluebell:** gratitude and humility
- **Chamomile:** complaining, patience, perseverance
- **Poppies:** Blood of Christ and resurrection of the Lord
- **Hyssop:** cleansing and redemption
- **Iris:** hope, faith, trust

## Correlating Animal: THE PEACOCK

The Peacock teaches us to love our true colors. The Recoverist has life experience that teaches others how to love, forgive, and own their stories.

By sharing your true colors, you give others the comfort and inspiration to own theirs. The peacock is also a symbol of integrity. Integrity is one of the qualities many people lose while struggling with their addictions and can be challenging to regain even after sobriety. As you live your life of sobriety, ask yourself, "What does integrity look and feel like to me? How can I embody integrity? How can I stay in alignment with my integrity even when situations are difficult for me?" Peacock medicine is here to assist you in coming from your most authentic and integrous place.

**Power Words:** surrender, hope, faith, trust, authority, power, forgiveness, self-forgiveness

## People, Places, and Periods That May Resonate with You

- **People:** inventors, scientists, explorers, rebels and outlaws
- **Places:** Rome, Frontier America, Europe, France, Mexico, China, England, and India
- **Periods:** Iron Age, Industrial Age, Mexican Revolution, French Revolution, the 1700s, 1920s, 1960s–1970s, early 1990s

## Common Struggles

**Common Triggers:** fear of the past, fear of the future, fear of your own weaknesses, shame, guilt, helplessness, the unknown

**When Triggered, the Recoverist Can Become:** anxious, impulsive, irresponsible

**Common Personal Struggles:** In programs such as AA, there is a typical formality where a person speaking introduces themselves, then says, "I'm an alcoholic." The reasoning behind this is to admit that the person has a problem, which is considered the first step of recovery. However, on a spiritual level, this affirms not that a person struggles with a condition, but that they *are* the condition. You are not an addict; you are a person struggling with addiction who can be delivered from your addiction. God did not create addicts; He created you in the image and likeness of Himself. You may struggle with this problem in your life, but you are not that problem. By affirming that The Recoverist is an addict, they make this belief firm in their consciousness and are thus chained to it. The Latin root word *Addictus* means "slave of" or "bound to." The word *addiction* was originally the term for debtors sentenced to slavery under Roman law. The Oxford Dictionary defines the historical use of the word as, "the formal delivery of a person or property to an individual, typically in accordance with a judicial decision." Meaning, that the words *addict* and *addiction* are defined as "slavery to a master."

The mythological story of Addictus tells the story of a slave whose master one day sets him free. Yet Addictus, so used to being a slave and wearing his chains, continued to wear them even though he was free and drug them along with him as he walked the lands. Similarly, many addicts drag the chains of their addiction along with them. Affirming the words, "I am an addict," affirms the negative: "I am a slave to, or bound to, my addiction."

Years ago, I spoke to a man who struggled with heroin addiction who explained why he used. "I use because I try to forget all the horrible things I have done. Then I feel worse because I used again and am stuck in this vicious circle of guilt, shame, and relapse." For people who struggle with addiction, it is as though addiction offers the illusion of solutions, forgetting, or numbing. The person suffering can become so overwhelmed with their inner turmoil that life can seem unmanageable, and tolerance for life's situations and adversity may reside at a lower threshold. The relationship, therefore, is an abusive one: "I hate you, but I need you. And I need you because I cannot live, forgive, or forget without you."

**Common Spiritual Struggles:** Another struggle is that The Recoverist may have some understanding of God or the Bible based on meetings, or may even read the Bible, but does not stay committed to either. As with all programs, the continuous practice of faith allows for vast improvements in recovery as well as sustaining it. Sometimes, people who struggle with addiction can feel as though they have a handle on their addiction, which is usually when relapse occurs. Your hard work and devotion to recovery may keep you sober, but it is through the grace of God that you will stay sober. Staying sober is not simply an act of abstaining from a substance or thing; true sobriety is no longer being chained to, or a slave, of something. This comes from spiritual advancement and personal development. Even Alcoholics Anonymous founder Bill Wilson was a student of Edgar Cayce and in communication with Carl Jung and other occultists. He spent his life devoted to recovery but was equally, if not more so, committed to his spiritual advancement in conjunction with his sobriety. By combining programs, support, and abstinence with your spirituality, you can become the master, remove your chains, and free yourself from your addictions.

## Mythology, Folklore, Symbolism, or Correlating Story

### Tarot Card: The Moon

The Moon card for The Recoverist represents the illusions and false promises addiction seduces them with. Its symbolism includes a full moon with a half-moon within. In the background there is a tower on each side, which represents the unknown, a daunting yet unavoidable part of life, the spiritual journey, and recovery. We see a dog and a wolf in the middle-lower part of the card. These images represent the tame part of The Recoverist, who can play by the rules and live life according to the "healthy standards" of society, their friends, their family, or themselves. However, there is the mirror image of the wolf, an untamed and savage animal, which shows the duality of The Recoverist's nature. Lastly, at the bottom of the card, a crayfish attempts to find footing and security on land, yet falls back into the unknown of the water. This shows The Recoverist's attempts to gain a sense of self and security in their sobriety and how it can always feel as though they are losing their solid ground and falling back into the abyss within themselves.

### The Prodigal Son

"A certain man had two sons. The younger of them said to his father, 'Father, give me the share of the property that falls to me.' So, he divided the estate between them. A few days later, the younger son gathered together everything that he had and traveled to a distant country, and there he wasted his fortune in reckless and immoral living. Now when he had spent everything, a severe famine occurred in that country, and he began to do without and be in need. So, he went and forced himself on one of the citizens of that country, who sent him into his fields to feed pigs. He would have gladly eaten the pods that the pigs were eating but they could not satisfy his hunger, and no one was giving anything to him. But when he finally came to his senses, he said, 'How many of my father's hired men have more than enough food, while I am dying here of hunger! I will get up and go to my father, and I will say to him, Father, I have sinned against heaven and in your sight. I am no longer worthy to be called your son; just treat me like one of your hired men.' So he got up and came to his father. But while he was still a long way off, his father saw him, was moved with compassion for him, and ran, embraced, and kissed him. And the son said to him, 'Father, I have sinned against heaven and in your sight; I am no longer worthy to be called your son.' But the father said to his servants, 'Quickly bring out the best robe for the guest of honor and put it on him; and give him a ring for his hand, and sandals for his feet. And bring the fattened calf and slaughter it, and let us invite everyone and feast and celebrate; for this son of mine was dead and is alive again; he was lost and has been found.' So they began to celebrate.

"Now his older son was in the field; and when he returned and approached the house, he heard music and dancing. So he summoned one of the servants and began asking what this celebration meant. And he said to him, 'Your brother has come, and your father has killed the fattened calf because he has received him back safe and sound.' But the elder brother became angry and deeply resentful and was not willing to go in; and his father came out and began pleading with him. But he said to his father, 'Look! These many years I have served you, and I have never neglected or disobeyed your command. Yet you have never given me so much as a young goat, so that I might celebrate with my friends; but when this son of yours arrived, who has devoured your estate with immoral women, you slaughtered that fattened calf for him!' The father said to him, 'Son, you are always with me, and all that is mine is yours. But it was fitting to celebrate and rejoice, for this brother of yours was dead and has begun to live. He was lost and has been found.'" (Luke 15:11–32).

The Recoverist is similar to the son who has left and lived outside his father's estate. Yet when the son returns, the father is not disgraced, cruel, or judgmental toward his son. Like a good father, he embraces his son and is grateful and relieved that his son is safe and has returned home. God rejoices when His children return to His estate. He is not making lists of all our wrongdoings and holding them up to shame, blame, and ridicule us when we return. We, like the prodigal son, are the ones who are ashamed and beg to be made a servant, but God says, "Quickly bring out the best robe for the guest of honor and put it on him; and give him a ring for his hand, and sandals for his feet. And bring the fattened calf and slaughter it, and let us invite everyone and feast and celebrate; for this son of mine was dead and is alive again; he was lost and has been found." Regardless of where you have been or what you have done, it is never too late to humble yourself and return to the estate of your Father with humility, sincerity, and the desire to make your life better.

## Spiritual Guidance

Preacher and healer Smith Wigglesworth told a story about a woman he met in Liverpool who came to him and said, "I have a drunkard husband, and every night he comes into the home under the influence of drink. Won't you join me in prayer for him?" Smith Wigglesworth asked her if she had a handkerchief, which she gave him, and he prayed over it, telling her to lay it on the pillow of the drunken man. She obeyed and put the handkerchief on her husband's pillow, which he slept on. Wigglesworth said, "He laid his head on more than a pillow that night, for he laid his head on the promise of God." Then, in Mark 11:24 he read, "Whatever things you ask when you pray, believe that you receive them, and you will have them."

The next day the man went to a saloon on his way to work, but when he tasted his drink, he believed it had gone bad or was poisoned. He went to the next bar where his drink was soured again, and he believed it was poisoned. He began accusing the bartenders of conspiring to poison him and was finally thrown out for causing a scene. After work, he attempted to buy himself another drink with the same results. Again, he believed they were trying to poison him, and was thrown out of the saloon. He went home and told his wife what had happened and that he believed they were trying to poison him. She responded, "Can't you see the hand of the Lord in this, that he is making you dislike the stuff that has been your ruin?" The man felt something come over him when his wife spoke those words and had a revelation that he had not had before. His heart was forever changed, and he went to a meeting and got saved.

Addiction is one area where people feel helpless to an invisible force that seems like it has absolute power. Feeling the powerlessness of addiction and the self-hatred that perpetuated the need to feed that addiction is a ruthless and degrading feeling. For many people who struggle with addiction, this is the catalyst to continue using. It is a vicious cycle of guilt, shame, and self-hatred while sober, then numbing the guilt, shame, and self-hatred by using. Working the steps, having support, and learning important details, such as triggers, are invaluable in recovery. However, it is through God's grace, mercy, and love that we can learn to love and forgive ourselves. Beyond programs and groups, The Recoverist must find their relationship with God. Programs give actionable steps while God provides supernatural solutions.

You, dear, are not powerless. Your flesh may be weak, but your soul is God-breathed and capable of anything. God instilled in you power and authority, which is yours as an inheritance. A person in a position of authority gains the confidence to use their authority by knowing the laws of their field and exercising those laws based on the power given to them accordingly. Luke 10:19 says, "Behold, I give unto you power to tread on serpents and scorpions, and over all the power of the enemy: and nothing shall by any means hurt you." This includes your addiction. There are laws that govern the spiritual world, just as there are laws that govern the physical world. Learn the laws of your power and authority and use them to overcome your greatest adversary: your addictions.

## Affirmations:

- *I AM the image and likeness of God.*
- *God is stronger than my addictions, the voice of the enemy, and even my own will. I can overcome anything.*
- *I surrender my weaknesses to You, God, and ask for strength in Jesus' name.*

## Prayer:

"Father, give us courage to change what must be altered, serenity to accept what cannot be helped, and the insight to know the one from the other."—Reinhold Niebuhr. Or pray the revised version known as "The Serenity Prayer": "God, grant me the serenity to accept the things I cannot change, courage to change the things I can, and wisdom to know the difference."

## Additional Resource:

*The Bible*
*Blame It on the Brain?* by Edward Welch
*The Recovery Bible* by Bill W., Emmet Fox, James Allen, Henry Drummond, William James, and more
*The Big Book* by Bill Wilson

# THE WITCH

The Witch has a strong belief in themself, which enables them to create magic in their life. Although they may not literally practice magic, they have an innate ability to manifest. They are powerful in your intuitive abilities, regardless of whether or not you have yet harnessed those powers and their full potential.

The Witch understands their power and the power of the divine feminine. The Witch often finds themself in the occupations of a midwife, herbalist, apothecary, healer, coach, or teacher. They are a feminist and, if female, may even work in a profession that primarily serves women. If they are male, they may find they are deeply in touch with their feminine side and have mostly female friends. The Witch prefers to be alone or among a small group of trusted allies who are usually female. They have mysterious and powerful energy, especially to outsiders, but are deeply loyal, loving, and committed to the few they let get close to them.

The Witch loves their home and considers it a sanctuary. It serves as a place of magic, recuperation, and to honor oneself. The Witch adorns their space, as well as themself, with vintage, antique, and handmade items that carry stories. They prefer old homes and historical places to modern living, although if they have a modern dwelling, they would furnish it with unique pieces. Reading books, drinking tea, sleeping, cooking, aromatherapy, candles, gardening, and old-fashioned crafting such as knitting, weaving, sewing, and embroidery are excellent self-care tools.

For the Witch, spirituality is about making their own rules. After suppression from the Church in the fifteenth century, the rise of witchcraft escalated. Many people wanted religious freedom but were not allowed to have their own beliefs. People began developing their faith and questioning the one-size-fits-all religion. The Witch incarnates this same rebel soul that cannot be tamed and does as they please spiritually and otherwise. They ask questions and question authority. The Witch has respect for the Earth and a live-and-let-live mentality. Because of the persecution they feel, they are accepting of the eccentricities of others and are usually nonjudgmental. However, they may also be on the other end of the spectrum and harbor resentment and bitterness for others because of the persecution they have experienced.

**Most Common Ascendant Spiritual Archetypes:** the Ancestor, the Mythologist, the Crusader, the Lightworker

**Colors of the Witch:** dark green, light green, red, black, rose pink, light purple

**When Balanced, You May Feel or Experience:** imagination, creativity, sexual energy, intuition, ability to resolve and dispel negativity and negative energies, self-care, confidence, a healthy reproductive system and ease of conception, happiness

**When Unbalanced, You May Feel or Experience:** an inability to accept yourself, feelings of limitation, lack of self-worth, codependency, sexual promiscuity, insatiable desires, victimization

**Governs:** pelvis, reproductive organs, bladder, colon, lower abdomen, spleen

**Common Physical Ailments:** reproductive issues, including infertility, irregular menstrual cycles, impotence, urinary tract and bladder problems; fungal overgrowth, such as candida; kidney infections; low-back pain

## Correlating Essential Oils:

**Clary Sage:** clarity, intuition, objective perspective
**Garlic:** protection and healing
**Rosemary:** "Where rosemary grows, the woman rules."
**Juniper:** Juniper is a tree of protection. In the Bible, the prophet Elijah's life is threatened by the evil Queen Jezebel. He retreats and sits under a juniper tree where an angel of the Lord comes to him, giving him food, drink, and messages from God (1 Kings 19: 2–5). Additionally, it is said that when Joseph and Mary hid with baby Jesus, their donkey rode them into a juniper tree that sheltered them from the massacre.

## Correlating Stones:

**Agate:** spiritual freedom; alignment; spiritual, mental, and psychical balance
**Sunstone:** Light in the dark months, or light in the dark moments. Once used by the Vikings for compasses, sunstone is used for finding your way.
**Opal:** independence, emotions, virtue
**Moonstone:** inspiration, magic, the awakening of the feminine
**Snowflake Obsidian:** correct thinking, the release of victimization, individuality
**Smoky Quartz:** focus, intention, transcendence into ones highest and best self
**Wulfenite:** female reproductive system, menstrual cycle, female hormones, menopause

## Correlating Plants:

- **Apple:** love, healing, immortality
- **Witch Hazel:** protection, chastity
- **Angelica:** protection, feminine power, blessings

## Correlating Animal: THE CAT

The Cat represents magic, independence, curiosity, freedom, and adventure. The Witch Spiritual Archetype tends to enjoy their solitude, which can keep them from living their lives to the fullest. The Cat encourages you to step out into the world in larger, more magnifying ways and remain curious about what life offers. Do not hold yourself back because of your desire to remain independent. Allow yourself to leap into opportunities and continuously create more magic.

**Power words:** magic, friendship, community, fighter, weaver, feminine

## People, Places, and Periods That May Resonate with You

- **People:** witch, abolitionist, freedom fighter, medicine woman, sorcerer, gypsy, fortune teller
- **Places:** Salem, Massachusetts; 1890–1910 France; England, Scotland Romania, Europe, Louisiana, New Orleans, Savanna
- **Periods:** Middle Ages, witch hunts of England and Germany between 1486–1660; 1400s Europe; 1647–1697 Connecticut; 1626–1730 Virginia; mid-1600s France

## Common Struggles

**Common Triggers:** being told what to think, feel, or believe; feeling hunted, hounded, or persecuted; seeing others being tormented; seeing others wronged; feeling helpless

**When Triggered, the Witch Can Become:** destructive, overly rebellious, headstrong

**Common Personal Struggles:** Witches have been falsely accused and persecuted relentlessly throughout history. They were victims of harsh punishment and were often put to death for their beliefs and practices or because of something someone said about them. Similarly, those with the Witch Spiritual Archetype are often misjudged and hold a strong victim mentality. You may find that you are often falsely accused and misunderstood despite your desire to be authentic. Because of your ability to manifest easily, you may find that when paired with a strong victim mentality, you manifest stressful and condemning situations relating to money, relationships, and work. This may present itself as being passed over for raises, promotions, or jobs you are qualified for, not being as successful as you desire, attracting unhealthy and abusive relationships, or having feast-or-famine cycles.

**Common Spiritual Struggles:** The female Witch loves being a woman but is greatly displeased with how women are perceived and feel this injustice predominantly in their lives. Through centuries of persecution that was, at times, for no greater reason than simply being a woman or minority, those with the Witch Spiritual Archetype retain these feelings of oppression and may either be aggressively vocal or passive-aggressive with their anger. While the Witch has a deep connection to the feminine, they must still practice healing around their own femininity. The Witch has their own resentments toward the feminine. You may feel like being a woman, or the female part of yourself is often your most blessed and cursed trait. This also creates deep-seated bitterness toward men, the "man's world," and God Himself, who is portrayed as our Father. People with the Witch Spiritual Archetype have issues with how women are seen and symbolized in the church, which can reflect their relationship with God and cause them to rebel against Him because of it.

## Mythology, Folklore, Symbolism, or Correlating Story

In the early days of the Christian church, after the death and resurrection of Jesus, there lived a rich and proper woman named Thecla, who lived in the city of Iconium. When the apostle Paul came preaching to the city, Thecla was enthralled with his teachings of the beatitudes and sat at her window for three days listening to him preach the gospel. Thecla decided to give up her life to follow Paul and became devoted to sharing the Word of God. However, Thecla was betrothed to a man named Thamyris, who was furious by her change of heart and that she no longer wanted to get married and have his children. Outraged by the rejection, Thamyris had Paul arrested and thrown in jail for disturbing the peace in hopes that Thecla would decide to marry him again. Unfortunately for him, she became more adamant and bribed the jail guards into letting her see Paul in his cell so that she could hear him preach. Upon finding them, Paul was exiled from the city, and Thecla was sentenced to death by burning at the stake. At her execution, the wood was lit with fire; however, it would not burn and the flames could not touch her, so they let her go.

After her failed execution, Thecla traveled to Antioch where Paul was preaching. There, a city official became interested in her, but when she refused his advances, he convinced the governor to put her to death. She was tied to a lioness and paraded in an arena with wild beasts. Yet when the male beasts attempted to eat her, the lionesses and female animals protected her. Commanding that she would baptize herself, Thecla threw herself into a large basin of deadly sea creatures. Before the fatal serpents could harm her, lightning struck them dead. Frightened, the people insisted she be released, and the officials let her go. Thecla followed Paul to Myra where he commissioned her to preach the gospel. She remained a healer and preacher of the Word of God for the rest of her life, performing miracles and teaching about God. Thecla became a saint in the Catholic Church and has been revered by many people, especially women, since the death and resurrection of Jesus.

While there were men who attempted to chain her to their ideas, desires, and beliefs, God delivered her from harm in miraculous ways. Though many teachings about women have been altered or misconstrued over the years, God has anointed many women to do amazing things in the world throughout history. Mother Mary was anointed to give birth to the Son of God, and Mary Magdalene was the first person to preach the gospel by announcing that Jesus had risen. Many women have done holy and anointed things throughout history, and it's important to differentiate between what is God and what is the persecution of man. Shifting these misperceptions can do wonders for our life and spiritual path.

## Spiritual Guidance:

We all have misperceptions and judgments about the masculine and feminine. It requires balance because one cannot exist without the other. When out of harmony internally, it will manifest externally. Remember that masculine qualities are not bad. While men in positions of authority may have abused their power, that is not who God is. The masculine and feminine aspects of God are perfect. Although people may abuse those attributes in this world, it does not make one or the other bad. Your spiritual path will require deeper development of these two energies and will present itself in your life until you heal your feelings toward them. Releasing and forgiving any harbored resentments toward male and female energy will create changes in leaps and bounds. For instance, male energy is giving, while female energy is receptive. By not balancing these energies, you will create more of one of these traits in your life—either by perpetually giving without reward or selfishly receiving without giving to others. If you are experiencing money issues in your life, this may be the root of your problem.

Lastly, letting go of victimization can be extremely difficult. Often, as soon as this is discovered and discussed, our initial response is to deny or defend this mindset. We usually begin justifying exactly why we feel "just" in our attitude of victimization. Until we take responsibility for our lives and belief systems, we will continue to experience our patterns of victimization. This way of thinking will affect our lives, money, relationships, and business endeavors. We cannot proceed spiritually, physically, emotionally, or mentally if we remain in this frame of mind. When we realize that our life is being created for us, rather than it happening to us, we can begin to create more desirable outcomes.

### Affirmations:

- *God is both Mother and Father. God is a parent, a guardian, and a loving, supportive presence in my life.*
- *I release all persecution I have felt and forgive anyone and everyone I believe has persecuted me.*
- *I create magic and miracles in my life and am open and receptive to the magic and miracles God creates for me.*

### Prayer:

"God, I release and forgive all negative emotions toward males and females. Assist me in seeing my brothers and sisters equally through Your heart and Your eyes."

### Additional Resources:

*Healing the Heart and Soul* by Michael Mirdad
*Ho'oponopono: The Hawaiian Forgiveness Ritual as the Key to Your Life's Fulfillment* by Ulrich E. Duprée
*Man's Search for Meaning* by Viktor E. Frankl
*Mirror of His Beauty: Feminine Images of God from the Bible to the Early Kabbalah* by Peter Schafer
*The Book of Thekla* by Thecla
*Women Who Run with the Wolves* by Clarissa Pinkola Estes

# THE ANCESTOR

The Ancestor knows the power of the wisdom, knowledge, and practices of our forefathers and foremothers. They love learning through our predecessors' stories, myths, and philosophies. They respect the lessons and teachings of indigenous people, tribes, and elders and aspire to honor and incorporate them into their life and spirituality. They understand how the world works as a whole to deliver God's messages, from nature and the animals to the Earth's omens to the energy and life force of all things. Wisdom and spiritual discernment can come from everywhere; they simply need to listen and strive to master this ability. Listening, belonging, healing, and honoring are essential aspects of their path and are key attributes they wish to share with others.

The Ancestor sees the footsteps of the past as lost treasures to who we are and the future of our world. They know that so many answers to life's biggest questions can be found in the truths of our past. The ways of our ancestors taught us how to listen to our bodies, connect with the Earth, and utilize nature in our lives and spirituality. They see the separation and segregation that has occurred through time and how this has bred a problem that only worsens in our modern living. Pain and suffering negativity affect us all, and they are on a mission to create resources, opportunities, and liberation accessible to everyone equally. They desire to reconnect with nature, their past, and themself, creating more authentic and organic living.

At their core, the Ancestor consists of earth and water, grounded yet fluid. They connect with the earth and breathe with its rhythms. If female, they may work with their cycle to the ebb and flow of the moon phases. Both males and females might work with the solstice and equinoxes and channel these powerful energies into their life and spiritual practices. They also carry the element of fire and are a fierce warrior, ready to go into battle. And they harness air, making them innovative, curious, and virtuous. They are the only Spiritual Archetype to personify all four major elements so potently. In doing so the Ancestor can channel the strength of the Vikings, the community of ancient civilizations, the wisdom of the greatest sages, and the nurturing quality of a loving mother.

**Most Common Ascendant Spiritual Archetypes:** the Neoteric Shaman, the Witch, the Eastern Philosopher

**Colors of the Ancestor:** deep red, forest green, light brown, dark brown, terra-cotta, crystal blue

**When Balanced, You May Feel or Experience:** harmony, equality, growth, peace, happiness, grounded, fluid

**When Unbalanced, You May Feel or Experience:** oppressed, anxious, helpless, frustrated, angry, resentful

**Governs:** feet, stomach, heart, reproductive organs

**Common Physical Ailments:** autoimmune disorders, candida, reproductive issues, swollen feet, bunions, acid reflux, leaky gut, IBS

## Correlating Essential Oils:

**Neroli:** happiness, purity, weaving emotions
**Ginger:** healing, stimulation, warmth
**Red Raspberry Leaf:** fertility, nourishing for women, love, passion
**Shephard's Purse:** wisdom in nature

## Correlating Stones:

**Malachite:** stone of wisdom, the stone of healers
**Bronzite:** stone of courtesy for being in the line of service and care
**Celestite:** prayer, wisdom, discernment, understanding, mindfulness
**Moss Agate:** stone of Mother Earth; environment, birth and rebirth, balance
**Stichtite:** healing, forgiveness, promotion of love and compassion

## Correlating Plants:

- **Sage:** cleansing, healing, transmutation
- **Palo santo:** The South American indigenous "holy wood" cleanses, protects, and is used in prayer and ritual.
- **Cedar:** Cedar was one of the most versatile and giving plants to the Native Americans. Like cedar, the Ancestor transforms to the form most needed for the situation.
- **Sweetgrass:** community, connection, ceremony, healing, peace, and in some cases is placed on graves or sacred sites
- **Tobacco:** absorption
- **Ginger:** health and immunity

**Power Words:** heal, grow, nurture, wisdom, medicine, earth, womb

## People, Places, and Periods That May Resonate with You

- **People:** naturopaths, herbalists, apothecaries, midwives, acupuncturists
- **Places:** Old England, Old Ireland, Old France, Ancient China, New England States, the Pacific Northwest
- **Periods:** 1200–600 BC, the Iron Age; 1500s–1730; early 1800s; early 1900s

## Correlating Animal: THE BUFFALO

Buffalo medicine is about balance; the balance of male and female, prayer, abundance, life, and birth. It is also about knowing that God is present in all things and that our greatest strength does not come from our wisdom; instead, it comes through our surrender to let God do the work through us. The Ancestor uses ancient techniques and wisdom in their philosophy of life and work but sometimes forgets that it was not just the ancestors who came up with all this ingenious information. They were in communion with God who gave it to them. Buffalo medicine reminds us that without God, our knowledge stays with the Earth, But with God, our wisdom transcends Earth and becomes holy. Buffalo was known to the Plains people as a great provider and honored its life. They saw the sacrifice of its life for the greater good of the people, providing food, shelter, and clothing. By sacrificing part of our worldly selves, we transcend our consciousness for the greater good of ourselves and the world.

## Common Struggles

**Common Triggers:** seeing others tread on marginalized people or people who have less of a voice in society, feeling like you contribute to the problem or that you cannot help enough, seeing the depths of others, feeling that your wounds are endless, wanting to honor others and never feeling like your work is good enough

**When Triggered, the Ancestor Can Become:** immobilized, ashamed, pessimistic

**Common Personal Struggles:** You are plagued by the oppression of others, particularly indigenous people or historically and/or currently marginalized communities. You see the connectedness of us and that there are no isolated problems in the world. You see this oppression in the world daily through news, social media, or in your communities and feel overwhelmed by the pain and injustice. Sometimes it can feel difficult to live your life knowing that others are struggling on such large scales, regardless of your struggles. This knowledge can taint your experience and hurt your heart in ways that feel insurmountable.

**Common Spiritual Struggles:** The Ancestor carries an onerous burden. You love and empathize with missions that may be entirely unseen by others, and you are warriors and saviors to many. This can weigh heavily on your heart, mind, and psyche. Like a mother who cares for her children, you see yourself as a parent to those in need—children, animals, or Mother Earth. Each success is a victory, but each loss is a battle wound that cuts you deep. Remember, friend, God places each person where they are meant to be. Therefore, every contribution you make impacts the lives of others and the world in ways that you cannot even imagine. The Ancestor is like a weaver who spins a thread with every mission and weaves those threads into a masterful tapestry that cannot exist without each filament. Let God guide and direct your hands as you weave, and let Him be a part of your work and purpose. A Master Weaver of the finest handiwork, God can help take the burden off your shoulders while giving you the support, nurturing, and love needed for your soul.

## Mythology, Folklore, Symbolism, or Correlating Story

There was once a pharaoh in Egypt who, looking at his kingdom, saw that the Israelites who inhabited his city had become far greater in

number then the Egyptians. He realized that if there were an upris-
ing or war, his people would lose and have far too many enemies. He
ordered that every son born of the Israelites would be thrown into the
Nile River, and every living Hebrew would become a slave to the Egyptians. A mother gave birth to a baby and hid him for months, fearing he
would be put to death like the thousands of other children. When she
couldn't hide him any longer, she put him near the riverbank in a tiny
ark. When the pharaoh's daughter went to the river to bathe, she saw
the baby and took him in, raising him as her own.

When the baby grew up, he saw and was pained by the oppression
of his people. One day, he saw an Egyptian hurting another Hebrew,
so he killed him out of protection for the other man. In fear, he fled to
the city of Midian and hid there for many years. He married and had
a son, became a shepherd, and had a new life far from his past. But
his people still suffered and remained slaves. God heard their prayers
and pleas for help, so He appeared as a burning bush to the man,
Moses. He told Moses who He was and that He would deliver the
oppressed, sending Moses as his mouthpiece and servant. So, Moses
went back to Egypt, and what transpired is considered one of the
most monumental interactions God has ever had in this world with
His people. With God, Moses stood up against the pharaoh, and with
God's wonders, miracles, and sovereignty, the pharaoh finally agreed
to let the slaves go.

## Spiritual Guidance:

Moses was just one man who saw and was plagued by the oppression
of His people. He thought that one man could not make a difference,
and he was right; one man alone cannot change the world. However,
one man, infused with the power of God, can do wonders and create
miracles beyond anything in this world. The Ancestor can get into the
mindset that they are responsible for saving the world and thus feel
overwhelmed by the weight of responsibility. They often do not realize
that with God, they are unstoppable.

Additionally, many spiritual people believe in only prayer and lack action or are all action with no faith or prayer behind it. However, there is a time to pray and a time for action. Using both in harmony can be one of the most powerful and valuable tools for yourself and others. In the story of Exodus, the pharaoh decided to free the Israelites from slavery but then pursued them, and Moses, into the wilderness to kill them. In fear, the Israelites questioned whether Moses had brought them into the wilderness to die. Moses stopped and spoke to the Lord, but God said, "Wherefore criest thou unto me? Speak unto the children of Israel, that they go forward, but lift thou up they rod, and stretch out thine hand over the sea, and divide it: and the children of Israel shall go on dry ground through the midst of the sea" (Exodus 14:15–16).

God said to Moses that it is not time to stop and speak; it is time to take action. He also said that he would do God's wonders with his faith. To stop when the Egyptians were pursuing them would have been foolish, but to take action while exercising faith created one of the most monumental divine actions ever accomplished in this world. Sometimes we should stop to pray, and sometimes we need to take action. But whatever we do, we should do it with God to ensure wondrous things occur.

### Affirmations:

- *The Lord will deliver the oppressed and free the captives.*
- *Jesus has triumphed over evil. In His name, so can I.*
- *God has given us the resources we need for healing, health, and freedom.*

### Prayer:

"Lord, I surrender my feelings of helplessness to You. I ask that You remind me, and those in need, to remember our power and authority so that we can be delivered from our struggles and strife. In Jesus' name, I command the spirit of oppression out of my life."

### Additional Resources:

*Braiding Sweetgrass* by Robin Wall Kimmerer
*Evolutionary Herbalism* by Sajah Popham
*Folk Medicine* by D.C. Jarvis
*Duke's Handbook of Medicinal Plants of the Bible* by James A. Duke
*Herbs of the Bible: 2000 Years of Plant Medicine* by James A. Duke
*Ho'oponopono: The Hawaiian Forgiveness Ritual as the Key to Your Life's Fulfillment* by Ulrich E. Duprée
*The Earthwise Herbal Repertory* by Matthew Wood
*Healing Oils of the Bible* by David Stewart
*Women Who Run with the Wolves* by Clarissa Pinkola Estes

# THE SECTARIAN

The Sectarian is a person who was raised or is currently practicing Christianity or another organized religion. The Sectarian is usually raised on doctrine and has a well-developed understanding of its laws and beliefs. If coming from that background, their family is generally involved in the church. Whether a devout attendee, pastor, or minister, The Sectarian is essentially born into the church rather than through their discovery. The Sectarian usually goes to church regularly or at least has a church they and their family are members of. The Sectarian is surrounded by a community of like-minded people, such as friends and family, and communities like Christian schools or Sunday schools.

Many people in The Sectarian Spiritual Archetype strive to include God in all areas and use the Bible as their foundation for building their lives. They are generally well-versed in the Bible and may even be able to quote some of their favorite scriptures for related situations. For The Sectarian, life isn't just about ourselves and our isolated incidences; it's about God and the greater purpose of all things. There is a devotion in the mind of The Sectarian that helps them to see all things through a

Biblical lens. The Sectarian aims to include God and the Bible in all areas of life, such as family, business, self, and health. The books they read, the music they listen to, the movies they watch, and the professionals they work with all have a religious tone and attribute to their personal and spiritual goals.

**Most Common Ascendant Spiritual Archetypes:** the Recoverist, the Christian Mystic, the Sovereign, the Theologist

**Colors of the Sectarian:** gray, white, beige, yellow, light pink, blue

**When Balanced, You May Feel or Experience:** driven, passionate, determined, devoted, strong, capable, organized

**When Unbalanced, You May Feel or Experience:** overwhelmed, anxious, scared, worried, weak

**Governs:** head, heart, and feet

**Common Physical Ailments:** mental health issues, such as anxiety and depression; hormonal imbalances; adrenal dysfunction, weight issues; masses; cysts; tumors

### Correlating Essential Oils:

**Lavender:** calming, soothing, cleansing
**Lemon:** longevity, fidelity, ceremonial cleaning of hands
**Holy Oil:** Used in the Bible for ceremonies, healing, and anointing, holy oil is one of the most sacred oils that has ever existed. When God anoints a person or a person is baptized, it has been reported that some people smell the scent of holy oil even though it is not in the room. The scent is a mixture of cinnamon, olive oil, myrrh, and other plants common at the time of Christ, the smell is sweet and unmistakable.

**Holy Basil:** Renowned in various practices such as Hinduism and in ayurvedic and Chinese medicine, holy basil is not only delicious but nurturing and healing to the body and spirit.

**Frankincense:** When placed on the crown of the head, frankincense opens a strong connection with God while praying.

### Correlating Stones:

**Pearl:** innocence, wisdom, wealth, good fortune

**Apache Gold:** faith, grounding, healing, Heaven, Earth

**Angel Aura Quartz:** An angel aura quartz is a stone that undergoes extreme heat and is then coated with other metals, such as gold or silver. It is a beautiful stone representing the beauty that is birthed when we devote our hearts to God and come out of the fire with His glory upon us.

### Correlating Plants:

- **Aspen:** Known as Populus tremula in Latin, meaning "the trembling poplar," the aspen tree has many stories and myths associated with it. One of the stories of the aspen is that when Jesus was crucified on the tree, all the other trees bowed in honor and respect for Him. However, the aspen, being arrogant and prideful, refused to bow and was cursed to tremble for the rest of its days. It serves as a reminder that when we are arrogant and prideful, we curse ourselves to be fearful. But when we humble ourselves, we allow God to do magnificent things.

- **Apple:** The apple is, of course, one of the most prominent symbols in Christian literature. The apple is used as a reminder of our sinfulness and sinful nature. However, we were created in the image and likeness of God; therefore, we are His image bearers and have more value than just a sinful nature. Many people focus solely on sinfulness rather than the redemption that has occurred. Remember, the apple is what happens when we think we can do it alone. But focus on the God-created image and the authority and dominion given back to us instead of what was lost in the beginning.

- **Mustard Tree:** "And the Lord said, If ye had faith as a grain of mustard seed, ye might say unto this sycamine tree, Be thou plucked up by the root, and be thou planted in the sea; and it should obey you" (Luke 17:6).

**Power Words:** independence, self-discovery, love, heart, open-mindedness

### People, Places, and Periods That May Resonate with You

- **People:** scholars, historians, the apostles, Puritans, Protestants, preachers
- **Places:** Israel, Europe, New York, New England States, New York, California, Colorado, the Bible Belt, Utah
- **Periods:** The Great Awakening, the Second Great Awakening, the Revivals, early 1900s Wales

### Correlating Animal: THE RABBIT

The rabbit has been infamous in culture and folklore throughout the centuries. The meanings and symbolism of the rabbit are greatly disagreed upon, depending the culture; however, many of its meanings revolve around fertility and abundance. Sayings such as "multiply like rabbits" refers to the way that rabbits multiply in abundance and are said to be incredibly fertile. This shows the way that faithful followers see the abundance of God's glory in their life and are abundant in His blessings.

The rabbit also has a story associated with it involving its fearful nature. Jamie Sams tells the story of rabbits' fear in the book *Medicine Cards.* The story goes that once upon a time, Rabbit was a fierce and brave warrior. Rabbit was befriended by a witch named Eye Walker. They spent a lot of time together and became very close.

"One day Eye Walker and Rabbit were walking along and they sat down on the trail to rest. Rabbit said, 'I'm thirsty.' Eye Walker picked up a leaf, blew on it, and then handed Rabbit a gourd of water. Rabbit drank the water but didn't say anything. Then Rabbit said, 'I'm hungry.' Eye Walker picked up a stone and blew on it and changed it to a turnip. She gave the turnip to Rabbit to eat. Rabbit tasted it and then ate the turnip with relish. But still Rabbit didn't say anything.

"The two continued along the trail, which led into the mountains. Near the top, Rabbit tripped and fell and rolled almost to the bottom. Rabbit was in very sad condition when Eye Walker got to him. She used a magic salve on Rabbit to heal his great pain and mend his broken bones. Rabbit didn't say anything. Several days later Eye Walker went searching for her friend. She searched high and low but Rabbit was nowhere to be found. Finally, Eye Walker gave up. She met Rabbit quite by accident one day. 'Rabbit, why are you hiding and avoiding me?' the witch asked. 'Because I am afraid of you. I am afraid of your magic,' answered Rabbit, cowering. 'Leave me alone!'

"'I see,' said Eye Walker. 'I have used my magical powers on your behalf and now you turn on me and refuse my friendship.'

"'I want nothing more to do with you or your powers,' Rabbit countered. Rabbit did not even see the tears his words were bringing to the Eye Walker's eyes. 'I hope we never meet and I never see you again,' Rabbit continued. 'Rabbit,' Eye Walker said, 'We once were great friends and companions, but no more. It is within my power to destroy you, but because of the past and the medicines we have shared I will not do this. But this day forward I lay a curse on you and your tribe. From now on, you will call your fears and your fears will come to you. Be on your way, for the sweet medicines that bound us together as friends are broken."

"Now Rabbit is the Fear Caller. He goes out and shouts, 'Eagle, I am so afraid of you!' If Eagle doesn't hear him, Rabbit calls louder, 'Eagle, stay away from me!' Eagle, now hearing Rabbit, comes and eats him. Rabbit calls bobcats, wolves, coyotes, and even snakes until they come. As this story shows, Rabbit medicine people are so afraid of tragedy, illness, and disaster, and being taken, that they call those very fears to them to teach them lessons."

The rabbit is the animal totem for the Sectarian because the Sectarian knows and generally believes in the power of God, His miracles, and His wonders yet is often too insecure and fearful to want to believe in them fully. They are fearful that they, too, will be "taken," so they are leery of the ways God appears to them, delivers them, or how He speaks to them. Rabbit medicine for the Sectarian is a reminder that God's miracles can come in ways that almost seem to be magic. His force is infinite, and He is capable of anything. Remember that God's only limitation is the one we put on Him, but if we allow Him, He can create great wonders in our lives.

## Common Struggles

**Common Triggers:** feeling like your beliefs are threatened, feeling like the world is attacking you, abandonment, perfectionism, feeling like you are endlessly sowing but not reaping

**When Triggered, the Sectarian Can Become:** dismissive, holier than thou, anxious

**Common Personal Struggles:** Due to the upbringing of only being around people and situations that nurture their worldview, The Sectarian can be very narrow-minded. It is not intentional; however, this does make them unrelatable in many ways to the outside world and people outside of their worldview. This can make The Sectarian seem cold or unsympathetic to people who struggle with situations they do not understand.

**Common Spiritual Struggles:** The Sectarian can struggle with developing their own sense of self or their spiritual and religious beliefs. Many people leave organized religion because they don't nurture their own sense of self in their faith. They are often taught that religion and faith are things they must pursue or maintain but not something they have developed themselves. A professor I once spoke to shared a story about a similar experience. Throughout his life, he was a Baptist, just like his family, friends, and community. He went through school and eventually went to a Baptist college. On a mission trip overseas, he was sharing the gospel when someone asked him the most basic question, which was, "Why do you go to church?" Although it was incredibly simple, he said he froze, realizing that he had never asked why or questioned why he did. Going to church was just something his family did, so he did it too. From that experience, he began to explore his faith, ask questions, and challenge his own worldview in order to better stand behind his faith.

## Mythology, Folklore, Symbolism, or Correlating Story

*Camille Flammarion's Engraving, aka "The Vision of Ezekiel"*
The Camille Flammarion woodcut engraving from his book *L'atmosphère: météorologie populaire* published in 1888 is one of the most discussed and widely studied pieces of art in history. The art depicts a man defined by Flammarion: "A missionary of the Middle Ages tells that he had found the point where the sky and the Earth touch . . ."

In relation to The Sectarian Spiritual Archetype, the missionary is a man who has traveled the world with his earthly wisdom and knowledge. We see the duality of night and day with the sun on the right side and the moon and stars across the upper left of the sphere. The lands are bountiful and abundant with blooming foliage and rich soil, which represent the ability to have abundance in the world and in our faith. However, while the missionary is well-educated and well-versed in his studies, it is only by humbling himself and bowing his shoulders that he sees outside his sphere of perception. On the other side of the sphere, he sees the mysteries and secrets of the universe, one that is often compared to the wheel in Ezekiel's vision. Ezekiel was in training for his priesthood and had studied the Laws of Moses, but it was his communion and relationship with God that led to his anointing and prophesying. The dedication of the mind is only part of the journey. The humbling of oneself allows God to show us beyond the veil of the world and into the wheels of the heavens.

## Spiritual Guidance

Faith is not ours if it's just passed down. We must have faith on our own and know why we believe what we believe in order to get behind our beliefs. Kenneth Hagin once shared a story about his first son who had a chronic ear infection. While his son was young, Hagin prayed for him and laid hands on him, and the infection always went away. However, when his son became a teenager, the infection worsened and would not go away. A doctor eventually told him that if it persisted, his son could become permanently deaf. When Kenneth Hagin prayed on it, he heard the Lord tell him that his son was not developing his own faith because he was relying on his earthly father's faith. He was not getting strong in his own faith for himself. Kenneth Hagin told his son the message he received and supported his son in developing his faith and prayer life. Soon afterward, he was cured of his chronic ear infections.

Similarly, The Sectarian must develop their own faith and practice it in their lives as well. This may take some examining as to why you believe what you do and how you can connect with God in a way that resonates with you.

## Affirmations:

- *My heart is filled with the everlasting, infinite love of God and overflows with love in my life and faith.*
- *I am the image and likeness of God, which includes His heart and His love.*
- *I am open to a relationship with God that is His will, not mine.*

## Prayer:

"Lord, help me to feel impassioned with love for You and Your Word. Help me to feel Your presence in my heart, not just in my mind."

## Additional Resources:

*The Bible*
*God's Creative Power Collection* by Charles Capps
*God's Generals* by Roberts Liardon
*The Believer's Authority* by Kenneth E. Hagin
*The Pilgram's Progress* by John Bunyan

# THE NEONATE

The Neonate is a person who has recently had a spiritual awakening or who considers themself born again. They are newly developed in their study and understanding and look at their newfound revelation with the eyes of a child. Curious and inquisitive, they are full of wonder as they approach the topics of spirituality and religion. For The Neonate, the world almost seems like a new place, full of mysteries and symbolism they never imagined or noticed before.

Many spiritual people think of their spiritual awakening as the beginning of their path; however, each and every person is, and has been, on a spiritual path not only from birth but from lifetimes proceeding their current life. Additionally, people can have multiple spiritual awakenings. Your first spiritual awakening is the realization of your path. You may also have other spiritual awakenings where your soul further challenges your beliefs. This may come in the form of a Dark Night of the Soul, or as a time where you realize all of the things you have come to know or believe are challenged on a deeper level. Since healing and growth happen in layers, you may go through a spiritual awakening, feeling like you have everything figured out, only to have your soul push you into the next layer, which awakens you on a deeper level and either challenges everything you have come to know or confirms where you are by making you practice what you preach.

A spiritual awakening can feel like you've been listening to the radio your whole life, but the station is finally coming in clearly. All of a sudden, the static recedes and you feel tuned in. It can feel strange, and you may even ask yourself how you went so long not realizing there was static. But if we believe that static is the way things are, we don't usually question the interference. Yet now that the static is gone, you start hearing songs differently; the lyrics have more meaning, and for the first time you hear the melody crystal clear. All of a sudden, you will look at the same things you have always seen differently.

### Signs and Symptoms of a Spiritual Awakening:

- You begin to question the beliefs you had previously.
- You become aware of the supernatural and spiritual existence in the world.
- You feel or know things prior to them transpiring, and your intuition feels more connected.
- You may begin noticing strange coincidences that cannot be explained away.
- You feel an unshakable nudging or urging to explore God, spirituality, healing, or your soul's purpose.
- Your current life, friends, or way of living suddenly don't seem to fit. It's as though they have suddenly shrunk or you have grown, but you can no longer seem to fit into the things that once gave you joy or pleasure.

Of course, there is also an alternative side to the spiritual awakening. A spiritual awakening can feel like a drug and alcohol withdrawal or detox. For those who do not know this experience, it can be confusing as to why you feel like your eyes have been opened yet your body is feeling worse than ever. In short, your body needs to catch up to where you are. A spiritual awakening can be a confusing, frustrating, and difficult time as we transition from who we were and how we were living, to whom we are becoming and the new way we want to live. The symptoms a person experiences during a spiritual awakening will depend on their belief systems and how strongly their negative beliefs are being challenged by their spiritual awakening.

**Most Common Ascendant Spiritual Archetypes:** the Recoverist, the Sectarian, The Eastern Philosopher, the New Ager, the Lightworker, The Theologist

**Colors of the Neonate:** bright blue, white, light yellow, sage/lime green, bright purple.

**When Balanced, You May Feel or Experience:** perceptive, clear, insightful, observant, knowledgeable, wise, awake

**When Unbalanced, You May Feel or Experience:** judgmental, guilt, shame, out of place, disconnected, overwhelmed, chemicalization, a holier-than-thou mentality

**Governs:** brain, stomach, bowels, heart, third eye, thyroid

**Common Physical Ailments:** Some of the uncomfortable symptoms of a spiritual awakening are:
- Feeling wired and tired
- Lethargy
- Fatigue
- Random aches and pains
- Cold or flu out of nowhere with no apparent origin
- Depression
- Exhaustion
- The Enlightenment Trap see page 344 for full description
- Self-judgment and projected judgment

- Anger
- Frustration
- Confusion

## Correlating Essential Oils:

**Vetiver:** spiritual connection, letting go of the past, transformation
**Bergamot:** relieving of grief, authority, joy
**Frankincense:** spiritual attunement, grounding with God, humility
**Cedarwood:** interpretation, unceasing faith, spiritual quest

## Correlating Stones:

**Clear Quartz:** mind, body, spirit
**Labradorite:** intuition, communication, awakening
**Selenite:** clarity, spiritual connection, prayer, meditation
**Serpentine:** new beginnings, rebirth, resilience
**Sugilite:** birthing your authentic self

## Correlating Plants:

- **Sage:** cleansing, purification, higher consciousness
- **Peace Lily:** rebirth, healing, peace
- **Lotus:** enlightenment, rebirth, self-awareness, spiritual awakening
- **Holy Basil:** balance, spiritual and personal growth, spiritual enlightenment

**Power Words:** born again, awakening, growth, metamorphosis, evolution, enlightenment

## People, Places, and Periods That May Resonate with You

Because the Neonate is awakening to their path, they do not necessarily have common people, places, and periods that a majority of the Spiritual Archetype strongly resonate with. As they progress down their path, gain more understanding of their spiritual selves, and see which paths resonate with them, they will consequently discover which people, places, and periods resonate with them as well. However, many Neonates first relate to the people places, and periods of the Eastern Philosopher (see page 127) the New Ager (see page 184), or the Theologist (see page 250).

## Correlating Animal: THE BUTTERFLY

A spiritual awakening or spiritual rebirth is a metamorphosis. It is a process that occurs and can take days, weeks, months, or years to fully develop. Just as a caterpillar does not rush its metamorphosis, we must be patient with ourselves and let the process happen organically. While we do not see its transition in the cocoon, a long evolution takes place, and it emerges as a butterfly. For many of us, we believe a spiritual awakening is a representation of going from a caterpillar to a butterfly, but that is not the case. Having the awakening is just the beginning. Our awakening is the moment we realize we are a caterpillar and that we are destined to become a butterfly. The awakening, and everything that follows, is our evolution in the cocoon.

The advice I give anyone experiencing their own metamorphosis is to observe. By observing we allow our newfound self to integrate and we may also be divinely led to our next phase of healing. Changing our consciousness is not only about doing; it's equally about being.

After a spiritual awakening, a deeper part of ourselves is provoked, and while ready to shine, it is not forceful. It is content with its awakened state and happy to marinate while awaiting its next junction. The enemy and our own egos are what initiate these traps, telling us we aren't doing enough and that if we do not do more, we will become the person we fear most: our old selves. Our initial spiritual awakening may only last a moment, but it is speaking to our higher consciousness to lure us to reach our highest potential. An awakening is an opportunity to embark on a lifelong quest, and conquering the enemy that sets these traps is an essential part of that journey. By accepting our quest, we have the capability to transcend our enemy to a higher consciousness, thus leading to a happier, healthier, awakened self.

## Common Struggles

**Common Triggers:** feeling duped or deceived, heresy; people not walking the talk; false prophets, teachers, or gurus

**When Triggered, the Neonate Can Become:** combative, pugnacious, sacred

**Common Personal Struggles:** When a person has a spiritual awakening or becomes born again, theygenerally have four main personal emotional struggles that can be hindrances on their path: guilt, blame and judgment, identity crisis, and fear.

**Guilt:** Many Neonate people may begin their new conscious path feeling guilt or shame about their past. They may look at their mistakes and choices and feel that they "should have known better" or "done better" and feel a sense of regret or embarrassment. It can be difficult to compartmentalize these emotions but it is important to remember that you did the best with the skills, understanding, and perception that you had at the time. This seems like a simple solution; however, it is essential to recognize this. If you think of children, they are only capable of the skills their parents or caregivers, environment, and upbringing provide. Unfortunately, in many cases these days, those are not positive or nurturing situations. Instead, they create children and adults who lack the emotional intelligence, skillset, or communication skills to be able to understand their own selves, let alone know how to express anything to others. When you see a child at any age, they are at a limited capacity of understanding designated to their age group. We certainly do not blame children for not knowing consequences they could not possibly know. We do not accuse them of being at fault for things that could not possibly be their fault. Yet as adults, we assume we should be all-knowing, have it all figured out, and essentially be perfect. We shame ourselves for not knowing better, despite the fact that if we don't know something, we cannot possibly know it. If we do not kno w we do not know something, how can we possibly attempt to learn? The spiritual awakening is the first time you are realizing what you did not know, and now is the time to begin consciously learning. It is the time to realize where you may be childlike in your life and how you can learn new ways of being, communicating, and acting in your life. This is an opportunity to forgive yourself and others and you grow into this new phase. Because just as you did not know better, neither did the other people who may have wronged you or contributed to the guilt you may be feeling. Be kind to yourself during this time; love yourself and nurture yourself like a child. If you do not know what that looks like, now is the perfect time to learn.

**Blame + Judgment:** When people go through a spiritual awakening or become born again, there is often a feeling or need to blame and judge others. This may manifest as blaming parents for not doing a better job or introducing us to spirituality or to God sooner. It may be blaming others for what they did to us in the past. Or it could be blaming the world, the patriarchy, or anything else that comes up. It may look like judging those who don't have it together or judging people who know less than you. This is usually connected to the feelings of guilt and shame we experience about ourselves, which then becomes blaming and judging others. While there may be thousands of legitimate reasons everything is everyone else's fault or even our own, the reality is that it doesn't matter anymore. That doesn't mean there aren't still feelings that need to be worked on, let go of, or even worked out with the people in our lives. All of those actions may need to be taken. However, what's most valuable during this time is forgiveness. We can sit around and justify all the reasons we are mad, why our situation is what it is because of other people, or how we could have been further along on our path if it wasn't for so-and-so, but what you will come to realize is that anyone in your life who was "asleep" was just the unknowing leading the unknowing. Hurt people hurt people, and those who are asleep keep others asleep because they don't even know themselves that they are sleeping. It may not feel right, and it may not be fair, but we cannot expect too much from the wounded. This is where forgiveness sets us free from others and allows us to fully wake up even while they stay asleep.

**Identity Crisis:** As mentioned in The Enlightenment Trap on page 344, The Neonate often suffers with an identity crisis. It can feel like our world, perception, and identity are spinning and that we cannot find our center. Remember that when everything else is spinning, by keeping a focal point in your vision you will keep yourself from falling. Make God your focal point so that when all else seems to spiral or become blurry, God will catch you, and you will find yourself within Him.

**Fear:** When The Neonate has an awakening where they learn about spiri-tuality, realize the capacity of their spiritual self, or have a revelation about their path or God, they may become overwhelmed with crippling fear, panic, or anxiety. Many teachers will tell you that this is due to a type of detox you experience with awakening; however, this is not the case. In fact, the closer we become with God, the less we should feel or experi-ence these types of symptoms. Instead, the reason this happens is that the enemy sees your revelation and will do everything in its power to keep you restrained in some form or another. If we have been living outside of God's Word and have suddenly been called to it, the enemy sees the threat and will use any advantage it can to lure us back under its rule. What better way to do this than through our own psyche? This is why many born-again Christians become judgmental and overbearing; they are so afraid of their own past, mistakes, and sins that they judge others in an attempt to feel better about themselves. Yet they live in their own anxieties and are tortured by perfectionism, fearing any further mistakes. One of the best ways to combat this type of fear is through the unyielding power of forgiveness. By forgiving ourselves and our past, we disarm the enemy of its power and stronghold over us. Many Neonates will work on forgiving others but refrain from forgiving themselves. One born-again Christian I spoke to said, "I work really hard to forgive everyone for everything they have done to me in my life." Yet when I asked, "How about forgiving yourself?" he replied, "Oh, I can't do that."

The areas of ourselves that we ignore, neglect, or avoid are the parts of ourselves that the enemy uses to infiltrate our consciousness. By illuminating them, we remove the opportunity for it to become a weapon used against us. As you enter into your first or new phase of spirituality, awakening, or rebirth, keep forgiveness close at hand. Forgive yourself and let go of judgments toward yourself and others. God has already forgiven you; therefore, who are we to live in unforgiveness against ourselves?

**Common Spiritual Struggles:** One of the ways many people try to compensate for the guilt, shame, or embarrassment they feel about their past is by trying to know everything and even sometimes becoming a know-it-all. This can be a conscious or unconscious attempt not to fall into the trap of being deceived or ignorant, as you may have felt in the past. This may also stem from excitement. When we discover something amazing, it is in our nature as human beings to want to share it. People may feel like they also want to share their newfound information because they don't want others to feel what they felt before their awakening. It's almost like there is a secret key to freedom that you have discovered and you want to give the key to others for their freedom too. It can be incredibly helpful to others to hear from someone about what they are going through because there is always someone going through the same experience and hearing a firsthand account can feel like a godsend in our struggle. But it's important to realize that while sharing is a beautiful and helpful gift, we don't want to step into know-it-all syndrome for a couple of reasons.

First, it does not benefit us to believe we know it all because if we know it all, we aren't in a place of learning and being receptive. Spirituality isn't just something we learn and then teach; it's something that is lived and then shared. A child does not know everything because their parent tells them. They know by learning and experiencing life. And while children are like little gurus in their own right, they are also still developing their brain, skills, and abilities, which requires consistent experience to develop and fine-tune. If a child decided they knew enough, began teaching others, and stopped learning, they would actually stunt their own growth. Therefore, be receptive. No one is expecting you to have all of the answers. Allow this time to be a time of communion and development of your relationship with God, and don't worry about sharing every detail with others. The spiritual awakening is the birth of our new selves. Give yourself some time and space to reflect on your life and receive insight and revelation so that you can evaluate your own self before sharing everything with others. Remember: stay receptive to the new, incoming information.

### Spiritual Guidance:

When we are fresh on our path, you will be astounded by the amount of information, opinions, and resources that are available in spirituality these days. While this may initially seem like a blessing, it can quickly become overwhelming or, worse, lead us down a wrong path. There are many teachers and teachings that can mislead or deceive us making a spiritual awakening or introduction to religion a negative experience, which leads to a whole new set of problems. Instead of trying to find the perfect guru, teacher, or spiritual path, I would suggest instead that you make God your North Star and let Him guide and direct you from here. Many people want to find a teacher with all the answers, but God is the only one with all the answers. Others will try to find the right modality or belief system, but God's way is always the best way. Seek Him first above all else, and you will already be on the right path. That does not mean you have to go to a specific kind of church, dress a certain way, or model yourself after anyone. Instead, pursue God with all your heart, and allow yourself to grow into the image and likeness you are meant to become.

### Affirmations:

- *I am awakening to my authentic, true, and divine self.*
- *I am the image and likeness of God.*
- *I forgive myself and everyone in my past. If I contributed to anyone being*

*asleep, or vice versa, may we all awaken with love, peace, and compassion.*

**Prayer:**

"From the depths of slumber,
As I ascend the spiral stairways of wakefulness,
I will whisper:
God! God! God!

Thou art the food, and when I break my fast
Of nightly separation from Thee,
I will taste Thee, and mentally say:
God! God! God!

No matter where I go, the spotlight of my mind
Will ever keep turning on Thee;
And in the battle din of activity, my silent war-cry will be:
God! God! God!

When boisterous storms of trials shriek,
And when worries howl at me,
I will drown their noises, loudly chanting:
God! God! God!

When my mind weaves dreams
With threads of memories,
On that magic cloth will I emboss:
God! God! God!

Every night, in time of deepest sleep,
When my peace dreams and calls, Joy! Joy! Joy!
My joy comes singing evermore:
God! God! God!
In waking, eating, working, dreaming, sleeping,

Serving, meditating, chanting, divinely loving,
My soul will constantly um, unheard by any:
God! God! God!"
—Paramahansa Yogananda, "God! God! God!"

## Additional Resources:

*Dark Night of the Soul* by St. John of the Cross
*Feeling Is the Secret* by Neville Goddard
*The Four Agreements* by Don Miguel Ruiz
*The Power of Now: A Guide to Spiritual Enlightenment* by Eckhart Tolle
*The Secret* by Rhonda Byrne
*You're Not Going Crazy You're Just Waking Up* by Michael Mirdad

# THE WAYFARER

I f the spiritual path was an expedition to discover new lands, The Wayfarer would be the captain of the ship leading the voyage. Curious, adventurous, and sincere, they approach spirituality and God with vigor. They desire to explore spirituality through adventure, travel, and wanderlust. For the Wayfarer, life and spirituality are about discovery, and they seek to find it on their own terms. They want to feel liberated and seek to help others feel this liberation as well. Where others see limitations, they see possibilities. Their heart is their compass and their compass points to adventure. For them, nothing is insurmountable; it just needs the proper mindset, will, and execution to achieve anything.

The Wayfarer has innate spiritual qualities that they may be completely unaware of. For instance, they may have a strong intuition that guides them throughout their life. Due to the organic nature of their intuition, they may not even realize they are, in fact, intuitive at all. They may brush it off, believing that everyone thinks, feels, and understands situations just as they do, not knowing their discernment is a gift. They may also be effortlessly exceptional at manifesting or creating spiritual environments or situations. They may be given opportunities or put in situations that work out in their favor without much conscious influence on their part.

Regardless of how it is presented, they are constantly being nudged toward opening themselves up to their path. The reality is that these are all common ways that God, or the Holy Spirit, communicates with us. Yet if we are unaware, we may think of these as strange or odd coincidences rather than communications. Numbers may be guiding us. The animals may be sharing their medicine (symbolism and meaning) with us in order to confirm or advise us. There is a whole world that God uses to communicate with us, but if we are unaware of the languages, then the messages can get lost in translation. Being aware of our path and how God is speaking to us creates a kinship with God, our souls, and our lives, which creates continuity, abundance, and harmony.

**Most Common Ascendant Spiritual Archetypes:** the Recoverist, the Sectarian, The Eastern Philosopher, the New Ager

**Colors of the Wayfarer:** olive green, forest green, ocean blue, beige, light brown, dark brown, medium bold orange

**When Balanced, You May Feel or Experience:** independent, brave, adventurous, bold, free, levelheaded, liberated

**When Unbalanced, You May Feel or Experience:** confined, dull, lifeless, tapped, monotonous, aimless, duped, gullible, restless, directionless, mediocre

**Governs:** glands, testicles, womb, bladder, lower back, head

**Common Physical Ailments:** overactive bladder, ADHD, dyslexia, inflammation of the sexual organs, uterine cysts, sciatica, lower-back issues

## Correlating Essential Oils:

**Sweet Orange:** joy, adventure, happiness
**Grapefruit:** personal and spiritual power, refreshing one's emotions and mindset
**Arborvitae:** grounding, surrender, trust
**Cassia:** breaking free from boundaries, surrendering pride, anointing

## Correlating Stones:

**Aventurine:** adventure, positivity, perseverance
**Golden Aura Quartz:** Like the Phial of Galadriel from The Lord of The Rings, golden quartz is a light for dark places on your journey.
**Sugilite:** authenticity, direction in life and soul's purpose, enthusiasm
**Charoite:** synchronicity, inner strength, transformation

## Correlating Plants:

- **Strelitzia:** The plant of freedom, also represents joy and paradise
- **Freesia:** purity, trust, innocence, freedom
- **Nerine:** good fortune, freedom, union

**Power Words:** exploration, adventure, opportunities, movement, inquisitor, analytical, ambition, wanderlust

## People, Places, and Periods That You May Resonate With

**People:** explorers, leaders, forefathers, seekers, government, politicians
**Places:** Himalayas, Peru, Australian Outback, Tibet, Nepal, China, Costa Rica, Portugal, Thailand, Grand Canyon, Yellowstone, Sedona, California, Colorado
**Periods:** AD 793–1100; AD 1254–1324; AD 1371–1433; The Age of Exploration, the late 1800s–1940s

## Correlating Animal: THE WOLF

Independent, willful, wild, and loyal, the Wolf is the perfect animal symbol for The Wayfarer. The Wayfarer is an explorer and adventurer who seeks freedom and lives life without borders, just like the wolf who also loves freedom and wildness. With a keen sense of intuition, The Wayfarer, like the wolf, relies on instincts to protect themself and others. The wolf also represents strength, mirroring the inner strength of The Wayfarer, who is grounded, strong, and determined in their life and endeavors.

## Common Struggles

**Common Triggers:** feeling trapped, confined, controlled; feeling a lack of direction or aimless wandering; worrying about losing your freedom one day; feeling hurt and rejected from the people or things you become attached to

**When Triggered, the Wayfarer Can Become:** aimless, empty, resentful

**Common Personal Struggles:** The Wayfarer is afraid of being trapped, held back, or fenced in. Life and spirituality are an adventure and a journey, and you do not want anyone or anything to hold you back from it. This may manifest in a few different ways.

First, The Wayfarer may try to remain unattached from their life. Without attachment, they feel like they are safeguarding their freedom; however, this unattachment actually keeps them from fully participating in their spiritual path. It is almost as though they freeze themselves in time, refusing to participate because they do not want to become trapped by the people or things in their life. They may find themselves traveling without fully enjoying the journey. It's as though they are fed, but not quite satisfied; they have a drink, but their thirst is not fully quenched. Alternatively, there are many Wayfarers who do settle down and create a more "normal" or "stable" life and leave their adventurous spirit tucked nicely away in a safe place. They try to compartmentalize their ordinary spirit and their free spirit selves and live a normal, healthy, and balanced life. The issue with this, of course, is that they are never living either extreme to the fullest, and life feels as though it is lacking something. They may find themselves dreaming of getting away or wanting to leave their normal life out of frustration that they are no longer answering the call of their soul to seek more. It can become a difficult balance of tending to the "real world" and fulfilling the passions, dreams, and energy of exploring and experiencing life and spirituality in the way they long to.

**Common Spiritual Struggles:** For the Wayfarer, on the surface, your biggest fear is that your life will be boring, mundane, or monotonous, but underneath the surface, your biggest fear is really that your life will not matter or be of any epic importance. Unlike Spiritual Archetypes such as the Sovereign, who aim to do big things that the rest of the world can see, touch, feel, or hear, such as build skyscrapers or be the most famous person in their field, you strive to do big things by feeling and experiencing life in a monumental way. Climbing mountains, traveling the world, exploring, and changing your scenery are part of your soul, and to feel like you cannot fulfill that to the fullest, is like certain death.

What happens to many Wayfarers is that they cannot find the balance between normal, everyday tasks and being the adventurer within. How can one travel the world and pay their bills? How can someone have a long-lasting, fulfilling relationship when they don't want to be tied down? It is a struggle that happens; unfortunately, many Wayfarers do not meet that balance. Additionally, it can be difficult to create this balance between God and spirituality as well. How do I live in this world while leaping fully into my spiritual path?

The spiritual path can be a rich, abundant, and exquisite pilgrimage that evokes the possibilities of our souls, hearts, and spirits. To live on the surface of this adventure is like going through the most marvelous expedition with a blindfold. Do not be afraid to travel your spiritual path. Your soul is a map, and it will guide and protect you along your journey.

## Mythology, Folklore, Symbolism, or Correlating Story

The 1994 Disney classic *The Lion King* centers around a young lion cub named Simba. The young cub eagerly awaits the day he will be king of the kingdom known as the Pride Lands and rule "everything the light touches." The beginning of the film shows his desire to be brave, strong, and wise like his incredible father and king, Mufasa. He seeks adventure and risks his life and his friend Nala's life in an effort to show his bravery. Young, naive, and lacking humility, little Simba has some growing up to do, but his father's love and mercy is an unwavering presence in his life. However, his life is suddenly thrown into tragedy when his uncle, Mufasa's brother, Scar, kills Mufasa and tricks Simba into believing that the young cub was responsible for his father's death. Ashamed, grieving, and alone, Simba exiles himself into the desert where he meets a warthog and a meerkat, named Timon and Pumbaa, who teach him to forget his past and "hakuna matata," which means "to have no worries." However, back home, his kingdom is in ruin, his mother and friends believe Simba is dead, and they are suffering under Scar's reign. Simba is living in denial. He leaves his home, changes his meat-eating diet (because he's a lion) to a diet of bugs, and goes against everything he was taught by his father. All of this leads to a beautiful and powerful moment when Mufasa appears to him in the clouds with a godly, booming voice and heavenly glow where he tells his son, "You have forgotten yourself; therefore, you have forgotten me." And that his son must "remember who he is and join the great circle of life." The film concludes with Simba having to return back home to face his past and fight to retake his rightful place as king.

Similarly, The Wayfarer can live this way on the spiritual path. Ashamed, hurt, overwhelmed with grief or trauma, or just their own fears of being trapped, they may run from their lives seeking detachment and living with "no worries," trying to avoid what is happening spirituality, emotionally, or mentally. They may literally or figuratively exile themselves in order not to have to deal with what they are running from. Unfortunately, chanting "hakuna matata" doesn't change the past or heal the hurt. It is by knowing the truth of who we are and facing our past, enemies, and self that we are truly in the circle of life and living how God has intended.

## Spiritual Guidance:

The Wayfarer aspires to embrace the fullness of the world to its highest potential. They desire to live a boundless and legendary life, growing, exceeding, and expanding themselves and their consciousness. While their journey may begin and stay in this frame for much of their journey, the ultimate destination The Wayfarer can reach is the Promised Land within themselves. The adventure outside of ourselves is a form of relationship with God because it requires trust and reliance on God, but it is still an external communion. When we incorporate the adventure for the Promised Land within ourselves, we reach a new level of faith, knowledge, and manifestation in the physical.

When the Hebrews fled Egypt, they embarked on the greatest Exodus in history. It was a physical journey where they fled from their captors and into freedom. Yet as soon as they were free, they became afraid, questioned Moses and God, and many even wanted to return to their bondage rather than persevere. It was only the most faithful, trusting, and devoted who made it to the Promised Land because it required not only reliance on God but an inner determination that meant enduring and persisting beyond what was physically visible.

We can make the journey and set out on the physical quest, but it is the inner expedition into ourselves and our relationship with God that leads us to the Promised Land. This also allows us to balance the mundane parts of life and continue to have excitement and discovery wherever we are and regardless of what we are doing. God will bring happiness, contentment, and passion into all areas of our lives, business, and relationship if we allow it. Instead of separating life and adventure, our greatest adventure becomes the exploration and revelation of ourselves with God.

## Affirmations:

- *I am on a journey and an adventure, living my life to its fullest capacity in every moment, relationship, thought, and achievement.*
- *I bring joy, excitement, and exuberance into all areas of my life and spirituality.*
- *God breathed life into me, and with this breath, I will do, be, and achieve, great things.*

## Prayer:

"Help me to journey beyond the familiar and into the unknown. Give me the faith to leave old ways and break fresh ground with You. Christ of the mysteries, I trust You to be stronger than each storm within me. I will trust in the darkness and know that my times, even now, are in Your hand. Tune my spirit to the music of heaven, and somehow, make my obedience count for You.

Amen." —ST. BRENDAN THE NAVIGATOR, also known as St. Brendan the Voyager, who was a shipbuilder, monk, and explorer and is known as "The Irish Patron of Sailors"

## Additional Resources:

*The Celestine Prophecy* by James Redfield
*The Alchemist* by Paulo Coelho
*The Pilgrimage: A Contemporary Quest for Ancient Wisdom*
   by Paulo Coelho
*Zen and the Art of Motorcycle Maintenance* by Robert M. Pirsig

# THE MYTHOLOGIST

The Mythologist relishes in the magic of lore, mythology, and storytelling, daydreaming about the existence of unicorns, fairies, wizards, and mermaids. They believe in man's ability to induce magic and miracles into corporal form. They love stories, especially in-depth tales of faraway places that transport them from the modern day. They have a fondness for fantasy books and films and are fascinated by gods and legends.

They believe in sacred sites and the power they hold from lifetimes ago. They dream of or enjoy traveling to places like England, Ireland, Scotland, France, and Greece, which are rich with the tales of kings and queens, gods, and magic. They adore metals, tapestries, patterns, and textiles that remind them of these times. They probably have a large crystal collection or altar with pictures and statues that resemble their archetype, such as goddesses and warriors.

They are old-fashioned in their beliefs of the roles of male and female and believe women should be treated as goddesses and queens and that men should embody the spirit of kings. They admire how male and female roles used to be much clearer, and each position held immense value. They attract people in their life who fit into roles, such as the fairy, goddess, unicorn, knight, warrior, and witch. Without realizing it, they recreate (or relive) the magical realm they adore.

**Most Common Ascendant Spiritual Archetypes:** the Witch, the Ancestor, the Warrior, the Saint, The Crusader

**Colors of the Mythologist:** gold, medium blue, bright red, silver, deep orange, soft yellow, purple

**When Balanced, You May Feel or Experience:** imagination, optimism, a strong sense of personal power, victory

**When Unbalanced, You May Feel or Experience:** issues with self-worth, desire for power, materialistic, easily seduced, anxiety, fatigue

**Governs:** pancreas, liver and kidneys, colon, stomach, upper intestines, lower back

**Common Physical Ailments:** poor digestion, eating disorders, hepatitis, colon cancer and disease, ulcers, weight problems, gas

### Correlating Essential Oils:

**Dragon's blood:** empowerment, authentic love, mysticism
**Neroli:** bliss, purity, dreams, fantasy
**Bergamot:** awareness, dignity, honor, stability
**Fennel:** strength, admiration
**Clove:** Once a cherished and rare spice that could only be afforded by the wealthy, clove is associated with money and prosperity
**Ivy:** eternal love and eternal life, patience, attachment

## Correlating Stones:

**Amber:** stone for warriors, a symbol of the sun in ancient Greece
**Ruby:** nobility, purity, royalty
**Emerald:** love, integrity, unity, compassion
**Garnet:** adventure, travel, spiritual journeys, intense love and passion
**Rutilated Quartz:** illuminator, spiritual growth, pillar of light
**Aquamarine:** stone of mermaids, water, the sea, emotions
**Larimar:** enlightenment, communication of feelings, the stone of sailors
**Pink Tourmaline:** self-love, compassion for others and self, confronting fears

## Correlating Plants:

- **Ash:** protection, prosperity, sea rituals, health
- **Fig:** divination, fertility, love
- **Moss:** protection, abundance, growth
- **Glastonbury Thorn:** Planted in England after the death of Jesus by his uncle, Joseph of Arimathea, the holy thorn is a legend and symbol of Christ and the birth of Christianity since its roots. It has persevered through harsh conditions and blooms on Christmas and Easter each year.

**Power Words:** illumination, imagination, fantasy, creativity, adventure, knight, king, queen goddess

## People, Places, and Periods That May Resonate with You

- **People:** king, queen, knight, Viking, Anglo Saxon, Knight Templar
- **Places:** Ireland, Scotland, England, France, Greece, Scandinavia, Norway
- **Periods:** Renaissance, Edwardian Period, Ancient Greece, AD 700–1100

## Correlating Animal: THE DRAGON

The Dragon represents change, transformation, leadership, mastery, divine illumination, and power. The Mythologist has a deep connection to the need for the balance of the divine masculine and divine feminine. The Dragon acts as a foundation of this balance providing the masculine traits of earth and fire, and the feminine traits of water and air. The Dragon carries intensity and ferocity and is a strong protector while offering emotional healing and intuition. The Dragon is a reminder for you that you can be the power of your divine masculine while still keeping your fluid, intuitive, and receptive divine feminine.

## Common Struggles

**Common Triggers:** consequences, stagnation, monotony, anything boring, having to face reality

**When Triggered, the Mythologist Can Become:** dishonest (with self or others), manipulative, illusion-centric, disconnected from self and others

**Common Personal Struggles:** The fantasyland is alluring, but perhaps a little too much so. You may prefer the fantasy world to the point of not desiring to live in the modern world. You may be called aloof, airy-fairy, or unrealistic because you are essentially living in two worlds. Your imagination runs away with you, and you may have unrealistic ideals. When you own your power, you feel like royalty in modern times, but when you do not and succumb to self-doubt, you may begin to act like a beggar in a crown. This will negatively affect you by convincing you to accept breadcrumbs from the world. You may begin allowing others to treat you in inferior ways, beg for work you are exceptional at, and spend too much time trying to convince others of how fantastic you are while not believing it personally. This may also be a contributing factor in your relationships and may mean you attract abusive or overpowering romantic partners.

**Communication:** The Mythologist may struggle with communication and communicating their feelings. They may be sarcastic or bypass their own feelings in an attempt to seem easygoing or to refrain from causing problems or taking up space. This is largely due to the fact that often-times they do not know how they feel or how they "should feel" in situations. You may be protecting your heart and, therefore, lie to yourself or others about how you feel, or feel that you lack the ability to speak your feelings at all.

**Common Spiritual Struggles:** Your ideas of spirituality may also be stuck in the past, without much room for growth or advancement. If we are living in the past, we may never live in the present, which keeps our spiritual growth stagnant and stunted. Those with The Mythologist Spiritual Archetype may live in the past personally, holding on to painful situations or trauma that drive their desire to live in the fantasy world in the first place. When we do not focus on the present, we are unable to manifest properly. When focusing too much on the past, you may have difficulty manifesting the relationships, jobs, or opportunities that you hope for. While you may be doing the healing work you believe will propel you into betterment, you may find the progress is quite slow. This is because of holding on to the past, which is not allowing room for new blessings to manifest in the present.

## Mythology, Folklore, Symbolism, or Correlating Story

Odin was the Great Allfather of the Norse people. He created Asgard and Midgard where the humans lived. He taught them about love and the arts and how to live a peaceful life. One day he became devastated when he saw that the giants of Jotunheim had invaded Midgard and were killing his beloved humans and animals. "Why do they not protect themselves?" he asked his wife, Frigga. "Because they do not know how," she responded. "We taught them the arts and how to live peacefully, but they know nothing of war." Odin decided to go to Midgard to teach the people how to defend themselves. He disguised himself as an old man and called himself "Waywise" and lived among the people teaching them how to fight and defend themselves.

Finally, the day came when he decided it was time to leave and he bid them farewell and he went on his way. Although he had taught them many things, Odin wanted to know more about the powers of evil in order to know how to defeat it. He embarked on a quest until he reached a place where the circle of the sea meets the circle of the sky where he met the wise giant, Mimir, who guarded the Well of Wisdom. He told Mimir about his desire to help the gods and men and asked for a drink of the water of wisdom. Mimir told Odin, "Many before thee have sought this well, but it was decided by the fates that none may achieve it except by sacrifice." Therefore, Odin agreed, and with a knife plucked out his right eye in exchange for wisdom. With a drink, the book of knowledge opened in his brain and he was granted information about all things.

The Mythologist loves a quest and the spiritual quest is the greatest of all. The stories of heroes embarking on epic journeys are part of the allure and romance that attracts The Mythologist to stories, myths, and folklore. The Mythologist loves, admires, and relates to the heart, mind, and soul of the best warriors and champions. What many of The Mythologist Spiritual Archetype do not learn, or learn much later, is that the quest does not require you to sacrifice your health, body, mind, or spirit. Many on this path believe that the quest requires physical sacrifice, rather than spiritual initiation.

For instance, when a distraught king let his kingdom fall to ruin, his faithful knights set out on a great quest to find something they believed would revive him: a quest for the Holy Grail. The cup was said to be a myth, but it was the cup that Jesus drank from at the last supper. Each of the men endured harsh conditions, tragedy, and even death along the way. However, one young man named Perceval went through a spiritual quest, going within himself, which led him to the Holy Grail.

He returned and brought it to the king, saving him and the kingdom.

God does not require us to give our physical selves brutishly, carelessly, or frivolously. The journey is an inward one that does not require a physical quest to Mordor that leaves us broken for years after, nor does it require sex, starvation, or excessive initiation to achieve our spiritual quest. The Holy Grail is within you, and when you let go of the physical, just as the knight Perceval had to, you begin the real journey of finding the Grail within.

## Spiritual Guidance:

You must own your power and realize your worth. You are royalty. You wear an invisible crown that you must dust off and claim. The time of the fantasyland is beautiful, but you must also make peace with your present for a more fruitful life now. You cannot keep the crown on your head if you are whipping it around to look behind you. It is time to heal and let go of the past and live in a present world with magic integrated into it. Letting go of the past can create more abundant and beneficial lives, businesses, and relationships. If you are lacking in these areas, I suggest reciting the release and forgiveness of anyone you feel has ever wronged you, slighted you, or hurt you in any way.

Oftentimes, we long for a more magical world or fantasyland when we have had a traumatic or extremely difficult experience. It becomes an escape that feels safe and enchanting rather than the mundane or difficult adversity we face in our current life. If this is the case, the solution is to begin working on the issues that cause the instinct to flee. By living in the past, you also unknowingly keep any of your negative past experiences alive. Now is all there is, and being present in the now will help you create a life you do not desire to escape from. You may want to ask yourself why the fantasy world is far more appealing than reality, then harness those qualities into your present life. If you desire more magic, ask yourself where you can create more magic in your life.

## Affirmations:

- *I have all the magic and miracles I desire presently in my life now.*
- *I manifest all that I desire from the purity of my heart.*
- *I am a magical, powerful being. I am royalty and claim my right to the throne through Jesus, the Christ.*

## Prayer:

"May I live my life like the royalty I was born into. May I serve others and be receptive to receiving this kindness from others as well. May I emulate the kingdom of heaven on Earth. Amen."

## Additional Resources:

*Awakening the Heroes Within* by Carol Pearson
*Goddesses: Mysteries of the Feminine Divine* by Joseph Campbell
*Pathways to Bliss: Mythology and Personal Transformation* by Joseph Campbell
*The Archetypes and the Collective Unconscious* by Carl Jung
*The Hero and the Outlaw* by Margaret Mark and Carol Pearson
*The Lord of the Rings* by J. R. R Tolkien
*The Pilgrim's Progress* by John Bunyan
*The Power of Myth* by Joseph Campbell
*The Prophet* by Kahili Gibran

# THE WARRIOR

The Warrior is a person who embodies God's blessings of strength, perseverance, and skill. They are often athletes, military, veterans, or competitors in their field. The Warrior is an expert in precision and meticulous detail. They have trained themselves to perfection personally or in their field and strive to reach the highest possible achievements. They don't want to just be "good" at what they do; they aspire to be the best. This may make them competitive, not necessarily in a spiteful or egotistical way, but because they see the potential of themselves and others. They encompass the strength and endurance of humanity and how when we connect our body, spirit, and mind, we are capable of greatness. To the Warrior, life is an arena where you win, succeed, and triumph over your own fears, but it's also about restrictions. If they are told they cannot do something, it only drives them more.

While they may or may not have been brought up in a spiritual environment, The Warrior usually finds a new level of faith, passion, and understanding in their spirituality through a personal hardship or setback. Although they may have been raised with some faith, it is not until this personal awakening that they fully step into The Warrior mindset.

Travel and adventure are powerful for their psyche and nurturing to their soul. They may even mix their adventures with travel and go backpacking, hiking, or mountain climbing. The Warrior brings a modern and grounded interpretation of spirituality that makes it easily accessible and digestible to the common person. They are able to speak about spirituality, the power of thought, and philosophy in a way that is sensible and practical.

**Most Common Ascendant Spiritual Archetypes:** the Wayfarer, the Eastern Philosopher, the Mythologist, the Crusader

**Colors of the Warrior:** gold, dark blue, navy blue, bright blue, orange, yellow, red

**When Balanced, You May Feel or Experience:** equipped, strategic, courageous, in the zone, precise, focused, dignified, heroic, glorious, confident, valuable, non-expendable, competitive

**When Unbalanced, You May Feel or Experience:** hostile, weak, defiant, compulsive, stressed, overwhelmed, helpless, lethargic, depressed, insomnia, deep-seated anger or frustration

**Governs:** head, ears, eyes, sinuses, knees, ankles, hips, legs, ankles, knees, femur, arms, shoulders, brain

**Physical Ailments:** arthritis, muscle spasms, sprained, fractured, or broken bones, ligament ruptures, knee pains, fractured discs

### Correlating Essential Oils:

**Roman Chamomile:** Used by Roman soldiers in preparation for battle, Roman chamomile promotes the calming of nerves, provides clarity, and bolsters courage.

**Helichrysum:** The oil for the wounded warrior, helichrysum is healing for physical and emotional wounds. It gives a feeling of strength and endurance to those going through difficult battles.

**Eucalyptus:** Soothing to the body and lungs, eucalyptus is useful to The Warrior who needs mending of muscles or opening of the lungs. Eucalyptus is also helpful for concentration and organizing thoughts, which is beneficial for The Warrior to create plans and map out their mission.

## Correlating Stones:

**Garnet:** "The warrior stone," regeneration, stimulation, determination
**Arrowhead:** bravery, courage, defense, achievement
**Carnelian:** self-esteem, life force, positivity
**Bloodstone:** resilience, vitality, power, protection

## Correlating Plants:

- **Warrior's Plume (aka Indian Warrior):** A root parasitic plant, warriors' plume has the ability to attach itself to the roots of other plants for nutrients; however, it can also live and thrive on its own, like The Warrior, who can thrive individually or in a group.
- **Yarrow:** Used on the battlefield to heal wounds, yarrow was referred to as "soldier's woundwort."
- **Gladiolus:** strength, integrity, strong moral values
- **Mistletoe:** In Norse mythology, Balder was the beloved son of Odin and Frigg. Favored and adored by all, he was one of the most cherished of the gods. One day, Odin began having dreams about his son that foretold of an untimely death. Disturbed by these dreams, Odin rode to the underworld to meet a seeress who could tell him if these dreams would come to pass. She confirmed that Balder would soon be dead and joining her in the underworld. Odin rode home to Asgard, distraught and broken-hearted that he might soon lose his son. Upon telling his wife, Frigg, she decided to embark on a quest to save Balder. She went through the worlds and heavens, asking every creature

living and nonliving to swear an oath that they would not hurt Balder. However, when she came upon the mistletoe, she assumed it was too harmless and did not ask for an oath. She concluded her quest and returned home, letting all of the gods of Asgard know that Balder was immune to harm from any creature, living and nonliving. Balder and the gods decided to make a sport of it and all began throwing things at Balder in amusement that nothing could hurt him. But Loki, the god of mischief and a shapeshifter, disguised himself and went to Frigg, asking her, "Did every creature living and nonliving really swear an oath to not harm him?" Frigg admitted, "Well almost everything. The mistletoe was so harmless I didn't feel that it was necessary to ask for an oath from it." With that Loki rode off in search for mistletoe. When he found it, he wanted to be certain it had not taken an oath and asked it if it had done so, but the mistletoe answered, "I have not." Loki cut a branch of mistletoe and rode back to Asgard with it in tow. The gods were all still laughing and enjoying the game, all except one god, Hodr, who was blind. Loki approached him, asking if he, too, would like to play, telling him, "I will give you this branch and direct your hand where to throw it." Hodr, not knowing what would happen, agreed and took the branch from the trickster Loki. He threw the branch of mistletoe, and it pierced Balder, killing him instantly.

The Warrior always seems to be immune to everything, like Balder was immune to all creatures living and nonliving. But The Warrior must remember that their immunity only goes so far and that one should never tempt fate or become arrogant with their abilities, strength, or endurance.

**Power Words:** champion, fighter, hero, force of nature, courage, tenacity, brawn

### People, Places, and Periods That May Resonate with You

- **People:** soldier, patriot, warriors, Spartan, athlete, Olympian, militia, Viking

- **Periods:** the rise of the Roman Empire, 27 BC–AD 476; Revolutionary War; Eurasia 1206; the Civil War; World War II
- **Places:** Rome, Greece, American East Coast, Eastern America, Middle East, China

## Correlating Animal: THE RAM

The ram symbolizes the warrior spirit and the ability to drive forward headfirst into situations with ferocity, strength, and brute force. Like Aries, the ram signifies ambition, leadership, and being assertive. However, Aries can be impulsive, and the ram reminds us to think before we leap and instead approach situations with planning and organization. The ram encourages us to utilize skill and personal power to dual against the challenges in our lives with determination and success.

## Common Struggles:

**Common Triggers:** feeling weak, someone questioning their ability or competence, being accused of being cowardly, having their physicality threatened, being robbed, feeling incapable

**When Triggered, the Warrior Can Become:** aggressive, arrogant, competitive

**Common Personal Struggles:** The Warrior bases a considerable amount of their value on their body, physicality, stamina, and physical abilities. If and when that is threatened (which usually happens in some form or another), the Warrior is thrust into an identity crisis of worth. If the Warrior cannot fight, what is their significance? This can be particularly difficult if your family, loved ones, and friends have relied on your persona as the Warrior and can no longer place you in that position. This redirection of purpose and importance can lead in two directions: A downward spiral where The Warrior feels worthless and depressed, turning to medication or substances to numb the pain of their loss of self. Alternatively, this obstacle can lead to greatness and can force The Warrior into a deep growth phase, pushing their mind and faith to the level they have excelled with their body.

The Warrior also feels that a lot rests on their shoulders. Whether it be a sports game, Olympic event, or even war, the Warrior feels as though if they do not win, then they are a failure. And if they fail, others who depend on them may lose their livelihood or even their lives. It's an insurmountable amount of stress and burden that, when going well, makes The Warrior feel alive and validated, but when not going well, makes them feel worthless, weak, or incompetent.

**Common Spiritual Struggles:** The Warrior can achieve so much with their own mind and strength that it may feel peculiar to acknowledge that they, too, need help or support in areas of their lives. They may see it as a weakness to lean on others or foreign to ask for God's aid in a time of distress. It can feel personally defeating to admit you need help, but there is no shame in doing so, especially when it's God's help you are asking for. The Warrior holds themself to high standards. Your perfectionism, while useful for fine-tuning your skills, can actually be tearing you down. Let God be there for you in all areas of your life, and allow yourself to make a few mistakes. While you may have abilities that are unusually extraordinary, God isn't asking you to be a perfectionist. You can only do your best, and God will always think your best is good enough.

## Mythology, Folklore, Symbolism, or Correlating Story

In Greek mythology, Achilles was a half-man, half-god, and considered the greatest warrior to ever live. He appeared to be invincible and unstoppable to any earthly creature and was a force of nature. However, despite his brute force and incredible fighting skills, Achilles had one weakness. When he was a child, his mother, Thetis, wanted to keep him safe from harm, so she set out to make his body indestructible. She held him by his heel and bathed him in the river Styx until he was invulnerable, except, of course, for the one spot on his heel where the water did not touch because it was where she held him. This one spot on his body was his only weakness and thus, when Paris shot him in what we now call the Achilles tendon, he was defeated.

Like Achilles, the Warrior seems to be unstoppable and has abilities that may seem otherworldly. Yet, like Achilles, the Warrior also has their weakness, which can be crippling to their psyche or ego. One's Achilles heel may vary, depending on each person, but many of Warriors fear being average. You live as a man amongst men (or woman amongst women) and fear living without the glory and magnified living. Greatness is in your blood, and you strive to live it in all things. Yet if you leave your heel exposed, you may create a situation that brings you to your knees.

### Spiritual Guidance:

The Warrior is an exceptional person who garners attention and affection from adoring fans. From athletes to those in the military, there is a respect and adoration that the Warrior receives from others. The Warrior must remember not to let their ego or self-worth become attached to the opinions or thoughts of others. While the attention may be well-deserved, if you allow your worth to be based on the opinions and thoughts of others, you may find you lack any when the adoring fans leave. If the fans were to leave or you lost your abilities, would you love yourself as much? Abide by what God says about you, and you will find more worth within yourself regardless of what others say or think about you.

Additionally, the Warrior bases so much of their value on reaching the top that they can miss the world happening around them. Dedication and devotion to a skill or trade can require incredible amounts of time and discipline but remember you must also live your life. If you have family or a partner, remember there is a life outside of work, and you must do what you can to achieve greatness in that area as well. You and your loved ones will still be around even when the fans, clients, or customers leave, so remember to prioritize what is really important.

Your talents and abilities may seem like weapons, but with God, you have the battle. Just as when the young boy, David, went to fight the greatest warrior in the lands, the man balked at such a small young man coming to fight him. But David replied, "Thou comest to me with a sword, and with a spear, and with a shield: but I come to thee in the name of the LORD of hosts, the God of the armies of Israel, whom thou hast defied.

This day will the LORD deliver thee into mine hand; and I will smite thee, and take thine head from thee; and I will give the carcasses of the host of the Philistines this day unto the fowls of the air, and to the wild beasts of the earth; that all the earth may know that there is a God in Israel. And all this assembly shall know that the LORD saveth not with sword and spear: for the battle *is* the LORD's, and he will give you into our hands."

The battle is the Lord's, whatever it may be that you do, involve God, and He will win your battles for you.

### Affirmations:

- *My body is a temple of the Lord.*
- *I am my most powerful when I surrender to God and let Him move through me.*
- *I will create all my plans and tactics with God.*

### Prayer:

"Lord, use my body to glorify You. Guide me, direct me, and lead me in the ways I must go and use my body to achieve greatness."

## Additional Resources:

*Alexander the Great* by Phillip Freeman
*Body Mind Mastery: Training for Sport and Life* by Dan Millman
*General Patton's Principles for Life and Leadership* by Porter B
    Williamson
*The Way of the Peaceful Warrior* by Dan Millman

# THE EASTERN PHILOSOPHER

The Eastern Philosopher is a thoughtful, unchallenging personality, who seeks to discover and live their dharma and purpose. They are subdued and prefer to avoid confrontation and see the world's conflicts as mirrors of themselves. They are compassionate with a soft heart. They see beauty in the smallest of details and believe in letting everything be as it is meant to be. They look to the wisdom of Buddha and other ascended masters to assist them in their journey and on their spiritual path. They love to laugh and most likely have the loudest, most infectious laugh in the room. They love seeing other people smile and believe spirituality should combine ancient teachings with fun, contentment, and gratitude.

They have a profound understanding of the connection between body and mind. They recognize the power of thought and how what we think becomes our reality. Health is simply an extension of their mindset, and they notice the difference in their health when they are happy and peaceful as opposed to angry or stressed. While they love the teachings of the sages, they may also be interested in current studies, psychology, and modern techniques. It can be intriguing to the Eastern

Philosopher to see how science is beginning to catch up with some of the oldest teachings in the world.

Additionally, they see that self-awareness is one of our greatest gifts and superpowers. When in a place of gratitude, have a strong meditation practice, and are disciplined in their health, they feel unstoppable and create ripples in the world. For the Eastern Philosopher, spirituality is not just about mindset. Rather, their mindset is about living, embodying, and spreading wisdom in their lives as well as into the world.

**Most Common Ascendant Spiritual Archetypes:** the Neoteric Shaman, the Ancestor, the Recoverist, the Warrior

**Colors of the Eastern Philosopher:** green, yellow, gold, orange, earth tones, sage, or jade green

**When Balanced, You May Feel or Experience:** compassion, love, inner peace, stillness, friendly, outgoing, letting go, balance, and self-acceptance

**When Unbalanced, You May Feel or Experience:** anger, loneliness, self-sabotage, victimization, blame, emotionally closed off, and feelings of not belonging

**Governs:** heart, breast, chest, arteries, blood flow, circulation, upper back, thymus gland, respiratory system

**Physical Ailments:** heart pain, heart attack, high blood pressure, diabetes, gallbladder and liver issues, breast cancer, lung problems

### Essential Oils:

**Nag Champa:** purification, positivity, enlightenment, mediation
**Ylang Ylang:** opening of the heart, used in the healing of trauma
**Rose:** God's love, grace, and mercy
**Jasmine:** community, family, hospitality, good luck

**Sandalwood:** transcendence, letting go, surrender, release
**Frankincense:** When placed on the crown of the head (Baihui acupuncture point GV20), it creates a strong connection with God while praying.

## Correlating Stones:

**Sapphire:** royalty, abundance, clarity harmony, tranquility
**Jade:** peace, good luck, fortune, healthy relationships
**Malachite:** stone of transformation, assists in healing emotional family ties
**Rose Quartz:** unconditional love
**Peridot:** peace, compassion, friendliness
**Rhodonite:** the stone of compassion, used in the healing of past wounds

## Correlating Plants:

- **Henna:** healing
- **Bamboo:** strength, happiness, wealth, love
- **Bodhi Tree:** enlightenment
- **Cherry Blossom:** the beauty of the present, lessons, heart, wisdom
- **The Lotus:** resilience, rebirth, purity, growth through harsh or dirty conditions

**Power Words:** compassion, letting go, surrender, determination, strength, endurance, inner peace

## People, Places, and Periods That May Resonate with You

- **People:** Ayurvedic or Traditional Chinese medicine doctor, herbalist, samurai, monk, healer
- **Places:** Mongolia, China, India, Japan, Nepal, Bali, Thailand
- **Periods:** Ancient China, pre-Vedic and Vedic periods in India, Islamic Golden Age, the Ayutthaya Period

## Correlating Animal: THE CRANE

The crane represents family, success, balance, grace, and prosperity. The Eastern Philosopher carries the beliefs, struggles, and adversity of their ancestors. The Crane encourages you to use your past as a source of strength in the present. Everyone has past struggles, and the crane reminds us to use our past rather than to become or relive it. The Eastern Philosopher has a tendency to avoid their emotions and become overly intellectual. The Crane serves as a reminder to express, witness, and honor your emotions. Creativity and joy are powerful tools for the Eastern Philosopher to connect to their feelings and process them in a way that is healthy and useful.

## Common Struggles

**Common Triggers:** having to live up to others' expectations; lacking honor; being patient and not seeing a payoff; being the backbone for your family, friends, and community; not being seen.

**When Triggered, the Eastern Philosopher Can Become:** detached, angry, destructive

**Common Personal Struggles:** Because you are sensitive, if you share your emotions and do not feel properly supported, you may become hardened and closed off. You may feel betrayed by your emotions and the lack of support you receive when you share them, so you become overly intellectual and analytical. If this happens, you may be perceived as angry, careless, and disregarding, but the truth is that you really feel so much and have no outlet that you become angry with how much you care but do not understand what to do with your sensitivity and feelings.

You generally feel like others' truths are forced upon you. This may be challenging as you begin to uncover your own reality and see that it is not congruent with family, friends, or leaders you follow. You may notice your ideals about work are different than most or that you have a different view of the world. You may begin to realize that the things that were believed and taught in your family growing up actually no longer coincide with your thoughts and feelings. This is especially popular among old-school cultures. The reason is that these cultures have long and proud lineages, which allows very little room for growth. They prefer the tried-and-true methods of life and many times feel uncomfortable with change. When an Eastern Philosopher comes from a strong cultural background, or even a family deeply rooted in their old ways, they may have to face this backlash. As you begin to develop your authenticity, they may feel it is inauthentic to your culture and therefore see you as an outsider to their reality.

**Common Spiritual Struggles:** You lean on the side of the intellectual and physical realm rather than the emotional and would prefer to "do" rather than "feel." When a problem arises, you reach for texts, formulas, or rituals rather than listening to God or your own intuition to guide you. With so many ancient texts regarding elements, grids, herbs, and modalities, it can be difficult for you to integrate healing into your life outside of your designated healing. Everything becomes an external cure rather than processing or integrating the emotional or spiritual aspects. You may go to healers and yoga classes to help you connect to source, but outside of those sacred spaces, you are unsure of how to integrate those positive high vibes into your life.

### Mythology, Folklore, Symbolism, or Correlating Story

The Buddha was teaching in a village when an angry man began heckling him. This man disagreed with the Buddha's teaching and angrily yelled at the Buddha, calling him a false master. While he did so, the Buddha just stared at the man and peacefully continued talking, which only made the man angrier. Finally, the Buddha smiled at the man and asked, *"Tell me, if you buy a gift for someone, and that person does not take it, to whom does the gift belong?"* The man was confused and answered,

*"It would belong to me because I bought the gift." To which the Buddha responded, "Yes, and it is the same with your anger."*

We do not have to accept the feelings, beliefs, or limitations of our ancestors. It is their possession and if we choose not to take it, they do not have to belong to us. Additionally, we have the right at any moment to decide we no longer want to possess that which has been given to us and can donate it to God.

## Spiritual Guidance:

Building your own intuition and connection with God will aid you in connecting Heaven and Earth. The earth holds many secrets, remedies, and attributes to assist in our consciousness, but without the connection to God, these are still traditions made by man. When you learn to connect God more with your belief systems, you will be able to create a life that only references physical remedies rather than a foundation built on them. Being too intellectual sometimes gets in the way or stunts our growth.

Surround yourself with others who support your emotions and can encourage you to feel and share your thoughts and feelings. As previously stated, due to your internal emotional sensitivity, you may become angry or closed off when your feelings are not honored. Therefore, it is key to surround yourself with people who love you and are receptive to your thoughts and feelings.

Many Eastern Philosophers begin forming pseudo families outside of their own, especially if faced with the backlash of going against the family. You may find you feel more in tune with your yoga family or friends in a healing class rather than with your own family. This is an important time to remember friends are the family we choose. We are born into our families to end karma and assist us on our spiritual path, but if they are damaging to our emotional state or hinder our healing, we must detach from the toxic environment. If your family is unsupportive as you grow, it is acceptable to take a step back as you engage with others who can support your growth. As you begin to better understand your emotions, it is crucial to be near people who value and honor them, regardless of their relationship with you.

## Affirmations:

- *My heart is full of love, compassion, and gratitude.*
- *I AM the joyful, loving, and playful expression of God.*
- *My heart is receptive to all of God's love.*

## Prayer:

"My God, there is only You. Deliver me from the ideas of suffering and evil. May I know Your love and abundance in my heart, and may I shine it onto the world always."

## Additional Resources:

*Autobiography of a Yogi* by Paramahansa Yogananda
*The Alchemist* by Paulo Coelho
*The Four Agreements* by Don Miguel Ruiz
*The Prophet* by Kahlil Gibran
*The Tao of Pooh* by Benjamin Hoff
*Wheels of Life* by Anodea Judith
*Zen and the Art of Motorcycle Maintenance: An Inquiry into Values*
     by Robert Pirsig

# THE SAINT

The Saint is the Spiritual Archetype that relates to and resonates with the divine feminine of the Blessed Mother. They see the anointing of Mother Mary and the heart of her purpose and mission and feel admiration and appreciation. While much of religion focuses solely on God and Jesus, they cherish Mary's motherly words, wisdom, and love. Additionally, The Saint acts as a mother to those around them. They, too, are loved, admired, and cherished by those in their life, especially those they have mothered or been nurturing to.

While The Saint is known for their tender heart, they have a strong spirit that is made stronger by going softer. The Saint Spiritual Archetype is about doing big things while loving the simplistic. No one does this better than The Saint. For them, dreaming and gratitude go hand in hand, and this is part of their charm. Just like Mother Mary, who lived a humble life yet had one of the most monumental tasks of all time, they are grateful for all that they have but aspire to live God's purpose in their life in a big way.

The Saint is a dreamer and sees the world through rose-colored lenses. They are kind, supportive, nurturing, and optimistic. They see the possibilities in everything and are enthusiastic about helping others become the best parts of themselves regardless of who they are or their story. They believe in everyone and are a champion for the world. They help people feel heard, which is a rare quality with an authentic impact. They wrap their arms, words, and prayers around others, giving them a mother's embrace that is needed and appreciated.

**Most Common Ascendant Spiritual Archetypes:** the Sectarian, the Mythologist, the Christian Mystic

**Colors of the Saint:** royal blue, pink, white, peach, light green, lilac

**When Balanced, You May Feel or Experience:** peaceful, joyful, harmonious, kind, loving, generous, proud, creative, open, thoughtful, devoted, nurturing

**When Unbalanced, You May Feel or Experience:** anxious, worried, heartache, distant, detached, overwhelmed, small, insignificant, people-pleasing, resentment

**Governs:** stomach, heart, chest, breast, feet, fingers

**Common Physical Ailments:** fatigue, brain fog, anxiety, depression, nervous system ailments, wired or tired, insomnia, inflamed gallbladder

### Essential Oils:

**Rose:** love, kindness, peace. It is often said that the scent of roses accompanies Mother Mary when people have visitations or she appears
**Gardenia:** gentleness, innocence, purity
**Jasmine:** femininity, modesty, hospitality
**Vetiver:** nervousness, stress relief, perfectionism

## Correlating Stones:

**Rose Quartz:** love, compassion, healing
**Peruvian Opal:** peace, hope, love
**Pink Calcite:** harmony, nurturing, self-love
**Morganite:** sweetness, innocence, wisdom
**Kunzite:** heart, divine light, the woman's stone, the mother's stone

## Correlating Plants:

- **Roses:** God's love, devotion, faith, honor
- **Lilacs:** spirituality, tranquility, humility
- **Hydrangeas:** grace, understanding, sincerity
- **Peonies:** compassion, honor, gentleness
- **Lily-of-the-Valley:** It is said that when Eve fell from the garden of Eden, she cried and her tears became Lily of the Valley. This plant is a sign of humility and returning to grace.
- **Provence French Lavender:** comfort, nurturing, motherhood
- **Fleur-de-Lis:** While not an actual flower, the fleur-de-lis is a symbol of the lily and one of the most famous representations of Mary.

**Power Words:** feminine, nurturing, connection, happiness, soft, mothering, Sacred Heart

## People, Places, and Periods That May Resonate with You

- **People:** Mother Mary, Mary Magdalene, women from the Bible, saints, angels, preachers, teachers
- **Places:** Lourdes, France: Mary's Grotto; Glastonbury, England: Chalice Well; Avebury,England; Fatima, Portugal; Spain; Nazareth and Jerusalem in Israel; Bethlehem, Palestine; Italy
- **Periods:** Ancient Greece, 700–480 BC; The Middle Ages, AD 500–1500; the Renaissance, AD 1400–1600

## Correlating Animal: THE DEER

Deer medicine represents gentleness, sensitivity, and intuition. The stag is the king of the forest, nurturing, protecting, and considering all of the other animals in his kingdom. Similarly, The Saint's mission is to protect, nurture, and give guidance through gentleness rather than pushing or forcing. The Saint knows there is power in loving, supporting, and encouraging people with a loving hand instead of an iron fist. Deer medicine reminds us that softness is a strength, nurturing doesn't mean being passive, and that leading with heart is a beautiful and healthy way to help others heal, grow, and love.

## Common Struggles

**Common Triggers:** being put on the spot, being seen, negativity, being blamed, a lack of feeling safe, feeling like you have messed up or done something wrong, boundaries

**When Triggered, the Saint Can Become:** childish, aloof, passive

**Common Personal Struggles:** Many people with The Saint Spiritual Archetype come from a background with an alcoholic, angry, or mentally ill parent or household where they were not allowed to express their feelings and emotions. Therefore, they can sometimes fear stepping into their identity or strengthening their voice out of fear of hurting others, being disagreeable, or getting into trouble. You may hide behind others in order to not have all of the heat on you in case something happens.

The Saint has an innocent heart and mind, which can deceive them into being too trusting of others. You may be gullible or feel like you don't get what is happening in a conversation or situation. Remember that you can be loving and trusting without throwing caution to the wind. It is alright to protect yourself and have boundaries and keep yourself safe.

**Common Spiritual Struggles:** The Saint has a heart that is wide open for the world, which can be felt and experienced by everyone who meets you, but sometimes your heart being wide open leaves you exposed to hurt, heartache, and oversensitivity. How can someone with such a big heart reconcile the evil, pain, and suffering in the world? Remember, dear heart, that the evils in the world are not of God but are of the devil. With God on your side, though, you can quash, battle, and liberate people from evil. This is a common area of misperception people have and may ask themselves, "How can God let this evil in the world?" It is not God doing or allowing the evil, and when we realize and embody that knowing, we can go into the world with a big heart and feel more empowered to drive out the evil and share our hearts with those affected by it.

## Mythology, Folklore, Symbolism, or Correlating Story

There was once a girl who was excited to be moving away from home for the first time. While she loved her family, she had big dreams she was eager to pursue. She left home and moved to a faraway land where she lived for many years without seeing her family. One day, her mother came to visit and she was beyond happy. She planned many adventures and wanted to show her the amazing new city she called home. She introduced her to all her new friends and all the people she had come to know. One friend, in particular, took a liking to her mother and started becoming very close. He began calling her "Mom" and treating her as a mother. While the girl was used to this in a way because this often happened, this time, she felt jealous. She had not seen her mother in a long time and felt possessive over her being her mom. She felt irritated and annoyed and thought about it continuously during the days her mother was there and her friend wanted to be a part of their adventures. While mulling it over yet again, she said to herself, "Why is he doing this? She's my mother, not his." Then God spoke to her and kindly and lovingly replied, "Some mothers are mothers to the world." She was stunned by these words as the realization washed over her. Her friend did not have a close relationship with his mother. It was a difficult and painful relationship filled with trauma, pain, and heartache. To have a mother who treated him like a son, offering him love, support, patience, and acceptance, was not something he could receive from his mother but was something he could get from hers.

Some mothers are mothers to the world. Whether a mother with children of her own, a person who adopts children as their own, or a person who treats others with the love and kindness of a father or mother, some people are meant to bring this nurturing, patient, and supportive love into the world for others. People like Fred Rogers, better known as Mr. Rogers, gave this gift to the world, acting as a father-type who made everyone he spoke to, adult and child alike, feel heard, seen, respected, and honored in the most profound ways. This is the role of some people and is a precious gift to the world. This is the role of The Saint.

## Spiritual Guidance:

While the role and destiny of The Saint is to care, nurture, and guide others, keep in mind that this can affect your boundaries. Like a parent whose priorities are their children and who can easily lose sight of their own, The Saint can also lose sight of their own self-care and personal needs. Keep your well full so that you have more to give to others. Fill your reservoir with God's Word, His love, His support, His guidance, His compassion, and His healing so that He may multiply it for you to give to others.

## Affirmations:

- *My heart is vast, full, and rich. I spread my love, and God refills it.*
- *I bravely face the enemy to spread God's love, will, peace, and abundance to the world.*
- *I am an instrument of God's love. I will play His love for all to hear.*

## Prayer:

"Lord, grant that I may always allow myself to be guided by You, always follow Your plans and perfectly accomplish Your Holy Will. Grant that in all things, great and small, today and all the days of my life, I may do whatever You require of me. Help me respond to the slightest prompting of Your Grace, so that I may be Your trust-worthy instrument for Your honour. May Your Will be done in time and in eternity by me, in me, and through me. Amen."—Saint Teresa of Avila

## Additional Resources:

*Come Be My Light* by Mother Teresa
*Goddesses: Mysteries of the Feminine Divine* by Joseph Campbell
*Hail, Holy Queen: The Mother of God in the Word of God* by Scott Hahn
*Medjugorje: The Message* by Wayne Weible
*Mother Mary* by Robin Rose

# THE CHRISTIAN MYSTIC

The Christian Mystic believes in the power and authority of God and resonates with the spiritual and supernatural influence found in the Bible and mysticism. They are drawn to aspects of the Bible, such as the raising of the dead, angels, and healing of the sick. When Jesus commissions His apostles to go out and do the works of God, the Christian Mystic takes this personally and knows that they, too, can do all He did and more. For the Christian Mystic, God is a God of love, miracles, and omnipresence, and they seek to discover, understand, and embody these attributes in their life.

In many cases, the Christian Mystic may have been raised with a hurtful or abusive God or with people who used the name of God in offensive, negative, or harmful ways. Some people portray Him as though He is absent, uncaring, and cold and His power is limited, insignificant, or a thing of the past. The Christian Mystic knows there is more to God than most people acknowledge or inherit. You may seek to redefine who God is and bring that new definition to others to heal their relationships or realize their fullest potential, spiritually and supernaturally.

While they love to study and learn about God, the Bible, and mysticism, for them, learning is about intensifying their relationship with God. The Christian Mystic feels a deep, impassioned love for God and a strong sense of communion with Him. For them, spirituality is not something they practice in rare moments; it is something they seek to live and be immersed in.

**Most Common Ascendant Spiritual Archetypes:** the Shaman, the Witch, the Crusader, the Theologist

**Colors of the Christian Mystic:** cobalt blue, gold, rose gold, amethyst purple, white, pink, emerald green, deep red, orange

**When Balanced, You May Feel or Experience:** faith, wisdom, intuition, guidance, knowing, hope, authority

**When Unbalanced, You May Feel or Experience:** attached to your suffering, identify with your fear as a means of showing strength, judgment toward others, lack of faith, hopelessness, powerless, fearful

**Common Physical Ailments:** anxiety, fear, morning sickness, food intolerances and allergies, eating disorders, cancer, candida, feminine and masculine imbalances

### Correlating Essential Oils:

**Palma Christi:** The healing oil known as "The Palm of Christ" has been used for centuries and was a favorite of mystics, such as Edgar Cayce.
**Cinnamon:** An essential ingredient in holy anointing oil, the smell of cinnamon is present when someone is anointed. It has also been reported to be smelled after some people's baptisms.
**Cassia:** Another ingredient in holy anointing oil, cassia is an oil of devotion and servitude.

**Spikenard:** Used in the oil to anoint Jesus' feet before his crucifixion, spikenard is considered a holy oil.

**Rose of Sharon:** Mentioned in the Songs of Solomon, the rose of Sharon is similar to hibiscus. It represents love, beauty, and the church as Jesus' bride.

## Correlating Stones:

- **Urim and Thummim:** These stones were worn on the breastplate of the high priest: "And thou shalt put in the breastplate of judgment the Urim and the Thummim; and they shall be upon Aaron's heart, when he goeth in before the Lord: and Aaron shall bear the judgment of the children of Israel upon his heart before the Lord continually" (Exodus 28:30). It is also used in mysticism for divine divination.
- **Bloodstone:** Referred to as "the martyr's stone," legend states that when the blood of Jesus hit the ground, it mixed with the earth and formed bloodstone.
- **Diamond:** infinite love, virtue, light, faithfulness
  Black Tourmaline: one of the birthstones of the zodiac Scorpio, the zodiac sign of mysticism

## Correlating Plants:

- **Rose:** love, healing, protection, often the flower of saints
- **Grapevine:** Jesus, prosperity, the Church, connection to divine power and authority
- **Holly tree:** Christ, goodwill, peace, redemption, freedom
- **Palm Leaves:** victory for martyrs
- **Passionflower:** Named "passion" by the Roman Catholic church to represent Jesus, the passionflower has ten petals, which priests believed represented the ten apostles who stayed true and loyal to Jesus.

**Power Words:** love, devotion, authority, prayer, faith, hope, belief, signs and wonders

## People, Places, and Periods That May Resonate with You:

- **People:** disciple, missionary, revivalist, faith healer, students, saints, mystics, Knight Templars, crusaders
- **Places:** Bible Belt, France, England, Hungary, Spain, Poland, Italy, Israel, Peru, Wales, Japan, China
- **Periods:** 1095–1300s, 1400s, 1850–1950, 1970s–1990s

## Correlating Animal: THE LAMB

While many people take offense to being referred to as sheep, the lamb is trusting, childlike, sweet, and follows its shepherd. Shepherds love and protect their flock. They are humble, patient, and caring. Sheep know and follow their shepherd's voice and are dependent on their shepherd, trusting him unfailingly. The lamb represents the purity and innocence of the Christian Mystic but also represents sacrifice. The lamb has symbolism throughout the Bible, referring to the sacrifice of the flesh for the initiation of the spirit. The Christian Mystic, however, offers themself as the sacrifice and would do well to remember that the sacrifice has already been made. Instead of putting ourselves on the chopping block for others, keep in mind that there is a Savior. While we can do our best to help others, the work has already been done for us all.

## Common Struggles

**Common Triggers:** feeling unwanted or unloved; rejection; being thrown away; being consumed by your thoughts, worries, or fears; being made a fool of

**When Triggered, the Christian Mystic Can Become:** dramatic, obsessive, desperate

**Common Personal Struggles:** The Christian Mystic often fights a battle of self-worth, always wondering what their value is and not feeling good enough. They get stuck between the Old Testament God who appears to be putting them to the test and the New Testament God who gave them Jesus. With the best of intentions, they believe they are fighting crusades to bridge the gap between the two. This requires healing around the idea of who and what God is as well as debunking the myths about Him. With spiritual and religious trauma or wounds comes a resistance to let go of the old ideas, but this is the up-leveling that must take place to create an authentic and personalized relationship with God.

**Common Spiritual Struggles:** People with the Christian Mystic Spiritual Archetype have a tendency to place others in the role of being their God, such as a spouse, partner, parents, teachers, gurus, clients, and pastors, seeking their validation or approval of God Himself. This further fuels confusion around their definition of God, especially if the person placed in the role is negative, hurtful, or abusive. They may base their worth on what their partner says about them or seek too much approval from those they look up to.

## Mythology, Folklore, Symbolism, or Correlating Story

When Jesus was crucified and rose again, he commissioned his apostles to go and preach about what they had witnessed and experienced. Each of the apostles obeyed and traveled throughout the world preaching the Gospel. They spoke about the one living God, Jesus, the miracles of God, and everything that Jesus had taught them to do in their time together such as raising the dead, casting out demons, and curing the sick. While this was a saving grace and road to salvation for millions, the pagan nations who worshipped many gods, such as the Romans who ruled the government, did not care to share their power with a sovereign King. The governments who used fear and oppression to rule did not want their people to hear about a loving, merciful God or that their people had salvation outside of their authority. Because of this, the apostles were consistently jailed, threatened, beaten, and most of them were murdered for sharing the Word of God. While this was devastating and scary the disciples knew what was to be expected. After all, Jesus told them "Blessed are they which are persecuted for righteousness' sake: for theirs is the kingdom of heaven." (Matthew 5:10) and warned them, "If any man will come after me, let him deny himself, and take up his cross, and follow me. For whosoever will save his life shall lose it: and whosoever will lose his life for my sake shall find it. For what is a man profited, if he shall gain the whole world, and lose his own soul? or what shall a man give in exchange for his soul?" (Matthew 16:24-26)

Many Christians and the Christian Mystic Spiritual Archetype will allow struggles of persecution, and oppression, because of these scriptures. Their mindset tells them that they must be persecuted in martyr themselves to show the depths of their love and devotion for God. However, Jesus was not saying that we had to martyr or sacrifice ourselves for God. He was saying that because this world is committed to error, the belief of separation, and sin, that anyone who speaks or lives against those ideas, will be judged.

In the Pilgrim's progress, Christian Pilgrim finds a book (The Bible) that changes his life. He sets out to find the King of the Celestial City (Jesus) and endures hardship, strife, and adversity on his way. He and a friend named Faithful, who joins him on his journey, find themselves in a town called Vanity, where they host a debaucherous, gluttonous, and sinful fair that never ends. Christian and Faithful must walk through the crowd while being solicited by the townspeople. However, Christian and Faithful refuse everything and tell the townspeople they are only interested in buying the truth. This infuriates them and the townspeople take Christian and Faithful to court. The judge asks why they have been brought before him and the townspeople complain that Christian and his friend do not want anything they have or are selling and that it is ruining their fun. Christian and Faithful remain kind, meek, and humble throughout their torture, accusations, and cruelty but the townspeople and court twist their words and find fault with everything they do.

Ultimately, Faithful is sentenced to death, and Christian escapes and returns to his journey.

Similarly, the Christian Mystic may find that they too are persecuted for simply not participating in the vanity fair of the world. However, there is a difference between being judged for a lack of participation, and going into the fair and sacrificing oneself for God to try to prove a point. We do not need to set ourselves on fire for others; instead, we can stand in truth and reach into the flames to pull others out. There is no need to "suffer in vain." Share God's love and embody His love in your life. In doing so, you will be a walking testament to His grace, mercy, and glory, which can inspire and motivate others to leave the fair and join you on your quest.

## Spiritual Guidance:

You want an authentic relationship with God. In order to attain this, you must dismantle all preconceived notions and develop a relationship based on who God actually is and how that pertains to you as a divine being. You must release your previous notions of God in order to clear a faulty foundation and rebuild your relationship with God in a truthful and authentic light. When we truly reflect on what we know about God, most of the information we believe is taught by external sources based on their beliefs and perceptions. We do not realize that we are harnessing resentments toward God based on what others have said and that by simply altering our own perception or clarifying some of our deepest questions, we may achieve profound results in our relationship with God.

Relationships begin with getting to know each other, learning about each other, creating habits and rituals, and ultimately falling in love. We get to know one another based on our experience in the relationship. Why, then, do we not give God this same respect? We cannot fall in love with another person based on what others think of them, nor can we have a healthy and loving relationship with God based on others' opinions.

## Affirmations:

- *I forgive all those who persecute, judge, or condemn me. If God is for me, who dares be against me?*
- *I am the image and likeness of God.*
- *I am perfect. I am whole. I am holy.*

## Prayer:

"Take, Lord, receive all my liberty, my memory, my understanding, my whole will, all that I have and all that I possess. You gave it all to me, Lord; I give it all back to you. Do with it as you will, according to your good pleasure. Give me your love and your grace; for with this I have all that I need."—St. Ignatius of Loyola

## Additional Resources:

*The Bible*
*Authority of the Believer* by Kenneth E. Hagin
*Christian Mystics* by Matthew Fox
*Ever Increasing Faith* by Smith Wigglesworth
*Major Trends in Jewish Mysticism* by Gershom Scholem
*Kabbalah: The Way of the Jewish Mystic* by Perle Epstein
*The Autobiography of St. Teresa of Avila* by *St. Teresa of Avila*
*The Essential Writings of Christian Mysticism* by Bernard McGinn
*The Spirit of Saint Hildegard* by Barbara LeVan Fisher
*Your Power in the Holy Spirit* by John G. Lake

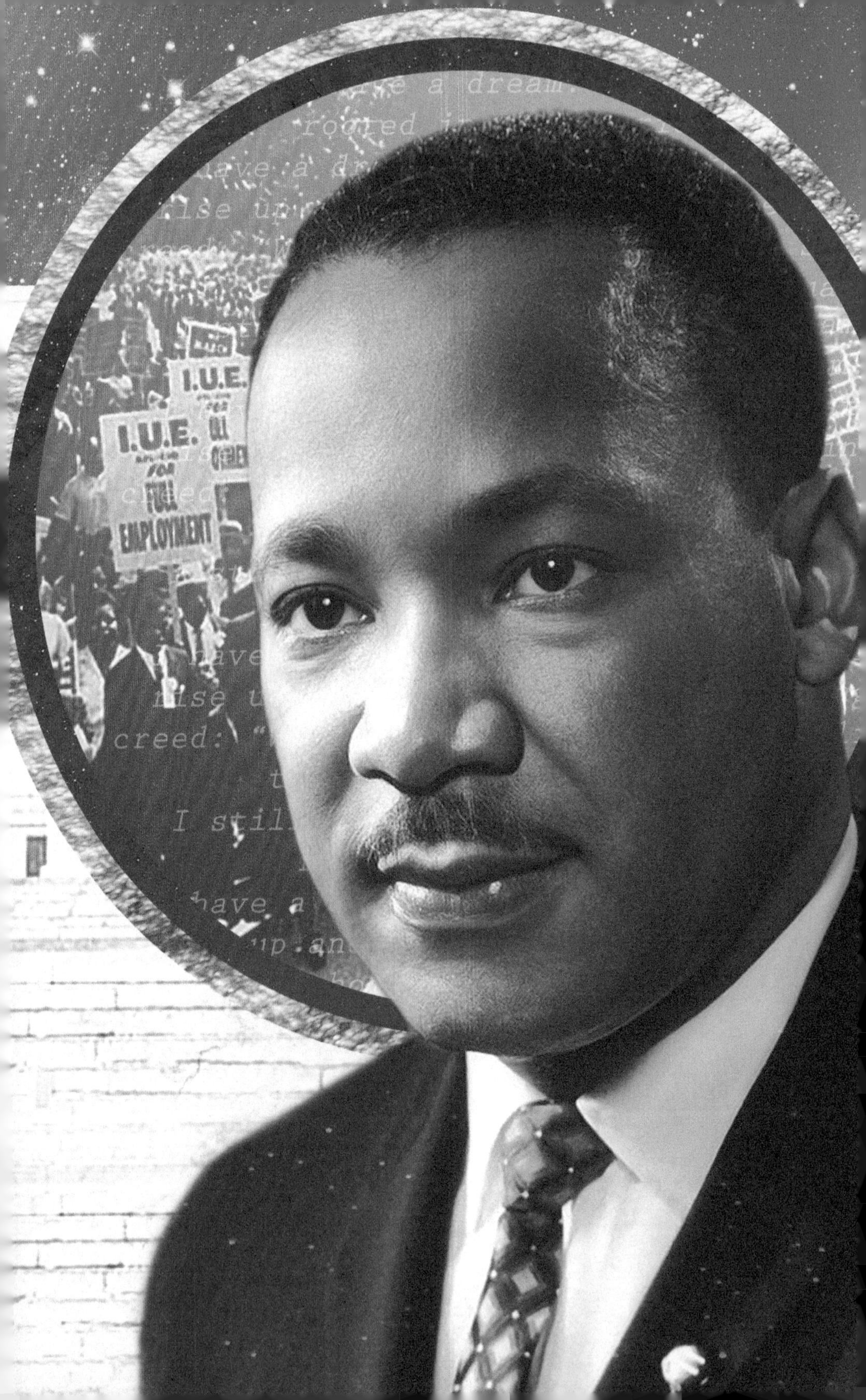
I.U.E.
I.U.E.
FOR
FULL EMPLOYMENT
rooted
creed:

# THE CRUSADER

The Crusader is a warrior with their words, actions, and beliefs. They fight against injustice, wrongdoings, and inequality to make a better world. While they may be fighters for the environment and animals, the Crusader is more of a social reformer, civil rights leader, and activist. Diplomatic, passionate, and strong-willed, the Crusader is a rebel against the status quo but a hero to those in need of change.

The Crusader is on a mission for advancement in areas that need attention and are lacking. They have seen or experienced conflict or oppression and are impelled to reform and evolve not only the situations but the consciousness and perceptions around them. Not only do they aspire to help those in need, but they also seek to educate to reduce the problem from the root.

Much of the Crusader's work revolves around speaking, writing, and using their words to influence change. Therefore, the Crusader is often eloquent and well-spoken. Words can be a weapon against the enemy if wielded correctly, so you strive to equip yourself for the battle.

The Crusader is good with people and can be friendly but is often serious. Due to the subject matters and issues they work with, there can be a more brooding side of them that is difficult to compartmentalize. Despite this, they seek to connect with people and/or animals. While it can be challenging due to the emotions involved in their work, at their core, they deeply love others and want to do everything in their power to help and be of service.

**Most Common Ascendant Spiritual Archetypes:** the Witch, the Ancestor, the Christian Mystic, the Theologist

**Colors of the Crusader:** bright-goldish yellow, red, green, bright blue, dark blue, deep purple

**When Balanced, You May Feel or Experience:** in control, directed, encouraged, influential, compelling, persuasive, credible, impelling, loving, peaceful

**When Unbalanced, You May Feel or Experience:** defeated, beaten, tired, powerless, abandoned, tyrannized, oppressed, distressed, subservient, inferior

**Governs:** heart, chest, aorta, throat, mouth, lower legs between the ankles and knees

**Common Physical Ailments:** head and brain issues, including seizures; ulcers from stress and worry; pleurisy; dysentery; appendicitis; high blood pressure; constipation and diarrhea

### Correlating Essential Oils:

**Cypress:** bravery, courage, transitions, and change
**Queen Anne's Lace:** protection, sanctuary, rebellion
**Rosewood:** confidence, self-esteem, encouragement
**Spearmint:** clarity, hope, peace

## Correlating Stones:

**Bloodstone:** courage, strength, the stone of heroes
**Sardonyx:** expression, communication, self-control
**Erythrite:** regulation of feelings, removing blocks, personal power
**Blue Halite:** resolution, empathy, confidence
**Kammererite:** initiation, insight, encouragement

## Correlating Plants:

- **Black-Eyed Susan:** justice, motivation, truth, endurance, survival
- **Blue Iris:** courage, hope, valor, faith
- **Thistle:** bravery, strength, determination, resilience, overcoming adversity
- **Pansy:** peace, free-thinking, loving actions
- **Chestnut Tree:** longevity, freedom, justice
- **Daisy:** new beginnings, optimism, thriving in the wild

**Power Words:** advocate, activist, justice, reformation, peace, strength, impact, power, authentic, vocalization, organic, transparent

## People, Places, and Periods That May Resonate with You

- **People:** abolitionists, writers, speakers, human rights activists, civil rights leaders
- **Places:** London, Mexico, Massachusetts, New York, Vermont, Chicago, Los Angeles, Seattle, Alabama
- **Periods:** 1773–1775, 1840–1920, 1960s–1970s

## Animal Totem: THE LION

Fierce, brave, and full of majesty, the lion is the reigning leader of the animal kingdom. The lion, like the Crusader, is a symbol of personal strength, courage, and authority in struggle and adversity. Lion medicine is fierce and reminds us to call upon its brawn in moments when you need vitality and tenacity. Lions are protective of their space, their young, and their pride. Similarly, the Crusader is protective of those whom they love and care about, whether in their life or through their cause. Lions are also willing to fight and will face a challenge head-on, like the Crusader who looks for change, progression, and advancement and is willing to fight for it.

## Common Struggles

**Common Triggers:** feeling overpowered, failing, feeling weak, being judged by those their fighting for, mutiny, giving up, feeling like you let people down

**When Triggered, the Crusader Can Become:** unrelenting, arrogant, vulnerable

**Common Personal Struggles:** The Crusader faces many personal struggles because they have put themselves in the position of fighting for a living. Fighting to make a difference, fighting to make changes, fighting for people's rights. You have put the burden upon yourself to perpetually struggle to make the world a better place, which takes its toll on your emotions, psyche, and heart. In Martin Luther King Jr.'s autopsy, it was reported that although he was only thirty-nine years old at the time of his assassination, his heart was like that of a sixty-year-old man. It was believed that due to the constant stress, hardship, and difficulties of his mission, Dr. King's heart was also negatively impacted. The Crusader takes their missions to heart and can feel the weight of the world on their shoulders. Sometimes it may feel like you have made a difference, that it's never enough, and the need to keep going and do more feels like too much. Or you feel that the win doesn't come often enough.

**Common Spiritual Struggles:** The Crusader sees injustice and inequality and wants to fight for what is right. However, when people fight, the line between constructive and destructive can blur. Keeping ourselves grounded in God's Word is essential to ensure that we are fighting for

His will, not our own. God wants us to love our neighbors, each other, and ourselves. He wants us to be generous, giving, and kind. He strives to abolish inequality, struggle, and suffering. By matching our will with His and using God's word to motivate our actions, we operate from a more persuasive, pure, and compelling place.

### Mythology, Folklore, Symbolism, or Correlating Story

The following is a transcript of an audio recording of a church sermon by Martin Luther King Jr. delivered at Dexter Avenue Baptist Church on or around November 17, 1957. While this is a lengthy text, it has been left in its entirety out of respect for Dr. King, and because I believe it is one of the best teachings on loving our enemies ever spoken.

*I am forced to preach under something of a handicap this morning. In fact, I had the doctor before coming to church. And he said that it would be best for me to stay in the bed this morning. And I insisted that I would have to come to preach. So he allowed me to come out with one stipulation, and that is that I would not come in the pulpit until time to preach, and that after, that I would immediately go back home and get in the bed. So I'm going to try to follow his instructions from that point on.*

*I want to use as a subject from which to preach this morning a very familiar subject, and it is familiar to you because I have preached from this subject twice before to my knowing in this pulpit. I try to make it something of a custom or tradition to preach from this passage of Scripture at least once a year, adding new insights that I develop along the way, out of new experiences as I give these messages. Although the content is, the basic content is the same, new insights and new experiences naturally make for new illustrations.*

*So, I want to turn your attention to this subject: Loving Your Enemies. It's so basic to me because it is a part of my basic philosophical and theological orientation: the whole idea of love, the whole philosophy of love. In the fifth chapter of the gospel as recorded by Saint Matthew, we read these very arresting words flowing from the lips of our Lord and Master: "Ye* have heard that it has been said, 'Thou shall love thy neighbor, and hate thine enemy.' But I say unto you, Love your enemies, bless them that curse you, do good to them that hate you, and pray for them that despitefully use you; that ye may be the children of your Father which is in heaven."

Certainly, these are great words, words lifted to cosmic proportions. And over the centuries, many persons have argued that this is an extremely difficult command. Many would go so far as to say that it just isn't possible to move out into the actual practice of this glorious command. They would go on to say that this is just additional proof that Jesus was an impractical idealist who never quite came down to earth. So, the arguments abound. But far from being an impractical idealist, Jesus has become the practical realist. The words of this text glitter in our eyes with a new urgency. Far from being the pious injunction of a utopian dreamer, this command is an absolute necessity for the survival of our civilization. Yes, it is love that will save our world and our civilization, love even for enemies.

Now let me hasten to say that Jesus was very serious when he gave this command; he wasn't playing. He realized that it's hard to love your enemies. He realized that it's difficult to love those persons who seek to defeat you, those persons who say evil things about you. He realized that it was painfully hard, pressingly hard. But he wasn't playing. And we cannot dismiss this passage as just another example of Oriental hyperbole, just a sort of exaggeration to get over the point. This is a basic philosophy of all that we hear coming from the lips of our Master. Because Jesus wasn't playing; because he was serious. We have the Christian and moral responsibility to seek to discover the meaning of these words, and to discover how we can live out this command, and why we should live by this command.

Now first let us deal with this question, which is the practical question: How do you go about loving your enemies? I think the first thing is this: In order to love your enemies, you must begin by analyzing self. And I'm sure that seems strange to you, that I start out telling you this morning that you love your enemies by beginning with a look at self. It seems to me that that is the first and foremost way to come to an adequate discovery to the how of this situation. Now, I'm aware of the fact that *some people will not like you, not because of something you have done to them, but they just won't like you. I'm quite aware of that. Some people aren't going to like the way you walk; some people aren't going to like the way you talk. Some people aren't going to like you because you can do your job better than they can do theirs. Some people aren't going to like you because other people like you, and because you're popular, and because you're well-liked, they aren't going to like you. Some people aren't going to like you because your hair is a little shorter than theirs or your hair is a little longer than theirs. Some people aren't going to like you because your skin is a little brighter than theirs; and others aren't going to like you because your skin is a little darker than theirs. So that some people aren't going to like you. They're going to dislike you, not because of something that you've done to them, but because of various jealous reactions and other reactions that are so prevalent in human nature.*

*But after looking at these things and admitting these things, we must face the fact that an individual might dislike us because of something that we've done deep down in the past, some personality attribute that we possess, something that we've done deep down in the past and we've forgotten about it; but it was that something that aroused the hate response within the individual. That is why I say, begin with yourself. There might be something within you that arouses the tragic hate response in the other individual.*

*This is true in our international struggle. We look at the struggle, the ideological struggle between communism on the one hand and democracy on the other, and we see the struggle between America and Russia. Now certainly, we can never give our allegiance to the Russian way of life, to the communistic way of life, because communism is based on an ethical relativism and a metaphysical materialism that no Christian can accept. When we look at the methods of communism, a philosophy where somehow the end justifies the means, we cannot accept that because we believe as Christians that the end is pre-existent in the means. But in spite of all of the weaknesses and evils inherent in communism, we must at the same time see the weaknesses and evils within democracy.*

*Democracy is the greatest form of government to my mind that man has ever conceived, but the weakness is that we have never touched it.*

Isn't it true that we have often taken necessities from the masses to give luxuries to the classes? Isn't it true that we have often in our democracy trampled over individuals and races with the iron feet of oppression? Isn't it true that through our Western powers we have perpetuated colonialism and imperialism? And all of these things must be taken under consideration as we look at Russia. We must face the fact that the rhythmic beat of the deep rumblings of discontent from Asia and Africa is at bottom a revolt against the imperialism and colonialism perpetuated by Western civilization all these many years. The success of communism in the world today is due to the failure of democracy to live up to the noble ideals and principles inherent in its system.

And this is what Jesus means when he said: "How is it that you can see the mote in your brother's eye and not see the beam in your own eye?" Or to put it in Moffatt's translation: "How is it that you see the splinter in your brother's eye and fail to see the plank in your own eye?" And this is one of the tragedies of human nature. So, we begin to love our enemies and love those persons that hate us whether in collective life or individual life by looking at ourselves.

A second thing that an individual must do in seeking to love his enemy is to discover the element of good in his enemy, and every time you begin to hate that person and think of hating that person, realize that there is some good there and look at those good points which will over-balance the bad points. I've said to you on many occasions that each of us is something of a schizophrenic personality. We're split up and divided against ourselves. And there is something of a civil war going on within all of our lives. There is a recalcitrant South of our soul revolting against the North of our soul. And there is this continual struggle within the very structure of every individual life. There is something within all of us that causes us to cry out with Ovid, the Latin poet, "I see and approve the better things of life, but the evil things I do." There is something within all of us that causes us to cry out with Plato that the human personality is like a charioteer with two headstrong horses, each wanting to go in different directions. There is something within each of us that causes us to cry out with Goethe, "There is enough stuff in me to make both a gentleman and a rogue." There is something within each of us that causes us to cry out with Apostle Paul: "I see and approve the better things of life, but the evil things I do."

So somehow the "isness" of our present nature is out of harmony with the eternal "oughtness" that forever confronts us. And this simply means this: That within the best of us, there is some evil, and within the worst of us, there is some good. When we come to see this, we take a different attitude toward individuals. The person who hates you most has some good in him; even the nation that hates you most has some good in it; even the race that hates you most has some good in it. And when you come to the point that you look in the face of every man and see deep down within him what religion calls "the image of God," you begin to love him in spite of. No matter what he does, you see God's image there. There is an element of goodness that he can never slough off. Discover the element of good in your enemy. And as you seek to hate him, find the center of goodness and place your attention there and you will take a new attitude.

Another way that you love your enemy is this: When the opportunity presents itself for you to defeat your enemy, that is the time which you must not do it. There will come a time, in many instances, when the person who hates you most, the person who has misused you most, the person who has gossiped about you most, the person who has spread false rumors about you most, there will come a time when you will have an opportunity to defeat that person. It might be in terms of a recommendation for a job; it might be in terms of helping that person to make some move in life. That's the time you must do it. That is the meaning of love. In the final analysis, love is not this sentimental something that we talk about. It's not merely an emotional something. Love is creative, understanding goodwill for all men. It is the refusal to defeat any individual. When you rise to the level of love, of its great beauty and power, you seek only to defeat evil systems. Individuals who happen to be caught up in that system, you love, but you seek to defeat the system.

The Greek language, as I've said so often before, is very powerful at this point. It comes to our aid beautifully in giving us the real meaning and depth of the whole philosophy of love. And I think it is quite apropos at this point, for you see the Greek language has three words for *love, interestingly enough. It talks about love as eros. That's one word for love. Eros is a sort of, aesthetic love. Plato talks about it a great deal in his Dialogues, a sort of yearning of the soul for the realm of the gods. And it's come to us to be a sort of romantic love, though it's a beautiful love. Everybody has experienced eros in all of its beauty when you find some individual that is attractive to you and that you pour out all of your like and your love on that individual. That is eros, you see, and it's a powerful, beautiful love that is given to us through all of the beauty of literature; we read about it.*

*Then the Greek language talks about philia, and that's another type of love that's also beautiful. It is a sort of intimate affection between personal friends. And this is the type of love that you have for those persons that you're friendly with, your intimate friends, or people that you call on the telephone and you go by to have dinner with, and your roommate in college and that type of thing. It's a sort of reciprocal love. On this level, you like a person because that person likes you. You love on this level, because you are loved. You love on this level, because there's something about the person you love that is likeable to you. This too is a beautiful love. You can communicate with a person; you have certain things in common; you like to do things together. This is philia.*

*The Greek language comes out with another word for love. It is the word agape, and agape is more than eros. Agape is more than philia. Agape is something of the understanding, creative, redemptive goodwill for all men. It is a love that seeks nothing in return. It is an overflowing love; it's what theologians would call the love of God working in the lives of men. And when you rise to love on this level, you begin to love men, not because they are likeable, but because God loves them. You look at every man, and you love him because you know God loves him. And he might be the worst person you've ever seen.*

*And this is what Jesus means, I think, in this very passage when he says, "Love your enemy." And it's significant that he does not say, "Like your enemy." Like is a sentimental something, an affectionate something. There are a lot of people that I find it difficult to like. I don't like what they do to me. I don't like what they say about me and other people. I don't like their attitudes. I don't like some of the things they're doing. I don't like them. But Jesus says love them. And love is greater than like. Love is understanding, redemptive goodwill for all men, so that you love everybody, because God loves them. You refuse to do anything that will defeat an individual, because you have agape in your soul. And here you come to the point that you love the individual who does the evil deed, while hating the deed that the person does. This is what Jesus means when he says, "Love your enemy." This is the way to do it. When the opportunity presents itself when you can defeat your enemy, you must not do it.*

*Now for the few moments left, let us move from the practical how to the theoretical why. It's not only necessary to know how to go about loving your enemies, but also to go down into the question of why we should love our enemies. I think the first reason that we should love our enemies, and I think this was at the very center of Jesus' thinking, is this: that hate for hate only intensifies the existence of hate and evil in the universe. If I hit you and you hit me and I hit you back and you hit me back and go on, you see, that goes on ad infinitum. It just never ends. Somewhere somebody must have a little sense, and that's the strong person. The strong person is the person who can cut off the chain of hate, the chain of evil. And that is the tragedy of hate, that it doesn't cut it off. It only intensifies the existence of hate and evil in the universe. Somebody must have religion enough and morality enough to cut it off and inject within the very structure of the universe that strong and powerful element of love.*

*I think I mentioned before that sometime ago my brother and I were driving one evening to Chattanooga, Tennessee, from Atlanta. He was driving the car. And for some reason the drivers were very discourteous that night. They didn't dim their lights; hardly any driver that passed by dimmed his lights. And I remember very vividly, my brother A. D. looked over and in a tone of anger said: "I know what I'm going to do. The next car that comes along here and refuses to dim the lights, I'm going to fail to dim mine and pour them on in all of their power." And I looked at him right quick and said: "Oh no, don't do that. There'd be too much light on this highway, and it will end up in mutual destruction for all. Somebody got to have some sense on this highway."*

*Somebody must have sense enough to dim the lights, and that is the trouble, isn't it? That as all of the civilizations of the world move up the highway of history, so many civilizations, having looked at other civilizations that refused to dim the lights, and they decided to refuse to dim theirs. And Toynbee tells that out of the twenty-two civilizations that have risen up, all but about seven have found themselves in the junk-heap of destruction. It is because civilizations fail to have sense enough to dim the lights. And if somebody doesn't have sense enough to turn on the dim and beautiful and powerful lights of love in this world, the whole of our civilization will be plunged into the abyss of destruction. And we will all end up destroyed because nobody had any sense on the highway of history. Somewhere somebody must have some sense. Men must see that force begets force, hate begets hate, toughness begets toughness. And it is all a descending spiral, ultimately ending in destruction for all and everybody. Somebody must have sense enough and morality enough to cut off the chain of hate and the chain of evil in the universe. And you do that by love.*

*There's another reason why you should love your enemies, and that is because hate distorts the personality of the hater. We usually think of what hate does for the individual hated or the individuals hated or the groups hated. But it is even more tragic, it is even more ruinous and injurious to the individual who hates. You just begin hating somebody, and you will begin to do irrational things. You can't see straight when you hate. You can't walk straight when you hate. You can't stand upright. Your vision is distorted. There is nothing more tragic than to see an individual whose heart is filled with hate. He comes to the point that he becomes a pathological case. For the person who hates, you can stand up and see a person and that person can be beautiful, and you will call them ugly. For the person who hates, the beautiful becomes ugly and the ugly becomes beautiful. For the person who hates, the good becomes bad and the bad becomes good. For the person who hates, the true becomes false and the false becomes true. That's what hate does. You can't see right. The symbol of objectivity is lost. Hate destroys the very structure of the personality of the hater.*

*And this is why Jesus says hate, that you want to be integrated with yourself, and the way to be integrated with yourself is be sure that you meet every situation of life with an abounding love. Never hate, because it ends up in tragic, neurotic responses. Psychologists and psychiatrists are telling us today that the more we hate, the more we develop guilt feelings and we begin to subconsciously repress or consciously suppress certain emotions, and they all stack up in our subconscious selves and make for tragic, neurotic responses. And may this not be the neuroses of many individuals as they confront life that that is an element of hate there. And modern psychology is calling on us now to love. But long before modern psychology came into being, the world's greatest psychologist who walked around the hills of Galilee told us to love. He looked at men and said: "Love your enemies; don't hate anybody." It's not enough for us to hate your friends because—to to love your friends— because when you start hating anybody, it destroys the very center of your creative response to life and the universe; so love everybody. Hate at any point is a cancer that gnaws away at the very vital center of your life and your existence. It is like eroding acid that eats away the best and the objective center of your life. So Jesus says love, because hate destroys the hater as well as the hated.*

*Now there is a final reason I think that Jesus says, "Love your enemies." It is this: that love has within it a redemptive power. And there is a power there that eventually transforms individuals. That's why Jesus says, "Love your enemies." Because if you hate your enemies, you have no way to redeem and to transform your enemies. But if you love your enemies, you will discover that at the very root of love is the power of redemption. You just keep loving people and keep loving them, even though they're mistreating you. Here's the person who is a neighbor, and this person is doing something wrong to you and all of that. Just keep being friendly to that person. Keep loving them. Don't do anything to embarrass them. Just keep loving them, and they can't stand it too long. Oh, they react in many ways in the beginning. They react with bitterness because they're mad because you love them like that. They react with guilt feelings, and sometimes they'll hate you a little more at that transition period, but just keep loving them. And by the power of your love, they will break down under the load. That's love, you see. It is redemptive, and this is why Jesus says love. There's something about love that builds up and is creative. There is something about hate that tears down and is destructive. "love your enemies."*

*I think of one of the best examples of this. We all remember the great president of this United States, Abraham Lincoln—these United States rather. You remember when Abraham Lincoln was running for president of the United States, there was a man who ran all around the country talking about Lincoln. He said a lot of bad things about Lincoln, a lot of unkind things. And sometimes he would get to the point that he would even talk about his looks, saying, "You don't want a tall, lanky, ignorant man like this as the president of the United States." He went on and on and on and went around with that type of attitude and wrote about it. Finally, one day Abraham Lincoln was elected president of the United States. And if you read the great biography of Lincoln, if you read the great works about him, you will discover that as every president comes to the point, he came to the point of having to choose a Cabinet. And then came the time for him to choose a Secretary of War. He looked across the nation, and decided to choose a man by the name of Mr. Stanton. And when Abraham Lincoln stood around his advisors and mentioned this fact, they said to him: "Mr. Lincoln, are you a fool? Do you know what Mr. [Edwin M.] Stanton has been saying about you? Do you know what he has done, tried to do to you? Do you know that he has tried to defeat you on every hand? Do you know that, Mr. Lincoln? Did you read all of those derogatory statements that he made about you?" Abraham Lincoln stood before the advisors around him and said: "Oh yes, I know about it. I read about it. I've heard him myself. But after looking over the country, I find that he is the best man for the job."*

*Mr. Stanton did become Secretary of War, and a few months later, Abraham Lincoln was assassinated. And if you go to Washington, you will discover that one of the greatest words or statements ever made by, about Abraham Lincoln was made about this man Stanton. And as Abraham Lincoln came to the end of his life, Stanton stood up and said: "Now he belongs to the ages." And he made a beautiful statement concerning the character and the stature of this man. If Abraham Lincoln*

*had hated Stanton, if Abraham Lincoln had answered everything Stan-
ton said, Abraham Lincoln would have not transformed and redeemed
Stanton. Stanton would have gone to his grave hating Lincoln, and
Lincoln would have gone to his grave hating Stanton. But through the
power of love Abraham Lincoln was able to redeem Stanton.*

*That's it. There is a power in love that our world has not discovered
yet. Jesus discovered it centuries ago. Mahatma Gandhi of India discovered it a few years ago, but most men and most women never discover
it. For they believe in hitting for hitting; they believe in an eye for an
eye and a tooth for a tooth; they believe in hating for hating; but Jesus
comes to us and says, "This isn't the way."*

*And oh this morning, as I think of the fact that our world is in
transition now. Our whole world is facing a revolution. Our nation
is facing a revolution, our nation. One of the things that concerns me
most is that in the midst of the revolution of the world and the midst
of the revolution of this nation, that we will discover the meaning of
Jesus' words. History unfortunately leaves some people oppressed and
some people oppressors. And there are three ways that individuals
who are oppressed can deal with their oppression. One of them is to
rise up against their oppressors with physical violence and corroding
hatred. But oh this isn't the way. For the danger and the weakness of
this method is its futility. Violence creates many more social problems
than it solves. And I've said, in so many instances, that as the Negro, in
particular, and colored peoples all over the world struggle for freedom,
if they succumb to the temptation of using violence in their struggle,
unborn generations will be the recipients of a long and desolate night of
bitterness, and our chief legacy to the future will be an endless reign of
meaningless chaos. Violence isn't the way.*

*Another way is to acquiesce and to give in, to resign yourself to the
oppression. Some people do that. They discover the difficulties of the wilderness moving into the promised land, and they would rather go back to
the despots of Egypt because it's difficult to get in the promised land. And
so they resign themselves to the fate of oppression; they somehow acquiesce to this thing. But that too isn't the way because non-cooperation
with evil is as much a moral obligation as is cooperation with good.*

*But there is another way. And that is to organize mass non-violent resistance based on the principle of love. It seems to me that this is the only way as our eyes look to the future. As we look out across the years and across the generations, let us develop and move right here. We must discover the power of love, the power, the redemptive power of love. And when we discover that we will be able to make of this old world a new world. We will be able to make men better. Love is the only way. Jesus discovered that.*

*Not only did Jesus discover it, even great military leaders discover that. One day as Napoleon came toward the end of his career and looked back across the years, the great Napoleon that at a very early age had all but conquered the world. He was not stopped until he became, till he moved out to the battle of Leipzig and then to Waterloo. But that same Napoleon one day stood back and looked across the years, and said: "Alexander, Caesar, Charlemagne, and I have built great empires. But upon what did they depend? They depended upon force. But long ago Jesus started an empire that depended on love, and even to this day millions will die for him."*

*Yes, I can see Jesus walking around the hills and the valleys of Palestine. And I can see him looking out at the Roman Empire with all of her fascinating and intricate military machinery. But in the midst of that, I can hear him saying: "I will not use this method. Neither will I hate the Roman Empire." [Recording interrupted] [ . . . ] just start marching.*

*And I'm proud to stand here in Dexter this morning and say that that army is still marching. It grew up from a group of eleven or twelve men to more than seven hundred million today. Because of the power and influence of the personality of this Christ, he was able to split history into A.D. and B.C. Because of his power, he was able to shake the hinges from the gates of the Roman Empire. And all around the world this morning, we can hear the glad echo of heaven ring: "Jesus shall reign wherever sun does his successive journeys run. His kingdom spreads from shore to shore, till moon shall wane and wax no more."*

*We can hear another chorus singing: "All hail the power of Jesus name."*

*We can hear another chorus singing: "Hallelujah, hallelujah! He's King of Kings and Lord of Lords. Hallelujah, hallelujah!"*

We can hear another choir singing: "In Christ there is no East or West. In Him no North or South, but one great fellowship of love throughout the whole wide world." This is the only way.

And our civilization must discover that. Individuals must discover that as they deal with other individuals. There is a little tree planted on a little hill and on that tree hangs the most influential character that ever came in this world. But never feel that that tree is a meaningless drama that took place on the stages of history. Oh no, it is a telescope through which we look out into the long vista of eternity, and see the love of God breaking forth into time. It is an eternal reminder to a power-drunk generation that love is the only way. It is an eternal reminder to a generation depending on nuclear and atomic energy, a generation depending on physical violence, that love is the only creative, redemptive, transforming power in the universe.

So this morning, as I look into your eyes, and into the eyes of all of my brothers in Alabama and all over America and over the world, I say to you, "I love you. I would rather die than hate you." And I'm foolish enough to believe that through the power of this love somewhere, men of the most recalcitrant bent will be transformed. And then we will be in God's kingdom. We will be able to matriculate into the university of eternal life because we had the power to love our enemies, to bless those persons that cursed us, to even decide to be good to those persons who hated us, and we even prayed for those persons who despitefully used us.

Oh God, help us in our lives and in all of our attitudes, to work out this controlling force of love, this controlling power that can solve every problem that we confront in all areas. Oh, we talk about politics; we talk about the problems facing our atomic civilization. Grant that all men will come together and discover that as we solve the crisis and solve these problems—the international problems, the problems of atomic energy, the problems of nuclear energy, and yes, even the race problem— let us join together in a great fellowship of love and bow down at the feet of Jesus. Give us this strong determination. In the name and spirit of this Christ, we pray. Amen.

## Spiritual Guidance:

Do all things in love. The soldiers of change can also be soldiers of love. It can be difficult to love and forgive the people whom we see as bad or evil but remember Dr. King's words: "There are a lot of people who I find it difficult to like. I don't like what they do to me. I don't like what they say about me and other people. I don't like their attitudes. I don't like some of the things they're doing. I simply don't like them. But Jesus instructs us to love people we find it hard to love. And loving is greater than liking. Love offers understanding, redemptive goodwill for all men, so that you love everybody, because God loves them. You refuse to do anything that will defeat an individual, because you have *agape* in your soul. And here you come to the point that you love the individual who does the evil deed, while hating the deed that the person does. This is what Jesus means when he says, 'Love your enemy.' This is the way to do it."

We can love a person and hate their actions and in doing so we can spiritually change them with our love. This does not mean we love and refuse to take action. Martin Luther King Jr., Gandhi, and Abraham Lincoln all took affirmative action to achieve their missions and goals, but they did so from agape. In turn, they changed lives and altered history.

## Affirmations:

- *I seek peace in the world; therefore, I seek peace within myself first.*
- *Love is my foundation, mission, and purpose.*
- *The Lord is my strength, my refuge, and my rock.*

## Prayer:

"My Lord, help me to tell the truth in front of strong people
   and not to lie to obtain the applause of the weak ones.
If you give me a fortune, do not take away my reasoning.
   If you give success, do not take away my humbleness.
   If you give me humbleness, do not take away my dignity.

Always help me to see the other face of the coin,
    do not let me think I betray others who do not think just as I do.
Teach me to love people as myself.
    Do not let me fall in pride if I succeed, nor in the desperation
    if I fail.
Rather remind me that failure is the experience that supersedes the
    triumph.
    Teach me that forgiveness is a greatness sign and revenge is a
    vile signal.
If you take success from me, give me encouragement to learn from
    failure.
    If I would offend people, give me encouragement to apolo-
    gize them.
    If people offend me, give me encouragement to forgive them.
Lord, if I ever forget you, please never forget me."
—Mahatma Gandhi


### Additional Resources:

*Book of Prayers* by Mahatma Gandhi
*Strength to Love* by Martin Luther King Jr.
*Where Do We Go from Here?* by Martin Luther King Jr.
*Sojourner Truth Prophet of Social Justice* by Isabelle Kinnard Richman
*Harriet Tubman's Intense Religious Faith in Maryland* by Phillip
    Thomas Tucker
The New Testament of *The Holy Bible*

# THE ARTIST

When used in sync with God, art is the creative expression of the Holy Spirit. The Artist can act as a conduit for that expression, bringing a connection and manifestation of God into the world that changes lives in ways no other format or medium can. Art can sincerely evoke the deepest emotions within ourselves, initiate healing, and communicate in a way that bypasses the ego and shoots straight for the heart.

The first mention of God filling someone with the Holy Spirit in the Bible is in Exodus, when God blesses Bezaleel with gifts, one of the most valuable being craftsmanship. Bezaleel became one of the most valuable and cherished artists in all of the lands. He built temples, and fixtures were not only remarkable but divine. Throughout the Bible, God calls upon artists to create art, designs, and architecture that are described as incomparable in their beauty, even by today's standards.

For the Artist, art, color, and texture are all a form of meditation and growth. Art is a way that they put themselves into the world, and this draws people to them who feel divinity through their work. The Artist is a special archetype because they see holiness and beauty where others often do not. One of the most precious spiritual gifts we can give to one another is to see the light within every person we meet; even when it seems there is only darkness. The Artist naturally has this ability and unknowingly practices it through their art and work.

**Most Common Ascendant Spiritual Archetypes:** the Shaman, the Witch, the New Ager, the Crusader, the Lightworker

**Colors of the Artist:** The colors of the Artist vary based on their own inspirational color palette. You may resonate with deep earth tones, light pastels, watercolors, gorgeous jewel tones, or white, gray, and black.

**When Balanced, You May Feel or Experience:** inspired, grounded, prolific, abundant, productive, outgoing, innovative, happy, gifted

**When Unbalanced, You May Feel or Experience:** poor, broke, uninspired, frustrated, willing to lower your standards, anxious, depressed, hopeless

**Governs:** heart, lungs, eyes, ears, hands

**Common Physical Ailments:** emotional imbalances, mental disorders such as anxiety or depression, arthritis, throat issues such as laryngitis or sore throat

## Correlating Essential Oils:

**Tangerine:** uplifting, bravery, courage
**Jasmine:** self-confidence, happiness, confidence
**Magnolia:** compassion and mercy for others and oneself
**Grapefruit:** creative and uplifting energy, personal restoration
**Clary Sage:** inspiration, vision, clarity

## Correlating Stones:

**Ametrine:** optimism, overcoming self-criticism and self-sabotage
**Fluorite:** vocalizing oneself, ability to flow (as derived from the Latin word fluor, meaning "flow"), spiritual sensitivity, and the ability to channel work and art
**Golden Obsidian:** ability to find and access skills and hidden talents
**Lolite:** self-acceptance
**Spinel:** setting aside of ego
**Picasso Jasper:** creativity, loving personal and work relationships, prosperity

## Correlating Plants:

- **Bleeding Heart:** passion, deep feelings, art, expressing feelings
- **Dahlia:** creativity, dignity, strength, allure
- **Narcissus:** Calm down! It's a plant that means hope, renewal, transformation and prosperity.

**Power Words:** create, creator, heal, flow, inspire, forge, surrender, design, color

## Past People, Places, and Periods That You May Resonate With

- **People:** artist, singer, painter, architect, blueprint designer, inventor, photographer, poet, musician, illustrator, cartoonist, actor, author, chef
- **Places:** Italy, Europe, France, Mexico, Spain
- **Periods:** Ancient Greece; 1300s Medieval Period; Renaissance Period; Mannerism 1527–1580s; Baroque 1600–1750; Romanticism 1780–1850; Industrial Revolution; Art Nouveau 1890–1910; 1900s Modernism; Art Deco 1920s; Pop Art 1950s–1960s

## Correlating Animal: THE SPIDER

The spider is nature's true artist, creating intricate webs of lace and design. Its medicine encourages you to create and allow yourself to flow with the creative energy that is natural to you. The spider also represents receptivity and feminine energy. There may be money or opportunities you are not seeing, and the spider reminds you to stay open and receptive to the abundance of your spiritual privilege.

In some cultures, people believe that the spider represents the shadow self. When a spider totem presents itself, it is asking you to face and love the parts of yourself you are ashamed of or dislike. By loving all aspects of ourselves, we become free from our ego, which makes us better people and artists.

## Common Struggles

**Common Triggers:** feeling like you will never make it, having other people not see or support your vision, rejection, feeling mediocre or uninspiring, losing talent or inspiration, being stifled

**When Triggered, the Artist Can Become:** narcissistic, unmotivated, dramatic

**Common Personal Struggles:** The Artist is an imaginative, creative, and innovative spirit who sees and thinks outside the box. Sometimes, getting people to see that vision can be difficult and frustrating. Some of the most famous inventors, creators, designers, and artists were ahead of their time but lacked the appreciation and credit they deserved during their life. This can make the Artist feel a need to prove themselves. They fear their time will never come or their vision will not matter. The Artist also has difficulty with their personal self and identity. While many artists, creatives, and inventors want to be acknowledged and appreciated for their work, they hide their innermost workings out of fear of rejection and judgment.

**Common Spiritual Struggles:** The Artist struggles with the ability to balance the channeling of creativity and anchoring themselves in this world. Take, for instance, electricity; it requires a power source and a place to ground to complete the circuit. However, the Artist channels the power but often lacks the ground within themselves to close the circuit. This can lead to depression, addiction, feelings of insecurity, and feeling inferior. The Artist may also use these emotions to perpetuate their work. As we have seen with many actors, they will put their health, safety, and well-being aside for the best performance, which has often led to breakdowns and even death. Many creative types will obsess about getting the perfect shot, overexert themselves to plan the best design or live unhealthily for the good of their projects. The Artist would do well to take themselves out of the role of power and focus on the grounding while the creative energy passes through.

## Mythology, Folklore, Symbolism, or Correlating Story

In Roman mythology, it was believed that people had a spirit called a *genius* that would accompany them at birth and was essentially assigned to them until they died. People believed the supernatural powers of the spirit gave the person their artistic, creative, intellectual, or otherworldly abilities. In Arabic mythology, the genius was known as a *Jinn*, which in their demonology is a spirit with supernatural abilities. But you may be more familiar with its other derivative, the genie, a supernatural being and spirit that grants humans wishes, usually for a price. While some were considered good, most were considered treacherous and diabolical beings. Even if they were friendly, they did not take lightly to feeling hurt, betrayed, or crossed and would punish or harm anyone who did. Some people believed that they were the cause of insanity, madness, illness, and disease. For those who believed that such beings were responsible for their talents, art, and abilities, a person must walk the straight and narrow in order to stay on the good side of their genius. Like a genie who grants wishes, the artist is without talents if the wishes run out.

While these beliefs are no longer widely prevalent today, they may explain the origins of the starving artist syndrome and why so many artists believe they have to suffer to be successful. The idea that a spirit can give or take away our abilities or that we have never earned our success can make anyone feel like they are on borrowed time. However, many artists were, or are, still seeking success for their own personal gain. Fame, money, adoration, and validation are a few of the many self-centered goals of the Artist. Therefore, if an artist is looking for these, they may be more likely to make a deal for their success because they are seeking fulfillment out of their desperation.

In an episode of the show *Supernatural* entitled "Cross Road Blues," the two main characters, Sam and Dean Winchester, are hunting hell hounds who are coming to collect the souls of people who have made deals with crossroad demons. They go to the apartment of a man named George Darrow, who, ten years prior, had made a deal and is now on the chopping block. Sam asks the man what he wished for, and Darrow says, "Of course I asked for talent. I should have gone for fame." Although he had sold his soul for talent, he never became successful and was now doomed for eternity. If people sought to serve a greater purpose, the blessings would be bestowed upon them without the negative consequences.

For instance, when God had delivered Moses and the Israelites out of Egypt, they were going to make a tabernacle, a place of worship for the Lord. God anointed two men, Bezaleel and Aholiab to design and build it. "And the LORD spake unto Moses, saying, See, I have called by name Bezaleel the son of Uri, the son of Hur, of the tribe of Judah: And I have filled him with the spirit of God, in wisdom, and in understanding, and in knowledge, and in all manner of workmanship, to devise cunning works, to work in gold, and in silver, and in brass, And in cutting of stones, to set *them*, and in carving of timber, to work in all manner of workmanship. And I, behold, I have given with him Aholiab, the son of Ahisamach, of the tribe of Dan: and in the hearts of all that are wise hearted I have put wisdom, that they may make all that I have commanded thee." (Exodus 31: 1–6)

God didn't just give Bezaleel and Aholiab talent; He gave them craftsmanship, wisdom, understanding, and knowledge in all manner of their workmanship. He gave them everything they would need to execute the plan properly, create the detail needed, and the wisdom and knowledge to produce the best results. Yet it was not for their personal gain that He gave them these skills or abilities. God blessed them because they were serving a greater purpose. When we make deals or seek our own personal gain, there is always a piece missing. Perhaps a person is the most incredible actor to ever live, but they have personal demons that haunt them and ruin their life. Someone could be the most talented singer but surround themselves with people who steal from them. Or, as in so many cases, you may be filled to the brim with talent but lack the confidence to put yourself out there in a way that is fulfilling, authentic, and organic to your soul. Artists are willing to take extreme measures for roles, or to get into their space of genius, but so many lack a relationship with God, which will lend to every area. If the Artist can design their personal and professional lives around serving God and bringing that intention into their work, God will bless you in ways you cannot fathom—without the consequences once believed in mythology.

### Spiritual Guidance:

Creativity is a physical manifestation of God. It is a way of being connected and is the Artist's way of manifesting that connection into corporal form. Your creativity is a gift from God. Creativity is spiritual expression; therefore, your connection, communion, and relationship with God is a significant conductor of your creative inspiration. If you're feeling blocked personally or spiritually, that can hinder your creative flow. The best way to bypass this is to develop your spiritual connection. When we feel connected to God, we can channel incredible pieces of art. Famous musicians, such as George Harrison, have spoken about how they could hear a melody in their heads and would have to race to write it down before it left. God was delivering the melody, and he was essentially the scribe. Al Pacino said that great acting is like a form of channeling. Our job as artists is to move out of the way and let God move through us. We must deepen our connection with God so that He moves more easily through us.

Our relationship with God is essential not only in our lives but in our work and our art. The more we strengthen our connection, the more we are inspired and able to release and move past our fear. The more you integrate spiritually into your life and work, the more you will experience major personal and professional changes. Surrender, connect, receive inspiration, create, and repeat.

Additionally, art is meant to glorify God and the attributes of God. While many people see all forms of media as "art," I would argue that true art is defined as work that produces the attributes of God: healing, understanding, love, inspiration, togetherness, connection, wisdom, knowledge, joy, peace, etc. If God is the ultimate Artist and Creator, and He creates only good things, and we are created in the image and likeness of Him, should we not only produce the good qualities of our divine nature?

### Affirmations:

- *God is my rock, foundation, and inspiration. I create to honor God, the divine within myself, and the divinity in others.*
- *God is the ultimate Creator, and I am created in His image and likeness. I will create from this place.*
- *God wants me to be successful.*

### Prayer:

"Lord, help me create art, work, designs, songs, and anything you want in this world. I release and surrender my own expectations and motives and humbly ask for You to put this in the hands, hearts, eyes, and ears that are meant to have it."

## Additional Resources:

*Cultural Apologetics* by Paul M. Gould
*The Actor* by Don Miguel Ruiz
*The Artist's Way* by Julia Cameron
*The Arts and Their Mission* by Rudolf Steiner
*The Lucid Body: A Guide for the Physical Actor* by Fay Simpson

# THE NEW AGER

I n the words of Vine Deloria Jr., "Religion is for people who believe
in hell; spirituality is for the ones who have been there." The New
Ager has been through the trenches and seeks to incorporate spirituality into every aspect of their life. They've spent their lifetime practicing spirituality in others' way and are ready to live and practice on their
terms. They most likely come from a background with a strong religious
figure, such as an overbearing or abusive Catholic parent. Therefore,
they may generally not be on the best terms with their immediate family and may be considered the black sheep. They celebrate life and see
their friends as the family they choose. They enjoy group gatherings,
conferences, expos, and tours with friends and familiar faces. Spirituality is a journey, and they enjoy traveling their journey with loving
souls who "get it." Being around others who understand the concepts of
spiritual beliefs such as past lives and karma helps them to freely express
their experiences without feeling odd or that they are being judged.

The New Ager has a difficult time living in the real world and would
prefer to spend their days reading about the secrets and mysteries of the
universe or going to healers throughout the world. They enjoy learning

about conspiracy theories, parallel universes, vortexes, and energy fields. They regret aspects of their past that keep them from wanting to make similar mistakes, which leads them to seek guidance from sources such as astrology, numerology, psychics, mediums, and anything else they feel can offer them guidance.

They are open and receptive to all ideas and possibilities. The New Ager Spiritual Archetype is generally more receptive to the unknown and trying on new modalities and practices than any other spiritual archetype. They have lived in a world with concrete beliefs and ideas and realize how much it limits growth. They understand man's limited perception and believe there are worlds and universes happening that we cannot even fathom. They do not have one religion but rather collect pieces from all faiths and spirituality they resonate with and then adopt them into their practices.

**Most Common Ascendant Spiritual Archetypes:** the Recoverist, the Mythologist, the Eastern Philosopher, the Artist, the Occultist, the Metaphysician

**Colors of the New Ager:** dark greens, grays, dark blues, dark purples, burgundy

**When Balanced, You May Feel or Experience:** a release of childhood trauma, forgiveness, the letting go of resentments, fearlessness, intuition, self-expression, communication, centered, living in the present moment, freedom of expression

**When Unbalanced, You May Feel or Experience:** headaches, lack of purpose, too analytical, afraid to voice your opinions or are overly vocal sharing opinions that stem from ego, lack of connection, depression, sore throat, paranoia

**Governs:** throat, ears, neck, shoulders, thyroid, mouth, tongue

**Physical Ailments:** immunity disorders, strep throat, thyroid problems, throat problems, speech issues, back problems, lymphatic problems, and strange illnesses doctors cannot diagnose

## Correlating Essential Oils:

**Eucalyptus:** healing, clarity, health, leadership
**Pine:** wisdom, longevity, peace
**Sandalwood:** prayer, meditation, divinity
**Patchouli:** spiritual growth, communication, courage
**Sage:** purity, protection, personal conviction

## Correlating Stones:

**Lapis Lazuli:** protection, inner truth, self-awareness, self-expression
**Lepidolite:** self-love, independence, emotional healing
**Sodalite:** clarity and truth
**Turquoise:** healing, cleansing, communication, wisdom
**Sapphire:** inner peace, royalty, spiritual development
**Amethyst:** wisdom, humility, strength, tranquility
**Morganite:** love, joy, heart, prayer and meditation

## Correlating Plants:

- **Flax:** money, protection, beauty, psychic powers, healing
- **Lavender:** love, protection, sleep, chastity, longevity, purification, happiness, peace
- **St. John's Wort:** health, power, protection, strength, love, divination, happiness
- **Aloe:** "the plant of immortality," healer, protector, good fortune

**Power Words:** secrets and mysteries, soul, awakening, sacred, ancient, mystic

**People, Places, and Periods That May Resonate with You:**

- **People:** astrologer, philosopher, medicine man or woman, writer, explorer, healer, Druid
- **Periods:** Atlantis, Ancient Egypt, Victorian Era, the Depression, the 1950s
- **Places:** Atlantis, Sedona, Washington D.C., England, Egypt, France, Ireland, Brazil

## Correlating Animal: THE SNAKE

The snake represents healing, transformation, primal energy, wisdom, and rebirth. New Agers tend to have painful and challenging pasts. The snake is your totem as a reminder that you can heal from your past and be reborn into your most divine and authentic self. The New Ager can also have a tendency to "space out" or become unattached to the present. The snake guides you in staying close to the earth while simultaneously looking to the heavens. One of the most common attributes of the New Ager is that they can sometimes look into too many modalities or belief systems or get swept up in something they are told without basing their commitment on facts. The snake asks you to fully digest the opportunities, information, and knowledge you receive in a more thoughtful and intentional manner.

## Common Struggles

**Common Triggers:** authority, organized religion, not being able to share your truth, being deceived or duped, being misled, putting your trust in the wrong people

**When Triggered, the New Ager Can Become:** passive-aggressive, manipulative, self-righteous

**Common Personal Struggles:** Because New Agers are so receptive to all ideas and possibilities, they are the most likely to be deceived by spiritual teachers or even unknowingly enter into cult-type situations. Your eagerness to heal fused with your trusting personality may leave you vulnerable to the manipulation or misguided teachings of leaders who take advantage of people's trust during a susceptible time on their spiritual path. This is especially common for New Agers with an unhealed history of overbearing or abusive parents. They unknowingly attract the same lesson in a different, holier seeming form.

**Common Spiritual Struggles:** You harbor many resentments and deep-seated anger toward the people in your life, mostly from your past. These negative emotions lead to health problems and issues with money, either not having it or being irresponsible with it. You guilt yourself too harshly and attempt to find reasons you have adverse outcomes in your life. You are generally willing to take responsibility for what you manifest, but because you have not healed the guilt and shame from your past, you overly accept responsibility or self-blame: "My car broke down because I'm not taking care of my body" or "I'm sick because in a past life I was a tyrant."

This also feeds into your "when" mentality. For example, you may find yourself saying things such as, "I will become wealthy *when* I forgive my past life as a thief," or "I will attract a healthy relationship *when* I release my trauma," and "I will be successful only *when* I do mindset work first."

God is a God of the present and gives freely. His blessings are limited based on how willing and able we are to receive them. Align yourself, your goals, and your life with God and see how quickly things manifest when God gives, and you are fully receptive.

## Mythology, Folklore, Symbolism, or Correlating Story

The story of *The Lion, the Witch, and the Wardrobe* by C.S. Lewis is a classic children's tale that chronicles the adventures of four siblings: Peter, Susan, Edmund, and Lucy. Sent to live with Professor Digory Kirke, the youngest girl, Lucy, discovers a mysterious wardrobe that transports her to the mythical world of Narnia. There she befriends

Mr. Tumnus, who tells Lucy about the treacherous White Witch, who is the imposter ruler of Narnia. Lucy returns home and tells her siblings the story, including the evil wiles of the White Witch, but only Edmund, the second youngest boy, believes her and decides to go to Narnia. However, Edmund finds himself in a different place in Narnia than his sister, Lucy, and instead of finding Mr. Tumnus, he arrives to see the White Witch herself. The White Witch lures Edmund with enchanted Turkish Delights, which he consumes excessively and greedily, and he is promised a position as the Prince of Narnia if he betrays his siblings and gives them to the White Witch. Having felt inferior to his siblings, he had always been nasty to them, lying, mistreating them, and being cruel, yet now he saw a chance to feel superior and hold the title of prince.

Eventually, all of the siblings go to Narnia, but they do not know or understand that there is a prophecy saying "Two Sons of Adam and two Daughters of Eve" will sit on the throne, and the true ruler, a lion named Aslan, is returning. Ignorant of his and his siblings' true importance and destiny, Edmund selfishly works with the White Witch for his own personal gain. His siblings, Peter, Susan, and Lucy go to find Aslan, who is preparing for battle against the White Witch. During the war, the White Witch turns on Edmund and is prepared to kill him. However, Aslan speaks with her, and it appears as though she has released Edmund. That night, Aslan goes to the Stone Table, secretly followed by Susan and Lucy, where they learn the horrible truth: Aslan sacrificed his own life for Edmund and gave himself in exchange for the White Witch letting Edmund go. There, the White Witch puts Aslan to death. Devastated, the girls stay with Aslan through the night and are shocked to see Aslan resurrected in the morning. Through the sacrifice of his own life for the life of Edmund, "Deeper Magic from before the Dawn of Time" resurrected him and brought him back to life. Aslan takes Susan and Lucy to the White Witch's castle, where she has turned dozens of Narnians into stone, and resurrects them all, breaking the White Witch's spell. Aslan then kills the White Witch, and Peter, Susan, Edmund, and Lucy (Two Sons of Adam and two Daughters of Eve) become the kings and queens of Narnia.

The New Ager has usually had a life and/or past filled with struggles, adversity, and turmoil. In many cases, this is what has been the catalyst for seeking spirituality and wanting to create more freedom in your spirituality. One area where this can become a slippery slope is when the New Ager, like Edmund, is driven by their own personal gain or retribution. Edmund felt insecure, unappreciated, and unimportant. With the promise of being Prince of Narnia and the craving for worldly desires, such as decadent candies, Edmund fell into the trap of being deceived and put his loved ones and himself in harmful positions and risked all of their lives. Because he cannot see past his own hurts and wounds, he cannot see the truth that is before him or the reality of their situation. The New Ager can also be distracted by their desire for control or power over their past and drive to have this in their present and future. Unfortunately, they may fail to see the present reality and that they may be hurting others and themselves just as Edmund did.

The beautiful evolution of Edmund is that once he realizes the truth, he becomes noble, honest, and brave, thus receiving the name "Edmund the Just." When he surrendered his will, humbled himself, and fought for the greater good, Edmund truly and authentically became the prince he was destined to become. When we step into our destiny, we no longer have to work so hard against others because we are no longer fighting against the grain; we are organically working with it. The New Ager, too, is destined for a throne of inheritance by God just as we all are. If you live and fight your spiritual battles with heart and humility, you will also be like Edmund the Just.

## Spiritual Guidance:

Everything we want in our lives is attainable the moment we choose to accept it. This does not require earning it or doing the work until we are worthy. That is not to say that we do not need to work hard for what we want. It means you do not have to work hard to be *worthy* of it.

With the mentality that we constantly have to earn our goals, visions, and dreams, they become a carrot on a stick you will never reach. This will create animosity because you see yourself as "doing the work," yet others seem to easily and effortlessly receive what they ask for without seemingly any difficulty or hard work. Until you let go of your past, forgive it, and see yourself as worthy here and now, you will continue to suffer and feel a lack of love, abundance, health, and worth.

Additionally, seek advice and information from all sources and outlets, but be cautious of devoting yourself entirely to one teaching style or teacher. Most spiritual teachers do not walk the talk or practice what they preach, but it is suggested that you attempt only to follow those who do, which may require some in-depth research. One way of connecting with teachers who emulate their teachings is by looking at the life they live. If your spiritual teacher reflects a life that you desire, they may be true to their word or at least have something to offer in this current stage of your life.

### Affirmations:

- *I forgive and release all whom I believe have hurt, judged, or slighted me in any form. I bless them and surrender them to God, here and now.*
- *I am worthy and accepting of God's love, health, and abundance.*
- *My Christ-self is my authentic self. I honor this truth in myself and others.*

### Prayer:

"Father, I accept Your abundance and wholeness of love, health, and prosperity in my life here and now. I surrender my will and belief that I must struggle or work hard to earn Your love. I AM the child of divine love, and I accept divine love now."

## Additional Resources:

*Edgar Cayce, My Life as a Seer: The Lost Memoirs* by Edgar Cayce
*Fingerprints of the Gods* by Graham Hancock
*From Karma to Grace: The Power of the Fruit of the Spirit* by John
    Van Auken
*Love Without Conditions* by Paul Ferrini
*Seven Initiations of the Spiritual Path* by Michael Mirdad
*The Dynamic Laws of Healing* by Catherine Ponder
*There Is a River: The Story of Edgar Cayce* by Thomas Sugrue

# THE METAPHYSICIAN

The Metaphysician is a student of science, mind, and spirituality. Educated, well-versed in theories, ideas, and facts, the Metaphysician seeks to bridge the chasm between science and spirit. The Metaphysician is a fascinating Spiritual Archetype because they have their mind in this world and are exceedingly intelligent, but also have a strong intuition and connection with their soul, the supernatural, and God. They are unique in their ability to connect with God through mathematics and science.

The Metaphysician is one of the most progressive, innovative, and ingenious of the Spiritual Archetypes. Their contributions to the medical, scientific, and spiritual fields are expectational and unrivaled. For instance, while some ancient civilizations had planted and harvested their crops according to moon phases, Rudolph Steiner not only revived the practice but also backed it with scientific proof of its benefits and effectiveness with his study, research, and teaching of biodynamics. Steiner was also one of the first scientists to encourage the use of plants in healing, which was later proved in the development of Bach remedies, created by fellow Metaphysician, Dr. Edward Bach. Bach was a well-educated doctor who lived from 1886–1936. While having never met Rudolph Steiner, Bach believed that plants held healing properties that could be proved by science and believed God directed him to this area of study. Bach devoted his life to writing about the connection between spirituality and health and developing the Bach flower remedies, which are still in use and deemed effective to this day. Without the most successful Metaphysicians in history, spirituality would not have the scientific backing and credit it does today. Additionally, scientific research with spiritual motives has become increasingly popularized due to the initial hypothesis of the greatest Metaphysicians.

**Most Common Adjacent Spiritual Archetypes:** the Neoteric Shaman, the Christian Mystic, the Crusader, the Artist, the New Ager, the Occultist

**Colors of the Metaphysician:** watercolors: yellow-gold, orange, red, blue, teal

**When Balanced, You May Feel or Experience:** clarity, determination, self-assurance, insightful, intuitive, connected, logical, rational, composed

**When Unbalanced, You May Feel or Experience:** overworked, exhausted, fatigue, overwhelmed, self-conscious

**Governs:** spleen, stomach, muscles, thyroid, heart, brain

**Common Physical Ailments:** stomach issues, nervousness, fatigue due to over overworking and overwhelm, mental fog and dissociation, muscle aches

## Correlating Bach Remedies originally created by Dr. Edward Bach:

**Aspen:** vague or unknown fears and anxiety
**Clematis:** focus and concentration
**Hornbeam:** procrastination, weariness, self-doubt
**Oak:** overworking, fatigue, overachiever

## Correlating Stones:

**Rhodonite:** self-love, self-care, self-esteem
**Brown Sphene:** study, knowledge, debating, thought
**Fiery Jacinth:** a reminder to put love and God before science and mind
**Violet Sapphire:** wisdom and good judgment
**Rainbow Quartz:** discernment, understanding, vision, harmony

## Correlating Plants:

- **Perovskia:** wisdom, knowledge, health
- **Mandrake:** The mysterious plant, whose roots resemble a human being, is an anomaly of science and well-conversed in spirituality and legends through the centuries
- **Fern:** humility, opening one's eyes, lighting the path, confidence
- **Mistletoe:** A favorite of Rudolph Steiner, who believed mistletoe was a great healing plant.

**Power Words:** medicine, healing, intuition, therapy, body, spirit, esoteric, cleanse, support, mind/body connection

## People, Places, and Periods That May Resonate with You:

- **People:** medical doctors, scientists, botanists, bacteriologist, homeopaths, philosophers, mathematicians, medical intuitive, naturopaths

- **Places:** Vienna, Switzerland, Croatia, Austria, Hungary, Russia, Germany, Italy, France, Persia, Sedona
- **Periods:** 600–200 BC, 1201–1274, 1598–1647, 1777–1855, late 1800s, early 1900s

## Correlating Animal: THE NARWHAL

A creature who embodies both the physical and spiritual, the "unicorn of the sea," has long been believed to hold magical powers. From the Vikings to the Intuit, the narwhal has captured people's attention for centuries. With its unique horn, believed to be used as a sensory organ, the narwhal is almost like a scientist of the sea with a witching wand in tow. Beautiful and majestic, their tusks (which can reach up to ten feet long) are spiraled, representing the connection to Earth and God, or worldly consciousness and spiritual consciousness, something the Metaphysician is constantly exploring and attempting to put into data and research.

## Common Struggles

**Common Triggers:** one's own limitations of time and self, getting other people to understand your vision, stagnation, doubt, self-condemnation, being put on the chopping block

**When Triggered, the Metaphysician Can Become:** smug, condescending, uncertain

**Common Personal Struggles:** The Metaphysician is known for overworking and even working themselves to sickness and death. Discovering and researching science and spirituality are ever-evolving, a rabbit hole that will never end. The Metaphysician tumbles down this rabbit hole, always wanting to know and discover more, which can lead to their own self-neglect of health, well-being, and relationships.

**Common Spiritual Struggles:** Scientists have long struggled to find tangible ways to explain, contain, or replicate God. Scientists are known for having a God complex and wanting to either play God or, in the case of the Metaphysician, make the spiritual tangible, creditable, and reputable. However, this is an endless battle, for even with science it all comes down to opinion. One scientist may have undisputable evidence that the spiritual exists, while another has irrefutable proof that it does not. Remember that while science is held in high esteem in this world, God is beyond science, mathematics, and experiments. We will never be able to explain all of the mysteries, abilities, and truths about God. This may be difficult to digest for such an educated and intelligent person. Remember, though, that the heart is more powerful than the mind, and the heart is where God resides. Use your heart in correlation with your mind and you will discover something science cannot.

## Mythology, Folklore, Symbolism, or Correlating Story

Rudolf Steiner was an Austrian-born esotericist, philosopher, teacher, and social reformer with a profound interest and knowledge of spirituality. One of his first stand-out spiritual experiences was when he was nine and saw the spirit of his aunt, whom the family was unaware had passed away. From this early age, spirituality and the physical world affected him. He became a writer and, in 1891 was awarded a doctorate in philosophy. He wrote books and articles, hoping to find an audience who was enthusiastic about philosophy. In 1899, he began speaking about his spiritual experiences and insights with the Theosophical Society, which he became an integral part of. In 1924, he held his first meeting for an agriculture course in a small village in Germany (which is now part of Poland), speaking on the detrimental habits of farming and the decline in the richness and quality of the soil due to poor agriculture. He shared his unique solution, which included replenishing vitamins and nutrients into the ground for better and more sustainable crops. Thus, biodynamic gardening was born and still thrives today. In 1919, he founded The Waldorf School in Germany, and in 1928 the first Waldorf school in the United States. While other schools were focused on standard studies, Rudolf Steiner sought to teach, nurture, and approach the whole child. His methods included a holistic approach, teaching not only the basics of math, English, science, and history but also art, music, gardening, and helping the child develop their spiritual, mental, and personal self through independence and philosophy. While these ideas are more popular and considered beneficial today, Steiner was the first to build the model for this type of schooling and was majorly successful in doing so.

Steiner was also incredibly intuitive, drawing and painting from his intuition and speaking about future events. He was an architect, a husband, a father, a teacher, a speaker, and an innovative thinker. He was a man ahead of his time who wanted to change the way of the future. However, his constant working, traveling, teaching, and personal exhaustion led him to an early grave at the young age of sixty-four. He became ill with an unknown stomach pain, which worsened from stress. Although he died at a young age, Steiner left many significant footprints in the world. Some, like the Waldorf school, biodynamics, and his many works, are still appreciated today.

### Spiritual Guidance:

The life of Rudolf Steiner is a fitting example of the Metaphysician. Your thoughts, personality, and goals generally coincide with that of Steiner. He knew from a young age that all we see is not all that exists, and he sought to share, inspire, and teach about the connections between the spiritual and physical world. Farming was not just farming; it was its own ecosystem that could be sustained, regenerated, and revived with each action. School was not just a place for children to become more intelligent; it was a place where children could grow personally, mentally, and spiritually to become a whole person in adulthood. While these may or may not be your specific areas of interest, the Metaphysician is personally driven to make a difference and think outside of the box. Additionally, you like to give and provide proof that the ideas are valid and beneficial. Biodynamic gardening has been proven to be more valuable than standard farming practices, and as the world converses about the need to shift and change our farming practices, more and more people have tampered with Steiner's idea from almost one hundred years ago. Without a doubt, the Metaphysician is precious to the world. This is, in part, why it is so important that the Metaphysician take better care of themself in an attempt to change and save the world.

Rudolf Steiner is not the only Metaphysician to run himself and his health into the ground. People like Dr. Edward Bach and Albert Einstein did not prioritize their health and put their science and worldly contributions before their own needs. When a person is such a powerful resource to so many others, they tend to put themselves last, which puts them and their lives at risk. Pulled in too many directions, the Metaphysician may have difficulty saying no or turning down opportunities to share their work. Remember that there is no value or excellence that happens from you putting yourself last. Time is one of our most valuable assets; however, our health is like gold, and there is no need for you to sacrifice yours. Take care of yourself, rest when needed, and prioritize your life and health.

### Affirmations:

- *The more I take care of myself, the more I have to give.*
- *I will put on my oxygen mask before helping others with theirs.*
- *God is my teacher, guide, and foundation in my work and in my life.*

### Prayer:

"God, please help me to prioritize You before all things, take care of myself, and glorify You in this world to others."

## Additional Resources:

*Chemistry of Essential Oils Made Simple: God's Love Manifest in Molecules* by David Stewart
*Heal Thyself* by Edward Bach
*The Bach Flower Remedies* by Edward Bach
*The Essential Rudolf Steiner* by Rudolf Steiner
*The Philosophy of Freedom* by Rudolf Steiner
*Wisdom Codes* by Gregg Braden

# THE ORACLE

The Oracle is an astrologer, numerologist, sacred geometrist, or someone who lives their life and spirituality based on numbers and cosmic influence. The Oracle is a cosmic counselor who gives intuitive and spiritual advice, guidance, and wisdom. While psychologists focus on a limited aspect of the human psyche by concentrating specifically on the brain and its functions, the Oracle is a metapsychologist who encompasses a more holistic view of the human condition by including the mind, body, and spirit relationship. Because of their line of work or interest, the Oracle has an innate ability to see people's uniqueness. In all of the world, and in all of the universe, the planets, stars, and numbers all align to make one specific person or event. The Oracle is a witness to the magic and awe of these events and heralds the news of these happenings. They are a messenger and a communicator who articulates to people who they can be and the lives they can live by working with their natural abilities, strengths, and characteristics. The Oracle is a seer of people's innermost workings, private selves, and secret aspirations. By seeing the hidden parts of people's souls, they are able to encourage and support them in a deep and meaningful way.

The Oracle adores evidence-based teachings that have shown their validity. If the numbers don't add up, they cannot get behind the belief. They are resilient and have gone through a tremendous lot in their life, making them wise beyond their years. This makes them compassionate yet warmly fierce in their awareness that people can overcome anything. They may have struggled in their life but now feel with astrology, numerology, or whatever they practice, that it is as though they have their head above water. They feel these have given them better insight, clarity, and meaning and have brought the knowledge of the past into the current world. They may use phrases for themselves such as, "Wisdom of an ancient mystic with a modern voice."

**Most Common Adjacent Spiritual Archetypes:** the Witch, the Christian Mystic, the New Ager, the Metaphysician, the Occultist, the Lightworker

**Colors of the Oracle:** purple, blue, pink, gold, white, black, holographic color

**When Balanced, You May Feel or Experience:** insightful, radical, adventurous, wise, therapeutic, empowered, content

**When Unbalanced, You May Feel or Experience:** depleted, chaotic, restricted, lost, perfectionism, uncertainty

**Governs:** eyes, third eye, mouth, throat, hands

**Common Physical Ailments:** eye disorders, menstrual issues, identity crisis, mental and emotional struggles

### Correlating Essential Oils:

**Clary Sage:** eye-opening, clarity, vision
**Frankincense:** communion with God

**Prophets Mantle:** prayer anointing oil, anointing oil for God's prophets

**Hyssop:** protection, blessings, cleansings, freedom, forgiveness

## Correlating Stones:

**Abalone:** intuition, tranquility, ancestry

**Labradorite:** the stone of healers, soothsayers, and seekers

**Opalite:** communication, connection, wonder

**Preseli Bluestone:** ancient stone of dreaming, vision, and intuition

**Kyanite:** communication, connecting with angels, self-expression, standing up for oneself

## Correlating Plants:

- **Bird of Paradise:** freedom, opportunity, identity
- **Papaya:** uniqueness, happiness, enjoying the fruits and juices of life
- **Cactus:** endurance, inner strength, adaptability
- **Laurel:** victory, success, awakening

**Power Words:** patterns, marrying ancient with modern, clarity, sacred, honoring, cosmic, systems, discovery

## People, Places, and Periods That May Resonate with You:

- **People:** astrologists; palm readers; fortune tellers; mathematicians; astronomers; cultures such as the Mayans, Native Americans, Aztec, and Jewish mystics
- **Places:** Mesopotamia, Babylon, Egypt, Rome, Israel, Greece, France, India, China, Mesoamerica
- **Periods:** Sumerian period; 2000 BC-AD 250 Yucatán; Islamic Golden Age; thirteenth century Europe; sixteenth-century France; late 1800s Europe; late 1800s–early 1900s New York; early 1900s–1940s Los Angeles

## Correlating Animal: THE OWL

Owls have long had meaning around intuition, wisdom, and prophecy. The owl is primarily associated with Athena, the goddess of art, war, wisdom, and council, who is often depicted with an owl. It was said that the owl shared its wisdom with Athena, telling her secrets and knowledge. Nocturnal in nature with large eyes, the owl represents the ability to see through the dark and where others cannot. Like the Oracle, who looks for secrets and wisdom in the universe, the owl guides us to see through seeming appearances and look for the truth and wisdom behind what others may not see.

## Common Struggles

**Common Triggers:** being judged, lack of clarity or direction, being misunderstood, being told what to do

**When Triggered, the Oracle Can Become:** misguided, dogmatic, destructive, and emotionally unbalanced

**Common Personal Struggles:** Many people in the Oracle Spiritual Archetype struggle with personal identity and self-discovery. Therefore astrology, numerology, and even archetypes can be a comfort to a person seeking to know themselves. There is a safety in the accuracy of the numbers that the Oracle can rely on. While some people use these as tools in their spirituality and life, some people in the Oracle Spiritual Archetype can reduce themselves to labels in an effort to know and describe themselves. For instance, they may say, "I am a leo with a pisces rising. My birth number is an eight. I am a type A personality. My psychological archetype is the hero, and my Spiritual Archetype is the Oracle." All of these words are meant to describe the person that you are instead of just letting people know you from their perception. While all of that may be accurate and describe you perfectly, it's alright and safe to know others, and yourself, as the soul of you and not just all the man-made labels that define you.

**Common Spiritual Struggles:** The Oracle loves facts, science, and evidence. This is partly what draws them to fields such as astrology or numerology. There is a science in the universe that is always working, and if we get into harmony with its numbers and cycles, we step into a higher potential for ourselves and our lives. One of the common struggles for the Oracle is putting their faith in the Creator of the universe, whose numbers and cycles they follow. Sometimes the Oracle relies on and trusts the physical more than the spiritual and can fall into the trap of putting their faith in their practices instead of God Himself. Without God, these things are just divination, but with God, we can be prophets. In the Bible, there are priests, priestesses, astrologers, and people who use divination as a means of fortune-telling and forecasting. Although they could get by on their crafts, God's chosen prophets were mightier than even the greatest soothsayers of the people. Prophecy is not a skill that can be taught; it is a gift from the Lord. If we are leaving Him out, what is left?

## Mythology, Folklore, Symbolism, or Correlating Story

### The Rider-Waite Tarot Deck

Created by Christian mystics Arthur Edward Waite (creator) and Pamela Colman Smith (illustrator), the Rider-Waite Tarot deck is considered one of the first tarot decks and is still commonly used today. While many forms of divination have existed throughout the centuries, the Rider-Waite deck was one of the first that had biblical influence and elements. No stranger to the Templar, Masons, and the Rosicrucians, Arthur Waite incorporated various symbols of these groups and Christian imagery into the deck.

First, the deck is broken down into four major suits. The first of these suits is Wands or Staves. This suit represents entering a new level of spirituality or consciousness. "And immediately, while he yet spake, cometh Judas, one of the twelve, and with him a great multitude with swords and staves, from the chief priests and the scribes and the elders" (Mark 14:43). In the Bible this is a paramount moment where Jesus is about to be betrayed and put on trial. While he is the Word made manifest, it is through His death and resurrection that He overcomes the Enemy and the world. The Staves represent overcoming obstacles and our resurrection spiritually.

The Sword in the Rider-Waite Tarot represents intellect, logic, and conquest. While we must sometimes fight for things in our lives, it is only with God that we truly overcome them. "Then said Jesus unto him, Put up again thy sword into his place: for all they that take the sword shall perish with the sword. Thinkest thou that I cannot now pray to my Father, and he shall presently give me more than twelve legions of angels?" (Mark 26:52–53).

Both the King of Swords and Queen of Swords cards notably have butterflies, which is a universal sign of transformation. They are no longer in battle, pierced, or bound to the sword like in the Two, Three, Four, Eight, Nine, Ten, or Knight of Swords, but have overcome the battle through transformation and now sit on the throne. The images of the King and Queen of Swords are similar to Jesus, who sat on the throne after the transformation of death and resurrection.

The Coins, or Pentacles as they are commonly called, represent the earth, earthly possessions, and money. Coins have a profound biblical influence as Judas infamously was paid thirty coins for turning Jesus over for trial.

The King of Pentacles shows a king sitting on a throne surrounded by an abundance of fruit, grapes, foliage, and a kingdom on the left side of the picture. While he is cloaked with a beautiful robe and crown, at the bottom, we see his armor, showing that the king has been in battles. The throne on which he sits is also decorated with bulls, which in the Bible symbolizes sacrifice.

Money and finances are commonly discussed in the Bible, and while sometimes sacrifices must be made for financial achievements, our most significant sacrifice is of self to fulfill God's will over ours. King Solomon was the wealthiest man who ever lived, and it was through God's anointing and will that he became so. We can choose to live with God's will, communion, and anointing over our lives and make worldly sacrifices for our well-being, or we can choose to sacrifice our souls for personal gains, such as Judas did for a few coins.

Lastly, the Suit of Cups represents the emotional aspect of ourselves. Cups are a representation of ourselves and a pinnacle part of Jesus' departing words to His disciples before being crucified. "And he took the cup, and gave thanks, and gave *it* to them, saying, Drink ye all of it; for this is my blood of the New Testament" (Mark 26:28).

The Ace of Cups symbolizes these aspects of Jesus and His departing words to His disciples. At the top of the picture is a dove, holding the bread (or body of Christ) with a cross symbol for "host" illustrated upon it. The dove brings the body into the chalice, which overflows with abundant water and is held by a divine hand descending from the clouds. The water flows into the water underneath that is covered in lily pads, which symbolize the rebirth of Christ.

The 78-card deck is filled with biblical symbolism and meaning. A.E. Waite was notorious for his mysticism and personal quest for knowledge. While that did not always stay biblically based, he did become a full-fledged Catholic later in his life. He sought to know God, looked for him in many groups, books, and modalities, and diligently incorporated his insights into his work.

The Oracle is also seeking, but for many Oracles, they no longer even realize that what they seek is God. Like Arthur Waite, the Oracle may look at stars, cards, groups, numbers, and symbols, searching for answers, but the answer is always found in God, not just His creations. The Rider-Waite deck may use countless symbols for God, but it is not the voice of God. Communion with God does not require any of these things but can be accessed through a direct relationship with Him. Without this, we can study the symbols and meanings of life but will never have anything more than our own interpretation if we do not allow God to be our interpreter.

## Spiritual Guidance

God created the Heavens and the Earth. He created the stars and planets, the moon and its cycles, and the sea. While it makes sense that they would have a divine purpose and power, it is invaluable to remember the Creator and His power rather than give all the power to His creations. God has used the Earth and the universe to show signs and events throughout history. A star led three wise men to the greatest King who ever lived. Yet it was not the star itself that held power but the Lord who put it in the sky to escort the King of kings into the world.

There are two types of destinies: the ones we cannot change and the ones we can. God gives us the free will to decide how to live and make choices on our paths. Therefore, nothing is set in stone unless decided by Him. Astrology, numerology, palmistry, and other forms of divination show our changeable destiny, but it is only with and through God that we gain revelation, insight, and guidance. Oracles see themselves as predisposed to their condition and see their conditions as aspects they must live with. In reality, this is backward, and the numbers and stars give us information about our life and purpose so we can lean into our strengths and heal or grow from the less favorable traits.

## Affirmations:

- *God aligns the stars to tell stories. I am His storyteller.*
- *There are patterns and divine synchronicities in the world. I am a part of the patterns and divine synchronicities, and they are part of me.*
- *My charts, zodiac, and numerology are only evidence of God's creation of me and my purpose in this life, but not the dictator of my life.*

### Prayer:

"Lord, help me to use Your creations to share Your knowledge, wisdom, and revelation to bring people closer to You and learn to hear You for themselves."

### Additional Resources:

*Edgar Cayce's Astrology for the Soul* by Margaret Gammon and
    W.H. Church
*Number in Scripture* by E. W. Bullinger
*Planetary Influences and Sojourns* by Edgar Cayce
*The Only Astrology Book You'll Ever Need* by Joanna Martine Woolfolk
*The Secret Teachings of All the Ages* by Manly P. Hall
*The Witness of the Stars* by E. W. Bullinger

# THE OCCULTIST

The Occultist thinks outside of the box in every area of life. They ponder the meaning of everything and are fascinated by the secrets of the universe. Occultists may find that they sometimes push things too far and walk the line of what is moralistic in regard to society's standards. They go through periods of genius where they become enveloped in studies and research. They love tumbling down the path of knowledge and lock themselves away to become completely immersed.

They love the supernatural and are drawn to the possibility of other dimensions. They may even connect to this side through ritual, or it may be drawn to them. The Occultist studies metaphysics, philosophy, and space. They love science fiction, supernatural lore, parapsychology, astrology, numerology, and learning about other occultists and metaphysicians. They could (and most likely do) spend hours researching space, alchemy, and philosophy.

They are intensely private, which gives them an alluring quality to those around them. They are massively intuitive and sensitive. Sometimes they cannot differentiate between what is seen by only them and what is evident to everyone. They surround themselves with other intelligent individuals and need constant mental stimulation.

**Most Common Adjacent Spiritual Archetypes:** the New Ager, the Metaphysician

**Colors of the Occultist:** dark blue, light blue, purple, beige, gray, kraft or antique paper brown

**When Balanced, You May Feel or Experience:** insight, intuition, knowledge, psychic vision, self-realization, self-expression, clairvoyance, clairaudience, willpower, telepathy

**When Unbalanced, You May Feel or Experience:** illusion, nightmares, depression, isolation, bipolar disorder, mood swings, addiction

**Governs:** nervous system, ears, nose, brain, eyes

**Common Physical Ailments:** frequent headaches; tonsillitis; neck pain; thyroid problems; chronic cough; sinus infections; mental health issues, including depression, bipolar disorder, schizophrenia, obsessive-compulsive disorder

### Correlating Essential Oils:

**Abramelin Oil:** The Occultists' version of holy oil from the book The Book of Abramelin
**Rose:** emotional stability, mothers love, calms anxiety
**Chamomile:** calming and peaceful for the restless or anxious Occultist
**Helichrysum:** Derived from the Greek word ἑλίσσω or helisso, meaning "sun" and χρῡσός, translated to chrysos, meaning "gold" because of their tiny yellow clusters of flowers. Helichrysum brings peace and light to the space of the Occultist.

## Correlating Stones:

**Quartz:** spiritual growth, awareness, vision
**Blue Lace Agate:** stabilization, calm, inner peace
**Black Tourmaline:** stone of magicians, grounding, electricity
**Citrine:** joy, light, transmutation of darkness
**Herkimer Diamond:** stone of attunement + alignment
**Iolite:** clear vision, imagination, inner strength
**Pyrite:** prosperity, good fortune, leadership

## Correlating Plants:

- **Ivy:** faith, eternity, friendship, fidelity, attachment
- **Angelica root:** Used throughout time as a powerful protector, Angelica root, also known as the "Holy Ghost" root, has been used in exorcisms, mojo bags, and healing.
- **Hellebore:** A plant that grows in shadows and thrives in the isolation of dim light and icy conditions of winter, yet it is one of the most marvelous, alluring, and fascinating of the species; just like the Occultist. Also known as Christe herbe, there is a legend that after the birth of Jesus, a young girl went to see the infant in Bethlehem. Seeing the gifts bestowed upon Him, she began to weep, for she was too poor to give Him anything. When her tears hit the ground, up sprouted the most beautiful flowers, the hellebore. So she gave the hellebore as her gift.

**Power Words:** insight, foreknowledge, health, satisfaction, light, clarity

## People, Periods, and Places you may resonate with:

- **People:** apothecary, chemist, scientist, inventor, Freemason, member of secret societies
- **Periods:** 520 BC–590 BC, AD 1100–1300, AD 1390–1425, AD 1300–1700, late 1800s, early 1900s, 1960s–1970s

- **Places:** France, London, England, Scotland, Ireland, Germany, Switzerland, Northern Spain, New York, Boston, Los Angeles

### Correlating Animal: THE RAVEN

The raven represents the master magician, mystery, mysticism, power of thought, creation, magic, self-knowledge, shape-shifting, and introspection. The raven symbolizes bringing light into the darkness, something the Occultist needs deeply. In many cultures, the raven symbolizes death, which embodies the transitions in life and the death and rebirth that takes place. The raven represents magic and the magic within you. They are persistent creatures and not easily intimidated.

In many cultures throughout time, raven medicine symbolizes magic and the transformation of consciousness. In Native American stories, the raven is a shapeshifter. Similarly, the Occultist is constantly growing in their consciousness both personally and spiritually. Sometimes healing requires us to go into dark spaces we didn't know lay dormant in our minds. In Native American folklore, the raven tricked the Gods into giving him the Sun so he could place it in the sky to light the world. The raven accompanies us into these dark places, illuminating them with light and casting out the darkness. Similarly, raven magic supports and empowers the Occultist to step into their divine power and bring light into the world. As you go through a phase of healing or growth, call on the medicine of the raven to assist you in bringing light to your situation and casting out the darkness of old paradigms and belief systems.

### Common Struggles

**Common Triggers:** anyone or anything you see as superficial, having your skills or knowledge challenged, seeing less-knowledgeable or "unworthy" people succeed, being forced into standard settings, being around ordinary people

**When Triggered, the Occultist Can Become:** isolated, egotistical, spiritually greedy, cultish

**Common Personal Struggles:** Due to the subject matter, the Occultist studies and is fascinated with how they use their mind, but many struggle with depression, bipolar disorder, or addiction. They may not realize it, but part of the purpose of addiction is to connect to the other planes and worlds they feel so in tune with yet cannot seem to connect with in their waking and sober life. The more artistic Occultists may also use their drug-fueled benders to inspire their work, essentially putting themselves on the chopping block for genius. Addiction may also become part of their social life and may feel like one of the only ways of connecting to others. The Occultist feels odd and out of place, but addiction becomes a common ground that makes them feel relatable.

The energy we emulate is the energy we attract; therefore, if you do not have a healthy mindset and participate in an unhealthy lifestyle, such as drug or alcohol addiction, negative spirits and people will attach themselves to you. The Occultist suffers from depression, obsessiveness, and even insanity if there is not proper attention given to increasing and maintaining your quality of life. While many Occultists prefer solitude and even darkness, these are actually things that can decrease the quality of their life. Because they are fascinated with the dark and mysterious, they attract people who walk that line. This only fuels their own darkness and increases their attachment to negativity. Being "normal" is one of their biggest fears and something they shy away from at all costs. Therefore, the Occultist acquires friendships and relationships with others who are a bit odd or off.

**Common Spiritual Struggles:** The Occultist has a tendency to become devoted to their "darkness," or "shadow side" as it may be called. Many Occultists will say things such as, "I own my darkness because it's part of who I am," or "I have befriended my shadow." What they fail to realize is that their shadow does not want to be their friend. Their shadow, or darkness, is looking for an advantage and a dictatorship, not a peaceful union. It has become more common in recent years to own your shadow in an attempt to gain control over it, or to let it be appeased. However, this can be detrimental to your health, mind, and well-being. Some of the most famous Occultists have made this same mistake and paid dearly for it with their emotional stability, sanity, and even their lives.

## Mythology, Folklore, Symbolism, or Correlating Story

In Greek mythology, the world was first a void and empty existence known as "Chaos." From Chaos, five initial beings were born, one of which was Erebus, the God of darkness and shadows. Erebus was responsible for tainting goodness and turning it into darkness. In Greek mythology, a Shade was a spirit or ghost of a dead person who was punished to roam the underworld for eternity. Although the Occultist believes their shadow, or darkness, is serving them, it is actually their greatest enemy. If the Occultist strives for the light instead of indulging in their dark side, they will overcome it and become more powerful in their spirituality than they ever imagined.

## Spiritual Guidance:

The Occultist is a powerful personality almost like Phoenix in *X-Men*, with too much power and too little control. Self-control is critical for the Occultist because without it, you may fall into addictions, develop an obsessive personality, and always push yourself to a fine line. Because you tend to associate with the dark side, you should refrain from alcohol or drug use. Mind- and energy-altering substances fueled by your intense energy can act as a beacon for negative entities, supernatural or otherwise. It is highly recommended that you associate with people who have lighter energies or who have healed some of their darker side. We are each unique in our ways, which is part of the human charm. However, surrounding ourselves with others suffering from the same afflictions will generally only worsen our issues. As you begin to work on yourself, you will begin to attract healthier people who bring out your own light. While it may seem difficult, it is highly encouraged for you to practice healthy, light-based modalities. You would benefit from turning your focus to more positive metaphysics and philosophy rather than engaging in the dark arts.

Keep your personal space and home clear of negativity. Smudging and cleansing rituals on yourself and in your space are highly encouraged. Refrain from letting strange or negative energy into your environment, especially your home. Mindset work is extremely powerful for you as you are skilled at manifesting. But due to the dark subject matter to which you are drawn and your darker thoughts, you attract darker people and situations. When you begin to notice your thoughts and tailor them to a more positive lifestyle, you will begin to see massive changes in your energy, mood, and thought patterns.

Lastly, God did not create intrusive, dark, or negative thoughts and actions. If God did not create them, and they are not of God, then you may be tapping into things that are going to harm you, your spirit, or your well-being. You do not need to love your darkness; instead, ask God to shine His light into it, dispelling the darkness. You are the image and likeness of God, and if your darkness is not God, then you are living an image outside of your authentic self, which will lead to deviation and a lack of alignment with your soul and purpose.

### Affirmations:

- *As above, so below. As it is in heaven, it is on Earth.*
- *My soul is the image and likeness of God. I dwell in Him and have authority over everything that is of the darkness.*
- *I AM created whole and accept the wholeness from God in my life, health, spirit, and mind.*

### Prayer:

"O blazing Light! Awaken my heart, awaken my soul, ignite my darkness, tear the veil of silence, and fill my temple with Thy glory."
—Paramahansa Yogananda

## Additional Resources:

*Atom-Smashing Power of Mind* by Charles Fillmore
*Demian* by Hermann Hesse
*Science and Health* by Mary Baker Eddy
*Master of the Mysteries* by Louis Sahagun
*The Consciousness of the Atom* by Alice Bailey
*The Kabbalah*
*The Secret Teachings of All the Ages* by Manly P Hall

# THE LIGHTWORKER

The Lightworker does not just practice spirituality; they make it a lifestyle. Spirituality is not a space of time carved out in their day to sit and meditate, pray, or study (although they do those things as well). Rather, it is something they strive to embody in the way they think, act, eat, exercise, and live. They may subscribe to other Lightworkers' newsletters and email lists, listen to spiritual podcasts, and attempt to fill their energetic field with high vibrational information at all times. Their bookshelves are full of spiritual literature. Even their material possessions, such as jewelry, are meaningful, high-energy pieces. They genuinely love the magic of the light and desire it to fill all facets of their life.

They are compassionate and loving. They love animals and nature and integrating the two into their spiritual experiences. They would love nothing more than to spend their day traveling horseback through the mountains to a lost temple for some energy work and toning or going to the beach for some exercise and prayer next to the water. They surround themselves with other Lightworkers who understand the spiritual realm and can discuss energy and mindset over morning tea or fresh juice.

They have experienced a lot in their life and on their spiritual path but are always eager to learn and grow. Because of this, they are incredibly nurturing and understanding of others. They have worked through many of their blocks and come out on the other side wiser and more peaceful than they could have imagined. They see every day as an opportunity to develop their spirituality and are constantly amazed by the clever ways God speaks to them to convey His messages. They feel the connection to God and desire to feel it more deeply and often.

**Most Common Adjacent Spiritual Archetypes:** the Saint, the Christian Mystic, the New Ager, the Oracle

**Colors of the Lightworker:** baby blue, light pink, off-white, emerald green, purple, mint green

**When Balanced, You May Feel or Experience:** compassionate, nurturing energy, joy, peace, intuition, empathy, in-tune, powerful, positive

**When Unbalanced, You May Feel or Experience:** spiritual cynicism and snobbery, lack of grounding, inability to manifest, lack of connection, depression, helplessness, and a loss of faith

**Governs:** head, ears, brain, eyes, nervous system, immune system

**Physical Ailments:** chronic pains, lower-back problems, upper-shoulder and neck tension and issues, depression, epilepsy, spinal problems, infertility, issues with nerves such as nerve damage or loss of control, hormonal imbalances, hair loss

### Correlating Essential Oils:

**Bergamot:** joy, happiness, surrender
**Rose:** heart, love, compassion, spiritual growth

**Neroli:** light, purity, confidence
**Vanilla:** water, the planet Venus (planet of love), simplicity

## Correlating Stones:

**Amazonite:** positivity, flow, and release of anxiety
**Quartz:** intuition, clarity, healing
**Opal:** peace, hope, purity
**Iolite:** water, direction (known as the Vikings' Compass),
overcoming fear
**Tourmaline:** compassion, love, friendship
**Azurite:** stone of heaven, truth, intuition, the pursuit of our
heavenly self
**Angelite:** angels, communication, positivity
**Celestite:** mindfulness, inner peace, harmony
**Labradorite:** shield of negativity, inner strength, self-worth

## Correlating Plants:

- **Succulent:** endurance, love, strength, beauty, harmony
- **Lady of the Desert:** Lady of the Desert are some of the most
  resilient and self-sufficient plants showing beauty that comes from
  struggle and can withstand the harshest conditions.
- **Bird of Paradise:** joy, self-expression, paradise
- **Lotus:** purity, compassion, transformation, enlightenment
- **Rose:** feminine energy, love, peace, holiness

**Power Words:** miracles, authenticity, guru, soul, spirit, vibration,
happiness, light

## People, Places, and Periods That May Resonate with You:

- **People:** priestess, healer, writer, environmentalist, social activist,
  animal rights activist, nomadic cultures and groups, speakers

- **Periods:** 1,000 BC–500 BC, late 1600s 1845–1920, 1950s 1960s–1970s
- **Places:** Hawaii, Florida, Bali, New York, Santa Monica, Venice Beach, Malibu, Australia

## Correlating Animal: THE DOLPHIN

The Lightworker usually finds the spiritual path through wading in life's difficult waters. Dolphin medicine is about rebirth, courage, and self-confidence, all traits you need on the spiritual path. If you are new to the spiritual path, call on dolphin medicine to assist you in your spiritual rebirthing. The Lightworker is a fun, happy, and energetic personality that lights up the room. Dolphin medicine reminds us to let go and be happy when life has become too serious. If you're not attracting what you desire, get into the vibration of Dolphin medicine to assist you in manifesting your desires.

## Common Struggles

**Common Triggers:** lack of support, spiritual bypassing, victim mentality, people who wallow in their problems, feeling disconnected, not following your own intuition

**When Triggered, the Lightworker Can Become:** abrasive, judgmental, self-righteous, anxious

**Common Personal Struggles:** Many Lightworkers come to this path through hardships, such as abuse, sickness—autoimmune issues, hormone imbalances, etc.—feeling depressed, detached from themselves, or as if life has a deeper meaning that they are unable to discover. Due to stress, trauma, or struggles, the Lightworker can be misled by superficial things. For example, some Lightworkers would rather dress the part by wearing the clothes, looking like a Lightworker, and talking the talk instead of delving deep into the trenches and going through the inner muck. This may be a form of self-preservation, especially if you have had past troubles, adversity, or struggles you would rather not face.

The Lightworker may seek "good vibes only" because they are afraid of getting trapped, controlled, or pulled down by the negative things that once seemed to have dominion over them. Unfortunately, it is only through the muck that we can reach the other side. A popular children's book, *We're Going on a Bear Hunt*, tells the story of a family that goes on a quest to find a bear and must go through water, mud, a forest, a snowstorm, and a cave, each time reciting that they "Can't go over it. We can't go under it. We've got to go through it!" It's a beautiful metaphor for our past, struggles, and circumstances. Although it looks tough and may be unenjoyable, "We can't go over it. We can't go under it. We've got to go through it!"

**Common Spiritual Struggles:** Many Lightworkers have strong intuition, manifestation skills, and spiritual understanding that can be beneficial on their path. One area of spirituality that can be lacking for some is having an actual relationship with God. Many Lightworkers refer to God as "The Universe" and treat it as an impersonal force. However, God is personal, and when we have a relationship with Him, we can reach depths of our spirituality we never knew existed. Alphonsus Liguori said, "Acquire the habit of speaking to God as if you were alone with Him, familiarly and with confidence and love, as to the dearest and most loving of friends." This is one area where many lack but do not understand why they do not feel this level of communion. If you have felt that your spirituality and spiritual connection feel impersonal, try adapting this habit of speaking to God more intimately and see how it affects your relationship with Him.

### Mythology, Folklore, Symbolism, or Correlating Story

*The Neverending Story* is a fantastic children's book and film from the late 1970s and early 1980s. The adventure centers on a human boy named Bastian, who reads a book called *The Neverending Story*. The story depicts a hero who is a great warrior boy named Atreyu. Atreyu is tasked with finding a cure for the Childlike Empress, who is sick and dying. Their world, called Fantasia, is also at risk of being destroyed.

An invisible force called "The Nothing" is eradicating their world, and Atreyu is the only one who can stop it. Atreyu sets out on an extraordinary quest to save the Childlike Empress and Fantasia while taking Bastian on the journey with him because Bastian is reading the story in the book. Atreyu faces many obstacles. His beloved horse, Artex, dies in the swamps of sadness. An evil wolf hunts him. It seems that all roads lead to nowhere—on an even longer journey than he expected. After a devastation that results in him feeling hopeless, a good-luck dragon named Falkor takes Atreyu to a gnome named Engywook. Engywook and his wife, Urgl, live at an observatory near the Southern Oracle, where Atreyu must pass through a pair of sphinxes that no man has ever passed through. As they watch, a knight approaches the sphinxes on horseback and attempts to pass through. When he enters their gaze, their eyes open, and a beam shoots the knight dead. Believing that he can pass through, Atreyu goes down to the sphinxes and begins walking toward them. He sees the dead knight in his path and begins to feel afraid. The eyes of the sphinxes start to open, and Engywook yells from the observatory, "Run Atreyu!" Atreyu runs and jumps just in time and is safe on the other side. Excited, Engywook rushes to Falkor and his wife and tells them that Atreyu made it but that he must now go to the "Magic Mirror Gate," where Atreyu has to face his true self. Falkor responds, "So what? That won't be too hard for him." But Engywook corrects him, saying, "Oh, that's what everyone thinks! But kind people find out that they are cruel. Brave men discover that they are really cowards! Confronted by their true selves, most men run away screaming!"

## Spiritual Guidance:

For the Lightworker, there is a part of themselves they are afraid to face, and may even deny. They may ride to their adversity in shiny silver on a noble steed, feeling like a warrior, but it is within the heart that the bravest warriors are born. If we hold onto our past, our hearts can become fragile or angry, striving to only live on the surface so as not to be hurt again. The healing that happens in the heart will make you unstoppable because it is then that you can share your light in a way that is truly authentic and fulfilling. You are here to love, share love, and reflect love. If you feel that something is lacking or that you cannot share that love in a way that feels true and organic, try letting God into your heart and asking Him to help you heal. With your surrender and God's love, you may be surprised by the impact and transformation you see.

### Affirmations:

- *I shine my light and see only the light in others.*
- *I AM God's image and reflection of love, abundance, and wholeness. I AM, I AM, I AM.*
- *All that is of this world is perishable. God is infinite.*

### Prayer:

"God, help me live, love, and learn through You today. I accept Your love and guidance in my life and seek to share Your divine light with others."

### Additional Resources:

*A Course in Miracles* by Helen Schucman
*Authority of the Believer* by Kenneth E. Hagin
*Lessons in Truth* by Harriet Emilie Cady
*Love Without Conditions* by Paul Ferrini
*The Disappearance of the Universe* by Gary Renard
*The Four Agreements* by Don Miguel Ruiz
*The Secret* by Rhonda Byrne

# THE MINDSET MASTER

The Mindset Master can do and achieve anything because they believe they can. Just like the great minds, such as Napoleon Hill and Dale Carnegie. The Mindset Master believes no limitation outside of themselves can hold them down because the power of their mind can break any chain, knock down any wall, and find a way where others believe there are none. The power of the mind is an unstoppable force that, when properly utilized, can achieve monumental success. Most Mindset Masters come from modest beginnings, which motivated them to create more for themselves. Sharing this gift with others is a driving force in their life. They see how influential the human mind is at creating our life and feel the need to share this knowledge with others.

The Mindset Master is a catalyst and cheerleader for others, supporting them, boosting their confidence, and encouraging them to be their highest and best selves. They have a way with words that generates energy within others, motivating and inspiring them to break out of their paradigms, circumstances, or struggles to see opportunities and possibilities where they may never have searched.

The Mindset Master uses their thoughts, words, and imagination to create their desired life. Visualization, vision boards, and journaling are all practices they may utilize in their mindset work to bring their goals to fruition. The Mindset Master lives by wise words like Mary Kay's when she said, "What you believe, you can achieve." Their mind is their greatest asset or greatest weapon, and they strive to make it their greatest companion.

**Most Common Ascendant Spiritual Archetypes:** the Neoteric Shaman, the Warrior, the Lightworker, the Sovereign

**Colors of the Mindset Master:** bright red, dark blue, royal blue, white, gold, brown

**When Balanced, You May Feel or Experience:** direction, clarity, growth, success, achievement, satisfaction, mindful, conscious, vigilant, positive

**When Unbalanced, You May Feel or Experience:** poor, rash, thoughtless, unaware, negative, remiss, deceitful, overly intellectual, discouraged

**Governs:** arteries, intestines, brain, lymph nodes

**Common Physical Ailments:** bowel issues, intestinal issues, plaque on arteries, swollen lymph nodes or blockages in the lymph node region, growths on the brain or pituitary, dyslexia, speech impediments, ADHD

### Correlating Essential Oils:

**Royal Hawaiian Sandalwood:** nervous system, tension, peace of mind, vitality
**Peppermint:** mental stimulation, intellect

**Vetiver:** known as the oil of tranquility; eases stress and worry
**May Chang:** mental fatigue

## Correlating Stones:

**Euclase:** connecting the heart to the mind
**Datolite:** connecting one's mind with their intuition
**Amethyst:** the stone of Aquarius; zodiac of intellect; used to promote inner peace, relaxation, self-realization, and intuition
**Citrine:** joy, happiness, refreshing one's thoughts, intellect

## Correlating Plants:

- **Anthuriums:** These heart-shaped leaves represent love and reminds the Mindset Master to work from their heart and incorporate it into their life and spirituality.
- **The Flannel Flower:** Ruled the "symbol of mental health" in Australia, the flannel flower is considered to be resilient and adaptable to all weather conditions in order to survive. This represents the power of the mind and overcoming mental adversity and struggles.
- **Strings of Hearts (aka Ceropegia Woodii):** beautiful vine plant that needs little care or watering; heart-shaped leaves a reminder to focus and be rooted in love

**Power Words:** think, thinking, thoughts, words, wealth, rich, imagine, brave, possibility, dream

## People, periods, and places you may resonate with:

- **People:** inventors, coaches, mindset gurus, intellectuals
- **Places:** Russia, Ukraine, New York, Los Angeles, Chicago
- **Periods:** early 1900s, 1930s, 1960s, 1980s

## Correlating Animal: THE TURTLE

Like the Mindset Master who usually comes from humble beginnings, the turtle is known to be capable of living in various environments. Additionally, the turtle proves that steady but persistent perseverance pays off. The Mindset Master knows that this type of patience, coupled with determination, may seem slow to others but is ultimately a winning combination. Remember, while you may have a goal in your mind and the will to get there, turtle medicine is also about inner peace and slowing down, within and outside of your mind. If you feel you have excessive racing thoughts or are being too hard on yourself, think of the turtle and the patience and space it gives itself to be, exist, and get to its destination in due time.

## Common Struggles

**Common Triggers:** ignorance, not reaching goals, appearing unknowledgeable, being outsmarted, not "making it," pressure of getting on top or staying relevant

**When Triggered, the Mindset Master Can Become:** shallow, pedantic, apathetic, money-driven

**Common Personal Struggles:** The Mindset Master has the power of the mind but can forget to incorporate the heart. Life, work, and your goals can always be about the next best thing rather than finding contentment in the heart. For instance, if you look at many of the teachers and leaders of mindset, their teachings are usually never complete. The secret to success is always in the following lecture, book, or class series, keeping the audience hooked for the next thing. While it may seem like a sales gimmick, and for some, it may be, this is primarily due to the fact that the Mindset Master has only mastered the mind but is lacking in the heart. If we only focus on the mind, we are engaging the human self and not integrating the spiritual self.

The Mindset Master can also be easily seduced by money and fame as evidence of their intellectual success. It's often believed that if one is successful, one will be famous and rich; however, that is not always the case, nor should it be the goal. If we seek first the kingdom of God, all else will be added unto us. This means seeking God above all else, and the rest will happen naturally.

**Common Spiritual Struggles:** While the Mindset Master is an expert in their mind, they tend to rely primarily on their own thoughts, words, and actions to create the life and business they desire while forgetting to incorporate God into their will. For instance, modern manifestation techniques encourage people to get whatever they want, and if they can dream it, they can achieve it. However, they never stop to think about the fact that what they want may not be what is in their highest and best good, and their will may not match God's will. People may use mindset techniques to get the relationship or job they want but end up unhappy with the results because they are exercising their supernatural ability to manifest as a spiritual being without aligning their vision with God's Word first. This creates a sort of backward effect. Instead of receiving God's blessings because we are in alignment with His Word, we often try to manifest worldly circumstances in an attempt to satisfy our worldly desires while bypassing the spiritual foundation. Keep in mind, that what is created in and of the world is subject to the world. Only God is infinite and eternal; therefore, only what is built in and through Him has longevity.

## Mythology, Folklore, Symbolism, or Correlating Story

"In Gibeon the Lord appeared to Solomon in a dream by night: and God said, Ask what I shall give thee. And Solomon said, Thou hast shewed unto thy servant David my father great mercy, according as he walked before thee in truth, and in righteousness, and in uprightness of heart with thee; and thou hast kept for him this great kindness, that thou hast given him a son to sit on his throne, as it is this day. And now, O Lord my God, thou hast made thy servant king instead of David my father: and I am but a little child: I know not how to go out or come in. And thy servant is in the midst of thy people which thou hast chosen, a great people, that cannot be numbered nor counted for multitude. Give therefore thy servant an understanding heart to judge thy people, that I may discern between good and bad: for who is able to judge this thy so great a people? And the speech pleased the Lord, that Solomon had asked this thing. And God said unto him, Because thou hast asked this thing, and hast not asked for thyself long life; neither hast asked riches for thyself, nor hast asked the life of thine enemies; but hast asked for thyself understanding to discern judgment; Behold, I have done according to thy words: lo, I have given thee a wise and an understanding heart; so that there was none like thee before thee, neither after thee shall any arise like unto thee. And I have also given thee that which thou hast not asked, both riches, and honour: so that there shall not be any among the kings like unto thee all thy days. And if thou wilt walk in my ways, to keep my statutes and my commandments, as thy father David did walk, then I will lengthen thy days" (1 Kings 3:5–14).

"And God gave Solomon wisdom and understanding exceeding much, and largeness of heart, even as the sand that is on the sea shore. And Solomon's wisdom excelled the wisdom of all the children of the east country, and all the wisdom of Egypt. For he was wiser than all men; than Ethan the Ezrahite, and Heman, and Chalcol, and Darda, the sons of Mahol: and his fame was in all nations round about" (1 Kings 4:29–31).

### Spiritual Guidance:

King Solomon was considered to be the wisest man who ever lived (other than Jesus) but was also the wealthiest man ever to live, even by today's standards. What's crucial to consider is that when God came to him and told him that he could ask Him for anything, Solomon did not ask for anything material, and it was not for his own benefit. Many people today would ask for fame, beauty, longer life, and money. King Solomon asked for wisdom to best serve his people. Because of his nobility and humility, God simultaneously blessed him with riches and fortunes, even though he did not ask for it.

Our minds are limited; they overthink, analyze, and judge. We cannot fathom what is best for us and our lives because only God knows. We may have an idea, but if we do not align it with God's vision, we risk making poor decisions. We may think money, moving, fame, a different job, or a relationship might be the solutions to our problems, but we may be way off course. When we ask God with our hearts, He will bless us beyond our capacity of thought or imagination.

### Affirmations:

- *I think, operate, and plan with my heart and God's Word.*
- *I make all goals, plans, and decisions with my heart and in alignment with God's plan for my life.*
- *Not my will but Yours, Lord.*

### Prayer:

"Lord, please let my mind be like the mind of Christ's so that I may do all things with love, humility, and good intention. I open my mind to Your thoughts, words, and revelations so that I may help and support others with wisdom and a good heart."

### Additional Resources:

The Book of Proverbs in the *Bible*
*The Dynamic Laws of Prosperity* by Catherine Ponder
*The Game and How to Play It* by Florence Scovel Shinn
*The Science of Getting* by Rich Wallace Wattles
*The Strangest Secret* by Earl Nightingale
*Think and Grow Rich* by Napoleon Hill

# THE SOVEREIGN

From Cornelius Vanderbilt, Henry Ford, and Andrew Carnegie, to John Rockefeller, some of the greatest influencers in the world and throughout modern history were people who started with nothing and utilized the power of their vision to make a profound impact. While some Sovereigns may come from a family of other Sovereigns, their goal is always to outperform, outdo, and make a name for themselves in the world.

The Sovereign Spiritual Archetype is about influencing the direction of the future. They see personal needs, the world's, or the environment's needs and aim to fill the holes. Whether it's a way to shop that provides ease or accessibility, a fresh spin on a creative project, or a new way to provide electricity, the Sovereign sees possibilities, opportunities, and advancement in ways that most people do not. They are often at the forefront of thought and can see what others cannot, which may make them question the Sovereign to begin with but they are always in awe of them after the fact.

The Sovereign is a king or queen in their field. They monopolize their field and position themselves in such a way that while others may try to compete, they cannot have competition because no one can be them. Power, authority, and sovereignty mean everything to them. Although it is their greatest fear to lose it, these traits are actually a part of their purpose, personality, and are integrated into their psyche.

The Sovereign practices spirituality in a dominant and significant way that is often integrated into their vision and purpose. For instance, John Rockefeller did not just believe his vision was important or valuable, which at the time it certainly was; he also believed that his life and business ventures were God-ordained and that people who got in his way were in battle against him. While the Sovereign may still attend church or have a spiritual practice, their spiritual zone of genius and communion with God often transpires during their revelations and planning. This space is a place of peace and clarity for them, which allows them to hear and speak to God more directly.

**Most Common Adjacent Spiritual Archetypes:** the Neoteric Shaman, the Warrior, the Mindset Master, the Theologist

**Colors of the Sovereign:** black, white, gunmetal gray, light gray, bright orange, electric blue, deep red, bright red, rich red, gold

**When Balanced, You May Feel or Experience:** powerful, authoritative, revered, listened to, prominent, significant, substantial, confidant, needed

**When Unbalanced, You May Feel or Experience:** inferior, weak, overthrown, subordinate, unimportant, conquered, underappreciated, undervalued

**Governs:** respiratory system, breast, heart, blood, lungs, colon, and kidneys

**Common Physical Ailments:** stress-related issues, such as high cortisol, alopecia, heart disease or pulmonary hypertension; nasal and sinus issues;

respiratory issues, such as pneumonia; skin rashes, such as eczema or rosacea; weak knees; blood-related health issues, such as diabetes

## Correlating Essential Oils:

**Vanilla:** luck, adoration, vitality, vocalization
**Patchouli:** grounding, business, wealth
**Frankincense:** Given to the King of all Kings, Jesus was gifted frankincense at birth. It is an oil of holiness and royalty and is often associated with the king's energy.
**Rose:** The scent of Mother Mary. Rose is the scent of the female energy of the holy Mother Mary, who gave birth to Jesus.
**Cinnamon:** money, stimulation, power

## Correlating Stones:

**Ruby:** fearlessness, passion, drive, royalty
**Emerald:** Revered as a stone of great royalty, associated with Alexander the Great and Cleopatra. Emerald is a stone of intellectual power, wisdom, discernment, vision, and healing.
**Diamond:** power, perfection, unconquerable
**Opal:** diversity in skill and talent, expression of self, wealth
**Sapphire:** royalty, nobility, self-discipline, structure, monarchy

## Correlating Plants:

- **Tobacco:** leader, respect, guidance
- **Black Pepper:** personal power, confidence, strength, intellectual stimulation
- **Galangal:** money, power, success with legal battles
- **Alstroemeria Mars:** devotion, achievement, prosperity, fortune

**Power Words:** power, authority, leadership, politician, ruler, influence, monopoly, sovereignty, king, queen

## People, Places, and Periods That May Resonate with You:

- **People:** emperors, queens, kings, rulers, leaders, chiefs
- **Places:** Seattle, Silicon Valley, New York, Colorado, Rome, Babylon, Greece, Egypt, Persia, England
- **Periods:** 1194–1184 BC, 700–480 BC, 356–323 BC, AD 1206–1368, AD 1781–1940, 1970s

## Correlating Animal: THE EAGLE

The eagle represents the Great Spirit and our connection to God. The eagle flies higher than any other bird, allowing it to see farther. Being a Sovereign means having to soar higher to bring the impossible into manifestation by seeing farther than others. Eagle medicine is about power, strength, and endurance. It is here to support you when you have trouble executing an idea or are unsure how to make something happen. It is also a reminder to let God in on the co-creation process. The eagle flies closer to the heavens than any other bird. It is in between the physical world and the spiritual world. This is the balance the Sovereign must attain to serve for the highest and best good of the world and themselves.

## Common Struggles

**Common Triggers:** having your throne or crown taken or stolen, being overthrown, being irrelevant, being powerless, anarchy, disarray, disorganization

**When Triggered, the Sovereign Can Become:** entitled, dramatic, out of touch with reality, self-centered

**Common Personal Struggles:** The Sovereign is driven, hardworking, and willing to make changes at all costs. They can become obsessed with their mission and work so intensely that they may begin to see people or things as casualties to a greater purpose. Remember that a great leader will be a servant of the people, not one who puts himself on the throne above others. Jesus was the greatest king who ever lived, yet He was born in a manger, lived among the people, and changed the world without seeking His own personal gain. Remain heart-centered in all that you do, and remember that any king or queen can dictate, but a man or woman of the people is revered, loved, and cherished.

**Common Spiritual Struggles:** The Sovereign is the most likely Spiritual Archetype to inherit a God complex, feeling unstoppable, above the law, and sovereign in their life and work. When a person's empire becomes exceptionally successful, and their reputation becomes otherworldly, it can go to their head. Morals, laws, and ethics can become relative, and the lines may begin to blur.

## Mythology, Folklore, Symbolism, or Correlating Story

Daedalus was a master craftsman and skilled tradesman in ancient Greece. Seeing his abilities, King Minos hired Daedalus to build a labyrinth to trap the half-man, half-bull creature called the Minotaur, who was the illegitimate son of King Minos's wife. The labyrinth was an elaborate structure that no one could escape unless they knew where the secret door was. When Theseus, a brave prince from Athens, journeyed to battle the Minotaur, King Minos's daughter, Ariadne, was struck by his beauty and instantly fell in love. Ariadne begged Daedalus to tell her how Theseus could escape the labyrinth so that he could live. Daedalus devised a plan and told her that Theseus could tie a thread to the entrance of the labyrinth and, after killing the minotaur, would be able to escape. Theseus did as Ariadne told him, killing the minotaur then escaped out of the entrance the thread was tied to. Upon seeing this, King Minos was furious and knew that only one person could have told Theseus the way out: the labyrinth creator himself. As punishment for betraying him, King Minos threw Daedalus and his son, Icarus, into the labyrinth. Being such a skilled architect, Daedalus himself could not find the way out. He realized that the only way out would not be through but above. He constructed wings made from feathers and wax and tied them to himself and Icarus, warning him not to fly too close to the sun. If he did, the wax could melt. They escaped the labyrinth and flew into the sky toward Sicily. Taken by the beauty of the sun, Icarus did not heed his father's warning and flew higher and higher toward it. As he grew closer, the wax of his wings began to melt and drip, causing the wings to break. Icarus fell into the ocean and drowned.

## Spiritual Guidance:

The story of Icarus has been retold for thousands of years and is often reinterpreted, but the one core moral of the story is that we must know and respect our limitations. For the Sovereign, it can be challenging to get your wings fastened, fly to new heights, feel the sun, and then just talk yourself back down to Earth. To be great, you must go above and beyond the norm, but it's essential to keep your compass pointing to what is most valuable: God and your soul. Your soul knows the direction of True North and can guide you back when needed. Just make sure that you are listening.

## Affirmations:

- *Give me God above all else, and let Him guide me in all my ways.*
- *God is the King of my kingdom, and I AM His humble servant.*
- *Let all I do reflect the grace, mercy, love, wisdom, generosity, and guidance of the Lord.*

## Prayer:

"O LORD, you have searched me [thoroughly] and have known me.
You know when I sit down and when I rise up [my entire life, everything I do];
You understand my thought from afar.
You scrutinize my path and my lying down,
And You are intimately acquainted with all my ways.
Even before there is a word on my tongue [still unspoken],

Behold, O Lord, You know it all.

You have enclosed me behind and before,

And [You have] placed Your hand upon me.

Such [infinite] knowledge is too wonderful for me;

It is too high [above me], I cannot reach it.

Where can I go from Your Spirit?

Or where can I flee from Your presence?

If I ascend to heaven, You are there;

If I make my bed in Sheol (the nether world, the place of the dead),

behold, You are there.

If I take the wings of the dawn,

If I dwell in the remotest part of the sea,

Even there Your hand will lead me,

And Your right hand will take hold of me.

If I say, "Surely the darkness will cover me,

And the night will be the only light around me,"

Even the darkness is not dark to You and conceals nothing from You,

But the night shines as bright as the day;

Darkness and light are alike to You.

For You formed my innermost parts;

You knit me [together] in my mother's womb.

I will give thanks and praise to You, for I am fearfully and wonder-

fully made;

Wonderful are Your works,

And my soul knows it very well.

My frame was not hidden from You,

When I was being formed in secret,

And intricately and skillfully formed

[as if embroidered with many colors] in the depths of the earth.

Your eyes have seen my unformed substance;

And in Your book were all written

The days that were appointed for me,

When as yet there was not one of them [even taking shape].

How precious also are Your thoughts to me, O God!

How vast is the sum of them!

If I could count them, they would outnumber the sand.
When I awake, I am still with You.
O that You would kill the wicked, O God;
Go away from me, therefore, men of bloodshed.
For they speak against You wickedly,
Your enemies take Your name in vain.
Do I not hate those who hate You, O LORD?
And do I not loathe those who rise up against You?
I hate them with perfect and utmost hatred;
They have become my enemies.
Search me thoroughly, O God, and know my heart;
Test me and know my anxious thoughts;
And see if there is any wicked or hurtful way in me,
And lead me in the everlasting way.
—Psalm 139, King David

### Additional Resources:

*Business for the Glory of God* by Wayne Grudem
*The Millionaire Next Door* by Thomas Stanley
*The Richest Man in Babylon* by George S. Clason
*The Richest Man Who Ever Lived: King Solomon's Secrets to Success,
     Wealth, and Happiness* by Steven K. Scott

# THE THEOLOGIST

The Theologist's mission in life is to know God in profound ways. They read the Scripture and ancient texts that describe the omnipotent presence of God and yearn to know this presence in their life. They believe that man holds the power to attain incredible aspects of our divine authority and seek to claim this in their life. They may be interested in biblical history and archeology. They are incredibly intelligent and study profusely. They have a library of leaders they follow and admire who will assist them in achieving success on their path. They look to God's guidance and realize inspiration and direction come from everywhere, everything, and everyone, despite its appearance. They use life as their teacher and are open to the possibilities and lessons it provides.

They seek balance in all aspects of their life. They have come to a place in their spirituality where they no longer learn lessons in horribly stressful or traumatic ways. Their masculine and feminine energies are balanced as well as their mental, emotional, physical, and spiritual centers. They understand food is nourishing but that God is their health. Instead of running for medicine, they turn to prayer. They are a good-natured person and a happy person who is not easily swayed by problems or drama. They do not become overly invested in the stresses of life such as bills or politics because they know they have no place in God. They do not vent or complain about their problems or give anything negative your prolonged attention.

The Theologist does not like participating in many every day, worldly things and often feels out of place. It may feel difficult to relate with others or care about material things other people care about. They may even find the world depressing and seek to disassociate from it. There are very few who walk the path of the Theologist and even fewer who understand it. The path is straight and narrow, which for many could be lonely, but you take solace in God, who strengthens your communion with Him.

**Most Common Adjacent Spiritual Archetypes:** the Sectarian, the Christian Mystic, the Saint, the Sovereign

**Colors of the Theologist:** white, purple, leather color, beige, blue, gold, silver, rich colors

**When Balanced, You May Feel or Experience:** wisdom, love, peace, synchronicity, joy, divine guidance, spiritual insight, intuition, inspiration, hope, and compassion

**When Unbalanced, You May Feel or Experience:** spiritual cynicism, lack of grounding, inability to manifest, lack of connection to Spirit, depression, helplessness, loss of faith, or anger and frustration toward others' poor choices

**Governs:** brain, pituitary gland, hypothalamus gland, cerebral cortex, nervous system

**Common Physical Ailments:** Tmj; Alzheimer's disease; thyroid and pineal gland disorders; neck and shoulder issues; problems with facial region, including, eyes, nose, mouth; neurological disorders; water retention (edema)

## Correlating Essential Oils:

**Holy Anointing Oil:** Used in the priesthood of Jerusalem, holy oil is one of the most holy oils in the world.

**Frankincense:** Given at the birth of the Lord, frankincense is a symbol of holiness and connection to God.

**Pure Nard:** sacred oil used to clean Jesus' feet

**Myrrh:** Given to baby Jesus as a gift, Myrrh is believed in many cultures to connect Heaven and Earth, which makes a fitting gift to the Savior at His birth.

## Correlating Stones:

The twelve stones that represent the twelve tribes of Israel:

Emerald

Topaz

Ruby (sardius)

Garnet (carbuncle)

Sapphire (ligure or Lapis Lazuli)

Turquoise

Diamond

Agate

Amethyst

Beryl

Onyx

Jasper

## Plants:

**Star of Bethlehem:** purity, hope, faith, happiness, good tidings

**Myrrh:** protection, healing, spirituality, power, strength, vitality

**Olive Tree:** spiritual and religious privilege, beauty, authority, prosperity, Christ

**Power Words:** truth, healing, Holy Spirit, faith, knowledge, authority, dominion, power

## People, Places, and Periods That May Resonate with You:

- **People:** priest, scholar, pharaoh, philosopher, king, queen, knight, crusader, kohen (Jewish priest), Jesuit, Brahman
- **Places:** Jerusalem, England, France, Damascus, Asia, Rome, Turkey
- **Periods:** AD 1095–1291; the First Great Awakening, 1730–1755; the Second Great Awakening, 1790–1840; Azusa Street Revival, 1906–1915; the Welsh revival, 1904–1905

## Correlating Animal: THE DOVE

The dove is a messenger from the Holy Spirit, reminding you of your connection to God. It reminds the Theologist to look at the world with innocence rather than with all the knowledge you have obtained. Knowledge has its place, but it is a mental process; whereas innocence is felt with the heart. Healing and helping others must be done from a heart-centered place. In psychology, the mind is defined as the ego. Therefore, if you attempt to help others with your mind, you will always be allowing ego to enter. Open your heart, not your mind, and you will live in God's consciousness.

## Common Struggles

**Common Triggers:** ignorance, lack of faith, church politics, skeptics, boring faith, being powerless in faith, people believing they are powerless, worldly restrictions

**When Triggered, the Theologist Can Become:** unsympathetic, self-righteous, preachy

**Common Personal Struggles:** Since the Theologist is so highly intellectual, they may find it difficult to turn off their studies and spend time in

the present. They may be so wrapped up in their thoughts and revelations that they ignore or forget the needs of others. One of the daughters of John G. Lake told the story of once being at dinner with her
father when he abruptly stated, "That's how I am going to end my sermon," then hastily left the restaurant, completely forgetting the dinner
and leaving his daughter there without a ride. Although it is not done
maliciously, the Theologist can be detached from their family and loved
ones. They are more comfortable in their mind than in their heart, and
others may feel as though they prefer their work and study over them.

The Theologist also struggles with participating in the world and
may find it archaic and arbitrary. This can breed animosity toward having to function and do things that the Theologist does not understand.
They may become unsympathetic and frustrated as to why others cannot seem to get themselves together. What starts as an empathic desire
for others to succeed may become a lack of compassion.

**Common Spiritual Struggles:** With a profound understanding of God,
life, and reality, the Theologist tends to fall into the trap of being and
acting holier than thou. One of the most common struggles is the
belief that the Theologist has no personal issues or that they do not
need to practice self-reflection. Many Theologists falsely believe they
are only alive and in the world to guide and help others and that they
do not have any issues to work on. This is generally an avoidance
tactic to attempt to outrun one's own problems. After some time
believing this falsity, they may begin to see everyone else as flawed
and start to dissociate from "less enlightened" human beings.

## Mythology, Folklore, Symbolism, or Correlating Story

### AN OLD LEGEND CURRENT IN THE VOLGA DISTRICT
*"And in praying use not vain repetitions, as the Gentiles do: for they think that
they shall be heard for their much speaking. Be not therefore like unto them:
for your Father knoweth what things ye have need of, before ye ask Him."*
—MATTHEW 6:7–8

A bishop was sailing from Archangel to the Solovétsk Monastery, and on the same vessel were a number of pilgrims on their way to visit the shrines at that place. The voyage was a smooth one. The wind favourable, and the weather fair. The pilgrims lay on deck, eating, or sat in groups talking to one another. The Bishop, too, came on deck, and as he was pacing up and down, he noticed a group of men standing near the prow and listening to a fisherman, who was pointing to the sea and telling them something. The Bishop stopped and looked in the direction in which the man was pointing. He could see nothing, however, but the sea glistening in the sunshine. He drew nearer to listen, but when the man saw him, he took off his cap and was silent. The rest of the people also took off their caps and bowed.

"Do not let me disturb you, friends," said the Bishop. "I came to hear what this good man was saying."

"The fisherman was telling us about the hermits," replied one, a tradesman, rather bolder than the rest.

"What hermits?" asked the Bishop, going to the side of the vessel and seating himself on a box. "Tell me about them. I should like to hear. What were you pointing at?"

"Why, that little island you can just see over there," answered the man, pointing to a spot ahead and a little to the right. "That is the island where the hermits live for the salvation of their souls."

"Where is the island?" asked the Bishop. "I see nothing."

"There, in the distance, if you will please look along my hand. Do you see that little cloud? Below it and a bit to the left, there is just a faint streak. That is the island."

The Bishop looked carefully, but his unaccustomed eyes could make out nothing but the water shimmering in the sun. "I cannot see it," he said. "But who are the hermits that live there?"

"They are holy men," answered the fisherman. "I had long heard tell of them, but never chanced to see them myself till the year before last."

And the fisherman related how once, when he was out fishing, he had been stranded at night upon that island, not knowing where he was. In the morning, as he wandered about the island, he came across an earth hut and met an old man standing near it. Presently, two others came out, and after having fed him, and dried his things, they helped him mend his boat.

"And what are they like?" asked the Bishop.

"One is a small man and his back is bent. He wears a priest's cassock and is very old; he must be more than a hundred, I should say. He is so old that the white of his beard is taking a greenish tinge, but he is always smiling, and his face is as bright as an angel's from heaven. The second is taller, but he also is very old. He wears tattered, peasant coat. His beard is broad, and of a yellowish- grey colour. He is a strong man. Before I had time to help him, he turned my boat over as if it were only a pail. He, too, is kindly and cheerful. The third is tall, and has a beard as white as snow and reaching to his knees. He is stern, with over-hanging eyebrows, and he wears nothing but a mat tied round his waist."

"And did they speak to you?" asked the Bishop.

"For the most part they did everything in silence and spoke but little even to one another. One of them would just give a glance, and the others would understand him. I asked the tallest whether they had lived there long. He frowned, and muttered something as if he were angry; but the oldest one took his hand and smiled, and then the tall one was quiet. The oldest one only said: 'Have mercy upon us,' and smiled."

While the fisherman was talking, the ship had drawn nearer to the island. "There, now you can see it plainly, if your Grace will please to look," said the tradesman, pointing with his hand.

The Bishop looked, and now he really saw a dark streak, which was the island. Having looked at it a while, he left the prow of the vessel, and going to the stern, asked the helmsman, "What island is that?"

"That one," replied the man, "has no name. There are many such in this sea."

"Is it true that there are hermits who live there for the salvation of their souls?"

"So it is said, your Grace, but I don't know if it's true. Fishermen say they have seen them; but of course they may only be spinning yarns."

"I should like to land on the island and see these men," said the Bishop. "How could I manage it?"

"The ship cannot get close to the island," replied the helmsman, "but you might be rowed there in a boat. You had better speak to the captain."

The captain was sent for and came.

"I should like to see these hermits," said the Bishop. "Could I not be rowed ashore?"

The captain tried to dissuade him. "Of course, it could be done," said he, "but we should lose much time. And if I might venture to say so to your Grace, the old men are not worth your pains. I have heard say that they are foolish old fellows, who understand nothing, and never speak a word, any more than the fish in the sea."

"I wish to see them," said the Bishop, "and I will pay you for your trouble and loss of time. Please, let me have a boat."

There was no help for it, so the order was given. The sailors trimmed the sails, the steersman put up the helm, and the ships course was set for the island. A chair was placed at the prow for the Bishop, and he sat there, looking ahead. The passengers all collected at the prow and gazed at the island. Those who had the sharpest eyes could presently make out the rocks on it, and then a mud hut was seen. At last, one man saw the hermits themselves. The captain brought a telescope and, after looking through it, handed it to the Bishop.

"It's right enough. There are three men standing on the shore. There, a little to the right of that big rock."

The Bishop took the telescope, got it into position, and he saw the three men: a tall one, a shorter one, and one very small and bent, standing on the shore and holding each other by the hand.

The captain turned to the Bishop. "The vessel can get no nearer in than this, your Grace. If you wish to go ashore, we must ask you to go in the boat, while we anchor here."

The cable was quickly let out, the anchor cast, and the sails furled. There was a jerk, and the vessel shook. Then a boat having been lowered, the oarsmen jumped in, and the Bishop descended the ladder and took his seat. The men pulled at their oars, and the boat moved rapidly towards the island. When they came within a stone's throw, they saw three old men: a tall one with only a mat tied round his waist: a shorter one in a tattered peasant coat, and a very old one bent with age and wearing an old cassock—all three standing hand in hand.

The oarsmen pulled in to the shore, and held on with the boat-hook while the Bishop got out. The old men bowed to him, and he gave them his benediction, at which they bowed still lower. Then the Bishop began to speak to them, "I have heard," he said, "that you, godly men, live here saving your own souls, and praying to our Lord Christ for your fellow men. I, an unworthy servant of Christ, am called, by God's mercy, to keep and teach His flock. I wished to see you, servants of God, and to do what I can to teach you, also."

The old men looked at each other, smiling, but remained silent.

"Tell me," said the Bishop, "what you are doing to save your souls, and how you serve God on this island?"

The second hermit sighed, and looked at the oldest, the very ancient one. The latter smiled, and said: "We do not know how to serve God. We only serve and support ourselves, servant of God."

"But how do you pray to God?" asked the Bishop.

"We pray in this way," replied the hermit. "Three are ye, three are we, have mercy upon us."

And when the old man said this, all three raised their eyes to heaven, and repeated: "Three are ye, three are we, have mercy upon us!"

The Bishop smiled. "You have evidently heard something about the Holy Trinity," said he. "But you do not pray aright. You have won my affection, godly men. I see you wish to please the Lord, but you do not know how to serve Him. That is not the way to pray; but listen to me, and I will teach you. I will teach you, not a way of my own, but the way in which God in the Holy Scriptures has commanded all men to pray to Him."

And the Bishop began explaining to the hermits how God had revealed Himself to men; telling them of God the Father, and God the Son, and God the Holy Ghost. "God the Son came down on earth," said he, "to save men, and this is how He taught us all to pray. Listen and repeat after me: 'Our Father.'"

And the first old man repeated after him, "Our Father." And the second said, "Our Father." And the third said, "Our Father."

"Which art in heaven," continued the Bishop.

The first hermit repeated, "Which art in heaven." But the second blundered over the words, and the tall hermit could not say them properly. His hair had grown over his mouth so that he could not speak plainly. The very old hermit, having no teeth, also mumbled indistinctly.

The Bishop repeated the words again, and the old men repeated them after him. The Bishop sat down on a stone, and the old men stood before him, watching his mouth, and repeating the words as he uttered them. And all day long the Bishop laboured, saying a word twenty, thirty, a hundred times over, and the old men repeated it after him. They blundered, and he corrected them, and made them begin again.

The Bishop did not leave off till he had taught them the whole of the Lord's prayer so that they could not only repeat it after him, but could say it by themselves. The middle one was the first to know it, and to repeat the whole of it alone. The Bishop made him say it again and again, and at last the others could say it too.

It was getting dark, and the moon was appearing over the water, before the Bishop rose to return to the vessel. When he took leave of the old men, they all bowed down to the ground before him. He raised them, and kissed each of them, telling them to pray as he had taught them. Then he got into the boat and returned to the ship.

And as he sat in the boat and was rowed to the ship, he could hear the three voices of the hermits loudly repeating the Lord's prayer. As the boat drew near the vessel, their voices could no longer be heard, but they could still be seen in the moonlight, standing as he had left them on the shore, the shortest in the middle, the tallest on the right, the middle one on the left. As soon as the Bishop had reached the vessel and got on board, the anchor was weighed and the sails unfurled. The wind filled them, and the ship sailed away, and the Bishop took a seat in the stern and watched the island they had left. For a time, he could still see the hermits, but presently they disappeared from sight, though the island was still visible. At last, it too vanished, and only the sea was to be seen, rippling in the moonlight.

The pilgrims lay down to sleep, and all was quiet on deck. The Bishop did not wish to sleep, but sat alone at the stern, gazing at the sea where the island was no longer visible, and thinking of the good old men. He thought how pleased they had been to learn the Lord's prayer; and he thanked God for having sent him to teach and help such godly men.

So the Bishop sat, thinking, and gazing at the sea where the island had disappeared. And the moonlight flickered before his eyes, sparkling, now here, now there, upon the waves. Suddenly he saw something white and shining, on the bright path which the moon cast across the sea. Was it a seagull, or the little gleaming sail of some small boat? The Bishop fixed his eyes on it, wondering. "It must be a boat sailing after us," thought he. "But it is overtaking us very rapidly. It was far, far away a minute ago, but now it is much nearer. It cannot be a boat, for I can see no sail; but whatever it may be, it is following us, and catching us up."

And he could not make out what it was. Not a boat, nor a bird, nor a fish! It was too large for a man, and besides a man could not be out there in the midst of the sea. The Bishop rose, and said to the helmsman: "Look there, what is that, my friend? What is it?" the Bishop repeated, though he could now see plainly what it was—the three hermits running upon the water, all gleaming white, their grey beards shining, and approaching the ship as quickly as though it were not morning.

The steersman looked and let go of the helm in terror. "Oh Lord! The hermits are running after us on the water as though it were dry land!"

The passengers hearing him, jumped up, and crowded to the stern. They saw the hermits coming along hand in hand, and the two outer ones beckoning the ship to stop. All three were gliding along upon the water without moving their feet. Before the ship could be stopped, the hermits had reached it, and raising their heads, all three as with one voice began to say: "We have forgotten your teaching, servant of God. As long as we kept repeating it we remembered, but when we stopped saying it for a time, a word dropped out, and now it has all gone to pieces. We can remember nothing of it. Teach us again."

The Bishop crossed himself, and leaning over the ship's side, said, "Your own prayer will reach the Lord, men of God. It is not for me to teach you. Pray for us sinners." And the Bishop bowed low before the old men; and they turned and went back across the sea. And a light shone until daybreak on the spot where they were lost to sight.

## Spiritual Guidance:

Sometimes The Theologist focuses on one aspect of spirituality or spiritual practice and teaches that as the way. They can become narrow-minded and see their area of study as better. However, God speaks to and communes with everyone in His own way. As long as it is scripturally sound, The Theologist should recognize and be open to all of God's ways.

Additionally, The Theologist is a part of this world, and as such, they are a part of the collective. Whether or not you have an enlightened understanding of God, you are also here to heal, grow, and accept your divine rights and authority. The Theologist can be a helpful leader, guiding and supporting others, but we all have a mission and purpose, which includes our healing, initiations, and soul's path.

## Affirmations:

- *I AM the power, wisdom, and love of God. I AM, I AM, I AM.*
- *I accept the healing power of God and accept my divine inheritance through Him.*
- *I AM open and receptive to the Word of God and am a mouthpiece for His word.*

## Prayer:

"God, thank You for Your divine love, guidance, and abundance. I AM a vessel for You and ask that Your will be done through me always. May I share Your Word, healing, and love with the world."

## Additional Resources:

*The Bible*
*A Common Sense Guide To Fasting* by Kenneth Hagin
*God, the Substance of All Forms* by Joel S. Goldsmith
*High Mysticism: A Series of Twelve Studies in the Wisdom of the Sages of the Ages* by Emma Curtis Hopkins
*The Great Physician* by Ernest C. Wilson
*The Healing Secrets of the Ages* by Catherine Ponder
*The Knowledge of the Holy* by A. W. Tozer
*The Pilgrim's Progress* by John Bunyan
*Science and Health with Key to the Scriptures* by Mary Baker Eddy

# THE HIDDEN PATHS

The hidden paths are Spiritual Archetypes that are not consciously participating in their spiritual path. As stated at the beginning of the book, we are all on a spiritual path regardless of whether we are aware of it or not. Since spirituality is all-inclusive, these paths are still included even though they do not appear as robust as the primary Spiritual Archetypes.

The hidden paths differ slightly from the primary Spiritual Archetypes in a couple of ways. The hidden paths are considered paths that have not yet converged onto a full primary spiritual path. People who are currently aware of, or intentionally practicing their spirituality will resonate with more specific Spiritual Archetypes and be more consciously aware of themselves and their spiritual path. Those who are unaware of their spirituality will be on a path that is seemingly not spiritual at all. This will continue until they find themselves through one or multiple paths. Because of this, these hidden paths do not include all of the same information as the Spiritual Archetypes. As they journey on their path, they will find themselves in one of the primary Spiritual Archetypes.

The hidden paths are in no way inferior to the Spiritual Archetypes and should not be viewed as such. In fact, some of the most devout, faithful, and holy people in history spent many years on the hidden paths and after having revelation excelled exponentially in their Spiritual Archetypes. Spirituality should never be measured by the quantity of time we have practiced but should be measured by the quality of time. Therefore, if you find yourself on one of the hidden paths, you are at the beginning of your quest and can fully devote yourself from here. The more you devote your mind, heart, and soul, the more growth, faith, and miracles you will experience. Let God be your guide, guru, and teacher, and a path will always be made for you.

# THE ILLUSIONIST

The most common Spiritual Archetype in the world, coincidently, has no idea they are even on a spiritual path. The Illusionist is what is referred to as being "asleep." They are asleep to the awareness of their spiritual self, and have little to no understanding of God, or of the universe conducting itself around them. They are adherent to the illusion that things are simply what they are and ignorant to the meaning and divinity of God. They may believe there is a God, be an atheist, have been raised with God, or know people that believe in God, but they themselves do not have a passion, desire, or personal drive to pursue a relationship with Him. The goal of the Illusionist is sensation and gratification. They seek to survive, and survive well, with superficial desires. Money, sex, thrills, entertainment, and pleasure are among their priorities. However, many Illusionists seek to suffer well, living with what is familiar regardless of how unpleasant, painful, or boring it may be. People who are unaware of their path are commonly referred to as being "asleep." This term has been referenced in various ways by many cultures, poems, and sayings such as Edgar Allen Poe's famous quote "All that we see or seem is but a dream within a dream." However, the term was popularized by A Course in Miracles, which states that Adam was put into a deep sleep in the Garden of Eden and that everything following was his dream. People who are asleep do not know or understand their cocreating abilities, their power as a soul, or their possibility of being created in the image and likeness of God. Most of the world is in a state of being asleep and living without any extensive investment into personal or spiritual growth. The Illusionist is mystified into believing they are powerless humans. Their mindset is essentially that the only certainties in life are death and taxes. They prefer cold, hard facts over faith and are more apt to listen to and obey science, statistics, and media over their own intuition, guidance, or faith. They feel disconnected from their inner man or soul, God, and their spiritual path.

**Colors of the Illusionist:** neutral colors, black, white, gray, anything popular or trendy.

**When Balanced, You May Feel or Experience:** empowered, alive, motivated, inspired, lucky, rich, successful

**When Unbalanced You May Feel or Experience:** stressed, like a hamster on a wheel, helpless, unmotivated, lackluster, worried, superficial, angry

**Governs:** genitals, back, heart, immune system

**Common Physical Ailments:** cancer, heart disease, depression, anxiety, stress, high blood pressure.

## Correlating Essential Oils:

**Rosemary:** Clears mental fogginess and mental fatigue.
**Black Spruce:** Strengthens the spirit and life force.
**Spikenard:** Spiritual connection, cleansing of physical self and anointing of spiritual self
**Cedarwood:** Personal power and strength, faith, purification

## Correlating Stones:

**Labradorite:** Inner peace, awakening, transformation, strengthening of personal will.

**Sardonyx:** Stamina, stability, self-control.

**Angelite:** Spiritual and personal purpose, spiritual awareness.

**Howlite:** Stimulates the desire for learning and knowledge, which is beneficial to the Illusionist who can use their newfound information to begin consciously walking on their spiritual path

## Correlating Plants:

- **Lavender:** Promotes peace, ease, and harmony of breath.
- **Holy Basil:** Relieves depression, balances hormones, balances heart and mind.
- **Palma christi(Castor Oil):** also known as the Palm of Christ, castor oil is one of the most healing oils in the world.
- **Mustard:** "And Jesus said unto them, Because of your unbelief: for verily I say unto you, If ye have faith as a grain of mustard seed, ye shall say unto this mountain, Remove hence to yonder place; and it shall remove; and nothing shall be impossible unto you." (Mark 17:20)

**Power Words:** believe, seek, allow, surrender, receive, faith, leap, trust, know, awaken

## Correlating Animal: THE VULTURE

The vulture is a bird that symbolizes scavenging and selfishly and aggressively taking care of one's own needs. The vulture spends its life looking at when it can take and thrive off of the misfortunes of others. This is not to say that everyone who is considered asleep is bad or acts badly. People can still be kind and loving even in the asleep state. Instead, it refers to the desperation that people feel, especially when they have no spiritual center. The world is focused on promoting desperation and wanting to feel desperate. The feeling of desperation creates reliance on authority, which gives power to those in that position. If people are afraid and desperate, they are easily controlled, which is the motive of those who seek power. Their greatest fear would be a global spiritual awakening that strips their authority by claiming our own. When we feel desperate and afraid, we can act in animalistic ways, and like the vulture, scavenge to meet our own needs.

However, the turkey vulture, a specific kind of vulture, is seen as a sign of adaptability, new opportunities, cleansing, and innovation. If the Illusionist can lean into the medicine of the turkey vulture, then they are no longer operating in the scavenger energy of the vulture. Instead of living as a scavenger, they can cleanse themselves of worldly desires and move into the more enlightened part of themselves, thus creating more enlightened situations, opportunities, and responses to life and its circumstances.

## Common Struggles

**Common Triggers:** work, money, relationships, health, life, television, the news

**When Triggered, the Illusionist Can Become:** angry, irrational, and superficial

**Common Personal Struggles:** The Illusionist is like the story of Mephibosheth, grandson of Saul. "Jonathan, Saul's son, had a son that was lame of his feet. He was five years old when the tidings came of Saul and Jonathan out of Jezreel, and his nurse took him up, and fled: and it came to pass, as she made haste to flee, that he fell, and became lame. And his name was Mephibosheth." (2 Samuel 4)

"Now when Mephibosheth, the son of Jonathan, the son of Saul, was come unto David, he fell on his face, and did reverence. And David said, Mephibosheth. And he answered, Behold thy servant! And David said unto him, Fear not: for I will surely shew thee kindness for Jonathan thy father's sake, and will restore thee all the land of Saul thy father; and thou shalt eat bread at my table continually. And he bowed himself, and said, What is thy servant, that thou shouldest look upon such a dead dog as I am? Then the king called to Ziba, Saul's servant, and said unto him, I have given unto thy master's son all that pertained to Saul and to all his house. Thou therefore, and thy sons, and thy servants, shall till the land for him, and thou shalt bring in the fruits, that thy master's son may have food to eat: but Mephibosheth thy master's son shall eat bread alway at my table. Now Ziba had fifteen sons and twenty servants. Then said Ziba unto the king, According to all that my lord the king hath commanded his servant, so shall thy servant do. As for Mephibosheth, said the king, he shall eat at my table, as one of the king's sons. And Mephibosheth had a young son, whose name was Micha. And all that dwelt in the house of Ziba were servants unto Mephibosheth. So Mephibosheth dwelt in Jerusalem: for he did eat continually at the king's table; and was lame on both his feet." (2 Samuel 9: 6–13)

The Illusionist sees themselves like Mephibosheth, not worthy of eating at a king's table, yet they do not see that they are heirs to the kingdom of God. They are willing to accept so little because they do not know they are capable of inheriting so much.

The Illusionist is essentially powerless in their life because they do not know or realize the power they have as spiritual beings. This means their life, energy, purpose, and communication are constantly in disconnect and misalignment, which manifests in their relationships, finances, personal self, and health. When we are disconnected from our inner man (spiritual self and soul), there is a feeling of stress, anxiety, tension, and feeling frazzled with our energy. Since they are, in many ways, accustomed to being comfortably numb, they do not necessary understand what is happening; they only know they do not feel their best and that feeling great may be a distant memory if a conscious memory at all.

In the film *Excalibur*, King Arthur discovers that his wife, Queen Guinevere, and his dearest friend and Knight, Lancelot, have had an affair. He is heartbroken and goes into a deep depression. His kingdom falls apart and he is inconsolable. The Knights of the Round Table set out on a life-threatening spiritual quest to retrieve the Holy Grail, in hopes that it will revive their king. When the knight Perceval returns with the goblet, he puts it to the mouth of King Arthur, who drinks the water from it. King Arthur awakens as if from a dream and says to Perceval, "I didn't know how empty was my soul . . . until it was filled." The Illusionist does not realize the emptiness they feel until they are refilled when they come to their spiritual path through revelation and spiritual awakening. It is as if they live in a dream, (or nightmare) unaware of why they are empty, or why certain themes, blocks, or problems keep showing up.

**Common Spiritual Struggles:** Since the Illusionist is not actively participating in their spiritual path, they tend to have various spiritual issues. Firstly, they lack any solid belief structure, which means they lack any solid spiritual beliefs. This means that their life, relationships, sense of self, work, and worldview all consist of going through the motions but not fulfilling these to the fullest. We are, by design, spiritual beings in a physical world. To live in the world operating as only part of ourselves, (the weaker and finite part of ourselves) greatly reduces the potency and quality we produce. By waking from their sleep, they awaken to not only their purpose but their ability to cocreate and live to the fullest.

## Spiritual Guidance

God is always willing to embrace us, eager for us to lay our burdens down and hopeful that we will surrender our lives to living the path we are meant to live. God is delighted when we leave our hurtful ways and accept a seat at his table. God loves you. He is a loving father who wants to have a relationship with you, support you, connect with you, and be there for you. The Illusionist often feels like "If there is a God, why would he care about me?" Because God is impassioned for his children. He would and will do anything for his children. One of the most famous scriptures is Matthew 18:12–14, which says, "If a man have an hundred sheep, and one of them be gone astray, doth he not leave the ninety and nine, and goeth into the mountains, and seeketh that which is gone astray? And if so be that he find it, verily I say unto you, he rejoiceth more of that sheep, than of the ninety and nine which went not astray. Even so it is not the will of your Father which is in heaven, that one of these little ones should perish."

Just the same, God will divide heaven and earth for the one child who needs him and calls out to him. If you are new to faith, have never had a relationship with God and are desperate for one, I invite you to learn about God's love and his will for you. This can be one of the most beneficial cornerstones to beginning a relationship with God and beginning a more intentional and fulfilling spiritual path.

### Affirmations:

- *I am a spiritual being in a material world.*
- *I am awakening to the possibilities of my spiritual self.*
- *I have power and authority over my life.*

### Prayer:

"Dear Lord Jesus, I know that I am a sinner, and I ask for Your forgiveness. I believe You died for my sins and rose from the dead. I turn from my sins and invite You to come into my heart and life. I want to trust and follow You as my Lord and Savior. In Your Name. Amen."
(The Sinner's Prayer or Prayer of Salvation as said by Billy Graham)

### Scriptures:

- "No one born of God makes a practice of sinning, for God's seed abides in him, and he cannot keep on sinning because he has been born of God" (1 John 3:9).
- "For God so loved the world, that he gave his only Son, that whoever believes in him should not perish but have eternal life" (John 3:16).
- "If anyone destroys God's temple, God will destroy him. For God's temple is holy, and you are that temple" (1 Corinthians 3:17).

- "Be not conformed to this world: but be ye transformed by the renewing of your mind, that ye may prove what is that good, and acceptable, and perfect, will of God" (Romans 12:2).
- "For all that is in the world, the lust of the flesh, and the lust of the eyes, and the pride of life, is not of the Father, but is of the world" (1 John 2:16).

## Additional Rescources

*A Course in Miracles* by Helen Schucman
*God's Creative Power Collection* by Charles Capps
*Happy for No Reason* by Marci Shimoff
*The Holy Spirit: Activating God's Power in Your* Life by Billy Graham
*The Secret* by Rhonda Byrne

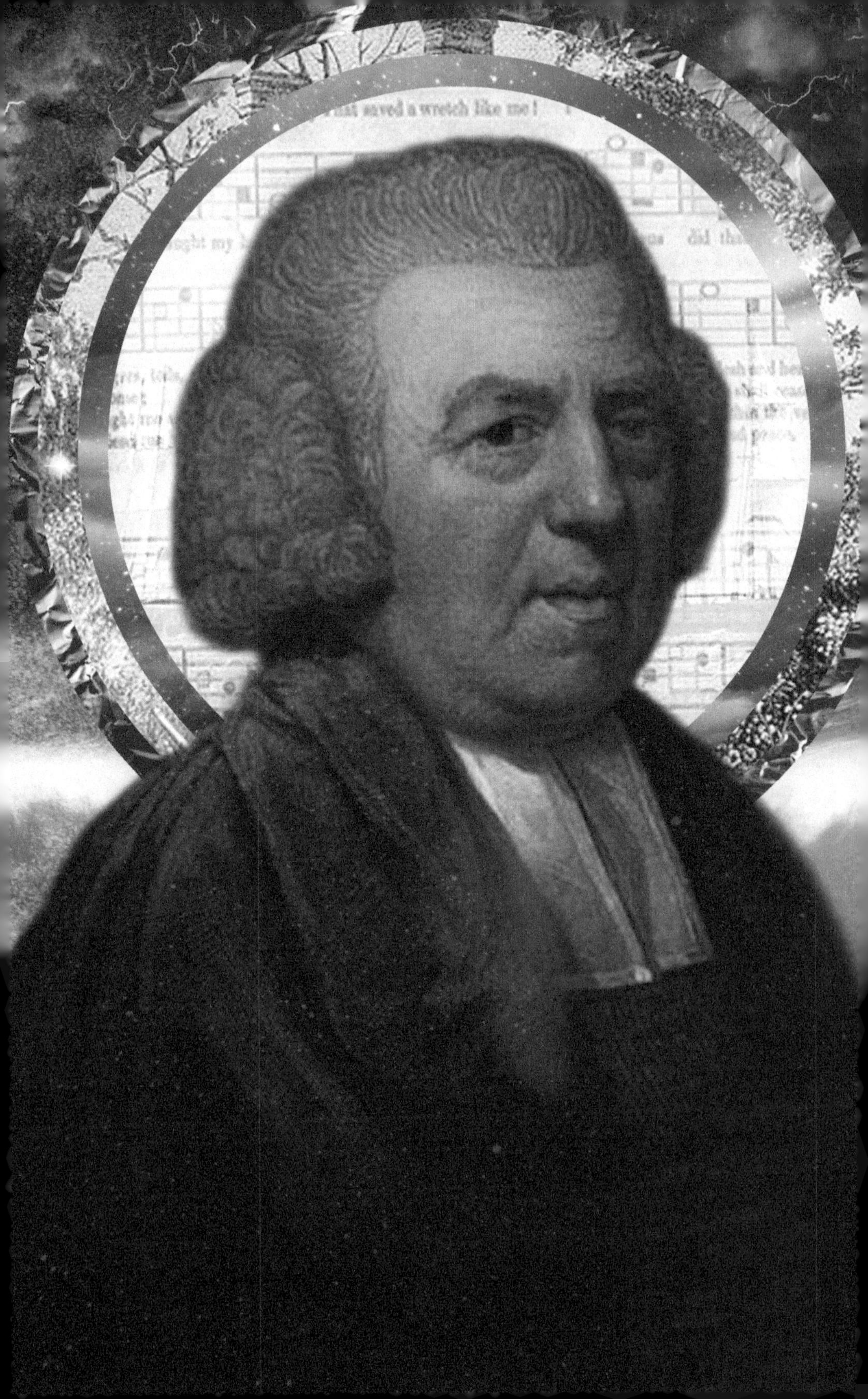
saved a wretch like me!

# THE DOUBTING THOMAS

The Doubting Thomas is the Spiritual Archetype who would be considered an atheist or unbeliever. They are not "asleep" or unaware of the spiritual world, rather they are usually well-educated and intelligent and have purposely and consciously chosen not to pursue a spiritual path. They do not like religion and spirituality and usually have well-thought-out, intellectual, arguments for anyone who does. They believe in science, evidence, proof, and seeing it to believe it.

However, the Doubting Thomas is one to reckon with. Thomas was an apostle of Jesus who doubted that Jesus had risen from the dead, despite hearing it from all of the others apostles. "Now Thomas, called the Twin, one of the twelve, was not with them when Jesus came. The other disciples therefore said to him, "We have seen the Lord." So he said to them, "Unless I see in His hands the print of the nails, and put my finger into the print of the nails, and put my hand into His side, I will not believe." And after eight days His disciples were again inside, and Thomas with them. Jesus came, the doors being shut, and stood in the midst, and said, "Peace to you!" Then He said to Thomas, "Reach your finger here, and look at My hands; and reach your hand *here*, and put *it* into My side. Do not be unbelieving, but believing." And Thomas answered and said to Him, "My Lord and my God!" Jesus said to him, "Thomas, because you have seen Me, you have believed. Blessed *are* those who have not seen and *yet* have believed." (John 20:24-29 NKJV)

While Thomas was doubtful and insisted on proof before he would believe, once he did believe he became one of the most faithful, loyal, and devoted of the apostles. He wrote *The Gospel of Thomas*, which is one of the most heartfelt and loving books of the Bible. When he had proof, he was unshakable in his faith. Once the Doubting Thomas has faith, it is profound and can change the world.

**Colors of the Doubting Thomas:** black, gray, white

**When Balanced, You May Feel or Experience:** articulate, eloquent, educated, intelligent

**When Unbalanced, You May Feel or Experience:** scattered, angry, judgmental, fearful, rude, abrasive

**Governs:** brain, kidneys, endocrine system, respiratory system

**Common Physical Ailments:** Cancer, weak kidneys or kidney failure, lung issues such as restrictions in breathing, pneumonia, and pulmonary edema, anxiety

## Correlating Essential Oils:

**Chamomile:** Depression, anger, anxiety
**Jasmine:** Overthinking, racing thoughts, calming the mind.
**Geranium:** Self-love, self-healing, calming of the nervous system

## Correlating Stones:

**Amethyst:** humility, truthfulness, healing

**Kunzite:** Surrendering resistance, opening the heart, emotion
**Rhodonite:** healing emotional wounds, open-mindedness, healing and releasing the past

### Correlating Plants:

- **Milkweed:** Spiritual resilience, perseverance, and identity
- **Rue:** Symbolizes regret and repentance
- **Honesty:** aka Lunaria annua represents sincerity and alchemy

**Power Words:** forgiveness, humility, compassion, understanding, love, awareness

### Correlating Animal: THE WHALE

The book of Jonah and the Whale tells the story of a man chosen by God who, overwhelmed by God's purpose for him, attempts to escape.

*"Jonah rose up to flee unto Tarshish from the presence of the Lord, and went down to Joppa; and he found a ship going to Tarshish: so he paid the fare thereof, and went down into it, to go with them unto Tarshish from the presence of the Lord. But the Lord sent out a great wind into the sea, and there was a mighty tempest in the sea, so that the ship was like to be broken. Then the mariners were afraid, and cried every man unto his god, and cast forth the wares that were in the ship into the sea, to lighten it of them. But Jonah was gone down into the sides of the ship; and he lay, and was fast asleep. So the shipmaster came to him, and said unto him, What meanest thou, O sleeper? arise, call upon thy God, if so be that God will think upon us, that we perish not. And they said everyone to his fellow, Come, and let us cast lots, that we may know for whose cause this evil is upon us. So they cast lots, and the lot fell upon Jonah. Then said they unto him, Tell us, we pray thee, for whose cause this evil is upon us; What is thine occupation? and whence comest thou? what is thy country? and of what people art thou? And he said unto them, I am an Hebrew; and I fear the Lord, the God of*

*heaven, which hath made the sea and the dry land. Then were the men exceedingly afraid, and said unto him. Why hast thou done this? For the men knew that he fled from the presence of the Lord, because he had told them. Then said they unto him, What shall we do unto thee, that the sea may be calm unto us? for the sea wrought, and was tempestuous. And he said unto them, Take me up, and cast me forth into the sea; so shall the sea be calm unto you: for I know that for my sake this great tempest is upon you. Nevertheless, the men rowed hard to bring it to the land; but they could not: for the sea wrought, and was tempestuous against them. Wherefore they cried unto the Lord, and said, We beseech thee, O Lord, we beseech thee, let us not perish for this man's life, and lay not upon us innocent blood: for thou, O Lord, hast done as it pleased thee. So they took up Jonah, and cast him forth into the sea: and the sea ceased from her raging. Then the men feared the Lord exceedingly, and offered a sacrifice unto the Lord, and made vows. (Jonah 1: 3-17)*

*"Now the Lord had prepared a great fish to swallow up Jonah. And Jonah was in the belly of the fish three days and three nights. Then Jonah prayed unto the Lord his God out of the fish's belly, And said, I cried by reason of mine affliction unto the Lord, and he heard me; out of the belly of hell cried I, and thou heardest my voice. For thou hadst cast me into the deep, in the midst of the seas; and the floods compassed me about: all thy billows and thy waves passed over me. Then I said, I am cast out of thy sight; yet I will look again toward thy holy temple. The waters compassed me about, even to the soul: the depth closed me round about, the weeds were wrapped about my head. I went down to the bottoms of the mountains; the earth with her bars was about me for ever: yet hast thou brought up my life from corruption, O Lord my God. When my soul fainted within me I remembered the Lord: and my prayer came in unto thee, into thine holy temple." (Jonah 2: 1-7)*

Like Jonah, the Doubting Thomas has fled from God, either knowingly and intentionally or ignorantly. The Doubting Thomas has attempted to live without God's word, or has walked away from the path God has intended for them.

## Common Struggles

**Common Triggers:** religion, suffering, blind faith, preaching, being made a fool of

**When Triggered, the Doubting Thomas Can Become:** rude, offensive, abrasive, crude, condescending, and pessimistic.

**Common Personal Struggles:** The Doubting Thomas most often comes to their unbelief through pain, hardship, and suffering. Through their trauma and heartache, they turn away from God and resent those who rely on faith. They may also see suffering in the world and, unable to reconcile how God allows the evils that exist, conclude that there is no God.

**Common Spiritual Struggles:** The Doubting Thomas is not just an unbeliever. There is a part of them that believes but they are angry at the loss, hurt, and sorrow they have felt in their life and blame God for not being there. Sometimes it is easier to tell oneself that there is no God than to try to understand what has happened and why.

Additionally, there is a long history of religious fanatics, cults, and trauma caused by religion and spirituality. For some, this can appear as though the root of evil is religion itself, which is not true. For example, money, like religion is not a living, breathing life. It is a thing, that has neither thought nor motive. Yet, people say "Money is the root of all evil." However, it is not money itself that is evil; it is the power people give it and the way they abuse it that makes it evil. Similarly, religion is not evil. But fear, lust for power, greed, and ignorance, are dangerous. This is an excellent example of why people should be educated in their faith, and a perfect reason to turn to learning more, rather than running from it.

## Mythology, Folklore, Symbolism, or Correlating Story:

John Newton was born on August 4, 1725 in Wapping, London. His father was a shipmaster and his mother was a devout and religious woman who taught John the Bible and prayed with him every night. At the age of seven years, his mother died of tuberculosis and he was sent to live in a boarding school. His religion and relationship with God ended at this time.

In 1743, he was captured by the Royal Navy and forced into imprisoned service. When he tried to escape, he was beaten and tortured in front of hundreds of his fellow naval officers. The abuse and imprisonment made him consider suicide but he did not and was transferred to another ship. His shipmates on the new ship did not like him and left him during a trip to Africa. He was given to an African slave dealer, who gave him to his wife, Princess Peye, who abused and tortured him. He was rescued about a year later by a friend of his father and returned home to England. Thereafter, he became the captain of slave ships over several years.

After years of slavery, abuse, and mistreatment, John Newton understandably became a hardened man. He described himself as a wretched man who was arrogant, reckless, and sinful. He once said, "I sinned with a high hand," he wrote, "and I made it my study to tempt and seduce others." He cursed, drank, and lived debaucherously. He relished embarrassing and harassing people who believed in and spoke about God and was considered the model of an atheist.

Then, on March 21, 1748, John Newton was sleeping aboard a ship on the North Atlantic when he awoke to a violent storm. He described it as a terrible tempest that crashed down wave after wave, tossing the ship around aimlessly. Despite their best efforts, and a life at sea, John Newton knew that they were all going to die in the storm. With his last effort he cried out, "Please, God, I know that I am a terrible sinner. No man has ever deserved Your mercy less than I do, but I beg You to help me!" Almost instantly the howl of wind died down and his shipmate informed them that somehow, the storm was passing. John Newton whispered, "Thank you, Father."

In 1772, he wrote about his experience living without God and what God's love and grace did for him, in what has become one of the most famous songs in history, "Amazing Grace."

*Amazing Grace, how sweet the sound*
*That saved a wretch like me*

*I once was lost, but now am found*
*Was blind but now I see*

*Was Grace that taught my heart to fear*
*And Grace, my fears relieved*
*How precious did that Grace appear*
*The hour I first believed*

*Through many dangers, toils and snares*
*We have already come*
*T'was Grace that brought us safe thus far*
*And Grace will lead us home*
*And Grace will lead us home*

*Amazing Grace, how sweet the sound*
*That saved a wretch like me*
*I once was lost but now am found*
*Was blind but now I see*

*Was blind, but now I see*

## Spiritual Guidance:

The Doubting Thomas is angry toward the people, religions, intuitions, or circumstances that have hurt them. This anger festers within us and creates unforgiveness that can be looked at or examined. When we release the fear and anger, we make space for the authentic God within us.

Forgiveness is the conscious act of releasing and surrendering a story that does not serve us. It is the letting go of a story between two or more souls and seeing the Go(o)d in the situation.

For every ailment you have, or any dissatisfaction you feel in your life, there is someone, somewhere you have not forgiven, which may also include yourself. Hatred and resentment fester in our minds and become physical manifestations in our bodies. Forgiveness alone can change the physical symptoms a person is experiencing and the lack they experience in their life. From money to health, forgiveness is a key that unlocks our wealth and abundance.

When it comes to forgiveness, we generally believe we can simply forgive the people of our choosing or the ones we believe to be deserving of our forgiveness. However, forgiveness is not discriminatory. The true practice and art of forgiveness is to forgive anyone, or anything, whom we feel has ever wronged us, hurt us, slighted us, or that we have had ill will toward. In his book, *A Sure Remedy*, Charles Fillmore, co-founder of the Unity movement, states,

"If you fear or if you are prejudiced against even an animal, mentally ask forgiveness of it and send it thoughts of love. If you have accused anyone of injustice, if you have discussed anyone unkindly, if you have criticized or gossiped about anyone, withdraw your words by asking him, in silence, to forgive you. If you have had a falling out with friends or relatives, if you are at law, or engaged in contention with anyone, do everything in your power to end the separation. See all things and all persons as they really are—pure Spirit—and send them your strongest thoughts of love."

True, deep forgiveness may take some time. We may have hatred and judgment on subconscious levels we are completely unaware of. But as you begin to forgive and persist in your forgiveness you will begin to realize just how many people you have persecuted in your mind. As they begin to surface you can simultaneously forgive and release them. If any negative thought or feeling toward another arises, you can practice this and may possibly even need to revisit people who feel you have already forgiven. When we are finally able to forgive our scariest demons, we release them from our path as well as release ourselves from the chains that bind us to them. By forgiving and letting go of our biggest assailants, we can finally break free of their stranglehold and the negative effects they emanate into our life and renounce their power. When we see the God within each person, we also honor the God within ourselves When this occurs, we are officially looking at others through the lens of God, rather than with our human mind.

## Affirmations:

- *I forgive all who have hurt, judged, or persecuted me, and I forgive all those whom I have hurt judged or persecuted.*
- *I forgive myself.*
- *I forgive you God.*

## Prayer:

"Lord, help me to surrender my ideas, thoughts, and feelings about you. Help me renew my perception and see with clarity. And help me to heal our relationship so that I can know you honestly and completely."

## Scriptures:

- "For it is impossible for those who were once enlightened, and have tasted of the heavenly gift, and were made partakers of the Holy Ghost, And have tasted the good word of God, and the powers of the world to come, if they shall fall away, to renew them again unto repentance; seeing they crucify to themselves the Son of God afresh, and put him to an open shame" (Hebrews 6:4–6).
- "If we confess our sins, he is faithful and just to forgive us our sins, and to cleanse us from all unrighteousness" (1 John 1:9).
- "Peace I leave with you, my peace I give unto you: not as the world giveth, give I unto you. Let not your heart be troubled, neither let it be afraid" (John 12:27).
- "For God hath not given us the spirit of fear; but of power, and of love, and of a sound mind" (2 Timothy 1:7).
- "There is no fear in love; but perfect love casteth out fear: because fear hath torment. He that feareth is not made perfect in love" (1 John 4:18).
- "For by grace are ye saved through faith; and that not of yourselves: it is the gift of God" (Ephesians 2:8).

## Additional Resources:

*Believing Is Seeing: A Physicist Explains How Science Shattered His Atheism and Revealed the Necessity of Faith* by Michael Guillen

*Darwin's Doubt: The Explosive Origin of Animal Life and the Case for Intelligent Design* by Stephen C. Meyer

*Return of the God Hypothesis: Three Scientific Discoveries That Reveal the Mind Behind the Universe* by Stephen C. Meyer

*The Case for Christ* by Lee Strobel

*The Language of God: A Scientist Presents Evidence for Belief* by Francis S. Collins

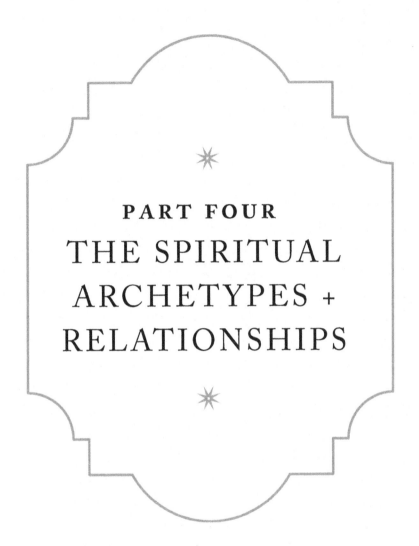

PART FOUR

# THE SPIRITUAL ARCHETYPES + RELATIONSHIPS

# HOLY AND WORLDLY
# RELATIONSHIPS

*Spiritual relationship is far more precious than physical.*
*Physical relationship divorced from spiritual is body without soul.*
—**MAHATMA GANDHI**

Relationships are some of the most spiritual endeavors in life. They can teach us lessons, bring us closer to God, and bless us in unimaginable ways. Regardless of the quality of our relationships, past, and present, they give us the opportunity to spiritually grow.

There are two types of romantic relationships: worldly (or ego) relationships and holy relationships. A worldly relationship is one that feeds, breeds, or contributes to making us feel separate from God and His will. These would be relationships that trigger, hurt, or abuse us, but also relationships that put us down, hold us back, or keep us from growing personally, emotionally, or spiritually. Worldly relationships are also superficial, based on looks, appearance, merit, or stature. They play games and keep us feeling crazy, uninspired, stressed, unhappy, and unloved.

A holy relationship puts God at the forefront of our will, desires, and motivations. A holy relationship dispels and unravels the lies of the enemy and feelings of separation. It holds truth for our partners and ourselves when we have become mystified. A relationship in God supports our soul, the part of us that is the image and likeness of God. It aims to promote our highest and best good. That doesn't mean it's perfect and that nothing uncomfortable will ever arise; it means that both people are committed to constantly growing, healing, and expanding their consciousness for the sake of themselves and their partner. When my husband and I got married, in my vows to him, I said, "I cannot promise you a bunch of things that haven't happened or that may never happen because I don't know everything the future holds, but I can promise you this, I will always do everything in my power to always put God first and for the sake of our marriage." The goal of a holy relationship is to do God's will within it for the sake of the greater good of the partnership or marriage. Sometimes that can be challenging when it goes against one's comfort, way of life, or personal aspirations, but when we unapologetically put God first, we will see the manifestation of it in our relationships. This creates holiness and purity that extends beyond worldly relationships and changes how we live and love. If we recognize where we are keeping ourselves from loving to the fullest and identify our strengths in love, we can open ourselves up to sacred intimacy that cultivates more devotion to our partner, increased self-awareness, and an enhanced understanding and love for God.

## The Neoteric Shaman in Love + Relationships

**When Balanced:** The Neoteric Shaman Spiritual Archetype is a blessing to those close to them. You are committed, loyal, and caring to your loved ones and would go to the ends of the Earth to protect your family and friends. The Neoteric Shaman typically stays in relationships for extended periods and has lifelong friendships. You stay with people through ups and downs and for better or worse, even if it may hinder or negatively affect you. In love, you are kind, patient, and understanding. The Neoteric Shaman can be romantic, thoughtful, and generally in tune with their partner's desires and needs. They can sense their emotions and energetic shifts, which makes them supportive and encouraging when their partner needs to talk or needs help getting out of a bad day.

**When Unbalanced:** Loving you is easy for others, although you may not extend that love toward yourself. There is a saying, "If your compassion does not include yourself, it is incomplete." Remember this and hold it close to your heart. You must love yourself first to love others properly.

**Lessons in Love:** The Neoteric Shaman is the most likely of the Spiritual Archetypes to fall into the mindset of, "Two halves make a whole," believing that together they will make one whole, and without each other, they are lost, destroyed, and hollow. While it makes for some of the greatest love stories, it can be a painful way to live. One of the best practices for the Neoteric Shaman is to put their value in their divinity, not what they do in this world. This world is circumstantial and impermanent; it will never give you the desired satisfaction. Recognize your value in God, and you will stop searching for it in other (wo)men.

## The Recoverist in Love + Relationships

**When Balanced:** The Recoverist is a partner who listens and can be understanding, patient, and compassionate.

**When Unbalanced:** The Recoverist does not like hardships, difficulties, or stress, no matter how big or small. They may run from these situations in order to avoid them altogether, leaving their partner to deal with them alone. Additionally, they may have trouble being in a positive, healthy, and loving relationship, especially if it is not something they are used to.

**Lessons in Love:** The Recoverist can be like the helm of a ship, directing the course of the relationship. If the Recoverist feels healthy, positive, and happy, the relationship is headed in a confident direction. However, if the Recoverist is feeling guilt, shame, or the desire to relapse, they, and the one on the ship with them, are headed for uncharted waters and troubles ahead. It can feel helpless to both the Recoverist and their partner to be driven by this force that can only lead to destruction, heartache, and failure. This is where the Recoverist must be willing to relinquish their own control and allow God to lead the way. In doing so, they are no longer determining the course for themselves and their partner but allowing God to lead, guide, and direct in a purposeful, divine, and healthy way.

## The Witch in Love + Relationships

**When Balanced:** You have a mystery about you that is alluring to others and keeps them wanting more. Your charm and independence are spellbinding, making it easy to fall in love with you. You have a great sense of humor but dislike being the center of a joke. Passionate, caring, and opinionated, you are unique and one of a kind. You care deeply for those around you and are fiercely loyal to the one you love and choose for your partner.

**When Unbalanced:** Your fear of being held back or persecuted may keep you from fully allowing yourself to open up in relationships. You might believe that if you show all of yourself and let the mystery fade, you will no longer cast your spell on your partner.

**Lessons in Love:** Relationships are not just about mystery. Relationships have longevity when both partners are comfortable and know each other through and through. Try to allow yourself to be fully transparent and trust in your worth enough to believe your partner will stay, knowing and loving all of you.

## The Ancestor in Love + Relationships

**When Balanced:** The Ancestor sees and creates love in many forms. For example, they may be a foster parent, stepparent, or an adoptive parent rather than only a biological parent. This extends to their love life and relationships as well. The Ancestor may be in a long-term relationship with roles designed and designated specifically for and by, each partner that may be unconventional or unusual but works well for you and your partner. The Ancestor may marry later in life and be a stepparent to their partner's children. However the Ancestor loves, they do so in a way that honors, respects, and reflects the type of life and spirituality they desire.

**When Unbalanced:** You feel as though your way of life and love is not respected. It feels as though your ways are not the norm; therefore, you are not given the same merit or esteem. This can make you feel as though you are an outsider and that you have to retreat to feel the reverence and consideration you deserve along with others.

**Lessons in Love:** The Ancestor may have anger and judgment toward the world because of how they, or the people and ancestors they love so dearly, are judged or hurt. This can make the Ancestor push harder to see change but unconsciously and inadvertently push away from those who may be harmless or innocent, like their partners. The desire to change the past is often born from the Ancestor's own personal wish that they could change the hurt, trauma, and adversity from their own past. Using our own experiences to help others is honorable and helpful, but if we try to facilitate change from a state of feeling broken, wired, and tired or from our unhealed wounds, then we are operating from triggers and pain. If this is the space we are living and loving from, then we may not be seeing or loving our partner or relationship clearly. Again, remember the saying, "We cannot solve our problems with the same thinking we used to create them." Similarly, we cannot create a relationship of love, peace, equality, and honoring the past when we are still living in our own past's hurt, pain, and chains. Let us instead try to honor, heal, and forgive our past while living in the present and creating a better future, trying to include our partner in the process where applicable.

## The Sectarian in Love + Relationships

**When Balanced:** You feel worthy of love and full of faith. You radiate this and share it with your partner so that they, too, feel love and faith in their life. In this space, it creates ease and lightheartedness in your relationship. You love group events, outings, and events with your partner. Everything seems manageable, doable, and exciting, and you relish in the fun of being in love with your partner.

**When Unbalanced:** You feel worried, which can translate to being controlling or complacent. When faced with extensive hardships or seemingly insurmountable stress, The Sectarian may forget to turn to God for help and become anxious. They may become controlling in order to try to fix their problems, thus being controlling of their partner. On the flip side, they may become passive, believing that they need not do anything and that God will do everything. This can affect our relationships when our partner trusts us to make good, healthy, and divinely guided decisions.

**Lessons in Love:** Keep God at the forefront of your relationship, and remember that there is a time to surrender and let God work, but there is also a time to take action. Also, instead of only praying for your wants, needs, and desires, pray to know and understand God's will in your life and relationship. Our wants may not align with God's Word or vision for our life, and His plan far supersedes ours. To have the most harmony and success in your relationship, try to be willing to surrender your five-year plans or ideas of what it should look like, and allow God to create something bigger and better.

## The Neonate in Love + Relationships

**When Balanced:** The Neonate feels excited, exuberant, ambitious, ready to learn, and hungry for more. You are being opened up to the potential of yourself as a soul and spiritual being and feel that the possibilities are infinite. You want to learn, study, integrate, and repeat. Relationships change a lot during these periods. You begin to see things differently and may change how you feel about certain things, develop different boundaries, or voice yourself in ways you have not before. You may also decide you want different things in your relationships and make space for change, growth, or healing, either in past relationships or in a current one.

**When Unbalanced:** You may feel confused, overwhelmed, and unsure of your new awakening and look to others to guide, direct, and lead you. Remember, this is a vunerable and somewhat fragile time in your awakening. Use discretion and caution with who you allow into your space and give your heart to, especially if they are a spiritual teacher, guru, or leader.

**Lessons in Love:** If the Neonate is in a relationship with someone who is considered "asleep" (they are not consciously walking on their spiritual path), they may have an issue with your newfound spirituality. Likewise, if you were practicing one faith or path that they agreed with and you are no longer on that same path, this may come as a shock or unwelcomed surprise. Sometimes a person may be a New Ager and become a born-again Christian, or they may be in organized religion and have new revelations about spirituality and God that conflict with their previous notions or understanding. It is important to realize that you must always honor God first, then yourself, then others. Whether this causes conflict or not in your relationship may be an issue, but staying true and steadfast to God is the most important relationship we will ever have. That being said, keep in mind that it is not your partner that has changed; it was you. And with change can come chaos, fear, and resentment. Try to do your best to include your partner in your spirituality, if possible, and make it a positive experience to grow together, not apart.

## The Wayfarer in Love + Relationships

**When Balanced:** The Wayfarer feels their love and relationship are one of the most extraordinary adventures. It is full of excitement and expeditions, but having a partner to join in the adventure is an experience all of its own.

**When Unbalanced:** You feel trapped, unable to commit, and afraid of being tied down.

**Lessons in Love:** The Wayfarer may commit to their work, adventures, and ideas rather than commit to love. The fear of being rejected or tied down can make them run from relationships, preventing them from being fully engaged in their commitments. For the Wayfarer, it is valuable to find someone who can ground you, while also letting you fly. This requires a partner who is confident with themself and willing to let you shine. Allow this partner to be a part of your process and ideas, and you can create a powerful, loving, lifelong bond.

## The Mythologist in Love + Relationships

**When Balanced:** The Mythologist has the ability to attract people with the power of presence. Your intuition, emotions, and ferocity make you a wonderful partner, always tuning into your partner's needs. The Mythologist believes in a love born from fables and tales. You know in your heart that love can be consuming, passionate, and never-ending. However, if you are not strong in yourself, your worth, and your values, you tend to be malleable, allowing yourself to be influenced by others' desires, thoughts, and opinions. Try not to throw yourself into love blindly for the sake of being in love. Keep your values and morals strong and you will attract people who resonate with them. The Mythologist tends to have fewer relationships, but their relationships are usually longer lasting and more intense and impactful than others, which means you may go longer periods of time without a relationship, but when you are in love, you make it count. Take your breaks as a time to heal, reflect, and love yourself.

**When Unbalanced:** The Mythologist wants someone to save them from their own fears and imagination but are too afraid and insecure to communicate what they want and need.

**Lessons in Love:** The Mythologist is a romantic, a love warrior, and a crusader for the sacredness of the ancient and mythical people, communities, and relationships. This is an aspect of your personality that can make you a great partner. Take caution that you do not fall for a person simply because they embody some of the characteristics you value. For instance, a woman might fall in love with a tough, aggressive, abusive man because he seems assertive, which gives her a false sense of safety. The more you value and love yourself, the more you will attract a partner who embodies qualities you love but in a way that is more conducive to your well-being.

## The Warrior in Love + Relationships

**When Balanced:** The Warrior may have adoring fans around the world, but the greatest warriors always went into battle with one love awaiting them back home. To be able to do the work needed and return to a faithful, grounded, and loving mate is a dream and goal for The Warrior.

**When Unbalanced:** You feel unable to give yourself to one person, feeling torn between work and love.

**Lessons in Love:** Remember that the work is just a job. It may leave you or change forms, but love is always worth fighting for. If you make love a priority, you will always be satisfied.

## The Eastern Philosopher in Love + Relationships

**When Balanced:** The Eastern Philosopher provides strength, balance, and peace to their relationship. They connect through good food, traditions, and feeling appreciated. The Eastern Philosopher also values simplicity and sees the beauty in the smallest moments. Being in beautiful and peaceful space with their partner is some of the Eastern Philosopher's favorite moments and memories.

**When Unbalanced:** The Eastern Philosopher feels rigid, betrayed, controlling, ungrateful, and unappreciated.

**Lessons in Love:** For the Eastern Philosopher, feeling honored and appreciated by their partner means a great deal. If they have a partner who seems ungrateful, it can have a deep impact on their self-worth. Remember that while it feels good to be appreciated, our self-worth does not depend on others validating us. One Eastern Philosopher client was having issues with this and began controlling their partner by saying, "I want you to show your appreciation for me in these ways," and when their partner did not, they would argue. What I suggested to them is to openly communicate to each other the way they liked to be appreciated, but also to share with one another how they liked to show appreciation. In doing so, they were able to look at the ways they each individually showed appreciation for one another. Instead of controlling each other, they could recognize the way they each communicated their gratitude. It's valuable to know how each person likes to be treated, but it's also important to see how others communicate their love for us as well.

## The Saint in Love + Relationships

**When Balanced:** The Saint feels happy, sweet, and fun. The Saint is a kind-hearted person who is romantic, simple, and a wonderful friend as well as devoted partner.

**When Unbalanced:** The Saint will feel anxious or guilty, or feel the need to cater to their partner and make sure they are perfect if they are feeling insecure. They deflect blame or responsibility so that they do not get in trouble.

**Lessons in Love:** The good-natured personality of the Saint can sometimes feel like too much pressure for others. Their angelic presence can feel like a lot for their partner to try to live up to or appease, which may cause frustration or conflict—especially because the Saint tends to attract someone that is a little more mischievous or outgoing in nature. What their partner usually doesn't realize is that the Saint is attracted to these types of people because they have qualities, they wish they possessed.

Instead of creating conflict because of the differences in personalities, the Saint and their partner can see, value, and learn from one another in these areas. If they can let each other be themself, as well and letting the other's good qualities rub off on them, it can be beneficial to both.

## The Christian Mystic in Love + Relationships

**When Balanced:** The Christian Mystic is passionate, romantic, and amorous. They are devoted lovers and will fight for their partners and relationships.

**When Unbalanced:** The Christian Mystic can become obsessive, abandoning their well-being or priorities to be with their partner or make them happy.

**Lessons in Love:** The Christian Mystic sees the good in everyone and has a tendency to fall for people who are unhealthy and not interested in changing, or try to help people who are not asking for it. They love hard and can get stuck on the roller coaster of emotions of their partners. Because the Christian Mystic generally has a confusing or traumatic upbringing with God and religion, they may put partners in the role of God, committing to overbearing, abusive, or controlling people. Remember the order of importance: God, self, others. Find someone who commits to that same foundation. This will ensure your relationships are always grounded in God, which will make them holy and better for your well-being.

## The Artist in Love + Relationships

**When Balanced:** The Artist is creative in all their endeavors, and their love life is no exception. They like to create their own rules for relationships and have partnerships that reflect their own style. The ways the Artist expresses love is always unique and incredibly special to them and the ones they share it with.

**When Unbalanced:** The Artist is afraid of being normal, mundane, or uninspired. Their fear can cause them to push away from their partner and in some cases create love triangles or affairs, possibly self-sabotaging in order to keep a sense of freedom.

**Lessons in Love:** The Artist is driven by inspiration, which can change from moment to moment. Their life, work, and relationships all flow with their mood, motivations, and interests. Therefore, to keep a relationship alive and working, the Artist will have to commit all of themself, which can feel scary but is essential for intimacy and success. As Jeff Bridges said about his forty-plus year marriage, "The easy answer about how to keep a marriage going is you don't get a divorce. It's when those big challenges, those upsets come up in your relationship, those are real opportunities to get to know each other more and become more intimate with each other, try to see what makes each other tick."

## The Crusader in Love + Relationships

**When Balanced:** The Crusader is devoted to one partner and, despite being intensely committed to their cause, are also loyally committed to their relationship. The Crusader tends to attract strong personalities that almost rival theirs. They love someone who is understanding of them and their mission, but also keeps them on their toes.

**When Unbalanced:** The Crusader's work is profoundly emotional and stressful. This may cause The Crusader to devote too much time to their mission and others instead of their partnership and/or family. They may also connect emotionally with others due to long hours and the personal relationships required in their field, which may sometimes cross lines.

**Lessons in Love:** Even while home, The Crusader's heart and mind are usually elsewhere. They are always living and breathing their purpose, which for others can feel as though The Crusader is not present. Being in the present with your loved ones can lend to the experience of your mission as well as bring more joy to the moments you are with your family or partner. As the saying goes, "If you want to change the world, start at home." Create your most successful relationship with God, yourself, and your partner, and you will magnify that satisfaction in all other things that you do.

## The Oracle in Love + Relationships

**When Balanced:** The Oracle seeks to discover and amplify the magic of the universe into the world as well as into their relationships. The Oracle also sees the characteristics of a person and tends to learn how to work with them. Instead of holding things against your partner, you see them for who they are and expect the same from them so that you can lean into and appreciate each other's strengths.

**When Unbalanced:** The Oracle can become judgmental, opinionated, and oppressed. They seek partners who validate and support them, but if they feel as though they are not being supported and validated, they can become destructive and irritable.

**Lessons in Love:** The Oracle sees the reasons behind behaviors and patterns. They see people as predisposed for certain elements of their behavior based on the numbers and signs, but also the makeup of the universe. For instance, they might say people are more emotional around the full moon or epic cosmic events. This makes them understanding and compassionate to their partners and themselves. However, his can be problematic if the Oracle makes excuses for people because of their predisposed natures. They may allow behaviors that are unhealthy because others "can't help it." This can also create issues if the Oracle refuses to take responsibility for their actions and instead blames it on sources outside of themself. It is through taking responsibility that we can grow, and if we cannot take responsibility where we could or should, we stunt our own growth and the growth of our relationships. Remember that we have power and authority over our outside circumstances, and we are influenced in so much as we allow. The less we allow the outside world to influence us, the more power we keep in our lives and our relationships.

## The New Ager in Love + Relationships

**When Balanced:** The New Ager has a childlike spirit that is fun, innocent, and playful. They offer a unique and fresh perspective to relationships and can make being in a relationship exciting and new. You don't have a generic model for how romance should be. Instead, you create relationships based on your needs and your partner's specific needs. This may seem unconventional to others, but somehow it works for you.

**When Unbalanced:** The New Ager feels like a wounded child. They feel big emotions but are unable to explain what they are feeling.

**Lessons in Love:** The New Ager tends to have a lot of deep triggers from childhood. This can be confusing and alarming to their partner, especially if they do not know or understand what the triggers are. Healing your past is the optimal way to create loving and fulfilling relationships in the present. Additionally, communication is key in helping your partner to support you through your wounded child work.

## The Metaphysician in Love + Relationships

**When Balanced:** The Metaphysician sees the spiritual part of their relationship. They see the soul within themselves and in their partner and can create a balance of spiritual and physical.

**When Unbalanced:** The need for answers supersedes the need for personal connection. They may overwork and spend more time in their quest for science and truth than with their partners.

**Lessons in Love:** The Metaphysician is a deeply intellectual person with a passion for the universe and spirituality. In love, this can translate to being detached or unemotional in love, which can make a partner confused or unsure of where the Metaphysician stands. Sometimes the Metaphysician can find one partner who understands them, and they can have a long-lasting relationship. Other times they may go through multiple marriages as they try to balance their intellect and work with their love life and family. To express love, emotion, and feelings is one of the Metaphysician's greatest challenges. If they feel as though they cannot give their partner the connection they are seeking, the Metaphysician may feel defeated and retreat into their work, which makes them feel accomplished. If the Metaphysician can learn to express their feelings and emotions, not to appease their partner but because it is a healthy practice, they can then offer a more well-rounded relationship.

## The Occultist in Love + Relationships

**When Balanced:** The Occultist is sweet, alluring, and protective of their love. Like their favorite secrets, they cherish love as a mystery and honor it like an oath.

**When Unbalanced:** The Occultist shuts everyone out, including their partners, and can isolate themselves to a point of destruction to themselves and their relationships.

**Lessons in Love:** The Occultist is the person people write novels about. Untamable, full of mystery and absolute wildness, people fall in love with the depths of your soul. Unfortunately, most people do not see the real you, only a version of you they conjure up in their own minds. The Occultist is reserved with who they let near them and tends to pick partners whose qualities are mostly seen only to them. The Occultist sees parts of others most do not see and spends too much time trying to convince their partners that those qualities exist within them. The Occultist is a person everyone wants, or wants to be. You are an enigma and force to be reckoned with. Your relationships never fit into a mold and are usually considered odd to others around you. But with the intense need for privacy, seclusion, and being in your own thoughts, plus the tendency to need adventure and excitement, whoever catches your eye needs to be up to the task of loving, honoring, and tending to all of the various aspect of your personality.

### The Lightworker in Love + Relationships

**When Balanced:** You feel in fluid harmony with yourself, your partner, and the world. You love to feel and live to feel good, which extends into your relationships as well. The Lightworker is loving, flexible, and easygoing. They are generally wonderful at communicating and are open and honest in the way that they speak. The Lightworker treats their partners the way they want to be treated. The Lightworker has feminine energy and exudes their feminine qualities of giving and receiving, balance, softness, and nurturing. They are sensual, powerful, and attuned to the ones they love. A Lightworker feels it all and emits it back into the partnership.

**When Unbalanced:** In order to not cause friction and stay positive, the Lightworker can become passive aggressive.

**Lessons in Love:** Many Lightworkers are intuitive or empathic, which can make them sensitive to their partner's thoughts, feelings, and energy. Because of this, without inner stability and solid self-worth, the Lightworker can lose themself in their partner. Being as fluid as you are, remember that you cannot let yourself flow with everyone around you. There has to be some solid foundation in order to keep yourself grounded. The more you love, the more you allow yourself to flow with your partner. Be sure to keep your center in God, and you will always have strong cornerstone, allowing yourself to flow with others while still keeping strong within yourself.

### The Mindset Master in Love + Relationships

**When Balanced:** The Mindset Master is able to articulate their feelings and emotions.

**When Unbalanced:** The Mindset Master has difficulty manifesting the types of the relationships they want and will attract the same type of person over and over.

**Lessons in Love:** Being so strong in their mind, the Mindset Master cannot understand if and why they cannot attract healthy love. They may have vision boards and journals and detail every aspect of the partner they want, then become frustrated when it does not manifest. The one big key here is that the Mindset Master may be asking for what they want, but it's not what God knows they need. Anytime we are asking for something and are not seeing it manifest is usually because it is not in alignment with God's Word or will for us. If the Mindset Master is looking for love and not seeing it, despite their best intellectual efforts, try praying to God for the type of partner and relationship He knows is best for you.

## The Sovereign in Love + Relationships

**When Balanced:** The Sovereign shares their throne and wants to build a kingdom together.

**When Unbalanced:** The Sovereign desires a sense of control and superiority over their partner, which can lead to dominance or manipulation to have things go their way.

**Lessons in Love:** The Sovereign can strive for control in their life and work, and their relationships are no different. If the Sovereign can learn to give a little and let their partner lead in some areas, they can create a powerful relationship. Ultimately, if the Sovereign can let God be the King in their relationship, then they can ensure they are always fighting for the greater good, not just their will.

## The Theologist in Love + Relationships

**When Balanced:** The Theologist is a strong foundation to those around them and usually is the one everyone turns to for advice, including romantic relationships. You are a rock for your loved ones and a centering place in the midst of overwhelming emotions or hardships.

**When Unbalanced:** The Theologist might use God or spirituality to romance, seduce, or create unequal roles in their relationships.

**Lessons in Love:** Due to the intellect of the Theologist, you are generally a teacher to your partners, which can tip the scales of equality. The Theologist, needing to feel that they are playing the role of savior, might attract people who need "saving" in order to feel they are properly playing their role. Generally, this is done out of innocence, but be careful not to play holier than thou with your partners. Relationships offer some of our most profound healing, but we should never act as the teacher or savior to our significant others.

PART FIVE

# THE SPIRITUAL ARCHETYPES + THE SPIRITUAL COMMUNITY

# THE UNIQUE EXPRESSION
# OF GOD WITHIN US ALL

*God has a higher purpose than making man an automaton.*
*God's highest is to bring out all the qualities of God in your own soul, to bring*
*out all the individuality that is in your life, not to submerge or destroy, but to*
*change it, to energize it, to enlarge it, until all your individuality and per-*
*sonality and being are of the nature and substance and quality of God.*
—JOHN G. LAKE

E very person, regardless of their path, has a Spiritual Archetype. Each path has its strengths, advantages, and value. They are reflections of our personality, style, and preferences and benefit us, each other, and the world. Throughout history, God has chosen people from all walks of life to do mighty and holy works. There has never been one path that is the right one, only that we seek God with all our hearts and live accordingly. Every person is capable of phenomenal works and wonders. Our experiences, backgrounds, and history all give us the potential to communicate, love, and heal in different, beautiful, and unique ways. God gave us our individuality, which is reflected in our lives and spiritual paths. We each have God within us and are the image and reflection of God.

In the 1940's film *Strange Cargo*, starring Clarke Gable, Joan Crawford, and Peter Lorre, and based on the 1934 novel, *Not Too Narrow, Not*

*Too Deep* by Richard Sale, Gable stars as Verne, a convicted convict on a penal colony on Devil's Island who is determined to escape his imprisonment. After another failed attempt to escape, Verne is released into his bunkhouse, where a mysterious new prisoner who acts and speaks a lot like Jesus and goes by the name of Cambreau (Ian Hunter) has suddenly appeared. None of the guards or other prisoners have seen Cambreau before, yet one by one the prisoners and people around him are affected by his presence throughout the film. In this particular scene, a religious prisoner named Telez reads from his Bible, which opens up a conversation and debate about God and the scriptures. Cambreau asks whether Vern has read the Bible, to which Verne (Gable) snarkily replies:

"It don't make sense, here, this one will start you talking to yourself, listen, 'So, God created man in his own image.' How do you like that? Now, take a look at me. Do I look like a god to you? This forsaken place is full of gods, I suppose. Only, they're not working at it right now, they're god's on a holiday! Answer that one."

To which Cambreau replies, "It sounds simple enough. I think it means that each man has some of the qualities of God inside him, if he wants them and if he looks for them."

Although sometimes we may look like "gods on a holiday," we were created in God's image and likeness, and God's qualities are inside each and every one of us. We each hold the reflection, nature, and characteristics of God within us that, while we may not be able to see blatantly, are there if we look for them. God is love. God is loving. He is full of grace, mercy, compassion, and understanding. As the image and reflection of Him, perhaps we could all give ourselves and each other a little more of His attributes. Regardless of our path, let us focus on love being the compass of our lives and the catalyst of our spiritual path. If we live, act, and think from a place of love in all that we do, then we will be echoing the God within us. Which, of course, is the ultimate purpose on our spiritual path and the thread that connects all of the Spiritual Archetypes.

## The Neoteric Shaman + the Spiritual Community

**Gifts + Qualities You Contribute to the Spiritual Community:** You offer strength, empathy, reliability, loyalty, support, and wisdom.

**Your Role in the Spiritual Community:** Male and female shamans are generally responsible for the health, spiritual teachings, and cultural traditions of indigenous people, tribes, and groups. With that responsibility comes reliability that others place upon them. Imagine being the doctor, spiritual advisor, storyteller, undertaker, and ancestral teacher all in one! Shamans are trusted, relied upon, and provide a feeling of strength, safety, and comfort to the community that the group may not have otherwise. Similarly, those with the Neoteric Shaman Spiritual Archetype are generally the backbone of their personal and spiritual communities. You may notice that people often open up to you and share their problems without being asked to. It is because you inherit an innate ability to comfort those around you, which makes them feel the desire to open up to you. The Neoteric Shaman also carries an internal strength that puts people at ease, especially those who feel they lack that same inner strength. Your community may look to you for guidance, support, or this strength.

## The Recoverist + the Spiritual Community

**Gifts + Qualities You Contribute to the Spiritual Community:** You offer compassion, understanding, empathy, forgiveness, perception, patience, sponsorship, encouragement, and inspiration.

**Your Role in the Spiritual Community:** Since the Recoverist has been through so much, they are often some of the most loving, understanding, and nonjudgmental people. Their ability to listen and witness for another person is a graceful gift they share with the spiritual community. While we persecute ourselves for our past, the Recoverist is the hand on the shoulder that says, "I am here for you," and encourages us that no one is too far gone to turn back and make a change. When a person has successfully completed the steps of a program, such as Alcoholics Anonymous or Narcotics Anonymous, they then have the choice to become a sponsor to a newcomer to the program. A sponsor acts as a mentor in the program, providing feedback, support, and guidance in maintaining and thriving in recovery. Their experience with addiction can yield understanding, empathy, and encouragement to those new to the program who may not be as understanding as someone without similar experience.

Similarly, the Recoverist may act like a sponsor to others around them. You communicate in ways that make people feel at ease and open up to you, thus encouraging healing and growth. You can support others during their struggles and find yourself in the role of mentor to those going through their battles.

Additionally, the Recoverist has experienced rock bottom. While this is a horrible feeling for anyone, it equips them with the understanding, acceptance, and lack of judgment that many others cannot. Although it is a terrible experience to have endured, God uses our worst experiences to strengthen us and uses this experience of the Recoverist to help others in the world and the spiritual community. Holding space for another person is one of the most loving gifts we can offer, and the Recoverist is blessed and guided in this area.

## The Witch + the Spiritual Community

**Gifts + Qualities You Contribute to the Spiritual Community:** You offer others the dignity of their civil rights and treat everyone with equality and tolerance. You have the grace of endurance, magic, and feminine power.

**Your Role in the Spiritual Community:** In the olden days, witches, midwives, and medicine women were trusted in their communities by people in dire straits. When conventional medicine failed, many people sought secret counsel and treatment from wise women who incorporated spirituality and medicine into their practice. Similarly, The Witch is a caring and fierce heart that loves their friends and community. The Witch is a dynamic contribution to the spiritual community with a strong shoulder to cry on, a sympathetic support system, and a powerful friend.

## The Ancestor + the Spiritual Community

**Gifts + Qualities You Contribute to the Spiritual Community:** You offer wisdom, insight, knowledge, lineage, advice, nurturing, and expertise, and show others how to honor the past by your actions, knowledge, and life experience.

**Your Role in the Spiritual Community:** The Ancestor is a sage, mentor, and master of ancient wisdom and bringing the elements of the past into the present. While there are many new spiritual teachers, modalities, and fusions of beliefs, The Ancestor reminds us that God, and our relationship with Him, have been practiced, nurtured, and respected since the beginning of time. Spirituality doesn't always need the new, but it can be accessed through the simplicity of the past.

## The Sectarian + the Spiritual Community

**Gifts + Qualities You Contribute to the Spiritual Community:** You offer innocence, organization, commitment, faith, unity, dedication, and devotion.

**Your Role in the Spiritual Community:** The Sectarian is devoted to their faith and will go to the ends of the earth for it. This devotion is inspiring, motivating, and sets a great example of the spirituality we can have when we leap fully and completely into the hands of God. When we are raised with a certain set of beliefs, we can inherit an unwavering faith that may be harder to obtain for others who were not given the same opportunity. This dedication can provide others with a strong foundation to look to if and when they turn to an organized faith or seek to know how to create the same dedication in their spiritual practice.

## The Neonate + the Spiritual Community

**Gifts + Qualities You Contribute to the Spiritual Community:** You offer fresh eyes, perspective, innocence, eagerness, excitement, and zeal.

**Your Role in the Spiritual Community:** The Neonate is a childlike perspective in the spiritual community. They offer a fresh perspective to anyone who may have been on the path for a long time. In many cases, when someone has been on the path for a while, they may lose touch with the fundamentals. It can be challenging to recall the time when they were new to their path. However, the Neonate requires us to go back to the fundamentals. They remind us to look at our own innocence and childlike nature. Similarly, children are some of the best teachers, and with the innocence of the Neonate, we remember that experience may make us smarter, but wisdom comes by continuing to learn.

## The Wayfarer + the Spiritual Community

**Gifts + Qualities You Contribute to the Spiritual Community:** You offer fun, adventure, excitement, exploration, and open-mindedness.

**Your Role in the Spiritual Community:** While many people in spirituality and religion follow rules, methods, and organized beliefs, The Wayfarer inspires us to think outside the box, ask questions, and explore options. While doctrine and laws can be beneficial and are in many ways the cornerstone of faith, the Wayfarer reminds us that spirituality and religion are not just meant to be learned in a church or a book; they are intended to be lived and experienced through the exploration and adventure of the soul. Sacred site trips are an incredible way for the Wayfarer to incorporate their spirituality and adventure, and they make fantastic tour guides to others seeking God in the experience of a personal, spiritual, and literal journey.

## The Mythologist + the Spiritual Community

**Gifts + Qualities You Contribute to the Spiritual Community:** You offer imagination, feminine and masculine attunement, lore, passion, nobility, honor, and royalty.

**Your Role in the Spiritual Community:** Throughout history, the most successful books, movies, songs, or plays are those that awaken a sense of magic, imagination, and wonder. Stories such as *King Arthur*, *The Lord of the Rings*, and *The Lion, the Witch and the Wardrobe* bring to life the feelings we have within us as spiritual beings that there is a supernatural to complement the natural. The artists of the Renaissance had profound ways of melding these worlds by painting pictures of humans and angels together in beauty and kinship. Poetry quickened the heartbeat as we read about knights on crusades clinging to the perfumed veils of their lovers awaiting them back home.

In a physical world that may seem dull and ordinary, you bring the magic of imagination; you bring creativity into spirituality. Your quality is otherworldly and can be felt by your friends and community. You carry the romance, passion, and love within you that the greats have written about, and the world is enchanted by. You are a reminder that all we see is not all there is, and life is meant to be passion-filled. The person on the spiritual path knows this in their heart and soul, yet it can be hard to remember there is something else when we see the physical world. Your presence allows people to touch that part of themselves where magic and imagination lie dormant within.

## The Warrior + the Spiritual Community

**Gifts + Qualities You Contribute to the Spiritual Community:** You offer strength, protection, power, stability, mastery, skill, vigor, vitality, security, pushing one's own limitations, endurance, resilience, motivation, and masculinity.

**Your Role in the Spiritual Community:** The Warrior is born to strive for mastery. Focus, determination, and accomplishments show others what is possible with drive, dedication, and action. The Warrior also provides a feeling of safety and security to those around them. The Warrior is the first to take action, protect others, and fight regardless of the situation. The Warrior will do the hard tasks others refuse or may not be equipped to tackle. Although in a perfect world there would be no war, struggle, or adversity, unfortunately these do currently exist. When faced with these, the Warrior is the one who will fight the good fight, and do what is needed to protect and defend.

## The Eastern Philosopher + the Spiritual Community

**Gifts + Qualities You Contribute to the Spiritual Community:** You offer endurance, patience, peace, perseverance, persistence, healing, knowledge of the elements, ancient knowledge, healing, and information.

**Your Role in the Spiritual Community:** From martial arts, which takes ages to perfect, or a bamboo shoot that takes years to grow, the Eastern Philosopher teaches the masterful skill of endurance and patience. In a society that wants everything here and now, or a spiritual community who can become impatient for enlightenment, the Eastern Philosopher knows that enlightenment is not an end game; it's a state of living that is perfected in the tiniest of movements or tailored until perfect. The Eastern Philosopher knows that it is not about the outward appearances but the inward feeling that matters. The peace that you feel resonates and infects those around you. It makes people question their lives and wonder where to get the sense of peace you so effortlessly seem to emulate.

The Eastern Philosopher also commonly connects with others through food and social gatherings involving cooking and big meals. They might have big events or small gatherings, but the focal point is food and connecting with loved ones through prepping, cooking, eating, and spending time together over a homecooked meal.

## The Saint + the Spiritual Community

**Gifts + Qualities You Contribute to the Spiritual Community:** You offer purity, humility, honesty, kindness, love, empathy, compassion, happiness, and positivity.

**Your Role in the Spiritual Community:** The Saint gives love and compassion to those who may never have had it or experienced it. You show the world that everyone deserves kindness, happiness, and empathy and that you can change the world with a tender heart. You cherish the simplicity and prove that less can be more, and being soft is an incredible strength. The Saint also has a way of bringing people closer to God without ever even mentioning God specifically. For instance, Fred Rogers, lovingly known as Mr. Rogers, attended seminary and was set to go into ministry until he saw the need for better childhood education and television programing. Thus, Fred Rogers began the show *Mister Roger's Neighborhood* which broadcast from February 1968 until August 2001. *Mister Roger's Neighborhood* is considered one of the best children's programs in history, teaching children how to live the attributes of God such as; forgiveness, love, communication, kindness, inclusion, self-love, doing what's right, family, and sharing, all while never even mentioning the word God. Like Mister Rogers, the Saint shows that we can live the attributes of God, and live His Word, while making everyone feel included, loved, and understood.

## The Christian Mystic + the Spiritual Community

**Gifts + Qualities You Contribute to the Spiritual Community:** You offer truth, integration, devotion, connection, relationship, love, and passion.

**Your Role in the Spiritual Community:** The Christian Mystic fuses the fundamentals of religion with passion and heart. They love God and Jesus and are deeply devoted to having a relationship with them that is loyal, authentic, and captivating. The intensity of the Christian Mystic's love for God and their spirituality can be a true testament to the kind of relationship that is possible and the miracles, blessings, and wonder that can come from loving God with all of our hearts. This can be wonderfully infectious to those around them and inspire others to seek this type of communion with Him. While many devout believers thrive on doctrine alone, the Christian Mystic reminds us to pursue God with love and heart.

## The Crusader + the Spiritual Community

**Gifts + Qualities You Contribute to the Spiritual Community:** You offer justice, freedom, activism, equality, drive, compassion, and empathy.

**Your Role in the Spiritual Community:** The Crusader is a champion for others, an advocate for those who cannot defend themselves, and a voice for the oppressed. The Crusader is often a political visionary or may be involved in supporting and promoting the rights of others, including animals, children, women, or indigenous people. Or you may find yourself promoting equal rights, human rights, affordable health care, or affordable education. You see the oppressed and aim to give them back their power. The Crusader hears those who cannot or will not be heard, and they offer themself as a mouthpiece to give the voiceless a voice. The Crusader sees injustice in the world and brings attention to ignored needs. You see possibilities for changes and speak about the ways we can manifest them into the world for a more harmonious society. By bringing these issues to the attention of others, you open their eyes to struggles and suffering they may otherwise be unaware of. Remember to do this with love, patience, and understanding. Not everyone understands the struggles of others or the reality of the issues you hold dear. This can be frustrating because it may seem like they don't care or realize the importance of the problems of the world, but your love and patience can be your greatest ally in teaching others. Sometimes people don't realize you can fight for what's right from a place of love. When done together, a fight for what's right from a place of love can be world-changing. Fight with love, and you will win your battles.

## The Artist + the Spiritual Community

**Gifts + Qualities You Contribute to the Spiritual Community:** You offer creativity, expression, imagination, inspiration, entertainment, and innovation.

**Your Role in the Spiritual Community:** The Artist brings a connection and manifestation of God into the world in a unique, powerful, and beautiful way. It is like what Yogananda said about flowers: "Humbly serving all with their beauty, flowers say more to us about God than anything else. Each one brings a message that the Heavenly Father is right here." It is through witnessing the flower's beauty that we witness God's creation and love. He is the best and most skilled artist, and with His blessing and anointing, we can also be artists that bring the "message of the Heavenly Father right here."

## The New Ager + the Spiritual Community

**Gifts + Qualities You Contribute to the Spiritual Community:** You offer unity, acceptance, inclusion, mystery, ancient traditions, and fusion.

**Your Role in the Spiritual Community:** The New Ager is an inclusive community that fuses many traditions and beliefs that make people feel welcomed and accepted. For those who have felt rejected by the religious communities, or may have felt outcast, this community can be a healing bridge back to creating a fulfilling and loving relationship with God. Many people on the spiritual path feel times of loneliness and as though they walk the path alone. The New Age community thrives on connection, events, and togetherness, which can be a blessing to those experiencing those feelings of unwanted solitude or looking for friendship.

## The Metaphysician + the Spiritual Community

**Gifts + Qualities You Contribute to the Spiritual Community:** You offer inquiry, curiosity, examination, a bridge for the spiritual and physical, knowledge, expansion, possibilities, science, and spirit.

**Your Role in the Spiritual Community:** In spirituality and religion, many beliefs, claims, and ideas have been introduced and invested in over time. The spiritual field, in some ways, is its own little scientific community, testing hypotheses and presenting ideas for further testing and research. However, unlike science with tests to prove or disprove a theory, the spiritual field holds no way to debunk a theory, regardless of its claims. Anyone can take the Bible and make it say what they want it to, in addition to other forms of spiritual teachings. This can lead to unhealthy or nonsensical claims, cults, or abuse of power in the spiritual field, which, unfortunately, occurs all too often. The Metaphysician is a voice of inquiry and a request for evidence in an area where so few ask for proof. While some people in the spiritual field may take a claim or theory at face value, the Metaphysician inquires and asks questions that others may not. The Metaphysician is adamant about knowing the ins and outs of claims to make informed decisions. They help the spiritual community to explore our beliefs, thus enhancing them, or we may discover we have a different view after our examination. Either way, the Metaphysician provides curiosity to keep learning, growing, and asking questions, which is an essential part of life and a crucial part of the spiritual path.

## The Oracle + the Spiritual Community

**Gifts + Qualities You Contribute to the Spiritual Community:** You offer counsel, direction, motivation, liberation, honesty, possibilities, planning, and the ability to reimagine and set clear goals.

**Your Role in the Spiritual Community:** The Oracle is like a counselor and a friend who offers advice, clarity, and feedback. They are also seekers of symbolism and finding truth in God's creations. The Bible contains astrology, numerology, and symbolism that, to the naked eye, may seem like nothing but happenstance. However, God does not create anything with meaningless intention, so each number, symbol, animal, message, prophecy, word, person, and action is done with purpose and meaning. The Oracle seeks to find and display these meanings in the spiritual community and to the world in a beneficial, useful, and digestible way for the average person.

## The Occultist + the Spiritual Community

**Gifts + Qualities You Contribute to the Spiritual Community:** You offer discovery, spiritual knowledge, transformation, and spiritual innovation. You see the magic in the ordinary and apply your studious nature and genius to initiate meaningful experiences.

**Your Role in the Spiritual Community:** The Occultist cannot stand the average, normal, or ordinary. With an innate ability to see the magic and secrets in the smallest of details, they aim to bring their knowledge, perception, and observations to the world to demonstrate the depths of spirituality in all things. With a fascination for knowledge, learning, and study, the Occultist propels us to look deeper, always be eager learners, and see the connectedness in everything and everyone.

## The Lightworker + the Spiritual Community

**Gifts + Qualities You Contribute to the Spiritual Community:** You offer love, light, community, friendship, positivity, femininity, flow, and ease of connection. You are skilled at aligning energies to help improve the personal and, thus the collective.

**Your Role in the Spiritual Community:** The Lightworker is one of the most active and prominent in the spiritual community. Motivated, positive, and influential, the Lightworker is eager to find the light and share it with the world. The Lightworker thrives off of connection and community and encourages the world to unify and form allegiance to create a better world. Also, a socially extroverted Spiritual Archetype, the Lightworker adores practicing spirituality with others, which can make our practice more powerful. Matthew 18:20 tells us, "For where two or three are gathered together in my name, there am I in the midst of them." When the Lightworker leads others into practicing God's Word, they profoundly impact their life, their group, and the world.

## The Mindset Master + the Spiritual Community

**Gifts + Qualities You Contribute to the Spiritual Community:** You offer encouragement, strategic thought, motivation, possibilities, positive habits, and affirmations. You are adept at new ways of thinking by reframing thoughts, actions, and feelings, which develop a new mindset.

**Your Role in the Spiritual Community:** The Mindset Master teaches people that they have power over their thoughts and actions, influencing our habits. Since our habits form the condition of our life, we can take control of our life. The Mindset Master teaches from their personal experiences and encourages people to take the reins, guiding their life in a direction that others may only dream about. For the Mindset Master, a dream is merely a goal that needs actionable steps. The Mindset Master helps people to lay out these steps to create the best life possible.

## The Sovereign + the Spiritual Community

**Gifts + Qualities You Contribute to the Spiritual Community:** You offer leadership, organization, confidence, success, wealth, initiative, direction, and innovation.

**Your Role in the Spiritual Community:** The world would not be the way it is today without the foresight, innovation, and leadership of the greatest Sovereigns throughout history. The Sovereign is always thinking about what can make life, culture, society, and the world of the future better. They strive to bring ideas and initiation that propel the direction of the future. Whether in the entertainment industry, food service, electrical, engineering field, or beyond, the Sovereigns have the drive, passion, and confidence to make their biggest and wildest dreams a reality.

## The Theologist + the Spiritual Community

**Gifts + Qualities You Contribute to the Spiritual Community:** You offer people structure and reliability. Your intellect, knowledge, and leadership allow you to be trustworthy in matters of law and liberation, highlighting your inner strength.

**Your Role in the Spiritual Community:** The Theologist doesn't just practice any spirituality; they practice tried-and-true religion that has been backed by information and evidence and has been proven effective. In spirituality, there can often be new ideas and beliefs that may or not be helpful or backed by truth, but with the Theologist, the proof is in the pudding. When the Theologist brings hard facts, they act as a pillar of truth in the community. If others get confused or falter, they can confidently rely on a Theologist while they find their way.

PART SIX

# THE
# SPIRITUAL
# ARCHETYPES +
# HEALING

# THE ESSENCE OF OUR
# BRIGHT NATURE

*I have heard thy prayer, I have seen thy tears: behold, I will heal thee.*
—2 KINGS 20:5

In *The Forgotten Books of Eden*, Adam and Eve were tricked by Satan and ate from the Tree of Knowledge of Good and Evil. In doing so, they fall from grace and fall to Earth, where they inhabit a cave as they begin their new life. Adam and Eve were distraught and confused about the new world and wept in sadness. Adam said, "O God, when we dwelt in the garden, our hearts were lifted up, we saw angels, that sang praises in heaven but now we do not see as we were used to do; nay, when we entered the cave, all creation became hidden from us." "Then God the Lord said unto Adam, 'When thou wast under subjection to Me, thou hadst a bright nature within thee, and for that reason couldst thou see things afar. But after thy transgression thy bright nature was withdrawn from thee' and it was not left to thee to see things afar off, but only near at hand; after the ability of the flesh; for it is brutish.'"

In Hindu mythology, our universe is created by the male deity Shiva, who represents unmanifest consciousness. Shakti is the divine feminine personification and creator of life and form. In her creation of life and the universe, Shakti created *maya*, which is known as "illusion."

Maya is not consciousness itself but is a projection of consciousness that disillusions us from omnipresent consciousness. Through the power of magic and illusion, maya creates the illusion of a veil of separation, thus mystifying people into believing in separation from omnipresent consciousness, each other, and ourselves.

In the story of Adam and Eve in the book of Genesis, the world and everything, including man and woman, were created perfect in God's image. When Adam and Eve ate from the Tree of Knowledge of Good and Evil, they lost their bright nature because it was covered in flesh, a veil (e-veil) of illusion (maya). This changed their perception because they were no longer ruled by God but by their own flesh. Their eyes no longer saw the truth; it saw the illusion. Therefore, healing is not the fixing of ourselves; healing is the recognition of the veil and the revelation of the truth through God that we return to our bright nature. Healing is about shedding the lies and false beliefs of the enemy (ego, devil, satan) to see the authentic God within ourselves, others, and the world. Oftentimes, people perceive healing as a process that we go through to get or be better and that when we get to the end, we will be perfect. However, healing is not an act of repairing something that is broken. Instead, it is the awareness and overcoming of the flesh by taking authority over it. Healing happens when we realize and reveal our bright nature and speak truth to the flesh and the world. Healing is possible because our bright nature, and the authority to overcome the flesh, are within each and every one of us. As we clear away the muck and mire of our illusions and false beliefs, we reveal the majesty of God and the authentic, bright nature that we are.

## The Characters of the Subconscious

In 1961, voiceover superstar Mel Blanc, who voiced famous characters such as Bugs Bunny, Daffy Duck, and Elmer Fudd, as well as many others, was severely injured in a car accident while driving home. In critical condition, Blanc fell into a coma and almost died. His son and wife were at the hospital for weeks, speaking to him and hoping for a sign he would recover, but he remained unresponsive. Doctors tried everything, but the situation seemed hopeless. One day, about two weeks after his accident, his neurologist decided to try something unconventional. Upon entering Mel's room in the morning, he loudly asked, "How are you feeling today, Bugs Bunny?" The other nurses and doctors were shocked by his unethical behavior . . . until they heard a small voice respond from the hospital bed: "Myeeeeh . . . What's up, Doc?" Although unable to speak or respond as himself, Mel was able to hear and answer as the characters he played. The doctor addressed Mel in his character names, including Tweety Bird, to which Mel responded as that character every time until he awoke from his coma and was once again personifying Mel Blanc. Our subconscious is a powerful fragment of our mind.

Even things we do not believe are causing us harm may be hurting us emotionally, mentally, and spiritually. Without realizing it, we may be letting one of our "character's" triggers or fears answer for us, instead of our inner self (soul) responding. Anyone who has endured an abusive relationship may have created characters as coping mechanisms while in survival mode. These characters take on the "fight, flight, or flee" qualities. If someone grew up in poverty, the character of "poverty consciousness" might come out, regardless of how much money they are currently making in their life. If someone has ever felt victimized, the character of "victim mentality" may show itself, even in situations that are not relevant. Mel's characters were distinct. They had names and personalities, were easily definable, and were created for fun and entertainment.

Motives are not always evident with our characters, and we may be expressing characters that were created in hardship and strife. Oftentimes, our characters were created for self-preservation. At one time or another, they provided a sense of security, love, prosperity, or safety because they were born to aid us in struggle, trauma, or adversity. Unfortunately, as our life changes or progresses, these characters become out of place, even inappropriate. They are playing a role in a film that has ended. Alternatively, they continue their lines, keeping us stuck in a movie reel from the past, unable to move forward or let go. Finding the root of these characters and allowing God to heal our wounds releases them, thus freeing us to live in the present. The characters and stories that play in our subconscious determine the reel that projects and manifests into our lives. When we heal and let go of the pernicious characters in our subconscious, we allow a new reel to play, allowing us to create the story and life we desire. In leaving the characters of our past behind, we can step into the role of a lifetime: the conscious reflection of the image and likeness of God and the reflection of our bright nature.

## You Are Honeycomb

A couple of years ago, I watched a video about processed foods. The video talked about all the things manufacturers put into our foods and the differences between processed and natural foods. It turns out there is a very distinct way to tell natural honey from processed honey. When you pour processed honey into a bowl, put water over it, and swish it around, the honey will spread out and become thin and runny. The reason is that this low-grade honey is filled with added sugar, so it dissolves. However, something magical happens when you do the same thing to natural, organic, unprocessed honey. If you put natural, unprocessed honey into a bowl, cover it with some water, and swish it around, the honey will arrange itself into a honeycomb design! The reason is that the honey holds the *genetic memory* of the honeycomb and will reshape itself to its natural state. I had to try this for myself, so my children and I tested it. Sure enough, our organic, natural honey arranged itself into a honeycomb design. Although it was a fun experiment, it got me thinking about the metaphysical aspect of it and how we are the honeycomb.

When we go through life in struggle, we spread ourselves, our energy, and our hearts thin. We become "processed" by life. Like honey, we no longer remember who we are as spiritual beings. On the other hand, when we go to our natural state, we remember our genetic makeup as divine beings and resemble the design of God. God made us in His image and likeness. We hold that divinity in our cells as part of our genetic coding. Regardless of who you are, what you have been through, or your path, you carry the genetic memory within you. When we feel we have been processed, it feels painful and even impossible to return to our natural state. Healing is allowing God to pour water over us and swish us around so we can return to the organic and holy versions of ourselves.

There is a famous story that many claim to be a Hindu legend, although the origin and author are unconfirmed. In this story, the gods are deciding where to put man's divinity. One of the gods calls a meeting among the gods and asks where they should hide it. The gods begin throwing out ideas, saying, "Let's bury it deep within the earth." The lead god replies, "No, humans will dig up the earth and find it." Another god recommends, "Let us hide it in the deepest ocean." But the lead god disagrees: "No, humans will learn to dive in the waters and will surely find it." Then another god suggested, "Let's take it to the highest mountaintop and hide it there." But the leader replied, "Humans will eventually climb the tallest mountains. We cannot hide it there." Eventually, the gods gave up and said, "Then we do not know where to hide man's divinity." After thinking for a while, the lead god declared, "We will hide divinity *within* each man. Humans will search for their divinity everywhere but will never look within themselves. So we will hide it within them."

Your divinity is within you. No matter what life has put you through, God is within your genetic makeup. No matter how it appears, you are the honeycomb of God. It is within you, even if you cannot see it. You may have looked for your divinity in the earth. Maybe you have plunged into the depths of the deepest oceans or trekked to the highest mountaintops to find it, but it will not be in any place outside of yourself. Your divinity will not be found in money, fame, or relationships. It cannot be sought in this world because it is not of this world. It is the breath of God within us that gives us life and makes up the totality of our being. It is our soul that resides within us, asking and nudging us to remember the truth about who we are and where we came from. Honey remembers its design; healing and walking our spiritual path require us to do the same.

# THE NEOTERIC SHAMAN + HEALING

**Practices + modalities you may have tried or areas of interest:**
Native American spirituality
Toltec Wisdom
Drumming circles
Sweat Lodges
Mystics and Mysticism
Nature
Water and water healing, sports, and being around water
Desert stories, folklore, and magic
Nature Spirits
Horseback riding and training
Healing with animals and animal magic

**Issues you may have worked on or have had difficulty with:**
Codependency
Boundaries
Abusive relationships
Fight or Flight aka Survival Mode
Overworking
Self-Worth
Self-Love

**The Neoteric Shaman Heals Best When:** The Neoteric Shaman Spiritual Archetype loves nature and does well healing outdoors or in a nature setting. Mediation and prayer outside are beneficial and will help you drop into a peaceful state faster and provide more quality. Depending on your preference, camping, boating, rock climbing, going for a walk, swimming, or spending time with animals can all be lucrative attributes to your healing.

## You might benefit from practicing and studying:

### *Self-Love*

Many with the Neoteric Shaman Spiritual Archetype have dabbled in the practice of self-love. The one-piece they are usually missing, however, is the critical piece that completes the puzzle. The Neoteric Shaman usually practices self-love by learning to see what they love about themselves, making lists of their traits, or looking at what they have accomplished, but they don't usually look at what God says about them. Without this fundamental piece, we cannot fully love ourselves because we do not even know why we are even loveable. Without this piece, we are merely loving the appearance of us, but not necessarily the soul within us. Man looks at the outside of a person and their accomplishments, while God sees a person's heart. Would it not be valuable to see what God says about us and how that gives us our worth? God says you are loved, valuable, unique, forgiven, blessed, and redeemed. God says you have authority over this world, that you are an heir to the kingdom, and that your body is a temple of the living Spirit. Everything outside of that is circumstantial but what God says about you is infinite, definite, and unwavering. Instead of looking at what the world, or even what you say about yourself, try looking at what the creator of Heaven and Earth says about you. This will open a new realm of self-love and silence the voices that oppose the truth of who you are and your worth.

### *Boundaries Practice*

I knew this excellent psychologist who taught me a fantastic tool for boundaries when I was a teenager. She told me to imagine a box. It didn't matter what size or color, just a box that worked for me. In this box were all the things I could handle in my life. It could be school, work, or a favor a friend asked of me, but it included everything that felt good to deal with or that I needed to do at the time. Outside of the box was everything that felt like too much. It could be something someone asked of me, something I felt uncomfortable with, something that stressed me out (that wasn't a priority or a must) too many commitments, etc. When a situation would arise, I could imagine this box and ask myself one simple question, "Does that fit in my box?" Meaning, "does that fit into my well-being, peace, health, etc., or will it make me over-committed, stressed, and anxious?" This became how I trained myself to not over-accept other people's demands, invitations, and needs, and it made me consciously aware of how my decisions and commitments made me feel. It also took away my feelings of being guilted into saying yes. Instead of it being a personal debate within myself, it became a simple fact, "that is just not in my box." Which then helped me detach from others' projection of guilt or upset that I couldn't give them what they wanted. I even began using the statement, "that's not in my box," when friends would ask me for something I couldn't commit to or deliver on, and it became a term that they adopted and used too. If you have an issue with boundaries, over-committing, and feeling guilty saying no, try imagining a box and putting in everything important, a priority, or a commitment that is a need, want, or must. Then, feel free to be unguilted by anything that falls outside of that box.

## THE RECOVERIST + HEALING

**Practices + modalities you may have tried or areas of interest:**
12-Step Programs
Owning responsibility
Personal inventory
Forgiveness
Meditation
Surrender
Codependency
Recovery
Sober living

**Issues you may have worked on or have had difficulty with:**
Addiction
Eating disorders
Obsessive-compulsive disorders

Abuse and trauma
Inferiority
Imposter syndrome
Anger
Helplessness
Self-Worth
Denial
Pride

**The Recoverist Heals Best When:** You feel loved, supported, and redeemable. The Recoverist has been through hell, and when people shame, blame or guilt them into recovery, it only adds to the internal negative dialogue. However, this love and support must also be the script you play in your mind because we cannot solely rely on others; we must rely on ourselves and God. You are loved, supported, and redeemable in God's eyes, so lean on Him harder in your most harrowing moments.

### You might benefit from practicing and studying:

*Authority*

Study, learn, and integrate your power and authority as given to you. This can be found throughout the entire New Testament and is one of the most powerful parts of the Bible for any person to learn.

*Pride + Faith*

Do not let yourself be fooled by your own pride into believing that "You've got this" and that you no longer need the tools that have formed, supported, or strengthened your sobriety. The Recoverist needs their connection with God to keep their sobriety in check and without it may be caught at the worst time feeling no connection, which can lead to relapse. Our spirituality is like a homeopathic; you must have it built up in your system for it to work. If you do not, then it won't work on the spot. Although God is capable of delivering us from the worst of situations, it is our job to have our faith built up in our system so that it can work when we need it. As they say in AA, it works if you work it.

### Recovery Programs + God

Keep in mind that most programs for addictions are not God-based. While many may have positive results from following actionable steps, it is not a substitute for your personal and spiritual relationship with God, which ultimately is the driving force behind recovery and deliverance from addiction. If you are in a program, it may be wise to consider God-based recovery programs through your local church or community center that incorporates the two.

If these are not available, perhaps look at ways to incorporate the two yourself in your studies and practice. Having the community's support with God as your foundation can profoundly impact your well-being and recovery.

### Equine Therapy for Addiction

One profound way people in recovery experience healing is through equine riding and therapy classes geared toward people struggling with addiction. God created animals for many purposes, one of which is their healing properties. This is why in many cultures it is referred to as "animal medicine." Horses are powerful in their healing and provide the medicine of strength, wisdom, endurance, and overcoming obstacles, but they are also intuitive, sensitive, and fiercely loyal. People who struggle with addiction also tend to focus on their problems, which creates and grows negativity. Equine therapy can help them focus on healing and positivity outside of themselves, creating a fulfilling bond and assisting them in their recovery.

## THE WITCH + HEALING

**Practices + modalities you may have tried or areas of interest:**
Paganism
Herbs and Herbal medicine

Herbal lore and history
History of women, witches, and/or witchcraft
Nature
Gender and cultural studies
Politics

**Issues you may have worked on or have had difficulty with:**
Victimization
Oppression
Persecution
Being misunderstood
Communication
Anger
Anxiety
Helplessness

**The Witch Heals Best When:**
You feel the freedom and independence to celebrate God in a way that feels authentic and radical.

## You might benefit from practicing and studying:

### *Healing Victim Mentality*
One of the most challenging aspects of the Witch's spiritual development is getting stuck in their victim mentality. While this has been mentioned, it is worth repeating because it is one of the greatest hindrances in their growth. Victimhood is challenging to overcome because it is such a strong voice from the past that cries to be appeased in the present, regardless of its validity. Victim mentality will dig in its heels and scream for everyone else to validate it, which can feel impossible and unfair to others. The more the victim mentality seeks validation, the stronger it becomes, and the more it needs approval. It is an ethos of famine, but outside circumstances cannot gratify the famine. The victim mentality must be quashed by living in the present and acknowledging

that any victimization that has taken place is in the past. If it is not, the Witch should take actionable steps to remove themselves from harmful, victimizing situations and lead the way for others.

Try to look at the positive in every situation rather than being cynical or pessimistic. Try to bring help, assistance, and positivity where there is none. Victim mentality can see the negative in everything and search for how they will be negatively affected by everything.

Victim mentality is a mindset of blame. People with this mindset will often blame others for everything that has gone wrong from their childhood and how it affects their current situation to why they are always late to work, gained weight, are sick, unhealthy, broke, etc. It can be challenging to reframe, but by realizing and owning our power instead of constantly viewing others as taking our power, we can claim our authority over our lives and create the life, situations, and circumstances we want.

Practice gratitude to combat the victim mentality that wants you to believe you have or are given less love, magic, and opportunities in your life.

Do not blame everyone else for your own choices or circumstances. Take responsibility for your part but also the authority you do have to create something better. Own your power and create from this place.

Heal past and present hurts and traumas and let them go. This doesn't mean they didn't happen or that what happened wasn't wrong. It just indicates you are no longer chained or bound to it. Our past is like a cage we allow ourselves to live in until we forgive, let go, and let ourselves fly.

### Forgiveness toward men and the masculine

It is easy to point fingers and blame one race or gender for all the world's problems. We can look through our history and say that one group is the cause of it all. However, the reality is that nothing is that simple and that while our history is full of unfortunate, sad, or evil doings, it has never been one person, group, gender, or race that is the cause. Fear, hunger for power, and ignorance are the cause of the evils of the world, and while it may seem beneficial to place that blame on one group, no one is immune to these things. If we cannot put the blame where it belongs, we will always be looking for a scapegoat. If we are always looking for a scapegoat, we live our lives divided, victimized, and accusatory. To move forward in our world, we must practice love, which means we should all begin forgiving one another, the past, and our spotted history.

As 1 Corinthians 13:4–7 tells us, "Love endures with patience *and* serenity, love is kind *and* thoughtful, and is not jealous *or* envious; love does not brag and is not proud *or* arrogant. It is not rude; it is not self-seeking; it is not provoked [nor overly sensitive and easily angered]; it does not take into account a wrong *endured*. It does not rejoice at injustice, but rejoices with the truth [when right and truth prevail]. Love bears all things [regardless of what comes], believes all things [looking for the best in each one], hopes all things [remaining steadfast during difficult times], endures all things [without weakening]. AMP We can change the world when we stand in this kind of love.

## THE ANCESTOR + HEALING

**Practices + modalities you may have tried or areas of interest:**
Ancestry
Herbs + Herbal Medicine
Ancient Civilizations
Folklore
History of Medicine
Climate change
Social Justice
Conscious Leadership
Liberation of self and others
Dismantling old outdated patterns, identities, and beliefs.

**Issues you may have worked on or have had difficulty with:**
Oppression
Guilt

Shame

Medical issues worsened by western medicine may have led you to discover herbalism, folk medicine, or natural remedies

**The Ancestor Heals Best When:** Deep connections and a sense of belonging are valuable to The Ancestor. This safely allows us to heal wounds and unravel the systems, beliefs, and structures that do not serve us.

### You might benefit from practicing and studying:

*Healing the past*

For the Ancestor, the past is spotted with pain, trauma, and wounds that are, in many cases, still raw and festering to this day. The land aches with the blood of indigenous ancestors and echoes the cries of the oppressed, sounds and feelings that can still be felt. The Ancestor carries this past on their back, carrying the weight of guilt and shame for how people were treated and how they are still treated. And while the Ancestor cares deeply for others and wants to feel and see the change with every fiber of their being, it is through their trauma and adversity that they feel driven to help others who are suffering. If their past wounds are left unhealed, the Ancestor might be trying to put on everyone else's oxygen mask while suffocating themselves.

Years ago, while praying, I asked, "How was Jesus able to heal others and live in this world without being attached to it?" The answer I received was, "As long as you are attached to your suffering, you will be attached to the suffering of others." It is not through our suffering that we heal; it is through healing and the transmutation of our wounds that we support others in healing theirs. If the Ancestor can focus on healing their suffering and wounds from their past, they will no longer be attached and consumed by the suffering of others but can support, assist, and lead from a place of transcendence. It does no one a service to set ourselves on fire for others. However, when we heal ourselves first, we can stand with our toes brushing the flames, with an outreached hand to those in the fire, and pull them out to a place of wisdom, love, and safety.

### *God, our oldest ancestor*

One of the most painful parts of the Ancestor's spiritual path is the harbored guilts of how our ancestors were treated, the colonization of their lands, and the domination of their ways of life. For some of the Ancestor Spiritual Archetypes, this may be a battle you face daily or an ache you forge through with hope, consciousness, and intention. The Ancestor does their best to honor our ancestor's lessons, patterns, behaviors, and lifestyles through their beliefs, medicines, and practices. There is incredible beauty, powerful knowledge, and a robust connectedness from ancient groups, tribes, and communities from which we are descendants by blood, memory, or in our hearts. In some cases, the Ancestor may find that despite their best efforts, practices, and devotion to the past, they still lack the sense of belonging they seek. One way we can find our sense of belonging is by celebrating the rituals and traditions of the past and finding our belonging in God. Connecting directly with God is like connecting with our most significant, oldest, and wisest ancestor. If you ever feel that you are missing a piece to the threads of the tapestry of our past, try weaving God in to see how it completes the whole piece and fills in areas we may not have known were missing.

## THE SECTARIAN + HEALING

**Practices + modalities you may have tried or areas of interest:**
The Bible
The Saints
The Prophets
Theology
God and Marriage
God and Parenting
Missions
Youth Group
Prayer

Prayer groups
Bible Studies

**Issues you may have worked on or have had difficulty with:**
Anxiety
Feeling trapped
Loneliness
Powerlessness
Addiction
Lack of passion and enthusiasm for life
Unworthiness + lack of self-worth
Stagnation
Empathy
Pride
Fear

**The Sectarian Heals Best When:** The Sectarian often believes that their community provides them strength, which can be true to some extent, but the Sectarian's faith and trust lead them to the highest results.

## You might benefit from practicing and studying:

### Empathy + Understanding

The Sectarian often grows up in a specific religion and has little knowledge or understanding of the world outside of theirs. This can lead to misunderstanding others' adversity and struggles and may even cause a lack of empathy. Remember that while we are all privileged to the Word of God, not everyone has had the same experiences and may not have had access in the way The Sectarian may have. Remember that having a solid spiritual foundation does not make one better or holier than thou and that Jesus would meet people where they were at.

In Acts 17:22-29, the apostle Paul speaks to the Athenians in Greece about the statues in the city. Walking through the square, he saw countless gods and goddess statues with names and labels; however, one remained nameless and was titled, "The Unknown God." Amid

Mars Hill, he spoke to them and told them about the God who was nameless to them. He began preaching about the living God and telling them many things about Him and us as his offspring. Paul leveled with the Athenians and spoke to them according to their beliefs for them to understand him. Meeting people where they are is one of the most loving things we can do for another person; however, we must take the time to see and understand them to do so. Often, The Sectarian goes into the world preaching their perception but does not take the time to understand other people's perceptions, limiting their ability to relate. While you do not have to make yourself "of the world," it can be beneficial to take the time to understand and empathize with others. After all, the most remarkable changes are inspired by love and understanding.

### Trust in God but tie up your camel

There is a common saying, trust in God but tie up your camel, meaning have faith but do not be foolish. I have known many Sectarians who have faith in God but choose not to take actionable steps to solve their problem when faced with adversity. There is a story that goes as follows:

During a flood, a man went up to the rooftop of his home. He began praying to God for help when the water continued to rise. Suddenly a man in a rowboat came and yelled to the man, "get in, I can save you." But the man on the roof refused and said, "No, thank you! I'm waiting for God to save me!" The man in the rowboat left, and then a man appeared in a motorboat and called out, "Get in! I can save you!" But again, the man responded, "No, thank you! I'm waiting for God to save me!" Finally, a helicopter flew in and yelled to the man, "Get in! I can save you!" But the man declined the offer again, saying, "No, thank you! I'm waiting for God to save me!" The waters then engulfed the house, and the man drowned. When he got to Heaven, he saw God and asked, "Lord, I had faith and prayed that you would save me, but you did not." God responded, "I sent three men to save you, one in a rowboat, one in a motorboat, and one in a helicopter, but you refused them all."

Sometimes when we pray for help, God sends us solutions in ways we do not imagine. Keep an open mind that it will be answered when you pray but your outcome may not look how you expect. Trust in God but take the necessary steps to ensure the best outcome.

### *Love God with all of your heart*

One area of difficulty I have heard and seen the Sectarian experience is that they go through the motions of their religion and faith but do not feel a passion for God within their hearts. For those I have worked with, this can be troubling and agonizing as they want to feel the love for and from God but instead feel a void. This happens because they are focusing too much on the Law of Moses and not the final commandment, which states that love is the fulfillment of the law (Romans 13:10). For those who feel inadequate, not good enough, or unworthy, they spotlight the Law of Moses but forget the final commandment, which fulfills the law. Without this, they are focused only on living up to an unreachable standard and lack God's love, which leaves an absence in their hearts. When we act in and from love, we will simultaneously fulfill all of the laws and commandants. If you are experiencing this, try reprioritizing your goals toward love and do everything from this space and you will notice that you feel more love for God while also feeling more love from God toward you.

## THE NEONATE + HEALING

**Practices + modalities you may have tried or areas of interest:**
Crystals
Astrology
Numerology
Aliens and UFOs
Energy
The Bible
Baptism
The Holy Spirit
The Gifts of the Holy Spirit
Ghosts and spirits
Psychic abilities

Spiritual awakening
Empaths
Chakras
Channeling
Soul Contracts
Atlantis + Lemuria

**Issues you may have worked on or have had difficulty with:**
God + Religion
Authority
Faith
Trauma
Money issues
Karma
Mindset
Manifestation
Triggers + Blocks

**The Neonate heals best when:** They feel they are given the space to process information and experience it in a way that feels credible, legitimate, and truthful to them.

### You might benefit from practicing and studying:

*Exercising Caution in finding teachers and studies*
The definition of the word "Neo" in Latin means "new", and the word "nate" in Latin is defined as "born" or "arisen." Thus, the word Neonate means to be a newborn or newly arisen. When we are children, aka, newborns to the world, we are like sponges. We take in our surroundings on energetic, emotional, mental, spiritual, and physical levels. We are influenced by the people, feelings, thoughts, mindsets, actions, and environment of our upbringing. While incredibly intelligent, perceptive, and wise, children are also shaped by the authoritative figures in their lives. Similarly, The Neonate is like clay in this period of their awakening. They can be easily molded and if not careful be molded in ways by teachers

and teachings, that ultimately do not benefit their personal and spiritual success. The reason being is that during this time The Neonate can be easily influenced, gullible, or naïve, trusting people they should not, or believing teachings that may hurt or negatively impact them. It can be helpful to remember that just because something is considered spiritual does not make it so. In fact, the word spiritual is derived from the French word, *espirituel* which means, "Relating to or concerned with the human spirit or soul." Therefore, if we use this as a guide, it becomes a bit clearer what is, and is not spiritual, as we transition through an awakening and begin healing. If our practice brings us closer to God, and our soul, then we are on the right path. If it does not, we might be headed down a path that leads us away from our human spirit.

## The Enlightenment Trap

Having spent my life in the spiritual, metaphysical, and new age fields, I have been a witness to countless spiritual awakenings. I have watched friends, family, coworkers, and acquaintances pass through awakenings that deeply impacted their lives. It's a paramount transition for anyone who experiences such a passage, but while it may be divine and intensely life-changing, it can also be a formidable transition. It can be a time of change, loss, progression, worry, excitement, and every feeling in between. Having seen so many of these awakenings, I have dubbed this transition: "The Enlightenment Trap."

The Enlightenment Trap is a trap many people fall into during and after their spiritual awakening. It is a period when they may begin to feel loss, grief, fear, and confusion by the shifts happening in their consciousness. If we fall into these traps, they can be massively debilitating. However, recognizing these traps before or during a spiritual awakening can help prevent falling into them. These may occur directly after an awakening, but may also be delayed depending on the person and the pace of their progression.

### *Trap One: Eliminating the "less enlightened"*
Going through a spiritual awakening can be awe-inspiring to those

who partake in it, but for friends, family, or coworkers, it might sound like we have gone mad and drank Kool-Aid. It may feel like we are suddenly outsiders to even our closest confidants, especially if they are still participating in unhealthy behaviors or are not spiritually minded. In many cases, I have seen people go through an awakening and eliminate loved ones immediately because they feel it's required to sustain their new consciousness. They believe that because others are not spiritual it will lower their vibration and take away from their new awakening. While sometimes it is the only option to walk away from people, primarily if they are participating in unhealthy behaviors that hinder our healing, I suggest taking a different approach.

As opposed to making a production of eradicating people from our lives, we can take a more passive approach, which is more lending to our experience, and less damaging to others. As we begin to change the way we are living, people in our lives who are not in alignment with that path may begin to fall away. Some people may react negatively to our changes because of their own fears, but it is important to realize this fear is being projected onto us and never take it personally. Jack Coe, a famous Evangelical revivalist once said that no one had a problem with him when he was drinking, but they sure had a problem with him when he found God and began preaching. When we change, we push people out of their comfort zone and shatter their ideas about us. While they should be supportive some people just don't know how to be. It can be difficult or feel unfair but leading by example can have a profound effect on the people around us.

Additionally, when we raise the quality of our life, words, actions, and beliefs, we will naturally begin attracting others who are supportive, loving, and understanding of our experience. Instead of creating unnecessary chaos by breaking up with everyone we used to know, we can focus on filling our lives with people who support us while simultaneously filtering out the negative, unsupportive people.

## *Trap Two: Self-Judgment*
Feeling such a powerful connection to God and suddenly knowing or being aware of that connection can be transforming. But when

that feeling wears off, we may begin judging ourselves harshly. After a spiritual awakening many people start looking at their love lives, sex lives, mistakes, diet, hobbies, and lifestyle and begin feeling ashamed or guilty for their life before their awakening. Feeling the love of an infinite presence of God can be humbling. This is a wonderful opportunity to do some inventory but blaming or shaming ourselves for not knowing what we didn't know isn't helpful or conducive to our growth. Whatever we have done in our past is what we were capable of at the time. Through conditioning, upbringing, or our own negative experiences, we believed that those things served us, no matter how dysfunctional we may now realize them to be. This is where self-forgiveness is imperative. As these feelings of personal condemnation arise, we can forgive ourselves for any behaviors we are now ashamed of or for not knowing how to do better.

In the first grade, I had an extremely difficult time spelling. I couldn't answer questions on the board and I struggled to see what my teacher was writing. My teacher would write a word on the board and ask us to repeat the spelling. Even though it was on the board I would still misspell things. It was not until later that I was tested for glasses and discovered I had weak vision. When I got my first pair of glasses, I was amazed at the world around me. A part of myself wondered how I could not have known that I couldn't see when it was so obvious the world was blurry. But if you don't see clearly, you cannot possibly know it's unclear.

A spiritual awakening is your soul putting on spiritual glasses and bringing things into focus. While it is essential to process the past, make amends where need be, or take responsibility, we must not be too hard on ourselves for not knowing how unclear our vision was before putting on our spiritual glasses.

### Trap Three: Addiction to Healing and Spirituality

Years ago, I had a client who spent thousands of dollars every few months on what she believed would be the key to her healing. She was putting her family in debt with her spending on courses, programs, services, and certifications, but she was frustrated because she still lacked results. As soon as she finished one modality, she would immediately rush to a new one. She was desperate for change but wasn't giving herself the time to integrate what she was learning and wasn't seeking a relationship with God.

Often people are so busy trying to find a new teacher, guru, modality, class, or workshop, that they forget that healing, expansion, and growth come from our communion with God. A person who spends more time with God, regardless of where they go, what they read, or what ritual they practice, will have a better relationship than those who seek him outside themselves.

It is motivating when we discover that we have the power to change our life. It's only natural to want to expedite the healing or spiritual growth process to start living the life we have dreamed of. I highly encourage everyone to try various classes, workshops, and services to see what is the best fit and the most helpful at each stage of our growth. When it becomes a trap is when we don't give ourselves the space to let the healing take place or look for God in the things, rather than communicate with Him ourselves. Instead of pressuring ourselves to consistently do more, we can sit a spell, allowing ourselves to incorporate the work we are doing, (which is how tangible healing occurs,) and focus on a relationship with God Himself. A couple can take all the classes they can find on marriage and love, but it is only by connecting and practicing the work together that their relationship can exist. A person can read about all of the trends in fitness and exercise but it is only by doing the work that they will see the results. Instead of becoming addicted to the next best thing or the new answer, we can commune with God who will do more and be more than anything in this world ever can.

## Trap Four: Changing to Resemble "The Enlightened"

There are many clichés of what spiritual people look and sound like. It is often believed that conscious minded folk do yoga, eat restrictive diets, only associate with other conscious minded people, and even dress a certain way. When people have a spiritual awakening, they may look to these clichés for direction to shape their new identity.

While some of these clichés may be true to some extent, people should do these things because they love them, not because other spiritual people do them. We do not have to force ourselves into the role we want to play, or even be spiritual the way someone else is. By healing, growing, and living better lives we begin to resemble a healthier, happier version of ourselves, not someone else we may believe to be enlightened. That may mean we bear a resemblance to other spiritually minded people, but by attaining those attributes through our experience it becomes mirrored through authenticity not imitation.

### Trap Five: The Identity Crisis

Whether we view our past as good or bad, it is a personality we identified with. Yet, in an effort to uplevel we don't realize how much we are letting go. All our habits, coping mechanisms, mindsets, relationships, and beliefs are being placed under a microscope and thrown out without the proper transition it takes to integrate new ones; which may lead to an identity crisis.

We may ask ourselves, "If I no longer want to be the person I was, but am not fully changed, then who am I?" This is why knowing what God says about us and who we are as spiritual beings is invaluable. When we try to find our identity outside our spiritual selves, we will always feel like we are looking for ourselves. We are not what others think or say, nor are we even what we think or say, but we are everything God says we are which is immeasurable.

A spiritual awakening is the beginning of our awareness of our spiritual path and journey. It is not something we achieve overnight; it is a progression that lasts the rest of our lives. Allow yourself the grace and mercy to go through the process.

## THE WAYFARER + HEALING

**Practices + modalities you may have tried or areas of interest:**
Meditating
Outdoor adventures + camping
Rock climbing
Extreme sports

Holistic practices such as chiropractic and acupuncture

Exploring + the history of exploring

Foreign lands

**Issues you may have worked on or have had difficulty with:**

ADHD

Poor academics and difficulty learning

Problems planning and organizing in ways other people understand.

Communication

Fitting in

Inability to commit

Creating unachievable goals

Anxiety

**The Wayfarer heals best when:** You feel the freedom to explore your feelings, thoughts, and opinions, without feeling boxed in or bored

## You might benefit from practicing and studying:

### *Finding God in the quiet and stillness*

While you may be accustomed to feeling and experiencing God in the ultimate settings and surroundings, and this may be a way that God communicates with you, you may also try speaking to God in the still, small, and quiet moments. The enemy loves the loud, crazy, and hectic because it keeps us out of our center which ultimately limits our communion with God. While you may love movement or adrenaline, try connecting with God in the simple, uninterrupted, and soft moments in your soul. This may be a different or new kind of connection but may be a welcomed new form of expression

### *Detachment vs. Unattachment*

In spirituality there is a concept known as unattachment. The premise of this is that we should have some sense of unattachment to this world and the happenings in this world. By being too attached to the world we can become overcome and ruled by the world. Our emotions lead us and we become irrational with emotion. If we are too emotional and excessively irrational, then we do not make good decisions and therefore live in our human selves rather than our enlightened selves. There is some truth to this; however, what many people leave out is that by denying the world, we must speak the truth to it. We, as spiritual beings have authority over it and should not be ruled by it, but it requires knowing the truth, knowing our authority, and then exercising that authority to be the governing voice over the world. With this clarity and authority, we then develop a sense of unattachment. For instance, when Jesus raised Lazarus from the dead, he was unattached to the grief that the others felt and unattached to the belief that Lazarus was dead, because he had the authority over the circumstances. Had Jesus been in the same state of mind as the people around them he would not have been able to do anything more than they did.

Where this can get confusing, and is something that commonly occurs for The Wayfarer, is that they believe that they are becoming more enlightened by being emotionally detached. They live their lives as wanderers, roaming, moving on, and keeping themselves detached, telling themselves they are spiritually evolving, but this is just a form of avoidance because they do not want to deal with their emotions. Unattachment comes naturally with spiritual evolution and knowing the truth of God so strongly that we can exercise it over our circumstances, therefore we are unattached to appearances because we know we have power over them. Detachment is a form of self-preservation, and an escape from our emotions, because they have too much power and authority over us. The saying "Seek first the Kingdom of God" means that all we will ever need comes naturally when we seek God. Instead of trying to become enlightened by being detached, seek God first and claim his Word for yourself, and unattachment will organically follow.

## THE MYTHOLOGIST + HEALING

**Practices + modalities you may have tried or areas of interest:**
Divine Masculine
Divine Feminine

Archetypes

Mythology

Sacred Sexuality

Sacred Sites such as Stonehenge, Tintagel, Lourdes, etc.

Love and romance

Love languages

Communication

Art and creativity

Intimacy

**Issues you may have worked on or have had difficulty with:**

Body issues, eating disorders, excessive working out.

Staying present

Letting go

Balance in relationships

Overly dominate partners

Being overwhelmed with emotions

Using your body and sexuality to achieve self-esteem or validation

Communication

Passive aggression

**The Mythologist heals best when:** Healing feels passionate, poetic, charming, alluring and mythical.

## You might benefit from practicing and studying:

The Mythologist is one of the most predominant Spiritual Archetypes who are attracted to sex, sexuality and finding their identity through sex. Proceed with caution as this can lead to identity crisis or loss of identity, pushing against one's values, and putting too much value on our bodies, which the Mythologist is already prone to. Sacred sexuality will not help us to find ourselves or God because it is an attempt to become spiritual through the physical. True sacred sexuality is the act of knowing God, treating our body as the temple of God, and sharing our temple with the temple of another in a relationship that embodies the attributes of God. Therefore, if God is love, peace, patience, forgiveness, joy, kindness, faithfulness, and self-control, then sacred intimacy should exhibit these attributes within yourself and your partner.

The Mythologist, more specifically, the female Mythologist, if there is a history of abuse or shame toward sexuality, may try to use sex as a form of liberation, expression, and vocalization. Remember that it is not the temple itself that is holy, but the communion with God within the temple that makes it hallowed. The temple may be a place where you receive revelation, but God is the one who provides it. Therefore, if you focus all of your energy, thought, and worship on the temple itself, you may not be prioritizing your connection with God. If you have been feeling this way in your life and/or practice, try to go directly to God for your healing, expression, and identity. When we see and understand the holiness we are as the image and expression of God; we tend to change how we see ourselves and how we treat our bodies, which simultaneously trickles into our relationships.

### Feeling and Emotions

Being a romantic and heart-based person, the Mythologist can sometimes live off emotion alone which can lead their life into turmoil, drama, or chaos, leaving The Mythologist feeling as though they have no footing in their own life. One study that may be beneficial for The Mythologist is the study of The Book of Proverbs. The Book of Proverbs is a fruitful, effective, and powerful tool that can be applied to every area of life, from romance, to work, parenting, friendship, morals, and everything in between. It is also like the sweetest, yet most powerfully spiritual poetry ever written. It is said that a person who lives by The Book of Proverbs will be successful in all things. This can be a useful compass for The Mythologist who may be looking at grounding, balancing, and owning their feelings and emotions instead of feeling owned or controlled by them.

## THE WARRIOR + HEALING

**Practices + modalities you may have tried or areas of interest:**
Warriors in Mythology

Athletics

Gymnastics

Dance

Martial Arts

Coaching

Military Training and/or Service

Sports recovery training

Physical education

Personal Training

Hiking

Mountain Climbing

Extreme Sports

Meditation

The history of war, military and/or battle tactics

**Issues you may have worked on or have had difficulty with:**

Self-worth

Loneliness

Isolation

Learning disabilities

Feelings of inadequacy

Social awkwardness and/or "fitting in"

Anxiety

Depression

Feeling trapped

Live's purpose

**The Warrior heals best when:** Their tough exterior is penetrated and they feel they have a meaningful connection with someone or something.

## You might benefit from practicing and studying:

*Meditation that focuses on heart and soul rather than physicality*
Since so much of your worth comes from movement and physicality, you may benefit from connecting in a way that doesn't promote

physicality such as breath work and meditation. This may be difficult at first, like working a new muscle, but you may enjoy having a multitude of ways to connect with God.

### Study ancient civilizations and mythology that integrate spirituality and war and athletics

Spirituality and athletics once had a strong union. Warriors integrated their spirituality into their battles, praying before, during, and after. Studying these ancient warriors might reveal some methods to assimilate your spirituality into your field and be a fascinating area of interest.

### Heal misperceptions or resentments around femininity and/or women

Some of the Warrior Spiritual Archetype may harbor resentments towards women or their own femininity. This can come across as archaic or chauvinist thinking. This may be rooted in resenting what may be perceived as "weak" or feeling the need to exert power over the weak to feel stronger. This is not the case for all of the Warrior Spiritual Archetypes, only some, but for those who struggle with this, you may benefit from working on balancing the male and female energies of yourself.

## THE EASTERN PHILOSOPHER + HEALING

**Practices + modalities you may have tried or areas of interest:**
Yoga
TCM
Ayurveda
Karma
Reincarnation
Tibetan Singing bowls
Sound therapy
Theta
Buddhist Death and Rebirth ritual
Cupping

Acupuncture
Martial arts

**Issues you may have worked on or have had difficulty with:**
Anger
Family beliefs and patterns
Dissatisfaction
Lack of direction or purpose
Depression
Stagnation
Confusion
Detachment
Empathy and Compassion
Confidence and Self-Esteem
Negativity
Anxiety and overthinking

**The Eastern Philosopher heals best when:** At retreats for yoga, Buddhism, ayurveda, etc., healing events, special training events, and classes that share ancient wisdom

## You might benefit from practicing and studying:

### *Gratitude*
The practice of gratitude is a weapon against stagnation, anger, and dissatisfaction. It reframes our minds from the negative or lack mentality, to the positive, and abundance mentality. If the Eastern Philosopher feels trapped, stagnant, or unhappy, you may benefit from beginning or revamping your gratitude practice. Gratitude also grounds us in the present. Instead of being angry about what was, or worried about what may be, gratitude roots us and brings our attention, energy, and focus to the present moment.

*Breaking Free from Limitations:*

One of the most challenging lessons for the Eastern Philosopher is breaking free from personal, family, or social limitations. These limitations may be generational, racial, personal, or spiritual, and come in all forms. One man I know is half Mexican, half Salvadorian and has long had dreams of traveling the world, living a free and adventurous life, learning about other cultures and discovering lands he has only heard of or read about. Having never left his city, and even though he appreciated all of the scarifies his family had made to make it in this country, he wanted more than what he had grown up with. However, his family's negative beliefs about how Hispanics should live differ significantly and they have been less than supportive of his dream.

I knew a woman of Chinese descent who wanted to be a healer and artist. She created incredible jewelry with spiritual meanings that incorporated her ancestry and honored her heritage. Unfortunately, her family made their success by all becoming doctors. Unless she too pursued medical school and became a doctor they would not support any other form of business or income.

A family I know is devoted to living the nine-to-five life, working for a union, and waiting for their pension and retirement. To them, manual labor is steady, consistent, reliable work, that while it may not be flashy or have a big payoff, is what made this country and should be what everyone wants. To their dismay, their children disagree and want nothing more than to be entrepreneurs and self-employed and never do manual labor in their life. They are constantly arguing their sides and never reaching a peaceful solution.

The reality is that sometimes people do not understand why others want what they want. Therefore, they cannot, or will not, get behind it. They see only what they believe or what has worked for them and are frightened by what it means for their paradigm if someone does something different.

For my Latino friend some of his family's unspoken, underlying questions were, "If you move away who will take care of your mother?" and "Who will support us if we no longer have your support?"

For the woman of Chinese descent, her parents were worried that her work would not bring the same level of achievement that being a doctor could. They had proof of how to make it in this country and were unwilling to accept her path since she could not prove that she could be successful in doing something else.

And for the family, they are afraid. The father is unhappy and does not enjoy his work or life. His children see this and are afraid too, "If I do that work, I will be stuck like he is stuck and I don't want to be unhappy." However, the father sees his children and worries for their future. "What if they never have a career? What if they never find good work? How will they live?" Which, for a parent, is terrifying. Both sides are afraid but do not voice their fears so they are lost in translation.

There is also one's pride. In many cases, people worry about how another person's decisions will make them look and are not willing to support compromising their reputation or appearance. For instance, a family might have a long line of attending prestigious universities until one day one of their children says they do not want to go to college. This may be more difficult for the parent for their own sake, making them act on their own behalf rather than in their child's best interest.

The Eastern Philosopher, more than any other Spiritual Archetype, has difficulty going against their families' beliefs and limitations and, in many cases, may choose not to in order to keep the peace. The Eastern Philosopher feels a sense of duty and commitment to their family that may make it feel that they are somehow betraying or leaving them behind by shattering their paradigm. Remember, friend, if you have a calling or dream in your heart, it may be your soul's purpose to pursue that path. God may direct or redirect you but it is only by moving forward that God can guide you to where you need to be. It is also not an accident that God has put you with your family. Living your purpose creates a ripple effect that may be needed for the rest of your family and friends. While they may not see the value in your choices, sometimes our mission is not to provide comfort but to facilitate growth in the most loving, positive, and confident way possible.

If you feel that you are still not living your dream or soul's purpose, it is never too late to transition into what fulfills your heart and makes you happy. You are not here just to appease the paradigms and limitations of others. Pray and ask for direction, guidance, and clarity on God's purpose for you and how a way can be made to transition into that as easily and effortlessly as possible.

## THE SAINT + HEALING

**Practices + modalities you may have tried or areas of interest:**
Boundaries
Type-A Personality
Women's groups
Mother Mary
Mary Magdalen
Women of The Bible
Motherhood and/or conscious parenting
Art
Traditions
Vegetarianism + Veganism

**Issues you may have worked on or have had difficulty with:**
Perfectionism
Boundaries
Anger
Resentment
Child of an abusive or substance abusive parent
Brain fog
Feeling flighty or spacey
Exhaustion
People pleasing
Feeling like you're going to "get in trouble" whether you have done something wrong or not

**The Saint heals best when:** They are treated softly, with love, kindness, and respect

## You might benefit from practicing and studying:

### *Healing perceptions about men*

While The Saint is drawn to more feminine energy, you may benefit from studying Jesus, especially if you have a past with an abusive male figure, father, partner, etc. Studying Jesus can heal those wounds while recalibrating your perception of men.

### *Mothering + Parenthood*

For the Saint who is a mother or parent, you may also enjoy studying the relationship between Mother Mary and Jesus. This can be healing to the mother/parent with a worried heart who also wants to love and support their child. The relationship between Mother Mary and Jesus is the most beautiful of any mother-son relationship. There are many beautiful lessons in this, such as how to be a mother to the son of the world. How can we be a mother, parents, or care for others while still respecting our mission and purpose? How do we surrender our will for the will of God, or the will of the people we love and care for? How can we be trusting and forgiving to those who are disillusioned and mystified? These are all monumental aspects of the Saint's path and if you have confusion, hurt, or issues around these, then studying Mother Mary, and Jesus may cause healing and revelation.

### *Healing mother wounds*

The Saint generally reveres mothers, especially if they grew up in hardship and view their mother as a savior. However sometimes there are unconscious resentments toward mothers. For instance, many people who grow up in households with abusive father figures tend to believe their anger and resentment are only toward him, but often come to realize they have buried animosity toward their mother for not saving them. Even though we may grow up and see these situations with more empathy or clarity, the child inside us may still be confused, hurt and abandoned. Forgiveness is a powerful tool in healing these wounds. It can also positively influence how we treat others, ourselves, and our children if and when we become parents, because the fuse has been extinguished. Healing mother wounds is deep and powerful work best done with loving motherly figures such as Mother Mary.

## THE CHRISTIAN MYSTIC + HEALING

**Practices + modalities you may have tried or areas of interest:**
Contemplative prayer
Religious history
Church History
Kabbalah
Christian Science
Signs and Wonders
Revivals
Divine Healing
Christian Monasticism

**Issues you may have worked on or have had difficulty with:**
Codependency
Depression
Feeling too emotional or controlled by your emotions
Empath
Masochism
Boundaries
Temperamental
Impulsive
Perfectionism

**The Christian Mystic heals best when:** They perceive God as loving, supportive, and nurturing

### You might benefit from practicing and studying:

### *Christian Mysticism*
Although this may seem obvious, many Christian Mystics are not practicing Christian Mysticism. Many of the Christian Mystics are people

who love God and Jesus but want to incorporate their intuition and spiritual self into their religion, spirituality, and practice. Christian Mysticism has a long and fruitful history of teachers and mystics that can be beneficial in studying to develop and blossom your interests. It can also bring new understanding, insights, and revelation to healing.

## God's Love

Suppose you have experienced seeing or learning about God as a hurtful or malicious God. In that case, you might want to learn about God with heart-centered material and let go of the false perception that God is cruel, spiteful, or judgmental. If you hear or read something that seems as such, pray on the material and ask God to show it to you through Christ's eyes. God is always loving, merciful, and full of grace. Try praying to feel God's love amid confusion and misperception and for discernment where needed.

## The Original New Thought Movement

The original New Thought movement 1850-1950 began with Phineas Parkhurst Quimby. It branched off into multiple other leaders and teachers over the next hundred years, including Mary Baker Eddy (Christian Science founder), Emma Curtis Hopkins, Harriet Emilie Cady, and Charles and Myrtle Fillmore (Founders of Unity Church). The New Thought movement brought a fresh approach to religion but also, for the first time in history, made God's love, divine healing, and mysticism mainstream. It also preached the equality of man, the right for every man to be free, and how God belonged to everyone, which had not been done on that scale and in such an unapologetic manner since the apostles first spread the Gospel. For anyone who wants to take in the richness of God, learn His Word, and study truth, the original New Thought movement can be a beneficial cornerstone of faith.

## THE CRUSADER + HEALING

**Practices + modalities you may have tried or areas of interest:**
Loss and grief

Bodywork and trauma release
Communication studies and practices
Anti-Racism and diversity
Psychology
Civil rights
Women's rights
Politics
Equality
Breathwork
History of social and civil rights movements

**Issues you may have worked on or have had difficulty with:**
Oppression
Persecution
Victimization
Brutality
Abuse
Suffering
Forgiveness
Self-Love
Feeling heard
Surrender
Letting Go
Anger

**The Crusader heals best when:** They feel their mission and purpose are divinely aligned and guided

## You might benefit from practicing and studying:

### *Forgiveness:*
Forgiveness is the greatest weapon we have toward our enemies. While it may feel challenging to forgive such evil or oppressive behaviors, especially if they are still transpiring, forgiveness can be practiced and is beneficial at all times. In her book The Dynamic Laws of Healing,

author and spiritual healer Catherine Ponder offers a powerful solution to anyone finding difficulty in forgiving our most negative relationships and encounters, stating: "It is easier to forgive those you are inclined to condemn, resent, even hate, when you remember this: They have not really failed nor disappointed you. They have not even let you down. They may have stumbled while crossing your pathway. But in reality, they are sons of God who temporarily lost their way. If they crossed your pathway, it was because they needed and wanted your blessing. They were unconsciously looking to you to be steadied and set right. Your progress has not been hindered, no matter what they did. They cannot keep your good from you. They crossed your pathway by divine appointment, even though they seemed to hurt you for a while. When people bother you in any way, it is because their souls are trying to get your divine attention and your blessing. Give them that."

### The life and teachings of Jesus and God-based activists

One of the reasons that men like Martin Luther King, Abraham Lincoln, and Mahatma Gandhi were so great is that they founded their mission and purpose in the Word of Jesus. They not only studied and appreciated his Word, but they also applied it to their lives and crusades. In doing so, they were affected personally, which translated into their work. Abraham Lincoln was known as "Honest Abe" and was said to be graceful, humble, and kind. Gandhi was known to be peaceful, loving, and truthful. Martin Luther King was compassionate, eloquent, and determined. While other people may exhibit these qualities, these three men are famous for their passion, drive, and caring demeanor, which they each established in their faith, love, and loyalty to God and Jesus. If you aspire to be like any of these great men in your heart, life, or work, you might want to look at the leader these great leaders followed and were devoted to.

## THE ARTIST + HEALING

**Practices + modalities you may have tried or areas of interest:**
Counseling
Art therapy

Self-worth
Spirituality and art
Spiritual and/or religious coloring books
Meditation
Art retreats
Spiritual retreats
Spirituality and religion in art

**Issues you may have worked on or have had difficulty with:**
Smoking
Excessive drinking
Recreational drug use
Fear of abandonment
Fear of losing talents
Fear of rejection
Insecurity
Overworking

**The Artist heals best when:** They are challenged. Artists love to challenge themselves and push themselves out of their comfort zone. This is a space where they allow themselves to surrender and let God move through them.

## You might benefit from practicing and studying:

The Artist thinks outside the box and is creative in many areas of their lives, including their spirituality. The Artist may enjoy mixing things up and trying new things, which can be beneficial in keeping your spirituality lively and fun. You may also benefit from a consistent spiritual practice such as church on Sundays, a study group, or even a spiritual book club. The Artist may tend to become very involved in something one week and then fall behind the next. By adding in these groups or events you can ensure that your spirituality is consistent, which can be incredibly beneficial.

## *Make God your compass*

For a creative personality we can often base our actions and motivations on feelings. This is part of what makes the Artist so extraordinary. However, if everything is based on feeling and emotions alone, we can run ourselves into the ground. Emotions are not stable and living on them can take our stability away. The solution to this is to make God our compass. God is stable in all things and his Word is actionable advice, information and wisdom in all situations and circumstances. If we live on emotions alone, we risk living on an emotional and unreliable rollercoaster. With God, He provides the foundation we need to live our most creative lives with support. Imagine a dance routine with two partners, a male and a female, where the male is firm in his foundation and footing. Knowing he can catch her, the woman can throw herself into his arms with trust, feeling free and unabashed. The more solid her partner, the more she can dance, letting go of her worries, and focusing on her art. Similarly, God is our most extraordinary of foundations and if we allow ourselves to leap into his arms, he will catch us with grace, strength, and love.

## THE NEW AGER + HEALING

**Practices + modalities you may have tried or areas of interest:**
Chakras
Kundalini
Reiki
Edgar Cayce teachings
Vortexes and grids
Aliens + UFOs
Conspiracy theories + theorists such as Davide Icke
Sound therapy
Past lives
Christ Consciousness
A Course in Miracles
Ego and Shadow work

Ancient Egyptian Spirituality
Inner child work

**Issues you may have worked on or have had difficulty with:**
Abusive parents or family
Overbearing or angry parents or family
Boundaries
Healthy Relationships
Manifesting
Money + Finances
Dark Night of the Soul
Attracting unhealthy, manipulative or dishonest people.
Sharing your truth + communication

**The New Ager heals best when:** They feel heard

## You might benefit from practicing and studying:

The New Ager is the other one of the most predominant Spiritual Archetypes who are attracted to sex, sexuality and finding their identity through sex. Proceed with caution as this can lead to identity crisis or loss of identity, pushing against one's values, and putting too much value on our bodies, as well as degrading ourselves. Sacred sexuality will not help us to find ourselves or God because it is an attempt to become spiritual through the physical. True sacred sexuality is the act of knowing God, treating our body as the temple of God, and sharing our temple with the temple of another in a relationship that embodies the attributes of God. Therefore, if God is love, peace, patience, forgiveness, joy, kindness, faithfulness, and self-control, then sacred intimacy should exhibit these attributes within yourself and your partner.

The New Ager, more specifically, the female New Ager if there is a history of abuse or shame toward sexuality, may try to use sex as a form of liberation, expression, and vocalization. The male New Ager might use sexuality as a form of domination to try to heal their own wounds around sexuality to make them feel empowered. Remember that it is not the temple itself that is holy, but the communion with God within the temple that makes it hallowed. The temple may be a place where you receive revelation, but God is the one who provides it. Therefore, if you focus all of your energy, thought, and worship on the temple itself, you may not be prioritizing your connection with God. If you have been feeling this way in your life and/or practice, try to go directly to God for your healing, expression, and identity. When we see and understand the holiness we are as the image and expression of God; we tend to change how we see ourselves and how we treat our bodies, which simultaneously trickles into our relationships.

### Forgiveness

Forgiveness is one of the most powerful resources available to us in our spirituality and, for the New Ager, can be keys to your freedom. Unforgiveness is like a malevolent spirit whose power, anger, and force grow over time. When it festers in our heart, soul, and psyche, it dominates our thoughts, actions, and motivations, either knowingly or unknowingly. The New Ager usually does not realize that while they think they will be pacified by sharing or expressing their truth, gaining power or control in their life, or retribution for past hurts, what they truly want more than anything is inner peace. Peace from the past, peace from needing to feel like they must control or avoid things to gain power, and peace from trying to make everyone listen, respect, and honor them. When the New Ager finds this inner peace, the rest of everything else they are seeking naturally and effortlessly will fall into place, creating ease that may be surprising. The beginning of this transformation begins with forgiveness.

### Connecting with the inner child

One of the New Ager's greatest assets is their childlike innocence and playfulness. This can be incredibly beneficial in healing, utilizing fun and innocent practices to aid your growth. Imagination, art, and even kids' activities such as building and Legos, can be soothing to a part of yourself you may not have realized and be healing to your inner child. Allow yourself to let your inner child out to play; you may be surprised by how much you grow.

## THE METAPHYSICIAN + HEALING

**Practices + modalities you may have tried or areas of interest:**
Social reformation
Philosophy
Intuitive Art
Medicine
Botany
Alchemy
Theosophy
Biodynamics
Anthroposophic Medicine
Applied Kinesiology
Bodywork
Rolfing

**Issues you may have worked on or have had difficulty with:**
Feeling misunderstood
Feeling ahead of your time or out of place in current society
Sharing your goals and vision
Bridging the gap between spirituality and science
Overworking
Exhaustion
Balancing work and life, family, etc.
Self-Care
Prioritizing personal needs

**The Metaphysician heals best when:** In solitude or conversation. The Metaphysician is always thinking; whether in solitude or bouncing ideas off of others, the movement and expression of your thoughts can help you sort and gain clarity from them.

### You might benefit from practicing and studying:

#### *Dream Interpretation:*

The Metaphysician gains revelation in their work, but many receive some of their most significant insights in their dreams. Therefore, dream interpretation can be extremely helpful for Metaphysician in understanding God's messages to them.

#### *Intuitive Art*

The Metaphysician has used drawing, painting, and any other form of art for many years. It is a valuable practice while also being meditative and relaxing. Especially for a left-brain intellectual mind, this can strengthen the right brain and help you tap into a different facet of God.

#### *Keep your priorities strong*

Keeping a solid spiritual foundation will help ensure that you also take care of yourself. If you make your priorities, God, self, and others, then you will always be putting your health and self-care at the top of your list.

#### *The God Particle*

Science has long tried to prove or disprove the existence of spiritual things. In many cases, it is evidence for those who have no faith. The Metaphysical however, strives to prove the validity of spiritual things with the power of science. This has created monumental leaps in our awareness of the metaphysical, making the Metaphysician arguably one of the most influential voices in the spiritual community because of their contributions to science and spirituality. For the Metaphysician, the quest for proof can hinder their faith, motivating them to always find physical evidence that may not be provable. One of the most significant spiritual laws is that "Faith is the substance of things hoped for, the evidence of things not seen" (Hebrews 11:1). If the Metaphysician is always seeking evidence in science, numbers, tests, etc. they are lacking a key element to their faith. If faith could be proven, everyone would have it. Unfortunately, that is part of the process which can be uncomfortable for a person who needs or wants proof. However, faith is about walking in faith, not by sight, (2 Corinthians 5:7), meaning that we must have faith in our hearts, not with our eyes. For the Metaphysician who relies on their sight, this will be an exercise of the heart. God is within us and resides in our hearts. When we connect there, the God particle will tie it all together.

## THE ORACLE + HEALING

**Practices + modalities you may have tried or areas of interest:**
Astrology
Numerology
Sacred geometry
Tarot
Runes
Palmistry
Social justice
Politics
Activism

**Issues you may have worked on or have had difficulty with:**
Identity
Self-worth
Faith
Life path
Karma
Breaking unhealthy patterns
Understanding blocks
Alignment
Intense health scares or near-death experiences
Self-Expression
Relationships

**The Oracle heals best when:** You feel you have clarity, purpose, and direction

## You might benefit from practicing and studying:

Pastor Kenneth Hagin was one of the most prophetic servants, teachers, and messengers of our time. However, he did not come by this gift at birth; it was almost fifteen years after becoming a teacher, and nearly twenty years after becoming a Christian that this miracle even happened. He stated that he prayed one prayer, from two chapters of the book of Ephesians, continuously over six months, which is when the visions and revelations began. The book of Ephesians was written by the apostle Paul to the church of Ephesus. However, Kenneth Hagin changed specific pronouns such as instead of saying "you," he would say "I" to refer to himself. In doing so, he continuously spoke the word of God over himself, which opened him up to God's word being revealed to him. Below are the scriptures of Paul written to the church of Ephesus as they appear in the book of Ephesians. When praying these scriptures, replace the word "you" with the word "I" or "me" to personalize it to yourself. This can also be prayed for others inserting their name where applicable.

## Original King James Versions

### *Ephesians 1:16–23*

"I Cease not to give thanks for you, making mention of you in my prayers; that the God of our Lord Jesus Christ, the Father of glory, may give unto you the spirit of wisdom and revelation in the knowledge of him: the eyes of your understanding being enlightened; that ye may know what is the hope of his calling, and what the riches of the glory of his inheritance in the saints, and what is the exceeding greatness of his power to us-ward who believe, according to the working of his mighty power, which he wrought in Christ, when he raised him from the dead, and set him at his own right hand in the heavenly places, far above all principality, and power, and might, and dominion, and every name that is named, not only in this world, but also in that which is to come: and hath put all things under his feet, and gave him to be the head over all things to the church, which is his body, the fulness of him that filleth all in all."

*Ephesians 3:14–21*

"For this cause I bow my knees unto the Father of our Lord Jesus Christ, of whom the whole family in heaven and earth is named, that he would grant you, according to the riches of his glory, to be strengthened with might by his Spirit in the inner man; that Christ may dwell in your hearts by faith; that ye, being rooted and grounded in love, may be able to comprehend with all saints what is the breadth, and length, and depth, and height; and to know the love of Christ, which passeth knowledge, that ye might be filled with all the fulness of God. Now unto him that is able to do exceeding abundantly above all that we ask or think, according to the power that worketh in us, unto him be glory in the church by Christ Jesus throughout all ages, world without end. Amen."

### Personalized Version

*Ephesians 1:16–23*

"I Cease not to give thanks for you, making mention of myself in my prayers; that the God of our Lord Jesus Christ, the Father of glory, may give unto me the spirit of wisdom and revelation in the knowledge of him: the eyes of my understanding being enlightened; that I may know what is the hope of his calling, and what the riches of the glory of his inheritance in the saints, and what is the exceeding greatness of his power to us-ward who believe, according to the working of his mighty power, which he wrought in Christ, when he raised him from the dead, and set him at his own right hand in the heavenly places, far above all principality, and power, and might, and dominion, and every name that is named, not only in this world, but also in that which is to come: and hath put all things under his feet, and gave him to be the head over all things to the church, which is his body, the fulness of him that filleth all in all."

*Ephesians 3:14–21*

"For this cause I bow my knees unto the Father of our Lord Jesus Christ, of whom the whole family in heaven and earth is named, that he would grant me, according to the riches of his glory, to be strengthened with might by his Spirit in the inner man; that Christ may dwell in my heart

by faith; that I, being rooted and grounded in love, may be able to comprehend with all saints what is the breadth, and length, and depth, and
height; and to know the love of Christ, which passeth knowledge, that
I might be filled with all the fulness of God. Now unto him that is able
to do exceeding abundantly above all that we ask or think, according to
the power that worketh in us, unto him be glory in the church by Christ
Jesus throughout all ages, world without end. Amen.

## THE OCCULTIST + HEALING

**Practices + modalities you may have tried or areas of interest:**
Ego and Shadow work
Alchemy
Chemistry
Literature and poetry
Astronomy
Astrology
Parapsychology
Psychology
Science
Psychic phenomena
Mysticism
Tarot
Hypnotherapy
Phrenology

**Issues you may have worked on or have had difficulty with:**
Depression
Anxiety
Bipolar or manic depression
Isolation
Addiction
Attracting difficult, dark, and unhealthy people and relationships
Racing thoughts
Obsessive tendencies

**The Occultist heals best:** When you are in a positive, healthy place in your life, mind, and spirit

## You might benefit from practicing and studying:

### *Kabbalah, Hasidism, Christian Mysticism, + Christian Science*

The Occultist is drawn to the supernatural elements of life and death and our innate supernatural qualities as souls. This often leads them into darker mysticism looking for answers to the secrets of our being and existence. The Kabbalah, Christian Mysticism, and Christian Science are all God-based teachings but include the supernatural and mystical elements of spirituality. For the Occultist, these teachings may be beneficial in satisfying your craving for mysticism while founding your study in a more positive, God-based way.

### *Letting Go*

Similar to how the Zodiac of Scorpio is drawn to mysteries and death, the Occultist is drawn to these darker aspects of life. Problems can arise for the Occultist when they cling too tightly to these darker parts of themselves and refuse to transcend them. Like an addict who continues seeing the same people, going to the same places, and acting out the same behaviors as when they were using, they cannot move past the addiction mentality, thus backpedaling their recovery. For the Occultist, the familiar is settling, regardless of how dark, depressing, or unhealthy it may be. In some ways, they almost find comfort in it. This is where letting go becomes the Occultist's greatest ally. To move forward on our path, we must let go of our attachment to our shadow and darkness. Spiritual teacher Michael Mirdad once said, "Do you know how you overcome your shadow? It's not through shadow work and validation; it's by turning to the light. When we face the light, our shadow disappears." Everything multiples after its kind. Therefore, focusing on darkness multiples darkness, focusing on pain multiples pain, and focusing on suffering multiples suffering. If we focus on our light, we will multiply our light. However, we must also let go of our need, desire, or attachment to our shadow if we are ever going to step into the light.

# THE LIGHTWORKER + HEALING

**Practices + modalities you may have tried or areas of interest:**
Kundalini
Yoga
Angel Cards
Sound Healing
Aqua therapy
Transcendental Mediation
A Course in Miracles
Animal healing
Reiki and energy healing
Chakras

**Issues you may have worked on or have had difficulty with:**
Lack of meaning and soul's purpose
Health issues
Eating and food-related issues
Drugs and/or drinking
Excessive partying
Existential crisis
Depression
Nervous breakdowns
Anxiety
Perfectionism

**The Lightworker heals best when:** You feel good

## You might benefit from practicing and studying:

When Helen Schucman was a little girl, she was saddened by her relationship with her father. Mr. Schucman, a cold, methodical, and unemotional man, seemed distant and as though he did not like her. When Helen told this to her mother, her mother assured her that her father did in fact love her but that he was just "different" and encouraged

Helen to appreciate her father. Helen tried to see the love her father had for her and tried to believe that even though he was different he did love her. As time passed, Helen grew tired of working so hard to see her father's love for her and told her mother that she just didn't believe it. Her mother grew irritated and told Helen that she just didn't appreciate her father. For Helen, a girl looking for a father to love her that she felt she could appreciate, the relationship with her father was devastating and had a profound impact on her relationship with God. Throughout her young life she had tried to find a relationship with God and was always disappointed.

Years after this conversation with her mother, Helen became incredibly ill and was told by doctors that she had to have an operation. Plagued by nightmares and terrified, she postponed the operation, getting increasingly ill. The doctor assured her that she should be out in a week or so, and she finally agreed. The night before the operation she once again prayed to God, telling him that while she no longer believed in him, she would put the operation in his hands. However, the operation did not go well and everything seemed to go wrong. What was assumed would be a week-long stint in the hospital grew to a four-month stay. Helen was angry and devastated that once again she felt God had let her down. Her nurse, a Catholic woman, told her that she was praying for her every day and that God had given her a miracle because Helen could have died during the operation but she lived. Helen did not see it that way. She was angry because it didn't appear the way she wanted it to, so she believed he had done nothing for her. The nurse then said something that had haunted Helen her whole life; her nurse told her that she would continue to pray for her but that Helen lacked appreciation for the miracle God had bestowed upon her.

Many years later, Helen Schucman healed her relationship with God and went on to write *A Course in Miracles*, which has gone on to become a best-selling book as well as a movement amongst lightworkers. And like Helen, many Lightworkers find themselves in the same situations where they feel angry toward a mother or father and are so deeply hurt by them, that they project that relationship onto God. To fill this void and feel a sense of power, they want to try to create their own miracles and use the universe as their tool, but the universe is only part of God's creation and does not fulfill the need for Himself. Like the girl in the beginning story of this book, we feel so hurt or betrayed by God for the wounds and pain in our lives, we try to become our own gods but it always leads to heartache. This was a battle that Helen faced for most of her life which ultimately made her turn away from God. That is, until she was chosen to write *A Course in Miracles*, which happened through one defining moment. As Helen tells the story in her biography,

"My own 'magic' phase ended abruptly with a particularly clear picture episode in which I knew I had made an irrevocable choice. I saw myself entering a cave cut into a rock formation on a bleak, wind-swept seacoast. All I found in the cave was a large and very old parchment scroll. Its ends were attached to heavy gold-tipped poles, and the scroll was wrapped around them so that they met in the middle of the scroll and were tied tightly together. With some difficulty I managed to untie the ends and open the scroll just enough to reveal the center panel, on which two words were written: 'God is.' Then I unrolled the scroll all the way. As I did so, tiny letters began to appear on both sides of the panel. The silent Voice which I had 'heard' before explained the situation mentally to me:

"'If you look at the left side you will be able to read the past,' said the Voice. 'If you look at the right side you will be able to read the future.' The little letters on the sides of the panel were becoming clearer, but I hesitated only a moment before rolling up the scroll sufficiently to conceal everything except the center panel. 'I'm not interested in reading the past or the future,' I said with finality. 'I'll just stop with this.' The Voice sounded both reassured and reassuring.

'You made it that time,' it said. 'Thank you.'"

God is, and while there may be a Rolodex of memories where it felt like the miracle wasn't there, or didn't appear the way you prayed or hoped, God is, always has been, and will always be, working miracles in your favor. It may be scary or uncomfortable to heal that relationship, just as it was for Helen, who felt angry and judged for not "appreciating" her earthly or heavenly father. Still, if we allow ourselves to heal these wounds, forgive these hurts, and open ourselves up, we might, like Helen, find the all-encompassing love of God we have been searching for. Part of the beauty of this is that when we create this relationship, the miracles will happen organically as we can surrender to the magic of God.

## THE MINDSET MASTER + HEALING

**Practices + modalities you may have tried or areas of interest:**
Affirmations
Manifesting
Life Coaching
Money Coaching, classes, training
Books, online courses, and workshops
Meditation
Visualization
Vision boards

**Issues you may have worked on or have had difficulty with:**
Poverty and money issues
Bullying
Victimization
Upper limits
Abusive parents
Breaking free from other people's limits and beliefs
Negative people
Negative self-talk
Self-doubt, worry, and fear

**The Mindset Master heals best when:** You see results

**You might benefit from practicing and studying:**

## The Book of Proverbs

The book of Proverbs is a wonderful foundation for anyone who wants to be in business and wants a solid spiritual foundation. Written by King Solomon, Proverbs details how to do all things with greatness, humility, wisdom, and communion with God. If anyone follows the words in Proverbs, they can have a fruitful, successful, and happy life.

## Listen, Learn, and Integrate

Many people interested in mindset will follow and explore mindset teachers and teachings. While this will be an area of interest, try also reading and exploring teachers with a powerful mindset with a solid spiritual foundation. In doing so, you may see how they integrated the two and how it positivity impacted their lives and spiritual practices.

## Heart-Centered Meditation, Visualization, and Planning

When you pray and meditate, try visualizing your heart center as you plan or design goals. Instead of just thinking words, try incorporating them into your heart by thinking or saying them aloud while imagining your heart. As you know, the mind is powerful; if you can believe it, you can achieve it. Therefore, think your thoughts into your heart to marry the two.

## The Fruits of the Spirit

The Mindset Master is an accomplished trainer of their thoughts and words. They train their mind to obey them and have it under their submission. This is a powerful tool for success, but is only one fraction of personal and spiritual mastery. When it comes to the spiritual, the true evidence of a master can be found in the Fruits of the Spirit, which are the signs and physical manifestations of a person's spiritual practice. These twelve attributes; love, joy, peace, longsuffering (patience), kindness, goodness, faithfulness, gentleness, self-control, faith, modesty, continence, and chastity, show how well a person is trained, not only in their mind but in their spirit. In some cases, the Mindset Master will use their mindset work as a practice; something they do at a specific time or in particular situations, however, spirituality is meant to be integrated into every aspect of our lives. They will feel amazing in the moments they practice but do not exhibit the Fruits of the Spirit outside of those moments. Since our lives and spiritual paths are entwined, there is never a moment that we are not practicing spirituality. If people can integrate their faith and spirituality into every aspect of themselves, not just the mind, they will begin to see the Fruits of the Spirit manifest in their lives.

# THE SOVEREIGN + HEALING

**Practices + modalities you may have tried or areas of interest:**
Organized religion
Tarot and readings
Palmistry
Secret Societies and their influence on the modern world
The most powerful empires and rulers throughout history
Astrology and numerology, especially for business ventures and big decisions
Intuition
Money habits of millionaires and successful people

**Issues you may have worked on or have had difficulty with:**
Motivation
Empathy
Detachment
Overworking
Control
Sensitivity and understanding
Impatience
Overthinking
Insomnia
Obsessing
Perfectionism
Betrayal and trust

**The Sovereign heals best when:** They approach spirituality and communion with God with humility, honesty, and an open heart.

## You might benefit from practicing and studying:

### Courage + Fluidity

The Sovereign fears chaos and anarchy and believes that peace and harmony come with order and control. To create order, they may take the reins of the leader. First and foremost, leading from a place of fear can be detrimental to one's ability to serve. Therefore, seek to lead from a place of courage, regardless of what field you are a leader in. Be confident in yourself but also seek God and put Him as your foundation. The most outstanding rulers and leaders of all time put God at the forefront of their leadership. By taking this approach, you are amongst the greats. Secondly, a leader must learn to flow with change. To refuse it can cause restriction and rigidity in the fluidity of the ever-changing world. To be fluid is to move, adapt, and grow. Do not fear change. God is infinite with infinite possibilities and ideas. Instead of seeing your current way as the only way, ask God to show you a new way and let Him guide you into a progressive vision for the future.

### Integrity + Trust

Today we are constantly at war with ourselves and others about whom we can trust and who truly has integrity. Over the years, it has become a fad to brand oneself or one's brand as being integrous in an attempt to get people to trust them. Politicians have become less professional and more casual to try to show they are just like the people they aim to serve. While this is the way of marketing, advertisers, professionals, and even the spiritual community these days, we trust each other less than ever and the world has become increasingly less integrous. The world needs kings, queens, and leaders who do not say what they are but embody it fully in their words, actions, and lifestyle. As parents, we are leaders, teachers are leaders, but even in our work, friendships and relationships, we can be leaders, guiding, protecting, and honoring those around us. Being a leader does not simply mean leading others toward some task, mission or job; it can and should be about leading people in the right direction, toward love, kindness, joy, happiness, giving, wealth, and compassion. By striving for these goals and working toward them in our own lives, we inspire others to do the right thing as well, which is what authentic leadership is about.

### Be the Light

Be the light you wish to see in the world, in turn, lighting the way for others.

### Humility

An arrogant and self-centered king named Nebuchadnezzar had a dream that greatly disturbed him. He called all of his magicians and astrologers to him to interpret the meaning behind his bothersome nightmare. However, when they arrived, he could no longer remember the dream. He insisted they tell him his dream and also the meaning, but of course, they could not. All except a young boy named Daniel who came to him and told him that he could tell him his dream and the meaning of it because God had revealed it to him. When King Nebuchadnezzar heard that God had indeed revealed the dream to Daniel "King Nebuchadnezzar fell upon his face, and worshipped Daniel, and commanded that they should offer an oblation and sweet odours unto him. The king answered unto Daniel, and said, Of a truth it is, that your God is a God of gods, and a Lord of kings, and a revealer of secrets, seeing thou couldest reveal this secret." (Daniel 2 46-47).

After hearing the dream's meaning and seeing God's power, Nebuchadnezzar changed his ways and his heart. He became a better person and a better king and humbled himself to the true King. The greatest kings knew that their rule on Earth is only temporary and that our reign is limited. Always remember that as powerful, sought after, or respected we may be on Earth, God is King, and to humble ourselves to his glory is the humblest act we can take.

# THE THEOLOGIST + HEALING

**Practices + modalities you may have tried or areas of interest:**
Faith Healing
Radical Initiations
Sacred Fasting
Church conferences
Sacred sites travel, especially to the Holy Lands.
Biblical archeology
Missions
The Holy Spirit
Genealogy of the Bible

**Issues you may have worked on or have had difficulty with:**
Boundaries (especially if you are a pastor or in the church)
Empathy
Compassion
Communication
Judgment
Condemnation
Heart filled faith

**The Theologist heals best when:** They can devote and dedicate themselves fully and entirely to their studies, practice, and teaching

## You might benefit from practicing and studying:

### Spiritual Fasting
I first wrote about this in the original guidebook for the Theologist and I received dozens of emails from people asking what it was and how to do it. Here is a general guideline but everyone must practice this according to how they are guided.

For the Theologist, spiritual fasting can be one of the most powerful and beneficial practices. Spiritual fasting is a practice that can be found throughout many cultures throughout history and is also mentioned in the Bible. It is reducing or denying food for a designated period of time in order to develop less dependency on our bodies, and more dependency on God.

For those new to fasting, it would be wise to begin with only one day. While that may not seem like much, if you are not used to this it will still have an effect on you. Most people will do a set of three days, and sometimes people even do more, but again, this is something you must be directed to do. Additionally, this is not something you should do if you have health issues that could flare up with a fast.

What spiritual fasting can do is bring us revelation and connection with God on a deeper level by depriving our physical senses in lieu of our spiritual senses. Many people do not realize that we are slaves to our bodies. Our bodies are driven by desire and pleasure, whether for food, sugar, alcohol, drugs, or sex, and are accustomed to illness, sickness, and ailments. In most cases, we do not have authority over our body, it has authority over us. However, we can, (and should, but it's everyone's choice,) claim our authority over our bodies. As the apostle Paul says in 1 Corinthians 9:27 "But I keep under my body, and bring *it* into subjection: lest that by any means, when I have preached to others, I myself should be a castaway." Fasting can be a catalyst to revoke our authority.

When we should fast will depend on the direction we receive but can be done especially when we are in a place of stagnation or seeking revelation. Revivalist Kenneth Hagin said there were times he fasted prior to a revival for better results. Many pastors and ministers will fast to receive information and clarity on a situation for guidance on the direction of their church. It can also be practiced for the sake of deepening or strengthening our dependency on God and allowing it to unfold organically.

How fasting is done, again, varies for each person, but can begin with going one day without food, or greatly reducing your intake (but still drinking plenty of water) and devoting your day to constant prayer, communion, and study of the Word. Sometimes people do just bread and water, or crackers and water, etc. This can be done at your discretion and what you feel is appropriate for your body and faith. For people who do not feel comfortable or who are unable to abstain from or reduce food, there are other forms of abstinence that could benefit you. For someone with excessive sexual activity, abstinence from sex for a period of time might prove more beneficial. At the same time, someone who uses drugs or alcohol would benefit from abstinence from these. Whatever your vice, remember that we are not merely abstaining from a thing; we are doing so with the intent of simultaneously increasing our communion, study, and prayer. We cannot simply take something away and hope for the best. By removing something and replacing it with God, we will see an impact and outcome. By allowing God more into each area of our lives, no matter how little to begin with and then increasing from there, we allow His hold on our lives in more significant ways.

*Note of caution:* Fasting should be practiced on a day off of work (or simultaneously with your work if you have a profession in spirituality or the church) so that you have time to fully dedicate to your fasting. This should not be done while driving long distances, traveling, babysitting, or doing open heart surgery, etc. Use common sense and proper discretion. If you have preexisting health issues such as diabetes or blood sugar issues, this will not be the best practice for you. Going without food for an extensive amount of time can be harmful and life-threatening so please be responsible, and when in doubt, always seek medical advice or attention when needed.

# CHEMICALIZATION

*Chemicalization means that things are coming out in a better state*
*of affairs than before. Regardless of what is happening . . .*
—CATHERINE PONDER

There is a process that can occur on the spiritual path that, without awareness of it, can make a person feel as though all they are practicing spiritually, and all their attempts at healing, are failing them. It is such a sizeable occurrence that regardless of a person's desire to change or uplevel their consciousness, they may, out of frustration and hopelessness, choose to give up entirely. This is known as chemicalization.

## What Is Chemicalization?

Chemicalization is a process that occurs when we have exposed deeply rooted negative belief systems. It is a physical and worldly reaction caused by a spiritual advancement. When pursuing healing and attempting to raise our consciousness or awaken spirituality, we shed our old belief systems, negative mindset, old fears, and commitment to our (victim) story. When revealing the lies or fears we are particularly committed to, physical manifestations may happen to combat the new truths being spoken to them.

For instance, if a person is sick or has an extensive history of sickness, then begins denying illness, they may become increasingly ill for a time. If a person has had issues with money and starts denying their scarcity mindset, which was initially born from lack and poverty, they may suddenly be hit with outstanding bills. If someone has had exceptional success in a particular area, it may suddenly seem to be falling apart.

The enemy (ego, devil) creates these lying symptoms to regain your engagement. What has happened is a conflict of beliefs and old conditioning. Through conditioning, negative programming, and the subconscious manifestation of our negative beliefs, we become invested in the lies we have come to believe. When we come to a place of realization and denial of these lies, an agitation occurs between the old and new ways of thinking.

Chemicalization does not happen to everyone, nor does it happen with every spiritual advancement. It mostly happens to people who are deeply committed to their false beliefs. The appearance of chemicalization in our healing is similar to cleaning a house. When we clean our home daily, we maintain its condition. However, when it comes time for deeper cleaning, such as clearing out the garage, basement, or attic, we are met with garbage and old rubbish we forgot we had. As we begin pulling out the old waste, dust and debris fill the air. There may be cobwebs and bugs hiding in dark spaces. With all our old belongings strewn about, we may wonder if our house will ever return to being clean and organized. But to clean and organize our homes effectively, we must go through the cleansing of the old to lay the foundation for the new. We must commence deep cleaning if we expect more profound results. Chemicalization is the mental, spiritual, physical, and emotional equivalent of this deep cleaning. When we begin attending to the dark, unattended crevices of our beliefs and fears, some dust and debris may become unsettled, and the upheaval may cause the appearance of chaos.

Emmet Fox said this about chemicalization: "It seems as though everything begins to go wrong at once. This may be disconcerting, but it is a good sign. Suppose your whole world seems to rock on its foundation. Hold on steadily, and let it rock, and when the rocking is over, the picture will have reassembled itself into something much nearer to your heart's desire."

## The Stages of Chemicalization

### The New Truth Is Introduced

The first step of chemicalization is when we begin to realize a new truth. When we have believed and committed to a lie and we suddenly introduce truth, our innards start to shift and quake. We begin questioning our old ways, and the seed has been planted for new growth. This is a crucial time when we must continue our studies and insist on this new truth. Abandoning the truth will leave worse turmoil than before. To win this battle, you must commit to braving the storm and continuing with the new truth until the smoke clears and you have reached the other side.

### The Upheaval

After new revelations are introduced, and we begin denying our false beliefs and affirming the truth, we transition into upheaval. This is the period where the enemy (ego, devil) creates chaos and argument, bringing in situations and people to convince us of our old lies and to abandon our newfound truth. People you know may begin to have issues with you and situations may arise that contend all your proceedings. Remain peaceful and free of fear, knowing that chemicalization is taking place and that peace and goodness are on the other side of the seeming chaos. Do not give up hope or embrace your fear by allowing it to reign over your thoughts and actions. Remind yourself there is nothing to fear and that you are birthing the manifestation of truth in your life. Pray through this period, affirming your authority over the situation: I AM the peace and stillness of God. There is nothing to fear. I AM in the truth of God and the truth of God is within me. I peacefully and joyfully accept God's truth in my life now.

### The Stillness and Shedding

After the loudness of the upheaval comes a period of great stillness and the shedding of that which no longer serves us. This is a space in time when we are no longer the person we were and can no longer go back to the same behaviors. This is also where we must let go of what we can no longer relate to. It can feel like a sad time, and you may experience feelings of loss as you release people, places, or things to which you have grown accustomed and attached. It may also feel confusing as to how we can love others yet not feel as though they fit into our new identity. This is not to say that we have become better than anyone or feel superior. It only means that the pieces of who we were and whom we are becoming no longer coincide or fit neatly together. As you go through the stillness and shedding, remember these words from *A Course in Miracles*: "Nothing real can be threatened, nothing unreal exists." Only the truth of God will prevail through chemicalization, and His truth cannot be threatened. Only that which serves you and your higher consciousness will remain; the rest will begin to fall away. Focus on the truth and let it be your beacon to guide you through your shedding process.

## The Fulfillment and Uplevel

At the end of the chemicalization process comes the glorious fulfillment you have been awaiting and working so passionately for. This is the final stage where the results occur and you finally see and feel the fruits of your labor. You may begin to feel healthier than you have ever felt, more prosperous and abundant than you ever have been, more successful than you deemed possible, or create healthier and more loving relationships than you ever imagined. Through chemicalization, you have up-leveled your consciousness to a place where your higher consciousness is more easily honored and governs more of your thoughts and actions.

It is an extraordinary feeling coming out on the other side, and it feels like a huge weight has been lifted. This final phase of chemicalization is a personal time where your new changes should be kept secret. Turning to God rather than sharing your newfound perceptions, ideas, and changes with the masses is important. Some experts insist that loudly sharing all your changes may even cause the effects to wear off or fade away. Being still with God is where we should remain during this time as we wait for the final pieces to fall into place and listen for our following insight or direction.

## *How to Peacefully Transition Through Chemicalization*

The more we deny our fears and old beliefs, the more intense chemicalization can become. The reason is that these old beliefs and fears appear to serve a purpose. When you deny them with the intent to eradicate them, they begin to kick and scream. However, if we gently eliminate them through the power of positive shifting, they are more apt to oblige. Imagine a child being told no for something they request. Upon being denied their request, they may throw a fit. However, if we gently communicate with them and lead their attention to something they *can* have, they are much more likely to feel peaceful about the situation. Instead of exclusively denying "there is no lack," you would do better to affirm, "I AM divine prosperity and abundance." By affirming rather than simply denying, you are leading your old self to the recognition that there is a more peaceful and fulfilling way.

Affirm the truth relentlessly. Despite all appearances and seeming failure, continue to affirm the truth of God. If you have seen lying symptoms of sickness, declare, "I AM the wholeness and health of God." If your life seems to be in upheaval, claim the words, "I AM the peace and stillness of God." Do not give in to the old ways begging for validation, or succumb to the belief that you are not advancing or have fallen from your path. Although chemicalization may feel or sound like a horrible process, it is the confirmation that our work, studies, and healing are taking place on grand levels. Commit to this truth and know that all you are desiring and working for is on the other side of this undoing process.

# COLLECTIVE
# CHEMICALIZATION

*The world we are experiencing today is the result of our
collective consciousness, and if we want a new world, each of
us must start taking responsibility for helping create it.*
**—ROSEMARY FILLMORE**

Just as we go through personal chemicalization, the collective does as well. As I mentioned, we tend to think of our path as exclusive to us and that we are the center of our little universe. However, we are a collective, and there are times when we see that play out in our world. Just as with personal chemicalization, it will seem like everything has gone wrong in the world. During collective chemicalization, we will see people reaching for their identity more desperately than usual, and some become more emotional, angry, or frustrated. This may play out in social norms, politics, social media, or day-to-day life. The global pandemic has escalated this chemicalization, bringing awareness to these issues that have been dormant or ignored. But as we clean out our collective, they begin to rise to the surface. The collective goes through the upheaval process, which creates chaos and argument in the world. We have seen this on a monumental scale throughout pandemics and other times in history where people have become ravenously unethical toward each other. They feel the chaos within themselves and seek identity outside of themselves, but their world has become unstable so instead they panic. Then comes the time of stillness and shedding; however, this isn't always something we can gain in the collective. This is when people start wanting their politics, religions, or laws to change to be free from their inner chaos. This usually does not happen. The issue with collective chemicalization is that since it appears to be happening outwardly, people tend to believe that is where they will find their answers. Unfortunately, they don't, and the healing often goes unutilized or missed. People seek the answers to their identity through the world instead of God, leading to more confusion and identity crisis.

People base their identity on whom they vote for, the color of their skin, their sexual orientation, the type of parent they are, and their zodiac sign—the list is endless. Yet people are more separated from each other than ever, and most are lost *within* themselves. When we go through chemicalization as a collective, people may want to see the changes in the world to accommodate them. But since the world cannot do that, we continuously go through a vicious cycle of upheaval and chaos, then search the world for answers and solutions. That doesn't mean we can't make laws in this world or stand up for injustices. This is a physical world, so of course it has its laws, and we must adjust ourselves accordingly to take care of our Earth and each other. But our identity is not in this world. Unfortunately, eons of trying to discover ourselves within this world have left people in a global identity crisis. There is a saying, "The definition of insanity is doing the same thing and expecting different results." Yet this is what the world keeps doing. Our identity is not in this world, nor has it ever been. That doesn't mean we don't identify with things in this world; but our true identity is not based in this world. People may love aspects of their personality, heritage, background, or hobbies, but that is something they like, love, or resonate with, not who they are as a soul.

The other issue with collective chemicalization is that a personal chemicalization can be self-focused whereas collective chemicalization can be blaming, shaming, or guilting others. When going through a phase of chemicalization personally, we can look at what is coming for us. Although it is a difficult period, it's still tailored to our experience, thoughts, and beliefs. We can identify themes that have been prevalent in our lives or look for patterns that are familiar from our past. In doing so, we can identify problem areas, hold onto what is important or valuable, then proceed accordingly. A collective chemicalization can appear in the form of its "them" that "they" are the problem, not "us," and that everyone else is responsible for the condition of the world. It's easy to get into the "us and them" mentality when things seem so bad. But if we look at our part and what is happening for us, it changes the process's dynamic entirely. Our collective consciousness will unearth the topics and conversations that must be addressed. Blaming one another does little in the face of chaos, which is why these processes tend to last longer, and the upheaval is far more intense. When the collective chemicalization happens, the most productive action is to look at what it brings up for us, heal or forgive anything we are holding onto, and see where we can be of service to others going through the process. Our spiritual path is not just about us; it is also about our collective brothers and sisters. If we genuinely want to do the work, we will support and carry those in need when the occasion arises.

PART SEVEN
# THE SPIRITUAL
# ARCHETYPES + GOD

# GOD IS.

*When will you find God? When all your desires for other things are finished. When you realize the only thing worth having is Him. When every thought, every feeling, is drenched with love of God.*
—PARAMAHANSA YOGANANDA

hile writing this book, I dreamt of sitting in a classroom with the twelve apostles. The apostle Paul wrote a list of attributes about God on a blackboard and asked, "Which of these attributes do you believe is the most important one people should know about God?" I looked at the list and thought for a moment before answering: "That God is love. If we are the image and likeness of God, then we are an extension of that love and should treat ourselves and each other as such." He smiled and said, "Then go out and teach about God's love."

If I could pray for one blessing in your life, it would be that you could see how much God loves you. Regardless of who you are, your experiences, or your past, God loves you with a love that we cannot fathom or fully understand. America's beloved preacher, Billy Graham, called God's love for us "the greatest love story," and it truly is. God's love, mercy, grace, forgiveness, compassion, and understanding far exceed any relationship we have or could ever have in this world. It is all-encompassing and infinite in its fairness, equality, and opportunity.

And yet, it is also fierce, protective, and loyal. Despite the evil perpetuated in the world—perhaps, at times, by our own doing—God will reach us in the worst of our despair, hopelessness, or defeat. Maybe you can see the moments where He was fighting for you or delivering you from the worst. Perhaps you need more clarity and revelation on where He was helping, and supporting you. But I assure you, He is, has been, and always will be fighting for you. His love is infinitely patient and merciful, and His presence is intelligent and purposeful. When we develop, honor, and trust our relationship with Him, we can live in an aligned, directed, and divine way.

The love, time, and energy we put into our worldly relationships may or may not be given back to us. However, our relationship with God will produce tangible results in our lives, thoughts, actions, finances, and health. Everything our soul seeks is found in our relationship with God because it is created from the essence of Him. Additionally, we all have, or have had, misperceptions about God. But when we create familiarity and relationship with Him, we reduce our misperceptions and gain insight, clarity, and revelation. When we peel back the layers of our misperceptions, we begin to see God for who He truly is, thus gaining a more accurate and authentic depiction of ourselves. In doing so, we can stand in complete and abounding love for God and ourselves. When we establish this kind of love for God, we are simultaneously filled with the love of God. When we become filled with this kind of love, it emanates from us, affecting those around us and impacting the world in the most spiritual ways. It is truly a wondrous miracle to behold and changes us on emotional, physical, mental, and spiritual levels. It is a love that cannot exist in this world outside of His presence. It is unapparelled in its impact and power. It can neither be sold nor bought. It can only be found by loving God and accepting the love God has for us. Although we can never fully grasp the capacity of His love for all of His children, I hope this is an invitation to explore this love on a new or deeper level than ever before.

## THE NEOTERIC SHAMAN + GOD

**Ways You Seek God:** You seek Him through rituals, prayer,and outdoor meditations, nature, water, movement, dancing, exercise, and work.

**Common Blocks + Misperceptions:** The Neoteric Shaman is used to having to work hard and/or suffer for their needs to be met. Oftentimes, this stems from the soul's initial belief that you must earn God's love, grace, mercy, prosperity, and favor. This may also manifest in our personal relationships. The Neoteric Shaman will give endlessly, believing that their family, friends, and relationships will give back equally, or at least give them love in exchange. This generally does not happen, and the Neoteric Shaman is usually the one giving too much and no one else can ever add up. Since we feel ashamed, unlovable, and underserving, the Neoteric Shaman believes that God must feel the same way about them.

**Ways the enemy Tricks, Deceives, or Lies:** The enemy sees your weakness and whispers lies, making you believe you need to work harder and that it all rests on your shoulders. He tricks you into making you think that you are a savior and that no one can manage without you. Since you are only one person, you are constantly spinning plates, attempting to keep yourself, your world, and other people's worlds from crashing. Although that task is impossible, you feel guilt, shame, and condemnation if you cannot keep the plates spinning; therefore, you think that you are not good enough.

### God Says:
- "For do I now persuade men, or God? or do I seek to please men? for if I yet pleased men, I should not be the servant of Christ" (Galatians 1:10).
- "But grow in grace, and in the knowledge of our Lord and Saviour Jesus Christ. To him be glory both now and for ever. Amen" (2 Peter 3:18).

- "I will lift up mine eyes unto the hills, from whence cometh my help. My help cometh from the Lord, which made heaven and earth" (Psalm 121:1–2).
- "Let us therefore come boldly unto the throne of grace, that we may obtain mercy, and find grace to help in time of need" (Hebrews 4:16).
- "For it is by grace [God's remarkable compassion and favor drawing you to Christ] that you have been saved [actually delivered from judgment and given eternal life] through faith. And this [salvation] is not of yourselves [not through your own effort], but it is the [undeserved, gracious] gift of God; not as a result of [your] works [nor your attempts to keep the Law], so that no one will [be able to] boast *or* take credit in any way [for his salvation]" (Ephesians 2:8–9 AMP).

## THE RECOVERIST + GOD

**Ways You Seek God:** You seek Him through support, community, loved ones, His Word, His grace, His mercy, and His forgiveness.

**Common Blocks + Misperceptions:** Your feelings of being unworthy or an imposter keep you from seeing and feeling the depths of God's love for you. You fear that God sees, judges, and condemns you the way you do to yourself.

**Ways the enemy Tricks, Deceives, or Lies:** Through your addictions, oppression, powerlessness, and hopelessness, and the false promise that your addiction can give you something that God cannot. Also, by making you believe you do not need the support, community, or spiritual connection that comes with sobriety and that you can do it all on your own.

*God Says:*
- "Watch and pray, that ye enter not into temptation: the spirit indeed is willing, but the flesh is weak" (Matthew 26:41).
- "Stand fast therefore in the liberty wherewith Christ hath made us free,

and be not entangled again with the yoke of bondage" (Galatians 5:1).

- "For the grace of God that bringeth salvation hath appeared to all men, teaching us that, denying ungodliness and worldly lusts, we should live soberly, righteously, and godly, in this present world" (Titus 2:11–12).
- "Submit yourselves therefore to God. Resist the devil, and he will flee from you" (James 4:7).
- "But I keep under my body, and bring it into subjection: lest that by any means, when I have preached to others, I myself should be a castaway." (1 Corinthians 9:27)
- "But God commendeth his love toward us, in that, while we were yet sinners, Christ died for us" (Romans 5:8).

## THE WITCH+ GOD

**Ways You Seek God:** You seek Him through strong female figures and female community, nature, animals, and the magic in the world.

**Common Blocks + Misperceptions:** Between 1450 to roughly 1750, the largest witch hunts in the history of the world transpired in Europe, resulting in up to one hundred thousand deaths of people accused of witchcraft. The main reason the witch trials escalated to the levels they did was not from random sources, but because of the spiritual and religious communities themselves. Books such as *Malleus Malefi-carum*, first published in 1486 and other propaganda, were widely dispersed, creating mania, fear, and hysteria throughout Europe, encouraging people to threaten, murder, and prosecute anyone who appeared to be a witch. In fact, in 1678, *Malleus Maleficarum* was the most popular book in the world, second only to the Bible. While witches have always had a tumultuous reputation in religion, it was not until the production of *Malleus Maleficarum* that the witch craze escalated. One prominent hypothesis by historians is that churches were using this propaganda to promote fear in citizens to drive them to their churches. Rivaling churches even used the material to bad-mouth other churches to convince people to come to their church rather than another. They used fear to convince people that evil was running wild and that they would be saved by coming to their church.

Horrors throughout history such as these have made people turn away from and even hate God. They see the evil done in His name and rebel against it, wanting nothing to do with God because of it. However, it is beneficial to remember that it was not God who did those horrible and disgusting acts; it was people, greedy for money and power. God is not victimizing us; only the ego and evil of man could do such a thing. For the Witch, it may be healing to begin dissecting this, as well as one's own experiences. When we realize that God is for us, not against us, and He is only working in our favor and not persecuting us, our perception and understanding of reality completely change.

**Ways the enemy Tricks, Deceives, or Lies:** The enemy will play on your victimhood. This may appear as being persecuted for being different, being falsely accused, or making you fearful of persecution or victimization in situations where there may not be any threat. You may look at situations and wonder, *Did they forget me on purpose?* Or *They said this, but did they mean something by that?* Your worry then creates situations that worsen your fears and keeps you in a cycle of feeling outcast, deceived, or cheated.

### God Says:
- "There is neither Jew nor Greek, there is neither bond nor free, there is neither male nor female: for ye are all one in Christ Jesus" (Galatians 3:28).
- "And the angel came in unto her, and said, Hail, thou that art highly favoured, the Lord is with thee: blessed art thou among women" (Luke 1:28).
- "Nevertheless, neither is the man without the woman, neither the woman without the man, in the Lord. For as the woman is of the man, even so is the man also by the woman; but all things of God" (1 Corinthians 11:11–12).
- "Come to Me, all who are weary and heavily burdened [by religious

rituals that provide no peace], and I will give you rest [refreshing your souls with salvation]. Take My yoke upon you and learn from Me [following Me as My disciple], for I am gentle and humble in heart, and you will find rest (renewal, blessed quiet) for your souls. For My yoke is easy [to bear] and My burden is light" (Matthew 11:28–30 AMP).

## THE ANCESTOR + GOD

**Ways You Seek God:** You seek Him through plant medicine, flower essences, herbalism, nature, bloodlines and ancestry, stories, folklore, and community.

**Common Blocks + Misperceptions:** The Ancestor believes in and strives to honor the ways of the past but also strives for the equality of those who still hold space and usher the past into the present. However, these tribes, groups, and communities had, and still face, many hardships. Therefore, the Ancestor longs for equality and inclusion for all. Since religion has long been viewed as exclusive, this can make the Ancestor feel as though perhaps God is exclusive when, in reality, He is not. God created all and loves each of His children infinitely. If we believe that God is not being inclusive or that He prefers one group to another, then we view Him as a Father who chooses favorites. It is invaluable to realize that any exclusivity or lack of equality is not from God; it is formed from people's fears, desire for power, and need for control. The exclusive mindset tries to bully and oppress those they believe are less than by their standards, beliefs, or personal gains.

**Ways the enemy Tricks, Deceives, or Lies:** He wants you to believe that things will happen without effort. Spirituality and religion often get us stuck into thinking that change comes solely from prayer or action, when in reality, it is both. Prayer is mighty when done correctly, but there is also a time for action. Let yourself live in the dance between the two, knowing that both hold extraordinary power.

## *God Says:*

- "And the Lord said, I have surely seen the affliction of my people which are in Egypt, and have heard their cry by reason of their task-masters; for I know their sorrows; And I am come down to deliver them out of the hand of the Egyptians, and to bring them up out of that land unto a good land and a large, unto a land flowing with milk and honey" (Exodus 3:7–8).

- "And, Thou, Lord, in the beginning hast laid the foundation of the earth; and the heavens are the works of thine hands" (Hebrews 1:10).

- "He raiseth up the poor out of the dust, and lifteth up the beggar from the dunghill, to set them among princes, and to make them inherit the throne of glory: for the pillars of the earth are the Lord's, and he hath set the world upon them" (1 Samuel 2:8).

- "The Lord also will be a refuge for the oppressed, a refuge in times of trouble. And they that know thy name will put their trust in thee: for thou, Lord, hast not forsaken them that seek thee" (Psalm 9:9–10).

- "For the Lord your God is the God of gods and the Lord of lords, the great, the mighty, the awesome God who does not show partiality nor take a bribe" (Deuteronomy 10:17).

## THE SECTARIAN + GOD

**Ways You Seek God:** You seek Him through doctrine, church, community, and structure.

**Common Blocks + Misperceptions:** The Sectarian thinks they know how God will work, but God does not work the same in all situations. There is also a possibility that we do not fully understand how He works. Remember to keep an open mind about God and your relationship with Him. It can match Scripture but also appear different than we may have perceived.

**Ways the enemy Tricks, Deceives, or Lies:** He wants you to believe that God is limited or only meant to make your suffering more comfortable.

Many Sectarians say things such as, "God is in the midst of your suffering," or "It is all God's will," even when they are struggling or facing adversity. God does not wish evil, struggle, or pain on us, and in believing such, we blame God for the enemy's work. Furthermore, people might see their conditions outside of God's authority. For instance, a woman I once spoke with believed that God could not heal her health issues because they were genetic issues. However, God's only limitations are the ones we place on Him. By believing that God could not heal a genetic disease, she was limiting His power in her life. The enemy will play on these limitations in our mind in order to convince us that God's power cannot deliver us or that God's power is ineffective for us.

### God Says:
- "How excellent is thy lovingkindness, O God! Therefore the children of men put their trust under the shadow of thy wings" (Psalm 36:7).
- "Charity suffereth long, and is kind; charity envieth not; charity vaunteth not itself, is not puffed up, Doth not behave itself unseemly, seeketh not her own, is not easily provoked, thinketh no evil" (1 Corinthians 13:4–5).
- "Then Jesus said to the crowds and to his disciples, 'The scribes and the Pharisees sit on Moses' seat, so do and observe whatever they tell you, but not the works they do. For they preach, but do not practice. They tie up heavy burdens, hard to bear, and lay them on people's shoulders, but they themselves are not willing to move them with their finger. They do all their deeds to be seen by others. For they make their phylacteries broad and their fringes long, and they love the place of honor at feasts and the best seats in the synagogues and greetings in the marketplaces and being called rabbi by others. But you are not to be called rabbi, for you have one teacher, and you are all brothers. And call no man your father on earth, for you have one Father, who is in heaven. Neither be called instructors, for you have one instructor, the Christ. The greatest among you shall be your servant. Whoever exalts himself will be humbled, and whoever humbles himself will be exalted" (Matthew 23: 1–12).
- "So we have come to know and to believe the love that God has for

us. God is love, and whoever abides in love abides in God, and God abides in him" (1 John 4:16).

- "And he said, The things which are impossible with men are possible with God" (Luke 18:27).

## THE NEONATE + GOD

**Ways You Seek God:** The Neonate will often ravenously seek spiritual information to curb their newfound craving. Remember to pace yourself with the information you ingest and be careful and cautious regarding who and where you get your information. The Neonate can be trusting to a fault, which can lead to more confusion and stress.

**Common Blocks + Misperceptions:** The Neonate can become focused on information and feelings during this time, yet often forgets to come from a place of love. Remember that having all of the answers, facts, and evidence will not make us holier. Following every feeling and sensation can make us and our path feel unstable and unreliable. But the pursuit of love and the commitment to think, act, and live from a place of love will always bring us to God.

**Ways the enemy Tricks, Deceives, or Lies:** He aims to keep you trapped in condemnation, fear, and judgment, or he plays on your pride.

### God Says:
- "For God hath not given us the spirit of fear; but of power, and of love, and of a sound mind" (2 Timothy 1:7).
- "Therefore if any man be in Christ, he is a new creature: old things are passed away; behold, all things are become new" (2 Corinthians 5:17).
- "Being born again, not of corruptible seed, but of incorruptible, by the word of God, which liveth and abideth for ever" (1 Peter 1:23).
- "That which is born of the flesh is flesh; and that which is born of the Spirit is spirit" (John 3:6).

# THE WAYFARER + GOD

**Ways You Seek God:** You seek Him through pushing the limits, expectations, and possibilities of yourself and others.

**Common Blocks + Misperceptions:** The Wayfarer fears being trapped, conforming, and being held back. They see a lack of movement as a way of slowly dying; therefore, they feel they must keep moving to be fulfilled. They often do not realize that even in the stillness, God is moving and leading them into the next phase, adventure, or opportunity. Like Joseph or Daniel in the Bible, who were both taken into captivity and made prisoners, God delivered them and made them great men. And while it could have appeared that they were trapped, God was working on raising them up and bringing them to their fullest protential and greatness. Even when we are still, God is still moving, working, and readying us for the adventure He has planned. Be faithful in the stillness, and know that God is always working on your journey.

**Ways the enemy Tricks, Deceives, or Lies:** The enemy wants you to believe that being still, or living a "normal" life, makes you small, insignificant, or meaningless. To be exciting or enjoyable, life does not have to be filled with consistent drama, adrenaline, or movement.

## God Says:
- "Then I beheld all the work of God, that a man cannot find out the work that is done under the sun: because though a man labour to seek it out, yet he shall not find it; yea further; though a wise man think to know it, yet shall he not be able to find it" (Ecclesiastes 8:17).
- "The Lord appeared to him and said, "Do not go down to Egypt; stay in the land of which I shall tell you. Sojourn in this land and I will be with you and bless you, for to you and to your descendants I will give all these lands, and I will establish the oath which I swore to your father Abraham. I will multiply your descendants as the stars of heaven, and will give your descendants all these lands; and

by your descendants all the nations of the earth shall be blessed"
(Genesis 26:2–5).

• "Delight thyself also in the Lord: and he shall give thee the desires
of thine heart" (Psalm 37:4).

• "Many times on journeys, [exposed to] danger from rivers, danger
from bandits, danger from my own countrymen, danger from the
Gentiles, danger in the city, danger in the wilderness, danger on the
sea, danger among those posing as believers; in labor and hardship,
often unable to sleep, in hunger and thirst, often [driven to] fasting
[for lack of food], in cold and exposure [without adequate clothing].
Besides those external things, there is the daily [inescapable] pressure of my concern for all the churches. Who is weak, and I do not
feel [his] weakness? Who is made to sin, and I am not on fire [with
sorrow and concern]? If I must boast, I will boast of the things that
reveal my weakness [the things by which I am made weak in the
eyes of my opponents]. The God and Father of the Lord Jesus, He
who is blessed *and* to be praised forevermore, knows that I am not
lying" (2 Corinthians 11 AMP).

## THE MYTHOLOGIST + GOD

**Ways You Seek God:** You seek Him through myths, stories, love,
romance, poetry, fantasies, tales of heroes and quests, and the divine
feminine and divine masculine.

**Common Blocks + Misperceptions:** In the olden days, it was believed
that great men and women came from great families. If a person was
born into a noble family, they were destined for greatness. Names, or
surnames, held powerful connotations and significance, which were
passed onto the children. While this could motivate and inspire the
children into greatness, it could also have the opposite effect and feel
like a burden. If a family had a stain or mark on their history, it could
make the children feel as though they had something to prove or overcome to be forgiven for the sins of their fathers. An example of this is
Aragorn in *The Lord of The Rings*. Aragorn is the lineage of Isildur, a

king of the past who was responsible for destroying the ring of doom. Overcome by the evil of the ring, Isildur instead kept the ring for himself and was eventually killed because of it. Aragon, being from the lineage of Isildur, was destined to be king of Gondor but greatly feared that the weakness of his ancestor was also within him and that he, too, might be foreordained to fail.

Similarly, the Mythologist fears the past of their family, name, and lineage. They worry that they may never measure up, or that they are destined to the fate of their fathers. Suppose a family is known for being unfaithful to their partners, unsuccessful with money, failed in a particular area of life, or was considered weak, hurtful, spiteful, or cruel. In that case, the Mythologist believes they are also condemned, or at the very least, they are concerned about being predestined to the same fate.

While it has long been believed that the ways of our family are passed down, it is only our behaviors that are inherited, and even those can be transcended. God is our rightful Father, and we are made in His image and likeness. We are not condemned to suffer the same fate as our ancestors if we choose not to.

In the Bible, Jesus quelled this belief when He was asked about the sins of the fathers. "While He was passing by, He noticed a man who had been blind from birth. His disciples asked Him, "Rabbi (Teacher), who sinned, this man or his parents, that he would be born blind?" Jesus answered, "Neither this man nor his parents sinned, but it was so that the works of God might be displayed *and* illustrated in him" (John 9: 1–3). This scripture means that not everyone is afflicted because of their sin or the sins of their fathers; instead, the world is ruled by sin, and God's power, healing, and omnipotence overrules it.

Additionally, it states, "The fathers shall not be put to death for [the sins of] their children, nor shall the children be put to death for their fathers; only for his own sin shall anyone be put to death." This means we are all responsible for ourselves and will not be condemned because of our family, lineage, or ancestry.

**Ways the enemy Tricks, Deceives, or Lies:** The enemy makes you believe that fantasy is better than your reality. Adam and Eve fell in the Garden of Eden, but not because the serpent made them. It was because they asked themselves one question: "What if?" The serpent had laid the temptation, but they questioned "What if?" which led to eating the apple. This question, "What if the mystery is better?" has been the cause of misery since. It is a Pandora's Box that leads to releasing the evil of the world. Do not allow yourself to eat the fruit of your temptations, for they will always lead you off course. In the story of *The Odyssey*, when Odysseus heard the sirens singing their alluring songs, he knew that, like so many sailors before them, he and his crew would be doomed if they listened. Instead of giving in, he put wax in his and his crew's ears to drown out the temptation. There are times in your life when you must do as Odysseus did and put metaphorical candle wax in your ears to drown out the temptations that will misguide you and crash you upon the rocks in your life.

## *God Says:*

- "Thine, O Lord is the greatness, and the power, and the glory, and the victory, and the majesty: for all that is in the heaven and in the earth is thine; thine is the kingdom, O Lord, and thou art exalted as head above all" (1 Chronicles 29:11).
- "For thy Maker is thine husband; the Lord of hosts is his name; and thy Redeemer the Holy One of Israel; The God of the whole earth shall he be called" (Isaiah 54:5).
- "For as the woman is of the man, even so is the man also by the woman; but all things of God" (1 Corinthians 11:12).
- "The Spirit itself beareth witness with our spirit, that we are the children of God: And if children, then heirs; heirs of God, and joint-heirs with Christ; if so be that we suffer with him, that we may be also glorified together. For I reckon that the sufferings of this present time are not worthy to be compared with the glory which shall be revealed in us" (Romans 8:16–18).
- "Our Father which art in heaven, Hallowed be thy name. Thy kingdom come, Thy will be done in earth, as it is in heaven. Give us this day our daily bread. And forgive us our debts, as we forgive our debtors. And lead us not into temptation, but deliver us from

evil: For thine is the kingdom, and the power, and the glory, forever. Amen" (Matthew 6:9–13).

## THE WARRIOR + GOD

**Ways You Seek God:** You seek Him through athletics, running, speed, adrenaline, competition, and the space of greatness where you go from an old level and push yourself into a new tier of performance or growth.

**Common Blocks + Misperceptions:** The Warrior has an intuitive knowing that God made them with innate physical abilities, but a part of them wonders if God's blessing, love, and favor will remain if they lose their physical abilities. This can make them fear personal failure and feel they have to earn God's love through their physicality.

**Ways the enemy Tricks, Deceives, or Lies:** The enemy wants you to believe that you and your abilities are only a result of your hard work. While this plays a significant factor in your success, remember that God has blessed you with your talents, but the glory is His. Athletes especially are known for praising and giving glory to God when they achieve a miraculous play because they know that they are blessed with their abilities and are grateful for them. Remember that God gave it to you and is with you through it all. The enemy will also use God's gift against you by making you think it's all you have so that if you lose it, you will have nothing. Remember, God is not the one taking away your skills and abilities; it's the enemy.

### God Says:
- "Ye shall not need to fight in this battle: set yourselves, stand ye still, and see the salvation of the Lord with you, O Judah and Jerusalem: fear not, nor be dismayed; tomorrow go out against them: for the Lord will be with you" (2 Chronicles 20:17).
- "Who is this King of glory? The Lord strong and mighty, the Lord mighty in battle" (Psalm 24:8).
- "Blessed be the Lord my strength which teacheth my hands to war, and my fingers to fight" (Psalm 144:1).

- "For the Lord your God is he that goeth with you, to fight for you against your enemies, to save you" (Deuteronomy 20:4).
- "I have fought a good fight, I have finished my course, I have kept the faith" (2 Timothy 4:7).

## THE EASTERN PHILOSOPHER + GOD

**Ways You Seek God:** You seek Him through movement (such as martial arts), Tibetan singing bowls, prayer, meditation, acupuncture, connection through good, TCM, ancestry, and family.

**Common Blocks + Misperceptions:** Many people project their relationships with their parents or caregivers onto God. For the Eastern Philosopher this may mean that you feel you have to live up to a narrow-minded view that perhaps your parents have enforced upon you. Since many parents show love through approval, you may feel like if God disapproves that He, too, will retract His love. However, parents often feel restricted in their views out of fear. They fear their child will fail, or they will fail them, which motivates them to push their child to succeed, regardless of whether the child is happy. But God's love is infinite. Regardless of whether we make mistakes or live rightly God's love, grace, and mercy are always infinitely and patiently waiting for us to find our way. While it may feel easier to focus solely on our parent's love, it will serve us to remember and focus on God's love, which never ceases.

**Ways the enemy Tricks, Deceives, or Lies:** The enemy makes you believe that you cannot live your dreams or that you are trapped by other people's rules.

### God Says:
- "He that is slow to anger is better than the mighty; and he that ruleth his spirit than he that taketh a city" (Proverbs 16:32).
- "Train up a child in the way he should go: and when he is old, he will not depart from it" (Proverbs 16:32).

- "Better is a dinner of herbs where love is, than a stalled ox and hatred therewith" (Proverbs 15:1).
- "Fathers, do not provoke your children to anger [do not exasperate them to the point of resentment with demands that are trivial or unreasonable or humiliating or abusive; nor by showing favoritism or indifference to any of them], but bring them up [tenderly, with lovingkindness] in the discipline and instruction of the Lord" (Ephesians 6:4 amp).

## THE SAINT + GOD

**Ways You Seek God:** You seek Him through parenting, humility, outreach programs, volunteering, and helping strangers, friends, and family. You also seek Him through feminine energy, such as Mother Mary. God is a parent and father; when we relate to this, we can understand and perceive God beautifully.

**Common Blocks + Misperceptions:** The Saint aims to do the right thing for everyone and be perfect, unbiased, and fair in all ways. If you cannot make mistakes, no one can judge you, right? Unfortunately, it is impossible to please everyone, and regardless of how hard we try, someone will be displeased or judge us for one reason or another. However, it is not God judging us. God is merciful, loving, and forgiving; whereas man can be condemning, cruel, and hypocritical. Like King David said in the Bible when he made a mistake, "I am in great distress. Please let us fall into the hand of the Lord, for His mercies *are* great; but do not let me fall into the hand of man" (2 Samuel 24:14). King David knew that God would be merciful and man would be merciless. The Saint already has God's grace and mercy. You do not need to earn it from the world.

**Ways the enemy Tricks, Deceives, or Lies:** The enemy gets to you through perfectionism. The Saint always wants to do and be better, for themselves, others, and God. They want to give and do more, but nothing you do ever feels good enough. An underlying fear of getting in trouble motivates you to overdo everything. Whether it's the small things (like not getting the house clean, missing a deadline at work, or making a mistake) or larger guilts (like being a parent who shames yourself for your off days, a teacher who wishes you could have helped one more child, or a doctor who relives the patients you couldn't cure), the enemy plays the reel of your "failures," making you always want to be better but never feeling like you are.

### God Says:

- "As one whom his mother comforteth, so will I comfort you" (Isaiah 66:13).
- "And so faith, hope, love abide these three; but the greatest of these is love" (1 Corinthians 13:13).
- "Then Mary said, Behold, I am the handmaiden of the Lord; let it be done to me according to what you have said" (Luke 1:38).
- "When Jesus therefore saw his mother, and the disciple standing by, whom he loved, he saith unto his mother, Woman, behold thy son! Then saith he to the disciple, Behold thy mother! And from that hour that disciple took her unto his own home" (John 19:26–27).
- "These things I have spoken unto you, that in me ye might have peace. In the world ye shall have tribulation: but be of good cheer; I have overcome the world" (John 16:33).
- "Now the Lord of peace himself give you peace always by all means. The Lord be with you all" (2 Thessalonians 3:16).
- "Blessed are the peacemakers: for they shall be called the children of God" (Matthew 5:9).
- "Blessed [inwardly peaceful, spiritually secure, worthy of respect] are the gentle [the kind-hearted, the sweet-spirited, the self-controlled], for they will inherit the earth" (Matthew 5:5).

## THE CHRISTIAN MYSTIC + GOD

**Ways You Seek God:** You seek Him through the spiritual, supernatural, and mystical aspects of Himself and His Word as described in the Holy Bible.

**Common Blocks + Misperceptions:** Due to the intense and dramatic nature of the Christian Mystic, you may feel that God is asking you to sacrifice yourself or that the adversity, struggle, and pain you feel is an ordained part of your path. The Christian Mystic will often look at the suffering of the apostles and other messengers of God and feel that they, too, must undergo similar judgment, scrutiny, and condemnation. However, God is not the one causing this strife, and it is not His will that anyone suffers. Those who serve God may eventually face condemnation in this world because this is not God's world, but it is also not His will that anyone be hurt or judged. The Christian Mystic may have this backward, believing they must suffer for Him or He requires it. Try reframing this to recognize God's role, the role of the enemy in this world, and the role we play as servants and missionaries for God. When we see the truth of the roles we all play, we can more clearly define the reality of each person's part.

**Ways the enemy Tricks, Deceives, or Lies:** The enemy distracts you by luring your attention to the sacrifice while keeping you from remembering or focusing on the resurrection. The Christian Mystic can become too infatuated with the death and the pain of the atonement, which holds you in the human realm of pain and suffering rather than experiencing the transcendence of the soul into the spiritual.

### God says:
- "We love him, because he first loved us" (1 John 4:19).
- "For God so loved the world, that he gave his only begotten Son, that whosoever believeth in him should not perish, but have everlasting life" (John 3:16).
- "Now we have received, not the spirit of the world, but the spirit which is of God; that we might know the things that are freely given to us of God. Which things also we speak, not in the words which man's wisdom teacheth, but which the Holy Ghost teacheth; comparing spiritual things with spiritual. But the natural man receiveth not the things of the Spirit of God: for they are foolishness

unto him: neither can he know them, because they are spiritually discerned" (1 Corinthians 2:12–15).

- "But he that is spiritual judgeth all things, yet he himself is judged of no man. For who hath known the mind of the Lord, that he may instruct him? But we have the mind of Christ" (1 Corinthians 2:12–16).
- "And he said unto them, Go ye into all the world, and preach the gospel to every creature. He that believeth and is baptized shall be saved; but he that believeth not shall be damned. And these signs shall follow them that believe; In my name shall they cast out devils; they shall speak with new tongues; They shall take up serpents; and if they drink any deadly thing, it shall not hurt them; they shall lay hands on the sick, and they shall recover. So then after the Lord had spoken unto them, he was received up into heaven, and sat on the right hand of God. And they went forth, and preached every where, the Lord working with them, and confirming the word with signs following. Amen" (Mark 16:15–20).
- "The next day John seeth Jesus coming unto him, and saith, Behold the Lamb of God, which taketh away the sin of the world" (John 1:29).

## THE CRUSADER + GOD

**Ways You Seek God:** You seek Him through your voice, mission, passion, communities, groups, and people. You also seek Him through your surrender because when you surrender, God works harder.

**Common Blocks + Misperceptions:** One of the most painful and confusing parts of life, especially for the Crusader, is to try to make sense of inequality and injustice. This can be confusing, frustrating, and maddening because the fear that creates inequality and injustice is senseless. Trying to understand it can make a person feel defeated and helpless. However, there is one cure for fear, which is love. And love has one source, which is God Himself. The Crusader wants to cure all of the world's problems or has one specific mission, but God is the cure for all. We cannot fight fear without love, and we cannot combat human error without a supernatural cure. Often, the Crusader sees this as separate, but the belief in separation has caused all these problems in the first place. Focus and meditate on the oneness of God and the oneness we all are. Despite people trying to pull away and segregate themselves, you will be able to remind people of their oneness and connection to others.

**Ways the enemy Tricks, Deceives, or Lies:** The enemy makes you believe that you must fight hate with hate, evil with evil, or that you must fight dirty to make changes happen. It can be difficult to fight hate with love, anger with peace, and fear with strength, but this is where real change happens. By reflecting the attributes of God into your mission, people will not be able to help being affected by it.

## God Says:

- "But I say unto you, Love your enemies, bless them that curse you, do good to them that hate you, and pray for them which despitefully use you, and persecute you" (Matthew 5:44). "Blessed are the peacemakers: for they shall be called the children of God" (Matthew 5:9).
- "The Philistine came and approached David, with his shield-bearer in front of him. When the Philistine looked around and saw David, he derided *and* disparaged him because he was just a young man, with a ruddy *complexion*, and a handsome appearance. The Philistine said to David, "Am I a dog, that you come to me with [shepherd's] staffs?" And the Philistine cursed David by his gods. The Philistine also said to David, "Come to me, and I will give your flesh to the birds of the sky and the beasts of the field." Then David said to the Philistine, "You come to me with a sword, a spear, and a javelin, but I come to you in the name of the Lord of hosts, the God of the armies of Israel, whom you have taunted. This day the Lord will hand you over to me, and I will strike you down and cut off your head. And I will give the corpses of the army of the Philistines this day to the birds of the sky and the wild beasts of the earth, so that all the earth may know that there is a God in Israel, and that this entire assembly may know that the Lord does not save with the sword or with the spear; for the bat-

tle is the Lord's and He will hand you over to us" (1 Samuel 17:41–47).

- "Then said Jesus, Father, forgive them; for they know not what they do" (Luke 23:34).
- "And be ye kind one to another, tenderhearted, forgiving one another, even as God for Christ's sake hath forgiven you" (Ephesians 4:32).
- "Judge not, and ye shall not be judged: condemn not, and ye shall not be condemned: forgive, and ye shall be forgiven" (Luke 6:37).
- "A new commandment I give unto you, That ye love one another; as I have loved you, that ye also love one another" (John 13:34).

## THE ARTIST + GOD

**Ways You Seek God:** You seek Him through music, painting, sculpting, acting, reading, crafting, film, dancing, designing, building, speech, and the body.

**Common Blocks + Misperceptions:** The Artist makes the mistake of believing that they and God are separate. Because of this, they may destroy themselves for their art, or use their art to spread pain, violence, and the enemy's will. Art, in any form, is a medium that can spread good or evil. If we look at most films, television, and media today, most of us can agree that it is not spreading the attribute of God. I once heard a woman say that she watched one of the most popular shows in the world, which was graphic, violent, and highly sexual. However, she said it was fine because she would *"balance her chakras before and after watching it."* Instead of refusing to allow this type of evil into her mind, consciousness and energy, she made excuses and created a space for it. While many people do not want to admit it, the shows and films we watch, the music we listen to, and the art we view, all contribute to the health of our spirituality and consciousness. Everything contributes to promoting our spiritual success or our worldly self, and the energy channeled into the art we consume greatly determines the direction we lean. Through art, it seems we can transcend space and time and channel words, music, images, and sounds in a way that resembles magic. We can be conduits for the attributes of

God or be the devil's advocate. The artist must ask themselves, "what am I channeling?"

**Ways the enemy Tricks, Deceives, or Lies:** He makes you feel inferior or like you need to suffer or starve to appease some hidden force to become successful. The enemy also wants you to believe that all creativity is art, which in this world is true, but real art reflects the Spirit and qualities of God.

## God Says:

- "For it is [not your strength, but it is] God who is effectively at work in you, both to will and to work [that is, strengthening, energizing, and creating in you the longing and the ability to fulfill your purpose] for His good pleasure" (Philippians 2:13).
- "Serve the LORD with gladness: come before his presence with singing" (Psalm 100:2).
- "And if it seems evil unto to you to serve the LORD, choose you this day whom ye will serve; whether the gods of the Amorites, in whose land ye dwell; but as for me and my house, we will serve the LORD" (Joshua 24:15).
- "No man can serve two masters: for either he will hate the one, and love the other; or else he will hold to the one, and despise the other. Ye cannot serve God and mammon" (Matthew 6:24).
- "But now, O LORD, thou art our father; we are the clay, and thou our potter; and we all are the work of thy hand." (Isaiah 64:8).

## THE NEW AGER + GOD

**Ways You Seek God:** You seek Him through creativity, playfulness, the Earth and its mysteries, and history.

**Common Blocks + Misperceptions:** The New Ager often has a convoluted and turbulent image of God. So much so that many New Agers find themselves avoiding words, phrases, or teachings that reflect God or the Bible. Unfortunately, this means they are missing out on the benefits of these practices and what they may have to offer. For instance, the words, *God*, *Jesus*, and *I AM* (as seen in the Bible) are the most powerful words in existence. However, since many New Agers have a history of hurtful people using God's name in vain, they refuse to use these words and shut themselves off from the power they hold. They do not realize that it is not God that they have issues with, but the people who hurt them that they are projecting their image of God onto. As one controversial rocker said, he never hated God, but he hated the god of the people he hated. Similarly, the New Ager harbors resentments toward God that have nothing to do with God at all; instead, they have to do with the people who hurt, abused, or shamed them.

**Ways the enemy Tricks, Deceives, or Lies:** He keeps you trapped in your shame, guilt, and the past. The enemy loves to dig deep into our psyche to drudge up the painful past and parade it around in the present. This can sometimes feel so real that in our hearts, minds, and emotions, it takes us back to the prison of our past. Forgiveness is your most powerful ally for others and yourself. Do not let the enemy make you believe that the past has power over you by chaining you to it.

## God Says:
- "The fear of man bringeth a snare: but whoso putteth his trust in the Lord shall be safe" (Proverbs 29: 25).
- "Let all bitterness, and wrath, and anger, and clamour, and evil speaking, be put away from you, with all malice: And be ye kind one to another, tenderhearted, forgiving one another, even as God for Christ's sake hath forgiven you" (Ephesians 4: 31–32).
- "Beware lest any man spoil you through philosophy and vain deceit, after the tradition of men, after the rudiments of the world, and not after Christ" (Colossians 2:8).
- "Brethren, I count not myself to have apprehended: but this one thing I do, forgetting those things which are behind, and reaching forth unto those things which are before" (Philippians 3:13).
- "From whom every family in heaven and on earth derives its name [God—the first and ultimate Father]" (Ephesians 3:15).

*Authors Note:* The Greek word *patria* means "family" and is derived from the Greek word *pater*, which means "father," because the idea, concept, and depiction of the family originated with God. This can be valuable for the New Ager, who believes in making their own family and that friends are the family we choose. The word *family*, regardless of whether blood or pseudo, can reflect God and His attributes.

## THE METAPHYSICIAN + GOD

**Ways You Seek God:** You seek Him through science, esoterism, spirituality, mathematics, art, writing, architecture, and intuition.

**Common Blocks + Misperceptions:** The Metaphysician sees themself as a conduit, a passage between the spiritual and physical. Sadly, they often allow themself to get burned out, which subsequently fries their conductor. They may believe that it's God doing this to them or that God wants to overload them, but this is not the case. We cannot overdose on God, but we can run ourselves into the ground in the physical. God is not pushing us to do, learn, or discover more; it is we who push ourselves. For the Metaphysician, discovery is everything, but remember to pace and nurture yourself and your needs. God is always working with and for us, so if we feel burned out, we need to consciously turn off and rest.

**Ways the enemy Tricks, Deceives, or Lies:** He wants you to believe that you must do more, give more, and be more. That you must sacrifice yourself, your health, and your well-being to give to this world.

*God Says:*
- "Keep that which is committed to thy trust, avoiding profane and vain babblings, and oppositions of science falsely so called: Which some professing have erred concerning the faith. Grace be with thee. Amen" (1 Timothy 6:21).
- "Therefore, take no thought, saying, What shall we eat? or, What shall we drink? or, Wherewithal shall we be clothed? For after

all these things do the Gentiles seek:) for your heavenly Father knoweth that ye have need of all these things. But seek ye first the kingdom of God, and his righteousness; and all these things shall be added unto you" (Matthew 6:31–33).

- "Come unto me, all ye that labour and are heavy laden, and I will give you rest. Take my yoke upon you, and learn of me; for I am meek and lowly in heart: and ye shall find rest unto your souls. For my yoke is easy, and my burden is light" (Matthew 11:28–30).
- "Come unto me, all ye that labour and are heavy laden, and I will give you rest" (Matthew 11:28).

## THE ORACLE + GOD

**Ways You Seek God:** You seek Him through numbers, the stars, the heavens, and Earth's patterns and designs.

**Common Blocks + Misperceptions:** The Oracle has been through a lot in their life and finally feels freedom in practicing their spirituality. When they feel that they are being controlled, judged, or condemned for their way of practicing, they may become stubborn, rebellious, or destructive against themselves and their spirituality to keep their feelings of independence and individuality. Many Oracles see God as condemning, judgmental, and cruel. Having felt this type of condemnation in their life, the Oracle shies away from God and may try to practice spirituality that leaves Him out ultimately. If the Oracle takes the time to see what a loving, graceful, merciful, and forgiving God He is and where the stars and numbers actually align with His word, they might see how they aren't so different after all. They might end up loving the Creator of the creations they adore so deeply.

**Ways the enemy Tricks, Deceives, or Lies:** He wants you to believe that your identity rests solely on chance rather than divine creation and purpose. It is no accident that you are who you are and have the life you do. Instead of looking at our numbers like the roll of a dice, we can instead shift our perception to see that God aligned all of the stars and numbers and brought us into this world at the exact moment he intended with a grand purpose so that we may be much more than we ever imagined. We are not the identity that our numbers and charts say we are. We are who we are because God created us to be the way we are. Our charts are just evidence of His planning for us.

## God Says:
- "Canst thou bind the sweet influences of Pleiades, or loose the bands of Orion? Canst thou bring forth Mazzaroth in his season? or canst thou guide Arcturus with his sons?" (Job 38:31–32) *Authors Note: Mazzaroth* is the Hebrew word for zodiac.)
- "Now faith is the substance of things hoped for, the evidence of things not seen" (Hebrews 11:1.)
- "Beloved, believe not every spirit, but try the spirits whether they are of God: because many false prophets are gone out into the world" (1 John 4:1).
- "Which things also we speak, not in the words which man's wisdom teacheth, but which the Holy Ghost teacheth; comparing spiritual things with spiritual" (1 Corinthians 2:13).
- "You are the Lord, You alone; You have made the heavens, The heaven of heavens with all their host (the heavenly bodies), The earth and everything that is on it, The seas and everything that is in them. You give life to all of them, And the heavenly host is bowing down [in worship] to You." (Nehemiah 9:6)

## THE OCCULTIST + GOD

**Ways You Seek God:** You seek Him through knowledge, books, information, and science.

**Common Blocks + Misperceptions:** Throughout the world's existence, there has been a misperception that God is both the Author or Creator of good and evil. Some people see scriptures like Isaiah 45:7, which says "I form the light, and create darkness: I make peace, and create evil: I the Lord do all these things," and can easily come to the conclusion that God does, in fact, create good and evil. For many, they can see this one scripture and paint a whole different picture of God. However, this scripture doesn't add up if you compare that to the rest of the Bible. Someone like the Occultist could see this scripture and stay committed to their darkness because, after all, isn't it all made by God?

The translation of the word *evil* stems from the Hebrew word, רָע, which is an adjective for evil that describes the manifestation of it. The etymology of the word *evil* from Old English more focused explicitly on evil as "being a moral lack of judgment, or moral depravity." In the King James Version of the Bible, the word *create*, when spoken by God, was translated in some cases with differing causation. Meaning, that in some places, God says He "creates" when in the Hebrew Bible, it actually more correctly translates to "permits" or "allows." So, when it comes to God saying, "I form the light, and create darkness: I make peace, and create evil: I the Lord do all these things," a blunter translation would translate it as: "God formed the light and created darkness (heaven and earth, night and day). He makes peace but allows or permits the repercussions of one's own sin (lack of moral judgment and moral depravity).

This is confirmed in the following scripture, which states, "Rain down, O heavens, from above, Let the clouds pour down righteousness [all the blessings of God]; Let the earth open up, let salvation bear fruit, And righteousness spring up with it; I, the Lord, have created it" (Isaiah 45:8). Meaning, "Let God's blessings shower onto those who seek to be saved, delivered, or protected from sin. And let their moral uprightness and virtue be born with the gifts of goodness, and goodwill.

For the Occultist, who loves knowledge and information, I implore you to seek the underlying truths of common misperceptions about God. They may be creating hindrances or blocks in your spirituality that can be extinguished through your exploration and discovery.

**Ways the enemy Tricks, Deceives, or Lies:** The enemy wants you to believe that your struggles, pain, trauma, anxiety, fear, depression, darkness, or shadows are a part of who you are. Your true identity is defined by God, though, and does not include any of these negative attributes. Take authority over your darkness, and watch your shadow flee in terror of your true, authentic, and divine self.

## God Says:

- "For You cause my lamp to be lighted and to shine; The Lord my God illumines my darkness" (Psalm 18:28).
- "For we wrestle not against flesh and blood, but against principalities, against powers, against the rulers of the darkness of this world, against spiritual wickedness in high places" (Ephesians 6:12).
- "Submit yourselves therefore to God. Resist the devil, and he will flee from you" (James 4:7).
- "Forasmuch then as the children are partakers of flesh and blood, he also himself likewise took part of the same; that through death he might destroy him that had the power of death, that is, the devil" (Hebrews 2:14).

## THE LIGHTWORKER + GOD

**Ways You Seek God:** You seek Him through water, the beach, nature, community, prayer, meditation, reading, and writing.

**Common Blocks + Misperceptions:** Many Lightworkers shy away from having a relationship with God and do not like working with God or Jesus directly. For example, many Lightworkers practice or study *A Course in Miracles* but refrain from working with Jesus. Some famous Lightworkers and ACIM teachers have claimed it has no ties to Jesus or God at all, despite the author, Helen Schucman's claims that the material was given to her from Jesus. Additionally, some Lightworkers will call on, manifest with, or speak of the universe but not have a relationship with God, the Creator of the universe. This goes back to the Lightworker's tendency to desire a light and happy spirituality that feels easy, which they often feel is more doable if the practice stays on a more surface level. While spirituality and spiritual growth should feel good, healthy, and beneficial, it can also have growing pains and take us out of our comfort zone, something the Lightworker does not particularly enjoy. However, this is not generally a conscious act; it is more out of self-preservation. The Lightworker's past has been a catalyst for their healing, but the pain of it can linger, making the Lightworker live off of feeling and instant gratification. This is why manifestation is so prevalent in the Lightworker community. Because it can produce instant results and instant gratification, it keeps the spiritual carrot out for the Lightworker to keep chasing it, which also appeals to their perfectionism. However, if we try to avoid pain and only feel good all the time, we are letting our past win, because it is still a dominating presence, controlling, dictating, and ruling over our conscious or subconscious. If we run to God, He will cast out and heal the past while leading us to the light. If the Lightworker can learn to trust, rely on, and have more faith in God, they will be able to let go of their perfectionism and anxiety. Instead of chasing the light and the trickles of light in their practices or the world, they become present in the light of God, which is ultimately what they are seeking.

**Ways the enemy Tricks, Deceives, or Lies:** He convinces you to stay in the "high vibe only" space and to seek "good vibes only." But if you read God's Word, it says, "Seek first the kingdom of God and his righteousness; and all these things shall be added unto you" (Matthew 6:33). The enemy lies to make you believe that if you seek feeling good, then you will find God. But it is by seeking God that you will feel good and find the highest vibration.

## God Says:
- "For You cause my lamp to be lighted *and* to shine; The Lord my God illumines my darkness" (Psalm 18:28).
- "And the light shineth in darkness; and the darkness comprehended it not" (John 1:5).
- "One thing have I desired of the Lord, that will I seek after; that I may dwell in the house of the Lord all the days of my life, to behold the beauty of the Lord, and to enquire in his temple" (Psalm 27:4).

- "Judge not according to the appearance, but judge righteous judgment" (John 7:24).
- "And be not conformed to this world: but be ye transformed by the renewing of your mind, that ye may prove what is that good, and acceptable, and perfect, will of God" (Romans 12:2).
- "And He will wipe away every tear from their eyes; and there will no longer be death; there will no longer be sorrow *and* anguish, or crying, or pain; for the former order of things has passed away" (Revelation 21:4).

## THE MINDSET MASTER + GOD

**Ways You Seek God:** You seek Him through your motivation, your support of others, your intuition, dreams, goals, positive thinking, and the power of your belief.

**Common Blocks + Misperceptions:** The Mindset Master often believes that because they want something, they are meant to have it. This is where a lot of the pitfalls of manifestation happen. People think, "I want this; therefore, I am meant to have it," and put all of their energy, prayers, affirmations, and sights on that specific goal. This causes an issue when people are putting all of themselves into a dream, goal, or vision, and doing all of the things, and either not getting what they want or getting it and being unhappy with it. The Mindset Master has a powerful mind, but be sure you match your mind with God's Word, which will bring you the most happiness, prosperity, and success. Instead of just speaking affirmations, which is often our will, try claiming God's Word over your life and see what transpires from it.

**Ways the enemy Tricks, Deceives, or Lies:** He makes you think the material world is the goal instead of the spiritual, and that material possessions prove your worth and the power of your thoughts and mind.

### God Says:
- "Lay not up for yourselves treasures upon earth, where moth and

PART SEVEN THE SPIRITUAL ARCHETYPES + GOD

rust doth corrupt, and where thieves break through and steal: But lay up for yourselves treasures in heaven, where neither moth nor rust doth corrupt, and where thieves do not break through nor steal: For where your treasure is, there will your heart be also" (Matthew 6:19–21).

- "And be not conformed to this world: but be ye transformed by the renewing of your mind, that ye may prove what is that good, and acceptable, and perfect, will of God" (Romans 12:2).

- "Set your affection on things above, not on things on the earth" (Colossians 3:2).

- "If there be therefore any consolation in Christ, if any comfort of love, if any fellowship of the Spirit, if any bowels and mercies, fulfil ye my joy, that ye be likeminded, having the same love, being of one accord, of one mind. Let nothing be done through strife or vain-glory; but in lowliness of mind let each esteem other better than themselves. Look not every man on his own things, but every man also on the things of others. Let this mind be in you, which was also in Christ Jesus: Who, being in the form of God, thought it not robbery to be equal with God: But made himself of no reputation, and took upon him the form of a servant, and was made in the likeness of men: And being found in fashion as a man, he humbled himself, and became obedient unto death, even the death of the cross" (Philippians 2: 2–8).

- "As in water face reflects face, so the heart of man reflects man" (Proverbs 27:19).

## THE SOVEREIGN + GOD

**Ways You Seek God:** You seek Him through visions, intuition, revelations, passions, drive, and dedication. You have the mind and heart of a warrior, but your battlefield is through innovation, influence, and leadership.

**Common Blocks + Misperceptions:** King Solomon was the richest and most successful king who ever lived. He was devoted to God's Word and communed with God at the beginning of his rule. However, toward the end of his rule, King Solomon started going against God's Word and letting other people influence him. Being a ruler in their own right, the Sovereign can lose sight of God and allow others to influence them. Remember to keep God as a pillar of your temple and the foundation for your kingdom. No kingdom should be built without love, mercy, grace, wisdom, and generosity—all born of God. Keep Him at the forefront, and His attributes will indwell in your empire.

**Ways the enemy Tricks, Deceives, or Lies:** The enemy convinces you that anyone or anything is expendable. Don't let yourself believe that anyone or anything is expendable in your pursuit of greatness.

### God Says:
- "For even the Son of Man did not come to be served, but to serve, and to give His life as a ransom for many" (Mark 10:45 AMP).
- "Do nothing from selfishness or empty conceit (through factional motives, or strife), but with [an attitude of] humility (being neither arrogant nor self-righteous), regard others as more important than yourselves" (Philippians 2:3).
- "For they loved the glory that comes from man more than the glory that comes from God" (John 12:43).
- "Know ye not that ye are the temple of God, and that the Spirit of God dwelleth in you" (1 Corinthians 3:16).
- "I will praise thee, O Lord my God, with all my heart: and I will glorify thy name for evermore" (Psalm 86:12).

## THE THEOLOGIST + GOD

**Ways You Seek God:** You seek Him through the Bible, books, doctrine, history, archeology, the Holy Spirit, fasting, speaking in tongues, revelation, and prayer.

**Common Blocks + Misperceptions:** The Theologist is known for their devotion and dedicated studies of God. They want to know everything about God and study the facts, evidence, and information about who and what God is, how He works, and the proven techniques for communing with Him. The one downfall many Theologists struggle with is that while we can study and read about God, our relationship with God is through the heart and can manifest in different ways for each of us. When this happens, they can become more focused on the mind of the Old Law rather than the heart and truth of the New Testament. This is what the Pharisees struggled with as well. They immersed themselves so intently in the Law that they missed the manifestation of the Word when it appeared to them because it appeared different than they imagined. If the Theologist can open their perception to allow other ideas, manifestations of God, and ways God communes with others, they may open their eyes and heart to the wonders of God they never knew could exist.

**Ways the enemy Tricks, Deceives, or Lies:** He wants you to believe that learning is all done in the mind. When it comes to God, learning is done in the mind and heart. It is not just computed, but rather something we experience. This is where the Theologist gets stuck in the law rather than the truth. In Romans 13:8, Paul states, "for he that loveth another hath fulfilled the law." Therefore, focus on the love of God and on treating everyone with love. In doing so, you will have simultaneously fulfilled the Law.

### God Says:
- "Do not let mercy *and* kindness and truth leave you [instead let these qualities define you]; bind them [securely] around your neck, write them on the tablet of your heart" (Proverbs 3:3).
- "Create in me a clean heart, O God; and renew a right spirit within me." (Psalm 51:10)
- "Lay not up for yourselves treasures upon earth, where moth and rust doth corrupt, and where thieves break through and steal: But lay up for yourselves treasures in heaven, where neither moth nor rust doth corrupt, and where thieves do not break through

nor steal: For where your treasure is, there will your heart be also."
(Matthew (6:19-21)

- "That if thou shalt confess with thy mouth the Lord Jesus, and shalt believe in thine heart that God hath raised him from the dead, thou shalt be saved." (Romans 10:9)

- "And thou shalt love the Lord thy God with all thy heart, and with all thy soul, and with all thy mind, and with all thy strength: this is the first commandment." (Mark 12:30)

# TO KNOW GOD IS TO
# KNOW THYSELF

Throughout history, many fascinating discoveries have given us clarity and revelation into the human psyche and soul. From ancient practices to modern medicine, we have had an infinite plethora of ways to better understand ourselves, our motives, and our purpose. However, if we are going to have a conversation about archetypes, we cannot do so without understanding the origin of our being. The definition of archetype is "an original that has been imitated." It is the reproduction or replication from an original model. When an art piece is reproduced, it does not change its authenticity or its creator. It does not take any from the beauty of the original piece, it is merely an extension of it. Thus, if God created us, it would stand to reason that we are the archetype of God. Just as an archetype is not the original model, only a replica, we too are the replica of our Creator. Although we are not God ourselves, the quintessential perfection of God is within us, inherited from His mold. We are God's handiwork, his finest creation and a replica of Him. Just as we learn about art by understanding the artist, we learn about ourselves by learning about the artist who created us. I once had a client ask, "If I let go of my ego, what is left of me?" My answer to her was, "the authentic part of you, which is the image and reflection of God." Our identity rests in God, not our ego, and not this world. Many people will spend their whole life seeking identity and personality in the world not realizing that our true self emerges when we realize who God is.

In a lecture by Dorothy B. Rieke, she shared the story of a young prince who, when he was very young, drifted from his nurse while on a walk in the woods nearby the palace. While wandering he came upon a band of Gypsies. Seeing that the boy was lost and not knowing to whom he belonged, they took the young boy and cared for him as one of their own. They dressed the boy as a Gypsy, taught him their language, and gave him a Gypsy name. After many years he appeared to be a Gypsy. One day, in his young adulthood, the Gypsy wagon was in the woods near the palace when a friend of the king saw the young boy. The friend had looked for the boy since his disappearance and although the boy now looked like a Gypsy, the friend was struck by how much the boy resembled the king. The king's friend approached the young man and, in the Gypsy language asked him, "Do you know who you are?" Puzzled the boy responded, "Of course I do." And he told the man his Gypsy name. The friend said, "Ah, but that is not your real name. The truth is that you are the son of the king." The young man shook his head and said, "you are mistaken. I am not the king's son. I am a Gypsy." The friend replied, I know that you seem to be, but the fact is you are not. You are really the son of the king." The young man said, "If that is true, there must be two of me, this Gypsy here, and the son of the king. I don't know where the son of the king is." But the friend persisted, "No, there is only one of you, and I am telling you about that one. That one is the son of the king." The young man thought for a moment then asked, "If I am really the son of the king, then where did the Gypsy come from?"

Then the friend explained to him that there was no Gypsy version of him. Despite the boy's appearance and belief that he was a Gypsy, he was still in fact, the king's son. The only truth about the boy being a Gypsy was in his misperception and ignorance of the truth about who he really was.

The boy identified with a personality he believed to be true but the truth was that he was always the son of the king. We too identify with our appearances, personalities, and perceptions as to who we are, but regardless of what we believe, misperceive, or identify with, we are still in the essence of our being, the sons and daughters of the King. The word personality is derived from the Latin word, persona, which is defined as "a mask that an actor wears." So much of the world is striving to identify, display, and fight for their personality, yet do not realize that they are only fighting for a mask, not their true self. When we discover that truth, we may have the same confusion as the boy. We may ask ourselves where our other identity comes from or wonder what is left if we transcend the misperceptions of our personalities. And while our masks may not be bad, or necessarily harmful, they are still not the truth of who we are.

C.S Lewis once said, "The more we let God take us over, the more truly ourselves we become – because He made us. He invented us. He invented all the different people that you and I were intended to be. . . It is when I turn to Christ, when I give up myself to His personality, that I first begin to have a real personality of my own." The attributes of God are within every one of us. These qualities make up the authenticity of our being and reflect our true selves, not a mask. By knowing our Creator, we finally know ourselves in our most accurate, authentic, and organic form. It is only by knowing the true essence of our being as the archetype and reproduction of God that we know who we truly are. Therefore, knowing and understanding God is the most beneficial undertaking because not only does it make us free to take off our masks; it allows us to leap into the possibilities of what that means for us as His replica and archetype.

# PROCEEDING ON YOUR PATH

*The truth has a million faces, but there is only one truth.*
—HERMANN HESSE, *DAMIEN*

After the initial release of The Spiritual Archetypes quiz and guidebooks, there was one question people often had. Many people emailed me, testifying to resonating with the material and how it had changed their life but would follow with, "Now that I know all of this, what do I do next?"

**The first part of proceeding on the spiritual path is to look at the fruits of the spiritual path:** In life, business, and finances, there is a term used to indicate how lucrative one's results are. This term is known as the *fruits of labor*. In business, the fruits of your labor would be the results of your work. If you are putting in long hours, doing overtime, and laboring, then you get a promotion, this would be seeing the fruits of your labor. If a person is working on their health and changing the way they think and feel about themselves, their food, and their body, they may begin to see changes such as losing weight, having more energy, and feeling better. Again, this would be the fruits of their labor. They are seeing the manifestation of their efforts. In spirituality, instead of the term fruits of labor, it is known as the *fruits of the spirit*. In spirituality, as with any other circumstance, we should see the results or manifestation of how much we put into our path.

In spirituality and religion people tend to see how much they do, study, the classes they go to, how many clients they have, or how much money they make, and take that as evidence of how well their spirituality is working for them. However, the best evidence is the fruits of the spirit. The reason this is the most authentic evidence is that it is not based on anything earthly. It is based purely on the spiritual attributes and characteristics we possess. Having money doesn't mean a person is spiritual, nor does not having any money. The fruits of the spirit are not about what we have or don't have in material form; it's about who we are as a person and soul, and how we practice those attributes in the world.

Having worked with many people around the world, it's always interesting when hearing how long people have been on their spiritual path and how unhappy they still are. Sometimes people believe that because they have been practicing spirituality for so long that that time must equate to happiness. However, our spiritual path is not about the number of years; it's about the quality of those years. It never ceases to amaze me how many people in the spiritual community are some of the angriest and most judgmental I have ever met. Alternatively, there are people in religious communities who have been in religion their whole life and still have debilitating anxiety and depression. That's not to say that when we are spiritual that we are perfect and never experience any negative symptoms. But spirituality is supposed to not only better our lives, it is also supposed to be full of miracles, profound insight, revelation, and offer supernatural cures to our natural human problems. There is a difference between an occasional obstacle and a perpetual struggle or issue. If someone is floating through life feeling a little bit better or suffering well, it might be worth examining their practice to see where they can deepen, strengthen, or fine-tune it. In doing so we can step into our full potential as supernatural beings.

For instance, if you think of your spirituality as a relationship, would you say it's loving, positive, supportive, and that you feel good most of the time in it? Do you feel inspired, and uplifted by it, or shamed and guilted? You would be surprised how much of religion and spirituality is shame-based and keeps people feeling like they need to be better and do more. Would you want to be with a partner or spouse that made you feel that way? Or would you prefer to be with a person who loves you, sees the good within you, and encourages you to be your highest and best self? If you were in a relationship that just wasn't working, wouldn't you want to know why? If it lacked passion, desire, and interest, wouldn't you want that spark back? Many people go through life with a relationship to their spirituality that is lackluster, uninspired, and unfulfilling. It's like a marriage they do not enjoy and stay in because they don't know how to make it better. Sometimes it's not until they witness a positive, healthy, loving relationship that they even realize something is amiss. This is why I encourage people to look at this spirituality and their spiritual path with objectivity and honesty. Is it assisting you and co-creating your best life? Or is it actually hurting you, hindering your growth, and keeping you stuck? That can feel difficult or offensive to look at because of course no one wants to feel like they aren't doing enough or that what they are doing is wrong, but acknowledging where we are stuck gives us the power to become unstuck. In programs such as AA they say, "The first step to recovery is admitting we have a problem." If we don't admit that we eat unhealthy food, we cannot change our diet to a healthier one. If we aren't happy in a relationship, we can never make it better by ignoring the problem. If someone has a money spending problem, they will never learn to budget without first admitting that there is in fact a problem. Instead of feeling bad about the things we do not know or the areas where we lack understanding, let's shift our perception and get excited for how much more fulfilled our soul can be when we know what and where something is stuck!

**There are twelve Fruits of the Spirit that show the quality of a person's spiritual practice:**
Charity (love, compassion, generosity)
Joy
Peace
Patience
Benignity (kindness)

Goodness

Longanimity (patience during hardships, endurance)

Mildness (gentleness)

Faith

Modesty

Continence (temperance, self-control)

and Chastity (surrendering worldly desires for spiritual self)

Although our human selves are not perfect and we may not feel we are strong in all of these areas, the fruits of the spirit are a great way to check in with ourselves. By seeing our strongest areas, and where we may want to spend more focus, we can create a more prosperous return on the fruits of our spiritual labor. Regarding spirituality, I always say, "The proof is in the pudding," meaning that whatever our practice, beliefs, and claims, we should see the results and manifestation of it within our daily actions, thoughts, words, and perspectives. Accordingly, if we are not seeing, feeling, or experiencing these qualities, we always have the opportunity to change or modify our practice or path to best get into alignment with these qualities. Our spiritual quest should be fruitful, and it can be helpful to ask yourself if you are seeing the fruits of your spiritual practice in your spirit.

**The second part of proceeding on our path is integration:** Integration is being in alignment with God and embodying those actions, thoughts, words, and feelings in our lives. Integration is, therefore, not a process we do after, or in between, spiritual practice; it is an encompassment of the holistic self. Spirituality is not moments we designate for connecting and communing; it is the constant communication evoked in our hearts, minds, and souls. To integrate spirituality is to live and breathe God and to mirror those qualities into the world. Integration is a oneness we feel and embody in all things. When we live in relationship with our spiritual integration, there is no separation. Instead of collapsing because we missed our morning meditation, or being controlled by the world, we are in constant communion and embodiment of God, which makes it more difficult to pull out of our center. In martial arts, there is a technique where two opponents stand facing one another with their arms touching one another. They move in a cycle, connected to one another the entire time, in a constant flow. If and when one of the opponents feels weakness or lessening of energy in the movement from the other person, they are supposed to pull the other one's arm slightly to signify they have felt the opponent's weakness. The more centered and more conscious each person is, the more difficult it is to pull them out of their center. It is not about strength, but rather focus and awareness. Similarly, the more we integrate our spirituality into our being and make it a part of our intention in all things, the less possible it is for the enemy to pull us out of our center. If we divert our attention and become complacent, we allow an opportunity to pull us out of our center. There are times that it may be a little tug out of place and others where we lose our footing completely. Integration gives us proper footing and grounds us into alignment with God, making it easier to flow while remaining solid within our spiritual ourselves.

**The third part of proceeding on our path is discovering and living your soul's purpose and destiny:** In the book *The Alchemist* by Paulo Coelho, he says, "To realize one's destiny is a person's only real obligation." The interesting part is that we all have the same soul's purpose: to glorify God's divine attributes. The unique manifestation of these attributes becomes our destiny.

By examining the Spiritual Archetypes, we see that each path exhibits and resonates with different attributes of God and that each person models those attributes in a way that resonates with them.

Ultimately, the Neoteric Shaman seeks to embody God's value and worth within themself. The Recoverist seeks to know God's redemption and salvation. The Witch seeks to know God's acceptance. The Ancestor seeks God's righteousness. The Sectarian seeks to trust in God's Word. The Wayfarer seeks to know God's omnipotence. The Mythologist seeks to know God's immanence and romance. The Warrior seeks to know God's victory and endurance. The Eastern Philosopher seeks to know God's patience and compassion. The Saint seeks to know God's mercy and kindness. The Christian Mystic seeks to know God's holiness and devotion. The Artist seeks to know God's creative beauty. The Crusader seeks to know God's justice and refuge. The Oracle seeks to know God's counsel and wisdom. The New Ager seeks to know God's impartiality. The Metaphysician seeks to know God's omniscience. The Occultist seeks to know God's mysteries and sanctification. The Lightworker seeks to know God's omnipresence and dependability. The Mindset Master seeks to know God's transcendence. The Sovereign seeks to know God's leadership and prosperity. The Theologist seeks to know God's Word and loyalty.

Every experience, situation, hardship, and adversity has brought us to the path of our Spiritual Archetype so that we can pursue the attributes of God that we most need in our lives and are most capable of helping others with. We seek to know, understand and integrate God within ourselves, our lives, and our spiritual practice. We are also seeking to embody these attributes not only for ourselves but for one another. Living our soul's purpose happens when we discover how to reflect these on our path and how to most authentically share them collectively.

You are the image and likeness of God, and your Spiritual Archetype is a part of that reflection. As you go forward on your journey, regardless of which path you walk, I pray these things for you: I pray that your path is conducive to your well-being, health, and enlightenment. I pray that your spiritual integration feels authentic, organic, and natural to your true state of being. I pray that you recognize your divine attributes and model them on your path for yourself and others. I pray that you trust and surrender to God's destiny for you and that it is abundant, prosperous, and poetically written. I pray that you know and discover God's infinite mercy, compassion, and grace and extend those attributes to yourself and others. I pray that you forgive yourself and bless others with the gift of forgiveness. I pray that you hold fast to spiritual truth and let go of what does not serve your highest and best good. I pray that you live in the love and expression of God and reflect the love and expression of God to the world. And lastly, I pray that God blesses you abundantly with everything you need, everything you may not know you need, and the wisdom to accept what you are given graciously. Remember that while the Spiritual Archetypes are the physical manifestation of your path, the pilgrimage is with God and within ourselves. If we allow God to be our compass, we will always find our way.

# ACKNOWLEDGMENTS

I would like to thank God for His infinite love, patience, grace, mercy, and persistence. God, you are good beyond words and I love you endlessly.

I want to thank my husband, Travis, for your support during the creation of this book and throughout our life together. Loving you and being loved by you is everything. Marrying you is the best decision I have ever made.

I want to thank my children for the magic, playfulness, and love we share every day. Truett, Hadley, and Revere, being your mother is my favorite experience. Thank you for picking me to be your mommy.

To my mother, who has believed in me and been such a wonderful support to my family. Thank you for all our long conversations and for always holding the truth for me. You are loved and appreciated beyond words.

To my father, who has taught me so much. Thank you for teaching me how to see the magic in everything. You have always been one of my favorite parts of my life.

To Geoff and Linda, who were catalysts on my spiritual path and propelled me to seek the truth. I love, respect, and cherish you both in the deepest depths of my heart.

I would like to thank Barbara LeVan Fisher for bringing the cover and design of this book to life. Barbara, you are a creative conduit, a mystic, and a friend.

Thank you, Vanessa Ta, for your amazing contributions and your devotion to editing this book with intuition, skill, and care.

Last but not least, thank you Depeche Mode.

# ABOUT THE AUTHOR

Although this page is meant to talk about the author, I would like to provide this space as an opportunity to shine a light on some organizations and charities that could use this platform to further their mission, purpose, and service. Please take a moment to get to know these fantastic causes, and if they resonate with you, please pray about how you might be able to donate your time or treasure to support their incredible missions.

# CHARITIES + ORGANIZATIONS

**Red Hawk Native American Arts Council**
"The Redhawk Native American Arts Council is a not-for-profit organization founded and maintained by Indigenous American artists, performers, and educators residing in New York and New Jersey. Since 1994, Redhawk has been dedicated to supporting the urban Indigenous community and educating the general public about Indigenous American heritage through song, dance, theater, and other works of art and cultural forms of expression with a diverse group of Indigenous artists from the Americas to around the globe."

You can find out more about their mission and how to support them at: www.redhawkcouncil.org

**Healing Warrior Hearts**
"Healing Warrior Hearts provides free retreats, plus other programs and resources for Veterans and their families, dedicated to healing the emotional, moral and spiritual wounds of war."

You can find out more about their mission and how to support them at: https://www.healingwarriorhearts.org

**Rainbow Therapeutic Riding Center**

"Rainbow is a non-profit organization that provides equine assisted activities to individuals with physical, educational, emotional, cognitive disabilities and other challenges. Our clients develop physical strength and better mobility, self-esteem and self-confidence while receiving benefits through an equestrian activity that accommodates their specific needs."

You can find out more about their mission and how to support them at: https://www.rainbowriding.org

# ABOUT THE ART

All of the artwork in this book was created by the author. Each piece was created to symbolize both the person and their correlating Spiritual Archetype.

## THE NEOTERIC SHAMAN: Black Elk

Black Elk was a holy man and medicine man of the Oglala Lakota people. He was a part of the Buffalo Bill Show, where he shared stories and dances of his tribe to teach the world about the Lakota people. He was a warrior who fought along his relative, Crazy Horse, in the Battle of Little Big Horn, and was a survivor who helped the wounded at the Wounded Knee Massacre. He is most notably known for his visions that were shared in the 1932 classic, *Black Elk Speaks*, which was compiled of interviews conducted by John Neihardt. *Black Elk Speaks* is considered to be one of the greatest spiritual works of all time, and shares the visions and experiences Black Elk began receiving at nine years old.

The image for Black Elk incorporates some of the major themes and elements from his visions: the animals and rainbow tent as well as the landscape where he lived with his tribe during his first visions.

### THE RECOVERIST: John Wesley

In the 1700's Methodist founder and theologian, John Wesley started what were known as Methodist penitent bands which met on Saturday nights. The intention of the meetings was for people to abstain from temptations such as alcohol. As the alehouses and alcoholism began to rise, people were looking for support in staying sober. Wesley, a preacher and holy man created the meetings where people heard and read from the Bible, sang hymns and supported each other through their issues, which in most cases was drinking. These meetings have been compared to the later model of meetings known as AA, and are considered by many, to be the first successful and organized sobriety group.

### THE WITCH: Ann Hutchinson

Ann Hutchinson is considered to be the first female spiritual teacher and activist in this country after the pilgrims came to America. She was a healer, herbalist, and midwife who practiced midwifery along with her preaching. She believed that the men teaching about God were only teaching part of God's Word and so she began teaching about God's grace. Her following began to grow, which infuriated others who then accused her of bewitching people. When one of the babies she delivered was born deformed, there were whispers and gossip that she was a witch working with the devil and that the baby was the manifestation of evil. As a member of the Boston Church, she accused the pastors and ministers of lacking the Spirit and said their teachings were incorrect. Angered by her influence, and that she had embarrassed them, the men took her to trial and she was eventually banished. She left with a group of her followers and founded what is now Portsmouth, New Hampshire.

Perhaps one of the most interesting details about Hutchinson was her volatile relationship with John Winthrop. Winthrop originally arrived in Massachusetts in a small town called Salem, which he felt was unfit for settlement, so he left for Boston. There he founded the First Church of Boston, of which Ann was a member. Winthrop envisioned a church that was based on the Old Testament and put women in a subsidiary role. Hutchinson challenged these beliefs and preached about the love and grace of God. He had an influential role in taking her to trial and even cross-examined her himself. Upon her death years later, he praised the Lord, believing that God's work had been done.

Years later, the Salem witch trials took place only miles outside of Boston, where this rivalry took place. Salem was the original village where John Winthrop first sought to settle but decided against it. The Salem witch trials were a case of mass hysteria where at least twenty people accused of witchcraft were killed. The presiding judge over the case was none other than Wait Winthrop, great-grandson of John Winthrop.

A few years earlier in the lesser-known Connecticut witch trials, the first person was hanged for witchcraft in the New World, and at least thirty-five cases subsequently followed. The governor of Connecticut at the time was John Winthrop Jr., son of John Winthrop.

While this is evidence of the abuse of power that men held during these times, it might also be said that there were evident karmic connections between these men and the rebellious female spirit often associated with "witches." It is also interesting how John Winthrop chose to leave Salem, yet his great-grandson still became an authoritative variable in the deaths of innocent people there.

The image of Ann Hutchinson features trees and landscapes of Massachusetts and New Hampshire. The crown around her includes plants and herbs to represent her midwifery and herbalism. The orange-hued layer is a mixture of the Bible, a map from 1600's New Hampshire, and the trees native to the areas she lived.

## THE ANCESTOR: Don Pedro Jaramillo

Don Pedro Jaramillo was a curandero (a healer) who combined folk healing, Catholicism, and traditional Spanish medicine. He was born in Guadalajara, Mexico. During a horse-riding accident, his face and nose were badly injured. One night, he was in such distress from the pain that he went to the edge of a pool of water and applied mud to his wound. His nose was miraculously cured, although it left a deep identifying scar, and he fell asleep. He awoke to a vision from God where God told him that he had blessed him with the gift of healing. He immediately began working as a faith healer, mostly working with families nearby who were either too poor to afford healthcare or were too far from town to travel to doctors. After the death of his mother, Jaramillo moved to Texas and became known as "the healer of Los Olmos Creek." He was famous for his healing and methods of using mostly water or mud on people while he prayed for them.

Jaramillo lived modestly, dressing like a shepherd or cowboy, wearing a cowboy vest and sombrero. He never asked for money for his services. People sent donations for his prayer and healing but he used the money to purchase wagonloads of food and would deliver them to churches. When he died, people found over 5,000 fifty-cent pieces for donations that he had not yet sent to local churches.

Don Pedro's art uses the landscape of his homeland, including cactus and flowers all native to that region. The flowers surrounding him show the gifts, blessings, and abundance that surrounded him in his life while remaining humble and modest.

### THE SECTARIAN: Mary Baker Eddy

Mary Baker Eddy was born on July 16, 1821, in New Hampshire. She was born and raised into strict orthodox religion yet felt that the cruel or unjust God that so many preachers spoke about was inaccurate. From a young age, Eddy felt that God was a good, merciful, and loving God who loved his children infinitely and equally. In her young adulthood, she began researching and studying Eastern religions and esoteric teachings but struggled a great deal personally. She had various bouts of sickness and accidents and struggled with anxiety. She became a devout student of Phineas Quimby, who introduced her to healing through a treatment she received from him. A few years later, she slipped and fell on some ice and was badly hurt. It was believed that she would not live and she lay in bed waiting for death. However, death did not come. Instead, she lay reading her Bible and a miraculous healing occurred, which caused her to get up and walk out of her room.

Her revelation and healing directed her to write a book outlining and describing the science behind divine healing. This book was called *Science and Health with Key to the Scriptures* and her teachings became known as Christian Science. After the release of *Science and Health with Key to the Scriptures*, Eddy became the most famous woman in the world. Her work, books, lectures, and teachings have continued gaining followers and inducing healing ever since. Christian Science continues to thrive and produce incredible healings, showing the power of God, but also the power of discovering and integrating spirituality for oneself.

The art for Mary Baker Eddy contains the seal from the Christian Science logo, which says, "heal the sick, raise the dead, cleanse the lepers, cast out demons." The next layer is a picture of the original portion of the First Church of Christ Science in Boston, which she founded.

## THE NEONATE: St. John of the Cross

Born June 24, 1542, John of the Cross was a Catholic priest and mystic and is called a mystical doctor. He is also the patron saint of mystics. In 1567, John became a priest and shortly after met Teresa of Ávila who had a huge impact on his faith, understanding, and spiritual mission.

In 1577, he was jailed for his religious beliefs and treated horribly. He was beaten regularly, kept in a tiny cell with little to no light, and fed water, bread, and scraps of fish. This lasted for nine months until he was able to escape. It was during his imprisonment that he wrote one of his most influential works, "The Spiritual Canticle," which also became one of the most beloved works in Spanish literature. "The Spiritual Canticle" is a poem about a bride who is searching for her groom and is anxious and in despair searching for him. This is a metaphor for the soul (bride) searching for Jesus (groom) and refers to the biblical reference of Jesus being the groom and the church being His bride. However, his most commonly referenced poem is "Dark Night of the Soul." The reason St. John of the Cross is used to symbolize the Neonate is that he was the one who identified and named the experience of the dark night of the soul, which is an experience that most people go through before or during their spiritual awakening. While the term "dark night of the soul" has become modernized and used frequently in New Age spirituality, it is of Roman Catholic origin and is a term that describes spiritual trials and tribulations in the quest for God.

St. John of the Cross also coined the terms "light and love" or "love and light," which has become a popular saying for Lightworkers and the spiritual community with his poem, "Dichos de Luz y Amor," which translates to "Sayings of Light and Love."

The artwork of St. John of the Cross is set at a cathedral in Spain, where he was from. The crown behind him shows the possibilities of the spiritual universe when we have a spiritual awakening. The colors used in this artwork represent colors often associated with spiritual awakening.

## THE WAYFARER: Gipsy Smith

Rodney "Gipsy" Smith was born in a Gypsy tent in England on March 31, 1860. Born into Gypsy patronage, Smith's family lived in a gypsy wagon and sold blankets and handmade goods for a living. When he was young, Smith's mother passed away from smallpox, which left him brokenhearted. After his mother's passing, his father turned to Christianity, which he had heard a jailor talking about while in jail for a minor offense. Smith's father became born again and took his children to a church meeting where he became overcome with the spirit. He collapsed and when he came to, he began shouting that he was a new man, which frightened Smith. Smith's uncles became born again and soon after his siblings began to convert as well. Smith, however, felt resistant and fought his conversion. Although he began to witness miracles and how faith was changing his family, it was a series of events that finally brought him to allow God into his life at the age of sixteen.

When Smith converted on November 17, 1876, he devoted himself to learning everything about God. Although he could not read, he purchased a Bible and dictionaries, vowing to learn to read and preach the words. He taught himself to read and began to preach and sing the words of the Bible. He became known as "the singing Gypsy" and later "the singing Evangelist." He began accepting speaking engagements and connected with a mission now known as the Salvation Army. Attendance grew everywhere he preached and he began accepting invitations to speak throughout the United Kingdom. In 1891, he came to America, where he drew large crowds.

After 1892, his ministry was called the Gipsy Gospel Wagon Mission. Although he refused the title, in 1896 he was called the greatest Evangelist in the world after speaking to a crowd of over 116,00 people in Boston.

Smith had a poetic and loving way of speaking to his audiences. Through his lineage of storytelling and tales, he was able to speak to people in a way that was artistic, unique, and touching. Smith was also able to help people resonate with the authenticity of God. Smith encouraged people to speak with God themselves, teaching that communion with God was a personal experience between each person. He once said, "St. Paul's cathedral is nothing but a glorified quarry if Christ be out of it, and my old gypsy tent is a cathedral when Christ is in it." Smith traveled around the world and used his heritage and background to bring people to God. An uneducated man who someone once referred to as "just a gypsy" devoted himself so wholeheartedly to God that he changed lives around the world. Considered an outcast because of his heritage, he once said, "I didn't go through your colleges and seminaries. They wouldn't have me ... but I have been to the feet of Jesus where the only true scholarship is learned."

His artwork includes the trees from the park where he was born, textures from blankets and hand-woven baskets, as well as an image of him with a group of Gypsies.

### THE MYTHLOGIST: J. R. R Tolkien

J. R. R Tolkien is one of the greatest writers and storytellers of myths and legends to have ever lived. The creator of *The Hobbit* and *The Lord of the Rings*, Tolkien was able to create worlds that transport readers to this day. As well as being an established writer, Tolkien was also a devout Christian whose faith and storytelling influenced another great author and Christian, C .S. Lewis.

Lewis, born and raised in religion, experienced a series of hardships that negatively impacted his life and faith. It was his friendship with Tolkien that influenced Lewis to explore God and faith through the power of myth, and ultimately lead Lewis back to his faith. Lewis went on to write *The Chronicles of Narnia*, as well as many other books and spoke about his transition from atheism back to God. Tolkien has continued to influence the world with the magic of his writing and the power of his faith.

The elements in this photo are pieces significant to Tolkien including a picture of his character Bilbo Baggins' window, a map of middle earth, and the inscription from the ring of doom.

## THE WARRIOR: Geronimo

A holy man, seer, and warrior of the Apache, Geronimo was a unique man, revered by his tribe and feared by his enemies. It is believed he had magical powers and special gifts that made it possible to walk without leaving footprints, could prophesy, and had a powerful intuition that allowed him to evade enemies. Some say he was able to magically survive gunshot wounds. Others testified that he could control the weather and elements. He was an advisor to his chief and was a medicine man who was respected for his spiritual abilities. His people and those who came to know him believed he was especially favored by their god and had special blessings.

When his entire family was murdered by troops, he became a fierce warrior, raging war against the settlers trying to take his tribal land and change his ancestors' ways. His battle tactics and spiritual protection allowed him to lead men successfully into war and made them follow him faithfully. At one point, at least 5,000 soldiers searched for him but were unable to find him, which only added to his mystery, and talk of his spiritual abilities.

The artwork for Geronimo shows the landscapes of his birth and the beloved lands he lived in during his freedom. The image of the men behind him is a real historical image of Geronimo leading his men into battle. In his later years, he was proud to learn how to write his name. His autograph is included in the image behind him.

## THE EASTERN PHILOSOPHER: Paramahansa Yogananda

Paramahansa Yogananda was a yogi, teacher, and guru from India who

influenced millions of people in the world. He had a profound love
and respect for Jesus and was able to bridge barriers between Eastern
and Western religions. At his birth it was foretold that he would be a
teacher and that would bring millions of people to God. His childhood
was filled with spiritual experiences, revelations, and visions. He began
practicing and teaching spirituality in India and upon having a vision
of America, Yogananda moved to the United States, where he lived
for the rest of his life. In 1925, he established his Self-Realization Fellowship Lake Shrine in Los Angeles, which still attracts thousands of
people a year. First published in 1946, his book *Autobiography of a Yogi*
has brought meditation and Eastern philosophies to the West, selling
over 4 million copies worldwide. Yogananda is one of the most influential teachers who inspired people like George Harrison, and Elvis
Presley—and songs like "Dreamweaver," written by Gary Wright about
Yogananda's poem entitled "God! God! God!"

Yogananda traveled and taught about God and spirituality for
almost the entirety of his life. He passed away at the age of 59, however,
Yogananda's passing was of unique circumstances. The day of his passing, he talked about how he would soon be leaving the Earth. He did
pass on that evening, and his book *Divine Interventions: True Stories of
Mysteries and Miracles That Change Lives* states that for three weeks after
his death, Yogananda's body "showed no signs of physical deterioration
and his unchanged face shone with the divine luster of incorruptibility."
Medical examiners and experts could not explain it, but there were no
signs of death, no odor, or signs of decay. The mortuary director at the
time stated, "The absence of any visual signs of decay . . . offers the most
extraordinary case in our experience. . . . This state of perfect preserva-
tion of a body is, so far as we know from mortuary annals, an unparal-
leled one. . . . Yogananda's body was apparently in a phenomenal state
of immutability. . . . No odor of decay emanated from his body at any
time. . . . For these reasons we state again that the case of Paramahansa
Yogananda is unique in our experience."

The artwork for Paramahansa Yogananda has elements of his
beloved country including landscapes, textiles from temples, and flowers from celebrations in India. The color of his robe is the color of the

robes he mostly wore throughout his life and teachings. The flowers represent the Eastern Philosopher's spiritual quest.

**THE SAINT: Mother Mary**

A figure and symbol of the ultimate earthly mother, Mary was the mother of Jesus, a faithful follower to God's Word, and a saint in her own right. While Mary had a profound understanding of her Son's mission and purpose, there are a few scriptures in the Bible that show that despite it all, she was still a mother and had the worry, care, and love of a mother.

"Now his parents went to Jerusalem every year at the feast of the Passover. And when he was twelve years old, they went up to Jerusalem after the custom of the feast. And when they had fulfilled the days, as they returned, the child Jesus tarried behind in Jerusalem; and Joseph and his mother knew not of it. But they, supposing him to have been in the company, went a days journey; and they sought him among their kinsfolk and acquaintance. And when they found him not, they turned back again to Jerusalem, seeking him. And it came to pass, that after three days they found him in the temple, sitting in the midst of the doctors, both hearing them, and asking them questions. And all that heard him were astonished at his understanding and answers. And when they saw him, they were amazed: and his mother said unto him, Son, why hast thou thus dealt with us? behold, thy father and I have sought thee sorrowing. And he said unto them, How is it that ye sought me? wist ye not that I must be about my Father's business? And they understood not the saying which he spake unto them. And he went down with them, and came to Nazareth, and was subject unto them: but his mother kept all these sayings in her heart. And Jesus increased in wisdom and stature, and in favour with God and man." (Luke 2:41-52)

Like a wonderful mother, Mary knew that while motherhood was a job bestowed upon her, it is truly God's job to care for his children. She was worried when she could not find her Son, but she knew that He was always in the care of God.

The artwork for Mary also centralizes the rose, which is a universal representation of Mother Mary. It is often said that when Mary appears to people, there is a scent of roses that accompanies her.

## The Christian Mystic: William J. Seymour

Born in Centerville, Louisiana, on May 2, 1870, African American Pentecostal (a Baptist in his childhood and young adult years) preacher William J. Seymour had visions and prophetic dreams beginning at a young age. In 1900, Seymour moved to Cincinnati, where he became a part of the Holiness theology, which emphasized divine healing. In 1902, he was stricken with smallpox, which left him blind in his left eye. His recovery from the fatal illness drove him to become a preacher. His gifts were amplified and in 1906, Seymour moved to Los Angeles, California. There he sparked the Azusa Street Revival, a movement that swept through Southern California and the American nation. Azusa Street Mission became known for its attendees being filled with the Holy Spirit, speaking in tongues, and being healed. Seymour's leadership and preaching abilities also bridged racial barriers. Azusa Street was not only a massive African American movement but also welcomed and drew people from other ethnicities; which was uncommon at the time for churches to mix races.

People flocked to Azusa Street Mission. All of the services were excessively full, even when they offered three services a day. While the Azusa Street Revival only lasted between 1906 and 1909, its impact rippled into the world. It was a catalyst for the Pentecostal movement and the faith healing movement. Hundreds of people were healed in the time of Azusa Street Mission and kept their healings years after. In the 1970s attendees of Azusa Street were interviewed about their healings, which had remained since the early 1900s.

Seymour spent the rest of his life traveling and spreading the Word of God. In 1915 he wrote his first book, *The Doctrines and Discipline of the Azusa Street Apostolic Faith Mission of Los Angeles.*

In the artwork, William J. Seymour is standing in front of his infamous Azusa Street Mission building. The newspaper article behind him is one of many that highlighted the miracles taking place on Azusa

Street. The light, gold, and fire around him show the power of the Holy Spirit upon him and his ministry.

## THE ARTIST: Hilma af Klint

Hilma af Klint was born on October 26, 1862 on a Navy base in Sweden, where her father was stationed as an admiral. By the age of ten, she was already enthralled with art and studying it passionately in school. In 1880, she was enrolled in a technical art school where she further developed her skill and interest. Around this time, her younger sister passed away at the age of ten, which spurred a lifelong interest in spirituality and the occult. She became deeply interested in the relationship between botany, science, and the spiritual realm, which led her to explore the work of Rudolf Steiner. She became a fan and follower of the Metaphysician Spiritual Archetype Rudolf Steiner, who was known for his intuitive artwork amongst many abilities. Af Klint first met Steiner in 1908, when she invited him to view her work, which he did.

As well as being a renowned and respected artist who was ahead of her time, Hilma af Klint was also a writer. When she passed away at the age of eighty-one, she left a box to her nephew with instructions not to open it for twenty years. In it was artwork that had never been publicly seen as well as over 150 notebooks filled with writings of her spirituality and life.

All of the artwork, elements, and pieces used in this collage are taken from Hilma af Klint's paintings including; *The Swan No16, Altarpiece No. 1 Group X, Group IX/UW, No. 25, The Dove, No. 1, Series VII, No. 7d, and The Dove no 14.*

## THE CRUSADER: Martin Luther King Jr.

Martin Luther King Jr. was a Baptist minister, preacher, and civil rights activist. With his love for God and people, and with a strong Biblical foundation, his ministry is one of the most historic, remembered, and honored to this day. In a turbulent time in history when African Americans and minorities were being oppressed by old beliefs, and being faced with new challenges, King spoke eloquently about peace, equality, and freedom. He lived and breathed his mission and purpose and walked his talk in a way that was admirable, respectable, and noble. He led marches for labor and civil rights, as well as the right to vote.

In 1955, while only in his twenties, King took the lead role in the Montgomery bus boycott, after another historic figure, Rosa Parks, refused to give up her seat on a bus to a white man. During the boycott, African Americans refused to ride the bus until they were treated equally and were allowed to sit anywhere on the bus. The infamous boycott lasted 385 days until the United States ruled that racial segregation was no longer legal on buses. King became a national figure and hero after enduring jail time and even had his home bombed.

On May 17, 1957, King led a Prayer Pilgrimage for Freedom, in which almost 25,000 people attended and prayed together. He was able to lead some of the largest and most effective nonviolent protests in history. His reputation and passion were inspirational and motivating.

On August 28, 1963 King delivered one of the most historic speeches of all time to a crowd of over 250,000 people, at the Lincoln Memorial in Washington D.C. His speech, which lasted almost twenty minutes, spoke of ending racism in America. Mahalia Jackson, a friend of King's and infamous gospel singer who sang at the event, suddenly called out to him during the speech saying, "tell them about the dream!" He followed by saying,

"I say to you today, my friends, so even though we face the difficulties of today and tomorrow, I still have a dream. It is a dream deeply rooted in the American dream. I have a dream that one day this nation will rise up and live out the true meaning of its creed: 'We hold these truths to be self-evident: that all men are created equal.' I have a dream that one day on the red hills of Georgia the sons of former slaves and the sons of former slave owners will be able to sit down together at the table of brotherhood. I have a dream that one day even the state of Mississippi, a state sweltering with the heat of injustice, sweltering with the heat of oppression, will be transformed into an oasis of freedom and justice. I have a dream that my four little children will one day live in a nation where they will not be judged by the color of their skin but by the content of their character. I have a dream today. I have a dream that one day, down in Alabama, with its vicious racists, with its governor having his lips dripping with the words of interposition and nullification; one day right there in Alabama, little black boys and black girls will be able to join hands with little white boys and white girls as sisters and brothers. I have a dream today."

These have become some of the most memorable, loved, and moving words in American history.

King endured hardship and struggle, and placed unfathomable responsibility onto himself to inspire change that is the right of every human being. He did so with selflessness and a personal commitment to uphold God's Word, and the ripples he created are still making waves today.

The artwork for Martin Luther King Jr. has the Lincoln Memorial where he spoke his most famous, "I Have A Dream" speech. Within the circle behind him is a picture from the March on Washington for Jobs and Freedom in 1963. Included is part of the transcript for "I Have a Dream." The colors in this image are used to represent his courage, persistence, passion, and Godly mission.

## THE ORACLE: Nostradamus

A French astrologer, occultist, and physician, Nostradamus is arguably the most accurate and famous psychic/prophet/oracle who ever lived. At the age of fourteen, Nostradamus entered medical school, only to be forced to leave a year later during an outbreak of the plague. After the school was shut down, he worked as an apothecary prior to pursuing his medical degree at the University of Montpellier in 1522. In 1525 he received his medical license and began traveling throughout Italy and France treating plague victims. His treatments using herbs and plants were incredibly successful, especially considering the mortality rate of the plaque.

Around 1538 he had a spiritual experience that changed him and led him to begin a lifelong interest in the occult. Soon after, Nostradamus began writing almanacs using astrology with great accuracy. He began writing volumes of predictions that always proved to be correct and have extended to modern times. Experts who have closely followed and interpreted his work state that out of over 6,000 predictions, over 70

percent have already transpired including World War II and the rise of
Adolf Hitler, the atomic bomb, the rise and fall of Napoleon Bonaparte,
the French Revolution, the assassination of John F. Kennedy, various
instances of economic inflation and depression, and even most recently,
the coronavirus. Nostradamus is without a doubt the optimal Oracle.

Well-versed in astrology, astronomy, lunar phases, and the occult,
the images around Nostradamus are all vintage images, some of which
he may have even used in his studies. The landscape behind him includes
Mont St. Michel in France, and the water surrounding it.

## THE NEW AGER: Edgar Cayce

Known as the father of holistic medicine, and "the sleeping prophet,"
Edgar Cayce was a banker turned healer, whose predictions, treatments,
and readings are still accurate, respected, and honored today. He was not
only considered the number one psychic in the world but was a great
prophet and one of the only people in history to successfully be able to
read the Akashic records. From ancient Egypt and Atlantis to past lives
and the life of Jesus, Edgar Cayce's readings have been proven time
and time again. His treatments, still sold through authorized companies
such as Heritage House, are considered industry standards—and his
rose tonic has become a revived favorite of a new generation.

Edgar Cayce spoke frequently about ancient Egypt. In the background of this picture are the pyramids and a circle of hieroglyphics
behind him. The plants surrounding him include the Ricinus, which
produces castor oil, a favorite remedy of Cayce.

## THE METAPHYSICIAN: Rudolf Steiner

Rudolf Steiner was an Austrian-born esotericist, philosopher, teacher,
and social reformer with a profound interest and knowledge of spirituality. From this early age, spirituality and the physical world had an effect
on him. He became a writer and in 1891 was awarded a doctorate in philosophy. He wrote books and articles, hoping to find an audience who
was enthusiastic about philosophy. In 1899, he began speaking about his
spiritual experiences and insights with the Theosophical Society, which
he became an integral part of. In 1924, he held his first meeting for an

agriculture course in a small village of Germany (which is now part of Poland), speaking on the detrimental habits of farming and the decline in the richness and quality of the soil due to poor agriculture. He shared his unique solution, which included the replenishing of vitamins and nutrients into the ground for better and more sustainable crops. Thus, biodynamic gardening was born and still thrives today. In 1919, he founded the Waldorf School in Germany, and in 1928 the first Waldorf School in the United States. While other schools were focused on standard studies, Rudolf Steiner sought to teach, nurture, and approach the whole child. Steiner was also incredibly intuitive, drawing and painting from his intuition and speaking about future events. He was a man ahead of his time who wanted to change the way of the future.

Rudolf Steiner's art piece includes his own art, watercolors, and writing. It also includes scientific elements such as the DNA strand, illuminated in light, symbolizing the connection of science and spirituality.

## THE OCCULTIST: Manly Palmer Hall

Manly Palmer Hall is considered the greatest Occultist in American history and one of the most respected in the world. Born in 1901 in Peterborough, Ontario, Canada, Hall moved to Los Angeles at the age of eighteen and quickly developed a name for himself as a master of esoteric studies. Soon after, at the age of 19, Hall began speaking at the Church of the People and quickly took over responsibility as the spiritual leader, counseling people. In 1920 Hall moved into the Oceanside home of Rosicrucian Fellowship leader Max Heindel (who had just passed away) and his wife, Augusta, to whom Hall became like a son, so much so that he called her "mother." Together they began what would be for Hall, the beginning of world travel to discover more about spirituality around the world. In 1928 he completed his masterpiece, *The Secret Teachings of All Ages*, which was an occult favorite to people including Elvis Presley and is still considered one of the greatest metaphysical works of all time. Aside from his expertise in spirituality and the occult, Hall also had a unique ability to speak on any subject with knowledge and expertise such as occultism in politics, karma, Jesus, and past lives. In 1934, he founded the Philosophical Research Society (PRS), which he said was "An institute for advanced study in philosophy, religion, and psychology." Hall became a friend and advisor to celebrities such as Helen Keller and Bella Lugosi, with whom Hall officiated his last marriage in 1955. His influence in Hollywood extended into film with the movie *When Were You Born*, a murder mystery based on astrology and an original story by Manly P. Hall. Released in 1938, *When Were You Born?* was one of the first occult-based movies in film history. Hall was a respected voice and authentic seeker until his passing in 1990.

The elements in this collage are taken from the Manly Palmer Hall collection of alchemical manuscripts, 1500–1825.

## THE LIGHTWORKER: Helen Schucman

Helen Schucman was born in New York City on July 19, 1909. From a young age Helen was a spiritual seeker. Through consistent spiritual experiences and exposure from nannies into religion, Helen had a deep yearning and desire to know God. Due to unfortunate life events, she renounced her faith and turned to psychology, which seemed more reliable and trustworthy. However, her spiritual calling continued and she was constantly being pulled back to her path. Ultimately, she could no longer ignore her mission and surrendered to scribing one of most famous books in history, *A Course in Miracles*. Today *A Course in Miracles* is one of the most famous spiritual books and teachings, inspiring some of the careers and books of spiritual authors. It has influenced thousands of groups and workshops worldwide and was the foundational teaching that began the movement known as Lightworkers.

This image of Helen combines the colors and style of the Lightworker. The background includes water, which is a favorite of the Lightworker, but also close to Helen as she grew up in New York. The triangle behind Helen is a favorite sacred geometry for the Lightworker and represents unity. *A Course in Miracles* is not only a teaching of unity and oneness but is often taught in Unity centers. The outer triangle has the flower and birds of paradise. The spiritual meaning of birds of paradise

are spiritual elevation, transcendence, joy, and self-expression. The rain-
bows along each side and connecting in the middle represent the bridge
that Helen was as the scribe of *A Course in Miracles*.

## THE MINDSET MASTER: Napoleon Hill

Napoleon Hill was born October 26, 1883 in a single-room cabin in
Pound, Virginia, into modest conditions. Throughout his young adulthood, Hill faced many failures and adversity. His mother passed away
when he was only nine, at the age of fifteen he married a girl and later
annulled the marriage, and he went to law school but was unable to
afford it and had to withdraw. He also had a slew of business failures
and ventures that were unsuccessful. In 1925 he released his first book
on philosophies of success called, *The Law of Success*, which was well
received. In 1930 he released his sophomore book, *The Magic Ladder
To Success*, which was also a commercial success. In 1937 he published
his most well-known masterpiece, *Think and Grow Rich*, a staple in
self-improvement and finance books to this day. Hill spoke about the
intuitive and spiritual inspiration he received to write these books and
said that he was greatly inspired by spirit visitations. His works have
changed the lives of millions and have gone on to influence some of the
other monumental works on finances and success.

The elements in Napoleon Hill's artwork include the cover of his
1937 piece, Think and Grow Rich, a layer of coins, and a layer of bills.
The coloring behind him represents the path of the Mindset Master
and the colors usually used in their work or marketing.

## THE SOVEREIGN: John Rockefeller

John Davison Rockefeller was born into extreme poverty in Richford
New York on July 8, 1839. In 1853 his family moved to Ohio, where his
conman father abandoned them and would infrequently return. Motivated not to follow in his father's steps, John had a great work ethic.
At the age of 16, John became a bookkeeper and excelled in the work-
force. In 1859 Rockefeller went into the produce commission business.
Their revenue skyrocketed during the American Civil War. Rockefeller became well skilled in making money and reinvesting it into other

businesses. In 1866, he partnered with his brother in the oil refinery business. In 1870, he ended their partnership and started the Standard Oil Company and grew the oil company to be one of the largest suppliers of oil and kerosene in the country.

In 1867 Rockefeller was set to travel on a train to Buffalo, New York, for a business meeting but missed it only by minutes. When the train reached Angola, New York, there was a series of mechanical features that failed, thus causing a massive accident and killing almost everyone on board. The event became known as the Angola Horror. For John D. Rockefeller, this was a divine intervention that became the catalyst for his life and business endeavors going forward. Rockefeller was a religious man who believed that God was the driving force behind his success and also saved him from misfortunes such as the Angola Horror. He was strict in his faith and abstained from alcohol, drugs, and cigarettes.

In the coming years, the oil business began to dry up as electricity became a household necessity and kerosene was no longer in high demand. Innovative and creative, Rockefeller found a use for gasoline, a byproduct of kerosene, and began producing the majority of gasoline for the new machine, the automobile. At a time when people saw gasoline as a useless byproduct, Rockefeller once again saw possibilities and in 1916 John D. Rockefeller became the first billionaire in the world.

The later years of his life were spent using his money for philanthropy and donating to charities. Being a Baptist himself, Rockefeller donated money to churches and church organizations.

The image of John Rockefeller has elements such as a piece of paper from the Standard Oil Company, a picture from his tea room, and New York from 1916 when he became the first billionaire.

## THE THEOLOGIST: John G. Lake

John Graham Lake was a Canadian-American preacher born in Ontario, Canadian on March 18, 1870. In 1886 he moved to America with his parents and family. During his childhood he witnessed eight of his sixteen siblings die from various illnesses. At the age of sixteen, he attended a Salvation Army meeting where he became born again. At age twenty-one, he married but his wife became ill and he once again had the threat of death in his life. He reached out to a well-known healer, Alexander Dowie, who prayed for Lake's wife and she was healed. John G. Lake became enthralled with divine healing and began studying it intensely. In 1901 Lake moved his family to Zion, Illinois, to further learn the gifts of healing at Dowie's ministry.

In 1908 Lake, along with his family and a group of other missionaries, moved to Africa where they started the Apostolic Faith Mission of South Africa. During his time in Africa, Lake was the catalyst of many incredible healings. At one point he needed to retire for the evening but people kept coming for healing. He blessed a tree stump and told everyone that anyone who touched it would be healed. Hundreds touched the tree stump and were immediately healed.

On February 1, 1913, Lake returned to the States where he began preaching and recording his sermons. On September 1914 he moved his family to Spokane, Washington, where he almost immediately began his own ministry called Lake's Healing Rooms. It is recorded that over 100,000 healings occurred at his Spokane location. After a fire at the Healing Rooms, Lake spent a few years in Portland Oregon before setting out on a tour where he opened more Healing Rooms in other states. Lake returned to Spokane, Washington, in 1931, where he continued his work until the end of his life. John G. Lake was called, "Doctor Lake" because he was able to heal more people than doctors.

John G. Lake's artwork has elements of Israel in the background because the Holy Land is meaningful and special to the Theologist who loves to study. The steps symbolize the higher consciousness or revelation of divine healing and the commitment of oneself it requires to walk this path. The coloring behind Lake is a fire to represent the Holy Spirit, which Lake spoke about frequently. The symbols behind him are from the Hebrew Bible.

Made in the USA
Coppell, TX
01 February 2024

28482918R00266